Spanish Romance in the Battle for Global Supremacy

Spanish Romance in the Battle for Global Supremacy

Tudor and Stuart Black Legends

Victoria M. Muñoz

ANTHEM PRESS

Anthem Press
An imprint of Wimbledon Publishing Company
www.anthempress.com

This edition first published in UK and USA 2022
by ANTHEM PRESS
75–76 Blackfriars Road, London SE1 8HA, UK
or PO Box 9779, London SW19 7ZG, UK
and
244 Madison Ave #116, New York, NY 10016, USA

First published in the UK and USA by Anthem Press in 2021

Copyright © Victoria M. Muñoz 2022

The author asserts the moral right to be identified as the author of this work.

All rights reserved. Without limiting the rights under copyright reserved above, no part of this publication may be reproduced, stored or introduced into a retrieval system, or transmitted, in any form or by any means (electronic, mechanical, photocopying, recording or otherwise), without the prior written permission of both the copyright owner and the above publisher of this book.

British Library Cataloguing-in-Publication Data
A catalogue record for this book is available from the British Library.

Library of Congress Control Number: 2020951133

ISBN-13: 978-1-83998-546-1 (Pbk)
ISBN-10: 1-83998-546-1 (Pbk)

This title is also available as an e-book.

CONTENTS

List of Figures		vii
Acknowledgments		ix
	Prologue: Translating Romance, Empire, and Spain	1
	The Structure of This Book	10
Chapter One	"Books of the Brave" English: Spanish Tales of Love and Arms in Translation	11
	Tales of Love and Arms	11
	"Books of the Brave" English	14
	Amadís Rejected	17
	A Sun Knight and His Moon Princess	22
	Apollo's Challenger	24
Chapter Two	Dream Visions and Competing Dreams: Rewriting the Spanish Model in America	39
	México in the Renaissance Imagination	40
	Dream Visions	43
	Competing Dreams	47
	"Empires fall and rise"	59
Chapter Three	Sun Kings and Moon Queens: The Courting and Uncourting of Spain	67
	Gloriana Triumphs	67
	Anglo-Spanish Contests	72
	Empire of Lust	77
	Conquering Lust	86
	Empire of Virtue	88
Chapter Four	Signs of England: Redcrosse Crosses the Ancient Boundary	95
	Beyond Thule	95
	Spain Founds the New Jerusalem	97
	Romancing Spanish Supremacy	99
	Signs of England	104
	Crossing into Faerieland	106

	Spenser Claims the Red Cross for England	109
	Thule Rewritten	119
	Coda	128
Chapter Five	Believing Bottom's Dream: Rationalizing Exploration from America to Australia	131
	Of Poets, Lovers, and Madmen	132
	In Search of Amazons	135
	El Dorado: Gilded for a Queen	139
	England "holds the chase"	143
	Reason and Unreason from El Dorado to Australia	151
	Going to California	156
Chapter Six	Unruly Readers: Anti-Spanish Sentiment and the Feminizing of Romance	165
	An Intellectual Black Legend	165
	Guilty Reading	174
	Quixotic Figures	185
	Epilogue: Spanish Literature in England before *Don Quixote*	191
	An Early Modern Space Race	191
	Spanish Romance before *Don Quixote*	196

Appendix I: English Readership of Spanish Romance, By the Numbers — 203
Selected Bibliography — 209
Index — 221

FIGURES

Cover: Thomas Cecil, *Elizabetha Angliae et Hiberniae Reginae &c, Engraving* (ca. 1625), © The Trustees of The British Museum.

1	George Gower (attr.), Armada Portrait, oil on canvas, (ca. 1588), Woburn Abbey Collection (George Gower, ca. 1588), Bedfordshire, UK, © The Duke of Bedford and the Trustees of the Bedford Estates	26
2	Woodcut map and plan of Tenochtitlán, in *Praeclara de Nova maris Oceani Hyspania Narratio* (Nuremberg, F. Peypus, 1524). Courtesy of Edward E. Ayer Collection, The Newberry Library	43
3	Tapestry depicting *Saint George and the Dragon,* on canvas (artist unknown, Palacio de Don Lope, Zaragoza, Spain)	114
4	1237 Battle of the Puig of Santa Maria (artist unknown, ca. 1410–20) temple and gilt on pine panel, © Victoria and Albert Museum, London	115
5	Publication trends for romances and other literature translated from Spanish to English	204
6	Genre breakdown of printed translations from Spanish into English, 1473–1640	205
7	Language and genre breakdown of literature translations printed in English, 1473–1640	206

ACKNOWLEDGMENTS

Many wits have helped me to realize this project, especially my colleagues, mentors, and friends from The Ohio State University (OSU), where this project originated as a doctoral dissertation. I especially credit the continued guidance of my thesis director, Jennifer Higginbotham, and the helpful insights of my thesis committee, Elizabeth Davis, Christopher Highley, and Luke Wilson. I further acknowledge the mentorship and feedback of my former professors, Jonathan Burgoyne, Richard Dutton, Alan Farmer, Hannibal Hamlin, Ethan Knapp, Elizabeth Kolkovich, Sarah Neville and Karen Winstead. I also credit my graduate cohort from the OSU Renaissance Dissertation Seminar: Jonathan Holmes, Manny Jacquez, Mira Assaf Kafantaris, Erin K. Kelly, Colleen Kennedy, Daniel Knapper, Justin Kuhn, Louis Maraj, Erin McCarthy, Carmen Meza, Ben Moran, Robey Patrick, Liz Steinway, David Sweeten, and Evan Thomas.

A further credit is owed to the members of the 2014–15 Folger Dissertation Seminar, especially the directors, Jean Howard and Pamela Smith, along with my fellow readers: Joseph Bowling, Amy Burnette, Alexis Butzner, Charlotte Buecheler, William Dean Clement, Heidi Craig, Rachel Dunn, Andrew Miller, Aaron Pratt, Ben VanWagoner and Katherine Walker.

A number of scholars have aided and informed this project along the way; in addition to the footnotes, I further acknowledge Elizabeth Evenden-Kenyon, Eric Griffin, Alexander Samson, and Louise Wilson for being gracious and inspiring scholars, and excellent seminar organizers. I also acknowledge Barbara Fuchs, whose groundbreaking work inspired the idea for this book.

I heartily thank Joyce Boro for her constant generosity in sharing work and feedback; Anne Cruz for her insights; Andrea Kouklanakis for her Latin translations; Sara Kozlowski for her art history consultation; Christine Hutchins for her constructive suggestions; and Alex Milsom and Elizabeth Porter for their expertise on the eighteenth and nineteenth centuries.

To all my colleagues and friends at the City University of New York (CUNY), I further express my thanks for their collective support; I especially thank Andrea Fabrizio, Tram Nguyen, and Andy Connolly, who assisted me with grant applications. Additionally, I credit the feedback and support of the 2019–20 CUNY Faculty Fellowship Publication Program: seminar leader Moustafa Bayoumi, and my colleagues, Christine Farias, Raquel Otheguy, Erica Richardson, Marisa Solomon, and Marta-Laura Suska. I also acknowledge the work of my CUNY student mentees and research assistants, Mohamed Aden, Gerlin Ball and Nelson Olmeda, who assisted with the graphs.

ACKNOWLEDGMENTS

Several institutions and organizations supported this project in the form of grants, programming, and other qualitative support: Anglo-Iberian Network, City University of New York, Folger Shakespeare Library, Modern Language Association, Northeast Modern Language Association, The Ohio State University, Renaissance English Text Society, Renaissance Society of America, Shakespeare Association of America, Sixteenth Century Society and Society for the Study of Early Modern Women. I also acknowledge the archives that supplied me with materials and images for this study: Biblioteca Nacional de Catalunya, Biblioteca Nacional de España, British Library, British Museum, Folger Library, Newberry Library, Real Maestranza de Caballería de Zaragoza, Victoria and Albert Museum, and Woburn Abbey.

I thank my mentors: Frederick Aldama, Cynthia Callahan, James Harris, Sheila Patek, Carolyn Skinner, and Yolanda Zepeda.

To my first mentor, Benedict Robinson, thank you for cultivating my interest in Renaissance studies.

Finally, the greatest honor is owed to my family, to whom this book is dedicated. To my sister, Dr. Martha Muñoz, thank you for your unwavering support and strong scholarly model. To my aunt, the late Dra. María del Carmen Caballero Alonso, thank you for inspiring me throughout my life.

PROLOGUE

TRANSLATING ROMANCE, EMPIRE, AND SPAIN

"Language has always been the partner to empire."[1] So remarked the Spanish humanist and philologist, Antonio de Nebrija, to Queen Isabel I (Isabella I) of Castilla (Castile) and León (1451–1504; ruled 1474–1504) in the dedication of his 1492 *Gramática de la lengua castellana*. This book, the first printed grammar of a romance language, served as prologue for the mass dissemination of Spanish language and literature, and especially of Spanish vernacular romance, throughout Europe and the Americas during the sixteenth and seventeenth centuries. Paired with the activities of the Spanish and Portuguese conquistadors in the New World, these diverse romance works translated the thesis of European civility across the globe with "the prerogative of a conqueror."[2]

Nebrija's observation therefore corroborates the view, commonly held among translation scholars, that translation forms part of a larger project of cultural imperialism.[3] This imperialist impulse also informed the early modern humanist program, which sought to recover lost works from the great writers of the Greek and Roman empires, in part to prepare the Christian princes of Europe for the demands of ruling. Nevertheless, this imperial reading of translation must be undertaken with care in order to avoid anachronisms, particularly in the context of Renaissance translations, which also incorporated a pluralist tradition of reading across time and space, as informed by Christian teachings. Indeed, the imperialist thesis of Renaissance translation could very easily be overstated, especially in the case of early modern Spain, where the linguistic umbrella had always been polyglot, encompassing Castilian, Catalán, Galician, Basque, Aragonese, Andalusian Arabic, and other regional dialects.[4]

---

1. Antonio de Nebrija, *Gramática castellana* (Salamanca: Juan de Porras, 1492), sig. A2r.
2. St. Jerome, qtd. in Hugo Friedrich, "On the Art of Translation" in *Theories of Translation*, Rainer Schulte and John Biguenet, eds. (Chicago: University of Chicago Press, 1992), 11–16 (13).
3. See, for example, Friedrich, "On the Art of Translation," esp. 12–13.
4. This heterogeneous culture of medieval and early modern Spain also evinced strong ties between language and genre. King Alfonso X of Castile (1221–1284; ruled 1252–84), for example, spoke Castilian, but he wrote his lyric poetry in Galician-Portuguese. Early modern Castilian competed with Tuscan (spoken in southern Italy) as the dominant lyric language even well into the seventeenth century, while such writers as Garcilaso de la Vega, Juan Boscán, Marqués de Santillana, Torres Naharro, Francisco de Aldana and Cosme de Aldana, Lope de Vega, Francisco de Quevedo, and Gabriel Bocángel dabbled in both languages simultaneously. Although the majority of works that were translated into English during the 1500s and 1600s

And yet, these hybridized conventions had limited impact on the political spread of Castilian during the fifteenth and sixteenth centuries as a major language of Spanish courtliness and commerce. The early modern construction of a Spanish vernacular tradition tied to the Spanish Habsburgs furthermore advanced a nascent *idea* of *the nation* prior to the emergence of nationalism as a concrete ideology, as Fernando Romo Feito explains:

> The dynastic union between two peninsular kingdoms achieved by the marriage of Ferdinand II of Aragon and Isabella of Castile, their conquest of the Muslim reign of Granada, and their support of Columbus's enterprise [to America] all served to define and consolidate the spread of Castilian across and beyond the peninsula, i.e., its conversion into "Spanish." This spread modified the status of the other Romance languages spoken in the peninsula, and it also changed the way that they were perceived. Due to these changes, the word "Spanish" acquired a political meaning, despite having an earlier origin.[5]

These were also, in effect, the underpinnings of empire; as the conjoined crowns of Aragón and Castilla concretized Spanishness as a political force in global politics, proto-nationalism and politico-religious conviction coalesced together in the humanist-evangelical missionary project of the Spanish viceroyalties in the Americas. Hence, when the first educational institutions were established in México and Perú, taught by friars and other state-sponsored clerics, indigenous students were taught Latin first, and Castilian next.[6] Even on the philological level, Spain had closely followed the model of the Romans of translating empire and culture in a common tongue.

While the renewed proliferation of romance literature during the sixteenth century traced the political rise of non-Latin romance languages, and of the Spanish monarchy,

---

were originally written in Castilian, the leading administrative and courtly language of early modern Spain, bilingual literary cultures with Castilian, by then also the primary language of education, were excelling in such regions as Galicia and Cataluña. In Portugal, the use of Castilian as *lingua franca*—particularly among the upper and middle classes—produced a bilingual culture whereby sixteenth-century writers habitually composed in both Castilian and Portuguese. Latin, meanwhile, represented the primary language of legal and ecclesiastical writing across Iberia. For more information, see Fernando Romo Feito, "Ideology and Image of Peninsular Languages in Spanish Literature," in *A Comparative History of Literatures in the Iberian Peninsula* (Amsterdam: John Benjamins, 2010), 456–74.

5. Feito, "Ideology and Image," 456.
6. Isabel's grandson, crowned Holy Roman Emperor Carlos V (hereafter Charles V) (1500–1558; ruled 1519–56), ordered that friars charged with delivering this curriculum teach the colonial subjects to speak, read, and write in Castilian. Although this proved more challenging than anticipated, many friars continued to enforce the use of Castilian throughout the reign of Charles's son, Felipe/Philip II (1527–1598; King of Spain from 1556–98), though he also encouraged colonial educators to learn the indigenous languages. For more information, see Juan Cobarrubias, "The Spread of the Spanish Language in the Americas," in *Language Spread and Social Change: Dynamics and Measurement*, Lorne Laforge and Grant D. McConnell, eds., Publications of the International Center for Research on Bilingualism (Saint-Foy: Les Presses De L'Université Laval, 1990), 49–92.

this genre also inculcated a particular *logic of empire* even while the larger European culture advocated an ethic of humanist pluralism. Unsurprisingly, the humanists all but disowned the writers of romance. The common humanist antipathy toward Habsburg Spain therefore may also help to explain why English writers were so often compelled to define their romances and romance translations against Spanish versions, or otherwise to pillage Spanish romances without attribution. Hence, the verb "Englishing," or *to make English*, emerged as a conventional mode for justifying one's ventures into the culture of the Other; and the discovery of an Other, as Fredric Jameson has noted, is a prime objective of romance.[7] Whereas to *hispanize* implied to turn backward, closely mirroring the cultural and religious implications of *turning Turk*, to "English" a work meant to metamorphose it in the positive direction, away from its seemingly primitive original, naturalizing whatever once was alien, and advancing it toward the cultural-linguistic expression of European civilization. In this capacity, English romance translations most forcefully endorsed the imperialist thesis of translation when invoked in the negative sense, as an act of rejecting and replacing the primitive Other, though individual writers might have protested otherwise.

Whereas my primary interest in this book is to tell the history of Spanish romance in England, showing how the genre factored into a larger ideological battle for global supremacy, I also unearth lost Spanish influences on Tudor- and Stuart-era writers. By helping to recover these works from the margins and gaps of historical posterity, I am continuing the important work of other scholars of England and Spain,[8] and particularly

---

7. Fredric Jameson, "Magical Narratives: Romance as Genre," *New Literary History*, 7, no. 1 (1975), 135–63 (161).
8. In the nineteenth and twentieth centuries, a few works of English and European criticism brought the influence of Spanish romance to light, such as John Garrett Underhill's *Spanish Literature in the England of the Tudors* (New York: Macmillan, 1899); Henry Thomas's *Spanish and Portuguese Romances of Chivalry: The Revival of the Romance of Chivalry in the Spanish Peninsula, and Its Extension and Influence Abroad* (Cambridge: Cambridge University Press, 1920); John O'Connor's *Amadis de Gaule and its Influence on English Literature* (Rutgers: Rutgers University Press, 1970); and Gustav Ungerer's *Anglo-Spanish Relations in Tudor Literature* (Bern: Francke, 1956). In the twenty-first century, scholarly interest in Spanish romance was marked by new editions in English, namely Helen Moore's edited volume of Book I of *Amadis de Gaule* (Aldershot: Ashgate, 2004), and Joyce Boro's edition of Margaret Tyler's translation of Book I of Ortúñez's *The Mirror of Princely Deeds and Knighthood* (London: MHRA, 2014); both are the editions used in this study. Donna Hamilton's *Anthony Munday and the Catholics, 1560–1633* (London: Routledge, 2005) underscored the political dimensions of Munday's Spanish romance translations, further reflecting the genre's Catholic associations. Louise Wilson has also studied the Spanish romance translations of Anthony Munday, particularly as they pertained to the work's English and European reception. See Wilson, "The Publication of Iberian Romance in Early Modern Europe," in *Translation and the Book Trade in Early Modern Europe*, José María Pérez Fernández and Edward Wilson-Lee, eds. (Cambridge: Cambridge University Press, 2014), 201–16; Louise Wilson, "'I maruell who the diuell is his Printer': Fictions of Book Production in Anthony Munday's and Henry Chettle's Paratexts," in *The Book Trade in Early Modern England: Practices, Perceptions, Connections*, J. Hinks and V. Gardner, eds. (Newcastle: British Library and Oak Knoll Press, 2014), 1–18. Leticia Álvarez Recio has also studied the English reception of Munday's translation of *Palmendos* and its role in the English book trade. See Álvarez Recio, "Spanish Chivalric

of Barbara Fuchs in *The Poetics of Piracy: Emulating Spain in English Literature* (University of Pennsylvania Press, 2013). Fuchs shows that England's appropriation of Spanish literature and general occlusion of Spanish influences formed an intellectual outgrowth of what is known as the *Black Legend of Spanish Cruelty*. Coined by Emilia Pardo Bazán (though often attributed to Julián Juderías), the *Black Legend of Spanish Cruelty* refers to various European propaganda movements that historically vilified Spaniards as racially impure owing to their cultural and genetic intermingling with West Africans, Muslims, Jews, Native Americans and other conquered groups, which then served as a European rationalization for Spaniards' inordinate cruelty as colonizers (i.e., *blackness*).[9] Ironically, this racist legend was first communicated in part through the anti-colonial tracts written by Spanish authors, especially the 1552 *Brevísima relación de la destrucción de las Indias* (*Short Account of the Destruction of the Indies*) by the Spanish Dominican friar Bartolomé de las Casas.[10] Las Casas was appalled by the atrocities committed by his own people under the guise of Christianity, and he implored the Spanish Crown to amend its practices, "for I do not wish to see my country destroyed as a divine punishment for sins against the honour of

---

Romances in English Translation: Anthony Munday's *Palmendos* (1589)," *Cahiers Élisabéthains: A Biannual Journal of English Renaissance Studies* 91, no. 1 (2016), 5–20; "Anthony Munday's *Palmendos* (1589) in the Early Modern English Book Trade: Print and Reception," *Atlantis: Journal of the Spanish Association of Anglo-American Studies* 38, no. 1 (2016), 53–69. Finally, Helen Moore's new book, *Amadis in English: A Study in the Reading of Romance* (Oxford: Oxford University Press, 2020) studies the cultural history of the romance in relation to readers. Recent years have also witnessed an outpouring of cultural and historiographical studies of early modern England and Spain, such as Alexander Samson's *The Spanish Match: Prince Charles's Journey to Madrid, 1623* (Aldershot: Ashgate, 2006); and Anne Cruz's edited collection, *Material and Symbolic Circulation Between Spain and England, 1554–1604, Transculturalisms, 1400–1700* (Aldershot: Ashgate, 2008). These have emerged alongside of an outgrowth in interest in Shakespeare and Fletcher's lost *Don Quixote* play, *Cardenio*, such as in David Carnegie and Gary Taylor, eds., *The Quest for Cardenio: Shakespeare, Fletcher, and the Lost Play* (Oxford: Oxford University Press, 2012); Terri Bourus and Gary Taylor, eds., *The Creation and Re-Creation of Cardenio: Performing Shakespeare, Transforming Cervantes* (New York: Palgrave Macmillan, 2013); and Roger Chartier, *Cardenio between Cervantes and Shakespeare: The Story of a Lost Play*, Janet Lloyd, trans. (Cambridge: Polity Press, 2013). Of related interest is Ronald Paulson's *Don Quixote in England: The Aesthetics of Laughter* (Baltimore: Johns Hopkins University Press, 1998) and Yumiko Yamada's *Ben Jonson and Cervantes: Tilting Against Chivalric Romances* (Tokyo: Maruzen, 2000).

9. Luis Español Bouché shows that although the term *Black Legend* has been erroneously attributed to Juderías, who undoubtedly contributed to its common usage, the term is rather indebted to Bazán. See Luis Español Bouché, *Leyendas Negras. Vida y obra de Julián Juderías (1877–1918); la leyenda negra antiamericana* (Salamanca: Junta de Castilla y León, 2007). For an interdisciplinary overview of the Black Legend, see Yolanda Rodríguez Pérez, Antonio Sánchez Jiménez, and Harm den Boer, eds. *España ante sus críticos: las claves de la Leyenda Negra* (Madrid and Frankfurt: Iberoamerica and Vervuert, 2015); Margaret Greer, Walter D. Mignolo, and Maureen Quilligan, eds. *Rereading the Black Legend: The Discourses of Religious and Racial Difference in the Renaissance Empires* (Chicago: University of Chicago Press, 2007).

10. Other important tracts to the formation of the Black Legend included the 1580 *Apology of William I, Prince of Orange* and John Foxe's *Actes and Monuments* (1563), as well as the anti-Habsburg testimonies of Iberian expats like the Portuguese claimant, Don António, Prior of Crato, and António Pérez, former secretary to Philip II, printed in diverse sources.

God and the True Faith."[11] As William S. Maltby recounted in *The Black Legend in England* (1971), however, the greater appeal of this critique was that its author was Spanish:

> The irony of the situation is inescapable. The most powerful indictment of Spain's cruelty and avarice is at the same time a monument to its humanitarianism and sense of justice. But men of other nations, writing in the heat of religious or national partisanship, could not be expected to recognize the all-important fact that Las Casas himself was a Spaniard. It is also noteworthy that while the *Brevissima Relación* was first published in 1551 [corr. 1552], it was not until 1583, when the growing enmity between Spain and England could no longer be disguised, that the first English language edition of the work appeared in the stalls of London booksellers.[12]

Tracing the roots of the Black Legend in England, Maltby uncovered the implicit biases in English perspectives of the Spanish conquest of America, noting, for example, that "[Las Casas] argued that cruel and barbarous men were engaged in the colonization of America and that their worst excesses should be legally curbed. It was his English translator who decided that the Spanish were an exceptionally 'cruel and barbarous nation.'"[13] But Maltby was mistaken when he remarked that "the English have shown little interest in criticizing Spanish intellectual standards."[14] As Fuchs shows, appropriation, occlusion, or erasure proved effective for English writers seeking to pillage Spanish sources; these practices reflected a larger anxiety about Spain's growing cultural influence in Europe (further activated by fears of miscegenation with Spaniards and their non-Christian, non-European ancestors)[15] as reflected by the wide dissemination of the country's literary products.

This book is particularly concerned with the Black Legend's intellectual responses to Spanish imperialism as expressed in European criticisms of Spanish literature and culture, particularly in England, where the undeclared war with Spain from 1585 to 1604 left a lasting impression of Spaniards as arrogant, luxurious, and inordinately vicious. This is not to say that Spanish explorers, slave traders, viceroys, and Catholic inquisitors did not commit the cruel acts for which they were roundly criticized by other European powers. Although exaggeration certainly proved effective in demonizing Spanish conquest, this was also counterbalanced by rosied defenses of colonial atrocities supplied by the likes of Hernán Cortés and Bernal Díaz del Castillo. The point here is not to excuse early modern Spaniards or to engage in ethically dubious debate over whether, for example,

---

11. Bartolomé de Las Casas, *A Short Account of the Destruction of the Indies*, Nigel Griffin, trans. (London: Penguin Group, 1992), 127.
12. William S. Maltby, *The Black Legend in England* (Durham: Duke University Press, 1971), 15.
13. Maltby, *The Black Legend in England,* 20. Las Casas informed contemporary notions of "barbarism" in his *Apologética Historia Sumaria* (completed 1553–54). For a reading of the *Apologética*, see Greer, Mignolo, and Quilligan, *Rereading the Black Legend,* esp. 6–8.
14. Maltby, *The Black Legend in England*, 6.
15. Spain tried to rectify the perception of the bastardy of Spanish blood though the expulsion of the Jews (1492) and Moriscos (1609), and through the institution of laws of limpieza de sangre (blood purity), starting in the fifteenth century.

their massacre of West Indians was more or less severe than the "deliberate extermination" later enacted by the Puritans of New England,[16] whether the Inquisition torture instruments were more or less brutal than those used by the English to punish state traitors and recusant Catholics,[17] or whether the actions undertaken by the Spanish were any less "monstrous" than those undertaken by any other European monopolies that filled Spain's place in this "fearsome [colonial] enterprise" that "sowed death and desolation on every continent."[18] This book does not seek to excuse; it seeks only to disabuse.

Early modern Spain has been given many names: universal monarchy, colonial empire, global empire, first superpower, and so on. Thus, in her opening statement to the 2019 "Iberian Romance and its English Afterlives" seminar (led by Joyce Boro and Louise Wilson) at the Shakespeare Association of America conference in Washington, D.C., Helen Moore suggested that the time has come to reassess what we mean by *Spain* in historiographical studies of early modern literature.[19] In order to address this question with any degree of satisfaction, it is important to first acknowledge that the signification of *Spain* or *Spanish* shifts according to one's scholarly vantage point, be it historiographical, philological, ontological, or otherwise. Second, since the Black Legend of Spanish Cruelty has so thoroughly confused the Spanish identity with the racist stereotypes emerging from the collective memory, it is befitting to note that the country remains constrained by politically contentious taxonomies.[20]

My Anglo-Hispanist approach to the romancing of empire is in fact less concerned with Spain itself, than with how the English narrativizing of the Spanish problem

---

16. See Maltby, *The Black Legend in England*, 18.
17. See Maltby, *The Black Legend in England*, 42–43.
18. Roberto Fernández Retamar, *Caliban and Other Essays* (Minneapolis: University of Minnesota Press, 1989), 58.
19. Helen Moore, respondent, "Iberian Romance and Its English Afterlives," Joyce Boro and Louise Wilson, organizers, 2019 meeting of the Shakespeare Association of America, Washington, D.C.
20. Hispanists generally prefer the term *Iberian* to describe the study of the literatures and cultures of Spain and Portugal, not least because Spanish and Portuguese as a discipline has traditionally subsumed the study of the Spanish Americas. *Iberian* is also more acceptable to modern separatist movements in such regions as the Euskal Herria (Basque Country) and Catalunya (Catalonia). Nevertheless, for the purpose of this study, *Spanish* will be the preferred term, specifically for its connotative use in English letters. *Spain* specifically refers to its discrete sixteenth-century iteration as a universal monarchy composed of colonial viceroyalties, superficially connected to each other by their common adherence to the Habsburg Dynasty and to the Catholic religion, though of course the lived reality of *Spanishness* was altogether distinct from place to place. For this study, *Spanish* could apply to parts of early modern Italy, France, the Netherlands, South and Central America, and Portugal, while for Spain's rivals, *Spanish* could also mean black, African, tawny, Moorish, Jewish, and of course, Catholic (i.e., imperial Roman). I reject all racist terms and elisions, but in order to place focus on the linguistic ties to empire attending to genre, and, in order to reconstruct English attitudes toward the Spanish monarchy as expressed in the way that authors talked about and through romance, which is my primary objective, I must also occasionally reify such distorted perceptions, treading delicately between England's view of Spain and Spain's view of itself.

(as expressed by Spain's conduct in the Americas) revealed an emerging sense of England and of Englishness—in effect, of the nation—by and through literature. It is in literature that the fiction of British exceptionalism first took root as a poetic-ethnographic *episteme of civilization*, and it is in literature that these ideas were inculcated to subsequent generations. For instance, England's proudly proclaimed independence from Spain was immortalized in the literature surrounding its famous naval victory against the attempted Spanish Armada invasion in 1588, widely romanticized as a providential escape from the clutches of Habsburg tyranny. Thus it became a defining moment in the construction of the English nation. Abject anti-Hispanism was certainly a far cry from concrete nationalism, but as Eric Griffin notes, "for a number of historically specific reasons, it was 'not-Spanishness'—or rather, not an ideologically motivated 'forging' of what it meant to be ethnically Spanish—that for several centuries gave the English their surest sense of national identity."[21] This narrative was well established by 1656 when Oliver Cromwell famously remarked in a speech at the meeting of the Second Protectorate Parliament that "truly, [England's] great Enemy is the Spaniard. He is a natural enemy. He is naturally so; he is naturally so throughout, by reason of that enmity that is in him against whatsoever is of God."[22] Moreover, given that a proto-national English consciousness manifested throughout medieval Arthuriana, as Geraldine Heng has demonstrated,[23] then consequently it may be surmised that fiction literature has always served (on one level or another) to disseminate the operative logic of an English empire as natural and predestined, perhaps no more so famously than in the foretold second coming of Arthur against the new Rome.

In this study, I concentrate on *tales of love and arms*, works that witness the chief romantic struggle between eros and adventure.[24] These books, poems, plays, and fairy tales advance versions of what Fuchs has called *romance strategies*, a series of "commonplaces and narrative maneuvers," inspired by the classical myths, folklore, and the epic, that idealize the wandering hero, probe the supernatural and the marvelous, and elide amorousness, adventure, and conquest as functions of erotic delay.[25] Although these strategies are not universally present in the primary works analyzed in this book, their common

---

21. Eric Griffin, "Ethos to Ethnos: Hispanizing 'the Spaniard' in the Old World and the New,'" *The New Centennial Review*, 2, no. 1 (2002), 69–116 (71).
22. Oliver Cromwell, "Speech V. Meeting of the Second Protectorate Parliament, 17 Sept. 1656," in Thomas Carlyle, *Oliver Cromwell's Letters and Speeches with Elucidations, in Four Volumes*, vol. III (London: Chapman and Hall, 1897), 267–310 (270–71).
23. Geraldine Heng, *Empire of Magic: Medieval Romance and the Politics of Cultural Fantasy* (New York: Columbia University Press, 2003). The work considers medieval romance's fascination with the East, by which proto-constructions of the nation-state began to form.
24. The inspiration was the preface written by bookseller and translator, Francis Kirkman, for his 1673 translation of *The Famous and Delectable History of Don Belianis of Greece* (London: Kirkman), in which he noted that in the Spanish romance: "there was *Love and Arms*, and some strange impossible adventures, for which I liked it the better." For a discussion of Kirkman and his translations, including this quotation, see Alex Davis, *Chivalry and Romance in the English Renaissance, Studies in Renaissance Literature*, vol. 11 (Cambridge: D.S. Brewer, 2003), 63–72.
25. See Barbara Fuchs, *Romance* (New York: Routledge, 2004), esp. 4–8.

unifying principle is that they idealize conquest as romantic, marshaling these *romance strategies* as major crucibles for the Age of Exploration.[26]

Since the sixteenth-century Spanish and Portuguese were so active in the project of global colonization, it is not surprising to find accounts attesting to the enormous influence of these tales of love and arms, or what Irving Leonard called *books of the brave*,[27] in spurring the martial spirits of Iberian knights, captains, and military commanders, and even the illiterate soldiers-in-rank, as the following anecdote from 1619 well attests:

> While a Portuguese commander had an enemy city under siege during the fighting in India, a number of his soldiers who camped together as comrades carried in their outfit a novel of chivalry with which they passed the time. One of these men who knew this literature less than the others regarded everything he heard read as true (for there are guileless people who think that there can be no lies in print) [...] When the time came for an attack this good fellow, stirred by what he had heard read and eager to emulate the heroes of the book, burned with a desire to demonstrate his valor and to perform a deed of knighthood which would be remembered. And so he heaped wildly into the fray and began to strike right and left with his sword among the enemy so furiously that only by great effort and much peril his comrades and numerous other soldiers together were able to save his life by picking him up covered with glory and not a few wounds. When his friends scolded him for his rashness, he answered: "Aw, leave me alone! I didn't do the half of what any of the knights did in the book that you fellows read to me every night." And from that time, he was exceedingly valorous.[28]

The writer also gave in evidence a "valorous Captain in Portugal, not surpassed by any in the Roman Empire, who with the imitation of a fictitious knight became the best of his era, just by imitating the virtues that were written of him" (my translation).[29]

Imitation of the *books of the brave* was not limited to Spanish and Portuguese readers, however. This study shows how the early modern English, eager to copy Iberia's voracious conquerors, keenly read, translated, and appropriated romance works, converting them into *books of the brave* English, though usually in ways that were more indirect, which points to a general sentiment of *guilty reading* that frequently accompanied the country's engagement with Spanish culture. Although this study concentrates on two romance cycles authored in Iberia, *Amadís de Gaula* and *Espejo de príncipes y cavalleros,* it also incorporates other works that deployed *romance strategies* as crucibles of conquest, such as the tragedy of *Medea* by the Hispano-Roman writer, Lucius Annaeus Seneca, or that

---

26. Patricia Parker has argued that elements of romance may be present in works that are not strictly defined as romance. See Parker, *Inescapable Romance: Studies in the Poetics of a Mode* (Princeton: Princeton University Press, 1979).
27. Irving A. Leonard, *Books of the Brave: Being an Account of Books and of Men in the Spanish Conquest and Settlement of the Sixteenth-Century New World*, second edition (Berkeley: University of California Press, 1992).
28. Francisco Rodríguez Lobo, *Corte en Aldea y Noches de Invierno* (Valencia: Salvador Faulí, 1798) (First edition in 1619), sigs. B2r–B2v; qtd. in translation from Leonard, *Books of the Brave*, 26.
29. Rodríguez Lobo, *Corte en Aldea y Noches de Invierno*, sig. B1v.

were used to romanticize colonization, as in the case of the *Orlando* epics. All of these, as I show, were deemed central to Spain's self-fashioning as a divinely ordained global empire, and so they likewise informed England's piratic self-fashioning as a world savior, divinely mandated to rescue the world from the thrall of Spanish tyranny.

While these tales of love and arms mobilized the colonizer mindset at the crucial levels of language and image, producing the era's most ambitious ideologues, these romantic fictions would not be fully realized by the English until much later during the Romantic and Victorian periods. The torch of empire would have to pass through the Netherlands, and France, and reconcile the events of the Thirty Years War (1618–48), all before England would emerge as a truly global player. The nineteenth century was certainly the era of most robust development of England's narrative of itself as world savior, but it may be that the scholarly predilection to track the money, the people, and the politics of British imperialism at its historical zenith has caused us to ignore the obvious fact that ideas dictate actions, and that ideology precedes administration.

Raymond Williams's work on cultural ideology, speaking of a dominant, residual and emergent culture, particularly illuminates the form of British imperialism that my book traces. If the dominant culture was most forcefully expressed in the nineteenth century, emerging in earnest during the eighteenth century with the official birth of the nation, then what Williams defines as the residual culture belongs to the sixteenth and seventeenth centuries.[30] Some historical touchstones were the English victories against the Armada and at Cádiz; and the sacking of Spanish-American viceroyalties and the founding of New Albion. And yet, when I speak of the ideological origins of the British Empire, I am also referring to something far more elusive than state propaganda or the progress of war. Williams observes that residual culture is especially active in "the literary tradition," particularly in the characterization of "what literature now is and should be."[31] And, during the early modern period what genre was more actively residual—and more predominately canonical—than romance, the cultural-imaginitive repository of Christian religion, and the *civilized* value-systems of "absolute brotherhood" and "service to others without reward?"[32] Evincing the natural linkage of literature and history, these romance books unified political *truths* by tropifying history as common experience: scriptural history, teleology, etiology, legend, and myth all appeared as part of the single fabric of *British* experience that would one day constitute a national epistemology. When I speak of romance translation as a project of cultural imperialism, I therefore mean a series of transmissive practices—from direct translation and adaptation to literary criticism and parody—that normalized culture in the common language, reformulating old world concepts in the new (e.g., honor, chivalry, crusade), and over time reinforcing the imperial power structures already set in place by the dominant regime.

---

30. Raymond Williams, *Marxism and Literature*, reprint (Oxford: Oxford University Press, 2009), 13.
31. Williams, *Marxism and Literature*, 123.
32. Williams, *Marxism and Literature*, 122.

The Structure of This Book

The chapters in this book represent separate case studies regarding the use of romance strategies and tales of love and arms more generally in the imperialist myth-making of early modern England against the threat of imperial Spain, particularly those which were first used by Spanish authors to justify Spain's own imperialist designs. Owing to the sprawling scope of this argument, touching on two national histories and literary traditions, and considering various sites of real or imagined conquest simultaneously, chapters have been organized by overarching themes, places, and ideas, rather than by a primary adherence to historical chronology. These show how the English colonial mindset developed through a concerted conversation with the reality of Spain's presence in the colonial world, particularly in the contentious sites of sixteenth-century México, Perú, Guiana, California, and Australia, with their widely contested borders and cultural taxonomies, producing emergent discourses of English nationalism and proto-imperialism as self-conscious responses to the so-considered *Spanish problem*.

CHAPTER 1

"BOOKS OF THE BRAVE" ENGLISH: SPANISH TALES OF LOVE AND ARMS IN TRANSLATION

The books of *Amadís de Gaula* and *Espejo de príncipes y cavalleros* came to England in the garb of military and rhetorical guidebooks. With an uptick in translation during the late 1500s, English culture developed a proverbial obsession with reading the *books of the brave* Spanish and Portuguese conquistadors, particularly during the war years of 1585 to 1604, when English men-at-arms prepared to meet Spaniards in battle. This was to be a hinge period in the conception of an English conquest fantasy, planting the seeds of England's aspirational imperialism, in and through romance.

Tales of Love and Arms

Ramón Llull's Català guidebook, *The Book of the Order of Chivalry* (1484), may not have been a fictional romance, but it certainly spoke of love and arms. It was, most fittingly, the first vernacular work of Iberia to be printed in English, the first in a developing series of translations that culminated with the period of most concentrated translation of Spanish romance during the Anglo-Spanish War (see Appendix I). In his youth, Llull had been a knight, seneschal, and courtier at the courts of James I, King of Aragón (1208–1276; ruled 1213–76) and of his second son, King James II (1267– 1327; King of Aragón from 1291–1327; King of Mallorca/Majorca from 1276–87 and 1295–1311). In the year 1263 at the royal court of Mallorca, Llull experienced a series of religious visions that enacted a major personal conversion, after which he turned to more exegetical and theoretical writings. Composed early in his career, *The Book of the Order of Chivalry* offered a didactic guidebook for inductees to the order of knighthood, typically men of noble birth who had closely served the king. Llull traced the origins of knighthood to the Creation, and he set down a set of virtues that bolstered the knight's crusading spirit, for "if you wish to find nobility of courage, seek it in faith, hope, charity, justice, fortitude, loyalty and the other virtues, for nobility of courage resides in them, and because of them the noble heart of the knight protects itself against evil, deceit and the enemies of Chivalry."[1] Touching on the classical divide between eros and adventure, love and arms, or what he called "lust and fortitude," Llull wrote:

---

1. Ramón Llull, *The Book of the Order of Chivalry*, Noel Fallows, trans. (Woodbridge: Boydell Press, 2013), 57.

Lust and fortitude engage in combat with each other; and the weapons with which lust fights fortitude are youth, handsome features, overindulgence in food and drink, ornate vestments, opportunity, falsehood, treachery, injustice, scorn of God and paradise, disdain for the torments of hell, and other weapons similar to these. Fortitude fights lust by remembering God and His commandments, and by understanding God and the benefits and sufferings that He can give, and by loving God because He is worthy of being loved, feared, honoured and obeyed; and fortitude fights lust with nobility of courage which refuses to submit to malicious and impure thoughts or descend from its high honour to be censured by the people. So then, since the knight is called a knight because he fights vices with strength of courage, a knight who has no fortitude does not have the heart of a knight, nor does he have the weapons with which knights must fight.[2]

This characterization of lust as antithetical to Christian community represented a major elaboration upon the classical understanding of eros, usually embodied in a woman, as a distraction or delay from the hero's voyage, as in Odysseus's entrapment by Calypso, or Aeneas's enthrallment with Dido. Whereas lust detained these heroes from their destined earthly kingdoms (Odysseus's rightful rule of Ithaca and Aeneas's destined founding of Rome), the Christian knight's cowardice denied him the greater kingdom of Christ. In this understanding of the struggle between love and arms, Christian conquest was divine, a reflected armament of faith, and carnal love was despicable, the disarming enticement of earthly delight. Writing in medias res, immediately following the Eighth Crusade led by King Louis IX of France (1214–1270; ruled 1226–70), Llull sought to reform the order of chivalry under the singular mission of pushing back the infiel (infidel), for which holy war served as a prime masculine function of holy knighthood.

From the moment of the book's first Català composition to its later English-language transmission in the interim of the War of the Roses,[3] however, a major transformation occurred. Spain was now the only country where the Crusades were ongoing. While England was largely divided by courtly and political ruptures among the remaining Plantagenets, the Spanish Crown was also undergoing a period of rapid unification following the 1469 dynastic marriage of the Catholic monarchs of Castilla and Aragón, which joined together both kingdoms' rich traditions in las órdenes de caballería (orders of chivalry).[4] Dedicating the translation to King Richard III of England (1452–1485;

---

2. Llull, *The Book of the Order of Chivalry*, 74.
3. The work is believed to have been translated from a French edition.
4. Originally, Spain's four major military orders, the Orders of Santiago, Calatrava, Montesa, and Alcántara, were affiliated with the local regions where they developed, but they gradually came under the direct tutelage of the Spanish Crown. Taking its rule from the Knights Templar, established earlier in the twelfth century, the Order of Santiago was founded in 1171 to fight invading Muslims and to protect pilgrims traveling to Santiago de Compostela. In the tradition of the Augustinian canons, the knights wore a white habit with a red fitchy cross. Their motto was "Rubet ensis sanguine Arabum" (May the sword be red with Arab blood). The order quickly became a wealthy international institution with landholdings in southern France, Italy, Palestine, Hungary, and England. It came under the Crown's administration in 1493. Formerly known as the Order of Saint Julián del Parero (founded 1156), the Order of Alcántara was a monastic militia of León. Alcántara became a national honorific order under the Spanish Crown in 1494. The Order of Calatrava derived its name from the Moorish castle of Qalat

ruled 1483–85), translator William Caxton treated the Spanish work as a model for the enduring mission of the Crusades that was alive in Iberia and which must be brought back to England to revive the declining masculine spirit. Addressing the knights of England, he asked, "Where is the custom and usage of noble chivalry that was used in those days?"[5] He added, "What do you do now but go to the public baths and play at dice? Leave all of this and instead read the noble volumes of Sir Lancelot and the Holy Grail, of Sir Galahad, of Tristram, of Perceval, of Gawain and many others. There will you see manhood, courtesy and nobility."[6] Caxton's edition of Thomas Malory's *Le Morte D'Arthur* was printed one year later. The work was instrumental in reigniting English interests in "the custom and usage of noble chivalry,"[7] especially during the ensuing age of the Tudors, who claimed descent from King Arthur to legitimize their dynasty, further translating chivalric traditions like the joust into national pastimes, or *past-times*, and promoting readership of these famous tales of Arthur and his knights of the Round Table.[8]

As Spain's cultural influence grew during the Siglo de Oro, contemporary romances, especially those of chivalry, further wed courtly love to erotic conquest, grafting the dominant discourses of martial masculinity unto the politico-religious missions of American colonization. These works developed the masculine call to arms as not only divine, required for entry to the kingdom of Christ, but also earthly, a first step toward the formation of a Messianic kingdom in the West, in the Americas ruled by the Habsburgs. Blending courtly love plots with scenes of astonishing fantasy, reconceptualizing the eastern Other in the mysterious West, tales of love and arms also linked the desire for a divine world with the epic spirit of adventure that formed the crux of Renaissance *bravery*. Juxtaposing romance's dominant *modes*, these proto-imperialist works eroticized the pleasure and terror of encounter with pagan Otherworlds (wonders), in the process legitimating conquest and conversion as integral to the hero's divine quest.[9]

    Rawah (the Castle of War), which was captured in 1147. From 1158 onward, the order was charged with defending the stronghold. The order's grand mastership passed to the Spanish Crown in 1487. The Order of Montesa was established in 1317 with the dissolution of the Templars. In 1400, the Order of Montesa also absorbed the Order of San Jorge de Alfama (Saint George of Alfama), which had been established in 1201 by King Pedro II of Aragón (1178–1213; ruled 1196–1213). The Alfama order followed the Augustinian rule and wore a white habit donned with the iconic red cross of Saint George. The knights of Montesa retained the white mantle but exchanged the red cross for a black one. They took their name from their headquarters at Saint George of Montesa, Valencia. The order passed to the Crown in 1587.

5. Qtd. in Kelly Devries and Michael Livingston, eds., *Medieval Warfare: A Reader, Readings in Medieval Civilizations and Culture: XXI*, Paul Edward Dutton, ed. (Toronto: University of Toronto Press, 2019), 62.
6. Qtd. in Devries and Livingston, *Medieval Warfare*, 62.
7. Qtd. in Devries and Livingston, *Medieval Warfare*, 62.
8. Such works as *Le Morte D'Arthur* complicated the conventional tension between love and arms by incorporating the Ovidian erotic tradition of desire as performative suffering. Courtly love represented both a promotion and obstacle to knightly celibacy. See Barbara Fuchs, *Romance* (New York: Routledge, 2004), esp. 42–50.
9. This imperial iconography undergirded by romance best corresponds with what Northrop Frye describes as the chronicle function, which occupies the juncture of thematic literature

For the avid reader of tales of love and arms, the global conquests of the sixteenth century derived legibility and justification through their allegorical embedment in romance's typological and topological wonder-worlds, obscuring the deadening brutalism of conquest with the enlivening idealism of fiction. This was a key readerly response to what Northrop Frye describes as the "creative fantasy," of naïve romance, or the romance of wonder.[10] The reader's capacity to identify with the hero's quest, coupled with his desire to reproduce its highly idealistic forms in ordinary life, cultivated *masculine wanderlust* as a key readerly impulse. As the hero's marvelous encounters turn upon erotic delay, specifically within these multipart and incomplete cycles, romance's major organizing structure also becomes its chief locus of meaning.[11] The tension arouses a ceaseless will for completion. The hero will either complete his quest, or the reader, stirred by romance's dilatory erotics, will complete the quest for him. He will become Don Quixote, called to arms by his wondering and wandering within the books of chivalry.

"Books of the Brave" English

England's sixteenth-century fascination with Spanish romance was benchmarked by two books of chivalry: *Amadís de Gaula* (*Amadis of Gaul*) and *Espejo de príncipes y cavalleros* (*The Mirrour of Princely Deedes and Knighthood*, hereafter *The Mirrour of Knighthood*). First published in 1508, *Amadís* was set down by Garci Rodríguez de Montalvo, municipal governor of Medina del Campo, who claimed to have corrected its first three parts (usually attributed to the Portuguese writer Vasco de Lobeira), and to have added the fourth and fifth books for *Las sergas de Esplandián* (*Exploits of Esplandian*) (1510). As I explain in Chapter 5, this sequel was particularly responsible for conditioning readers' impressions of the New World while the books of *Amadís* were altogether synonymous with American colonization. As such, they were frequently imported into the Spanish New World. For instance, on a 1540 inventory of books from the Seville-based Cromberger printing house, which held exclusive right to print books destined for the Americas during the first half of the sixteenth century, there were 446 copies of *Amadís*, along with 10 copies and 171 copies, respectively, of the spinoffs, *Lisuarte de Grecia* and *Florisel de Niquea*.[12]

---

and the romantic mode. It also evinces this mode's overlap with the high mimetic mode, particularly through creation of a strong nationalist sentiment, here treated as proto-nationalism. See Frye, "Historical Criticism: Theory of Modes," *Anatomy of Criticism* (Princeton: Princeton University Press, 1957), 33–68.

10. In imitation of "the wish-fulfillment dream," the romance "tends to absorb emotion and communicate it internally to the reader. Romance, therefore, is characterized by the acceptance of pity and fear, which in ordinary life relate to pain, as forms of pleasure. It turns fear at a distance, or terror, into the adventurous; fear at contact, or horror, into the marvellous, and fear without an object, or dread (*Angst*) into a pensive melancholy." Frye, *Anatomy of Criticism*, 37.
11. Patricia Parker, *Inescapable Romance: Studies in the Poetics of a Mode* (Princeton: Princeton University Press, 1979), 221.
12. Irving A. Leonard, *Books of the Brave: Being an Account of Books and of Men in the Spanish Conquest and Settlement of the Sixteenth-Century New World*, second edition (Berkeley: University of California Press, 1992), 98.

Amadís appeared regularly listed on inventories of Spanish inquisitors inspecting goods transported by voyagers to the New World; it was so ubiquitous that it is unclear whether the title was used to refer to the original work by Montalvo, to its sequels and imitations, or to any book of chivalry.[13]

The tale relates the adventures of the chivalrous knight, Amadís, born of a secret union between King Perión of Gaul and Princess Elisena of Little Britain. Elisena conceals the child by sending him upon a bark cast out to sea; he arrives in Scotland, where he is guarded and trained in chivalry by the knight, Gandales. As a youth, Amadís falls in love with the princess, Oriana, daughter of King Lisuarte of Great Britain, but the courtship is many times frustrated, often at the hands of the evil knight and necromancer, Arcaláus, whose tireless cunning is met by the prophetic wisdom of Urganda la Desconocida (Urganda the Unknown), who serves as Amadís's protector. Through many adventures Amadís, whose name recalls the love of God, eventually matures into a paragon of chivalry and a true devoté to Oriana, with whom he produces the great hero, Esplandián.

Book I first appeared on the English print market within Thomas Paynell's 1572 *Moste excellent and pleasaunt booke, entituled: The treasurie of Amadis of Fraunce Conteyning eloquent orations, pythie epistles, learned letters, and feruent complayntes, seruing for sundrie purposes*, which Paynell translated from a French collection originally published in 1559.[14] The French version, *Le thresor des douze livres d'Amadis de Gaule: assauoir les Harengues, concions, epistres, complaints, & autres choses le plus excellentes & dignes du lecteur François*, offered a selection of letters and speeches from the 1540 translation of Montalvo's Castilian edition, especially those that exhibited the tale's high rhetorical style. Many of these passages were of a sentimental quality, depicting the love correspondence between the main characters. For instance, included among its celebrated rhetorical discourses and love missives was "The complaint Amadis made when he received Oriane's vigorous Letter, declaring the nobility of fortune, by the which she banished him from her company." This long speech made the lady's cruel rejection of the Christian knight one of the first plotlines known to English audiences, crucial for Edmund Spenser, for example, in his characterization of Timias's torment at the rejection of Belphoebe in *The Faerie Queene* (1590; 1596), as I show in Chapter 3.

In his dedicatory epistle, Paynell highlighted the romance's pedagogical function for students of rhetoric. This discerning and disarming approach may have heightened *Amadís*'s mystique in England. Not only did Paynell translate the original published work from French, a language whose prestige dated back to the Norman Conquest, but he also

---

13. See Leonard, *Books of the Brave*, esp. 160–63.
14. An earlier version of this chapter, which has been split with Chapter 6, was published as "'Carried away with The Myrrour of Knighthood': Hispanophobia and the Rhetorical Feminization of Romance Literature," in Arthur F. Marotti, ed. *New Ways of Looking at Old Texts, VI. Papers of the Renaissance English Text Society 2011–2016* (Tempe: Arizona Center for Medieval & Renaissance Studies/RETS, 2019), 269–95.

introduced its titular character within what was essentially a carefully constructed style manual, offering readers:

> Wherout men may learne to be noble oratours, wise and prudent counsellours, excellent Rhetoricians, expert captains, amorous companions, feruent & honest louers, secrete messengers, obedient seruants, elegant enditers of louely Epistles, sweete pronouncers & true ortographers, of the french tong so pleasant, so highly commended, and so imbraced of all men.[15]

The collection was so impressive that in his *Defence of Poesy*, published posthumously in 1595, Sir Philip Sidney criticized the Spanish language for lacking English's poetic fluidity, nevertheless noting: "I have known men, that even with reading *Amadis*, which, God knoweth, wanteth much of a perfect poesy, have found their hearts moved to the exercise of courtesy, liberality, and especially courage."[16] A known Hispanist,[17] Sidney probably also consulted Paynell's *Treasurie* given that his remarks so closely echo Paynell's preface "To the Gentle Reader," where he said of *Amadis*, "What weake and cowardly heartes and stomackes have they that will not be stirred or moued with the rhetorical & eloquent orations [...] [and] fight stoutly and courageously, as Amadis, the king of England & France."[18]

Sidney well illustrates the phenomenon of a brave Englishman whose broad romantic formation gave him courage to take arms against the Spanish threat.[19] The epitome of the Renaissance gentleman, Sidney fought "stoutly and courageously" against the Spanish in the Netherlands, where he received a mortal bullet wound in the thigh at the 1586 Battle of Zutphen; he died less than three weeks later in October 1586.[20] The much-repeated circumstances of Sidney's wounding and conduct in battle, and of his subsequent death, were the subject of ample English legends, some apocryphal or exaggerated, constructing the portrait of a man utterly disposed "to the exercise of courtesy, liberality, and especially courage." These made him the immortalized subject

---

15. Thomas Paynell, "To the Gentle Reader," in *The moste excellent and pleasaunt booke, entituled: The treasurie of Amadis of Fraunce conteyning eloquente orations, pythie epistles, learned letters, and feruent complayntes, seruing for sundrie purposes. Translated out of Frenche into English* (London: Thomas Hacket, 1572), v–vi (vi).
16. Philip Sidney, *An Apology for Poetry (or The Defence of Poesy)*, R. W. Maslen, ed. (Manchester: Manchester University Press, 2002), 95.
17. An avid reader of Spanish romance, Sidney adapted portions of Jorge de Montemayor's *Siete libros de Diana* and Montalvo's *Amadís*, for *The Arcadia* (1590), a work that mingled aspects of chivalry (i.e., "Heroicall poetry") with pastoral love plots. Sidney also read Spanish. See Oliveira e Silva, "Recurrent Onomastic Textures in the *Diana* of Jorge de Montemayor and the *Arcadia* of Sir Philip Sidney," *Studies in Philology* 79 no. 1 (1982), 30–40; e Silva, "Sir Philip Sidney and the Castilian Tongue," *Comparative Literature* 34 no. 2 (1982), 130–45.
18. Paynell, "To the Gentle Reader," v–vi. Anthony Munday's first full-length, English edition of Part I did not appear in print until 1590.
19. Nevertheless, as I discuss in Chapter 6, the *Treasurie*'s explicit Francophilism may have partially obscured *Amadís*'s connotative Hispanism.
20. For a study of Sidney's foreign service, see Tim Crowley, "Sidney's Legal Patronage and the International Protestant Cause," *Renaissance Quarterly* 71, no. 4 (2018): 1298–350.

of Spenser's pastoral elegy, *Astrophel* (1595), and several other works that completed his panegyrical portrait as a lover and a gallant.[21]

Amadís Rejected

In 1569, *Amadís* caused a diplomatic scandal involving Spanish ambassador, Guerau de Espés del Valle (hereafter Ambassador de Spes), who referred to the work in a letter addressed to Antwerp-based royal financier, Gerónimo de Curiel. This "first crisis in Anglo-Spanish relations during Elizabeth's reign"[22] involved Spain's seizure of English shipping in the Low Countries in retaliation for a recent English capture of Spanish treasure. This event forced the newly appointed Spanish ambassador into house arrest, of which he remarked:

> If you hear say that they have detained me, do not be amazed, for in this island there are still the enchantments of Amadís, and Arcaláus lives, but I am healthy and well, a prisoner of the queen Oriana, and I think that without the need of either Urganda or of stirring too much trouble, all of this will end as a comedy.[23]

The Privy Council denounced the allusion as "slanderous" and "seditious" on charge of its excessive "levity" toward the queen.[24] A French Ambassador wrote, "[the Queen] became so indignant" that she exclaimed that "if he [Spes] had been her subject, she would have pursued him with the utmost rigor of the law."[25] A memorandum accused Spes of sedition, dubbing him a "calumniator of Princes."[26]

In his testimony, Ambassador de Spes successfully argued that his associating Queen Elizabeth with Oriana was a form of compliment commonly used in reference to great ladies at the Spanish court, but he failed to convince the Council that his mention of Arcaláus was not a libel against William Cecil (later Lord Burghley). In a previously confiscated letter to Don Fernando Álvarez de Toledo y Pimentel, third Duke of Alba and resident commander of the Spanish army in Flanders, Ambassador de Spes had complained of Cecil's evil enterprises, particularly in seeking to find possible evidence of his collusion with Mary, Queen of Scots (1542–1587; ruled 1542–67), though no such documents were found. Of Cecil's corrosive influence, Ambassador de Spes remarked

---

21. For a comprehensive study of Sidney's final year, see J. A. Van Dorsten, Dominic Baker-Smith, and Arthur F. Kinney, eds., *Sir Philip Sidney: 1586 and the Creation of a Legend*, Publications of the Sir Thomas Browne Institute, New Ser., no. 9 (Leiden: J. Brill/Leiden University Press, 1986).
22. Tim Crowley, "Contingencies of Literary Censorship: Anglo-Spanish Diplomacy and *Amadís de Gaula* in January 1569," *Sixteenth Century Journal* (2015), 891–926 (891).
23. Letter by Spes to Gerónimo Curiel, January 10, 1569, British Library, The National Archive, SP 70/105, fols. 87–88. Transcription derived from Crowley, "Contingencies of Literary Censorship," 922. All translations are my own.
24. Privy Council to Spes, January 14, 1569, English draft, British library, Cotton, Galba, C III, 155v; qtd. in Crowley, "Contingencies of Literary Censorship," 892.
25. Qtd. in Agnes Strickland, *Lives of the Queens of England, from the Norman Conquest*, vol. 4 (Philadelphia: Lippincott, 1893), 287.
26. Qtd. in Crowley, "Contingencies of Literary Censorship," 911.

that it was "a pity that so excellent a Queen should give credit to so scandalous a person. God will remedy it."[27] Unfortunate for the ambassador, Cecil could decipher the relevancy of this comment to the *Amadís* allusion: Spes was comparing Cecil's poisoning Elizabeth's mind against Spain's King Philip II (1527–1598; ruled 1556–98) to the false information that Arcaláus supplies to Lisuarte about Amadís; in both scenarios, a threatened war and dynastic marriage hung critically in the balance.

This was an additional cause for outrage: in using Amadís as a reference to the Spanish king, whose enchantments were still felt in "this Island," Spes was likely referring to not only England's oppression of Catholics and the general fear of collusion with Spain, but also Philip's own use of Amadís as his royal avatar. This association brought to mind Philip's former consort of Queen Mary I (1516–1558; ruled 1553–58), recasting the king in his familiar role as suitor to an English princess, all in an effort to condemn Cecil.

As proxy for the King of Spain, Ambassador de Spes had violated the boundaries of Elizabethan court politics, in which the subject of royal marriage went hand-in-hand with the queen's tense foreign and domestic policy. Hence, according to Elizabeth's biographer, William Camden, the Spanish ambassador "Spred abroad defamatory Libels, wherein he scandalously blurred the Queen's Reputation, under the name of *Amadis Oriana*."[28] Montalvo's work was published more than 60 years earlier, but Spes had used it—all too successfully—to converse with contemporary Anglo-Spanish politics. As Tim Crowley puts it:

> The Arcaláus, Oriana, and Urganda references, together, subtly imply sedition brewing within England and suggest that the outcome (though perhaps messy in its achievement) will be favorable to Spain and to English Catholicism [...] The logic of cultural poetics by which Spes argued that his Oriana reference was indeed harmless proved unconvincing due to the *Amadís* allusion's internal connection between its Arcaláus and Oriana components.[29]

The ambassador was confined to house arrest for an additional five months; two years later, when Elizabeth expelled him from England for his involvement in the Ridolfi plot, her explanatory letter to Philip circulated internationally along with a Privy Council report citing her offense at the ambassador's *Amadís* allusion from 1569.[30]

Perhaps the Spanish ambassader, writing in January, had reason to be optimistic after all that "all of this will end as a comedy," or in other words, a story ending in marriage. One month after Spes wrote his fateful letter, Philip's engagement to the Habsburg imperial princess, Anna of Austria (1549–1580), was publicly announced. The two were

---

27. Qtd. in Crowley, "Contingencies of Literary Censorship," 891.
28. William Camden, *The History of the Most Renowned and Victorious Princess Elizabeth Late Queen of England; Containing All the Most Important and Remarkable Passages of State, Both at Home and Abroad (so Far as They Were Linked with English Affairs) During Her Long and Prosperous Reign. The Fourth Edition, Revised and Compared with the Original, Whereby Many Gross Faults are Amended, Several Periods Before Omitted are Added in Their Due Places, ... with a New Alphabetical Index of All the Principal Things Contained in the History* (London: R. Bentley, 1688), 122.
29. Crowley, "Contingencies of Literary Censorship," 920–21.
30. Crowley, "Contingencies of Literary Censorship," 918–19.

married by proxy in May 1570, and Anna's arrival, some months later, was celebrated with a pageant featuring Amadís's wedding to Oriana.³¹ Based on two chronicles, one from Burgos and the other from Seville, Maria Mercedes Carrión relates how:

> Anna's arrival, welcoming the future bearer of the imperial crown's succesor to Spanish soil after three "unsuccessful" marriages by the king, was singularly characterized with a clear and present sense of Spanish history, the first time in Spanish pageantry that audiences witnessed the grandeur of Spain's historical memory [...] In fact, the masters of ceremonies spared no detail, evoking the highly ritualistic and legendary entertainments employed by Elizabeth I of England in Kenilworth and other British courtly spaces to build her single, imperially pregnant figura. This was surely a familiar (and, in more ways than one, rival) performance and plot for Anna, her husband-to-be, and their subjects, and the dramatic recreation of Burgos, in open dialogue with Elizabeth's *imago* of the Virgin Queen, placed the issue of eschewing marriage at the centre of its histrionic mirror. Offstage, under the scrutiny of her new subjects as she watched Oriana's fate, Princess Anna advanced on her way to become the fourth and last wife of King Felipe II, the next queen of the Catholic Universal Monarchy, and its last hope to remedy the crown's lack of succession.³²

Philip had found his true Ori-Anna. His royal entertainments permanently settled the question of an Anglo-Spanish marriage, showing the greater profit that was to be gained by the king's marriage to an Austro-Hungarian princess, heiress to the Holy Roman Empire that had been ruled over by his father, Charles (1500–1558; King of Spain 1516–56; Holy Roman Emperor 1519–56).

Philip's use of *Amadís* to mark this momentous occasion probably also encoded a degree of anxiety over the bad press that had recently plagued his love life as it was portrayed on the international stage. Europe stirred with rumors that Philip had killed his third wife, Isabel de Valois (1545–1568), over a purported sexual intrigue with his son, Don Carlos (1545–1568), whom Philip was also believed to have had murdered.³³ The suspected infanticide reinforced Orientalist characterizations of the Spanish king as a more *barbaric* than other European princes, *practically a pagan or Saracen*, and therefore unfit to lead a universal Christian monarchy, as one chronicler later intimated of the supposed "killing of his Sonne, Prince Charles":

> And heere is a Case to bee lamented eternallie, that those Parricidies, committed now in Spayne, after the manner of the Mahumetane Superstition; not as Crymes to bee repented,

---

31. Spain's public Philipine pageants regularly featured reanactments from Montalvo's romance, including the hero's famous nuptials with Princess Oriana.
32. Maria Mercedes Carrión, *Subject Stages: Marriage, Theatre, and the Law in Early Modern Spain* (Toronto: University of Toronto Press, 2010), 72.
33. Don Carlos was originally betrothed to Elizabeth of Valois, though for various reasons, Philip decided to marry the 14-year old princess instead. Elizabeth died of miscarriage in October 1568. In January of the same year, Carlos had been imprisoned by his father in 1568 on grounds of his documented instability; he is also believed to have plotted to have his father killed. This led to Carlos's arrest and imprisonment; he died alone in confinement in July 1568, just shortly before Elizabeth. The short time span between both deaths, and the bizarre details pertaining to Carlos's imprisonment were kindling for much anti-Spanish propaganda.

but as Religious Traditions, and Deeds of great Merite, when the life of one Man, or a few Men, if it were of our Brethren, or Children, are taken, and sacrificed, for preservation of the publicke Tranquillitie both of Church and State, chiefelie in great and Monarchicall Kingdomes, where Religion doeth shoot out, with a growing and flowrishing Empyre. Alace! is not this the Fyre of Moloch, and the sacrificing of our Children to those bloodie and savage Gods?[34]

European outrage also concerned the incestuousness of Philip's marriage to Anna, his own niece, for which the *Amadís* pageantry could also serve as redress. The most prominent points pertaining to Philip's salacious love life were later gathered together by William I, Prince of Orange (1533–1584) in his famous *Apologie* (1580), a major cornerstone of the Black Legend.[35] With these charges of Philip's depravity further spurring the Reformed League's armed resistance of Spanish tyranny on land and at sea, Elizabeth's determined chastity would soon appear as a supreme wisdom, part of her defense of England against foreign conquest, especially after 1588.

As she advanced in age, Elizabeth's own royal entertainments further highlighted her cultish beauty and great desirability as Protestant Europe's most eligible unmarried queen, capturing what Roy Strong has aptly called the queen's "mask of youth."[36] And so, despite the queen's expressed displeasure over Ambassador de Spes's comparison of her royal person to Oriana, at some point the queen must have come to embrace the fictional English princess as one among her many alter egos. In fact, a correspondence dated December 8, 1592 by the courtier, Philip Gawdy, reported that "Uppon the coronation day at nyght ther cam two Knightes armed vpp into the privy chamber. [viz.] my L[ord] of Essex and my L[ord] of Cumberland and there made a challenge that vppon the xxvj[th] of ffebruary next that they will runn wth all commers to mayntayne that ther M[ajesty] is most worthiest and most fairest, [quoth] Amadis de Gaule."[37]

---

34. Peter Hay, *An Aduertiseme[nt] to the Subjects of Scotland of the Fearfull Dangers Threatned to Christian States; and Namely, to Great Britane, by the Ambition of Spayne: With a Contemplation, of the Truest Meanes, to Oppose it. also, Diverse Other Treatises, Touching the Present Estate of the Kingdome of Scotland; Verie Necessarie to Bee Knowne, and Considered, in this Tyme: Called, the First Blast of the Trumpet* (Aberdeen: Edward Raban, 1627), sig. F1r.

35. For a reading of Orange's *Apologie* in relation to the Black Legend, see Jesús M. Usunáriz, "Envidia de la potencia del rey católico,": respuestas españolas a las críticas de sus enemigos en los siglos XVI y XVII," in Pérez and Sánchez Jiménez, y den Boer, eds., *España ante sus críticos*, 45–66, esp. 47–50.

36. For discussion of the "mask of youth," see Roy Strong, *Gloriana: The Portraits of Queen Elizabeth I* (New York: Thames and Hudson, 1987), 94–97 and 146–51; *The Cult of Elizabeth: Elizabethan Portraiture and Pageantry* (London: Thames & Hudson, 1977), 46–54; *Artists of the Tudor Court: The Portrait Miniature Rediscovered, 1520–1620* (London: Victoria & Albert Museum, 1983), 126–32.

37. Isaac Herbert Jeayes, ed. *Letters of Philip Gawdy of West Harling, Norfolk, and of London to Various Members of his Family 1579–1616* (London, J. B. Nichols and Sons, 1906), 67. I have restored "quoth" following Roy Strong, who compared the transcript of Gawdy's letter to the manuscript record. See Strong "Queen Elizabeth I as Oriana," *Studies in the Renaissance* 6 no. 1 (1959), 251–60, note 18.

The use of the famous Spanish work to defend Elizabeth's reputation seems altogether surprising for a monarch whose hatred of Spain was so often recorded, particularly during the period of greatest conflict during the Anglo-Spanish War. The equation evinced the particular utility that *brave* English readers found in emulating the warlike paragons of Spanish romance, particularly during wartime.[38] It must not be forgotten that the real test of bravery was for the courtiers, Robert Devereux, second earl of Essex, and George Clifford, third earl of Cumberland, who around this time were also respectively being engaged in skirmishes with the Spanish about the globe. Devereux had was charged with leading English troops in the ongoing Siege of Rouen, an attempt by King Henry IV of France (1553–1610; ruled 1589–1610) to recover Normandy from the clutches of the Catholic League. The joust may have been a bid to recover some favor with Elizabeth, the queen having been displeased with Devereux's frequent departures to Normandy, and with the mounting costs of his expedition. Clifford, meanwhile, was meant to depart on a mission to plunder the Spanish West Indies.[39] He had already distinguished himself as a *brave* Englishman, having served on Lord Charles Howard's council of war, and having fought courageously at the Battle of Gravelines. He would further prove himself as a privateer during the 1590s, and in 1598 make a glorious stand against the Spanish by taking San Juan. A great lover of chivalry and of the joust, Clifford had been made the queen's champion in 1590.

In effect, these men were using the *Amadís*-inspired display of chivalry to play out England's real-world encounters with the Spanish, further defending the queen's virtue and beauty in a bid for royal approval. This means that if Clifford had personally read the translation of Lord François de la Noue's *Political and Military Discourses* (1587), which Edward Aggas had dedicated to him, then the French Huguenot's criticisms of *Amadís*'s spurs to warfare must have served more as an advertisement than a warning, as I further discuss in Chapter 6. In fact, for men like Clifford, the Spanish romance must have served as a fictional manifesto on the character of Spanish *bravery*, inspiring English readers to be more like the warlike Spaniards whom they expected to meet in

---

38. Roy Strong speculates that "either Essex or Cumberland might have played Amadis." "Queen Elizabeth I as Oriana," 255. Jeremy L. Smith also analyzes Oriana's correspondence with Elizabeth in "Music and Late Elizabethan Politics: The Identities of Oriana and Diana," *Journal of the American Musicological Society* 58, no. 3 (2005), 507–58. Smith suggests that both men intended to play Amadís to defend two different ladies as Oriana, but this hypothesis misaligns with Strong's notes on the manuscript record.

39. He was detained by bad weather at Plymouth, so when the fleet departed to its new destination at the Azores, it was instead led by John Norton. Together with a royal fleet under Sir John Burgh, it captured the great Portuguese carrack the *Madre de Dios*, containing a large cargo of spices, silks, and jewels, worth about £500,000. Much of the profit from the voyage disappeared (probably stolen by the sailors) before arriving in London. According to Gawdy, "Ther is muche stir and contention about the carike goodes whilst some sweare that they be loosers therby. And my L. Treasurer will take order that all will come into her Maties hand and Sr Walter Raweleyes who still continueth in disgrace," *Letters of Philip Gawdy*, 67–68.

battle. Indeed, the book had already taught many European readers how to hispanize, or as the Lord de la Noue put it, to be "readie at all times to fight for a souse."[40]

A Sun Knight and His Moon Princess

Following Paynell's *Treasurie of Amadis* was Margaret Tyler's *The Mirrour of Princely Deedes and Knighthood,* a direct translation of Diego Ortúñez de Calahorra's *Espejo de príncipes y cavalleros* (1555). This was the first complete volume of a Spanish chivalric romance printed in English. It was also the first translation of its kind to have traveled from Iberia without first passing through the Pyrenees. First published in English in 1578 (STC 18859), containing only Book 1 of Part I, *The Mirrour of Knighthood* was quickly reprinted in 1580(?) (STC 18860) and again in 1599(?) (STC 18861). The quick turnover of a second edition in roughly two years suggests that the first print run was too small (perhaps just a few hundred copies) to accommodate demand.[41] More editions and more books were soon to follow, securing the romance's meteoric rise to prominence in England.

Inspired in part by the mirror-for-princes tradition, the tale chronicles the lives of two knights, Rosicleer and El Caballero del Febo/Donzel del Febo (Knight of the Sun), who travel about Europe and Constantinople embarking on holy missions and knightly exploits in order to distinguish themselves as paragons of chivalry. These eventually lead them to discover their true identities as the lost sons of the Greek emperor Trebatio. Trebatio married their mother, the Hungarian princess Briana, by killing her betrothed, Prince Edward of England, and then disguising himself for the nuptials, after which he was inadvertently separated from Briana, leaving her pregnant with twins.[42] As youths, Rosicleer and the Knight of the Sun are also accidentally separated, with the Knight

---

40. François de La Noue, *The politicke and militarie discourses of the Lord de La Nouue VVhereunto are adioyned certaine obseruations of the same author, of things happened during the three late ciuill warres of France,* Edward Aggas, trans. (London: T.C. and E.A., 1587), sig. I2v. A souse was a piece of pork.
41. Since unusually small print runs would have been unprofitable, it may be inferred that the second edition produced between 1,000 and 1,500 copies. (Although print run records are rather fragmentary, a range of 250 to 2,000 copies per edition seems to have been normal.) The second printing was probably larger (as many as 2,000 copies), but the Stationers' Company limited print runs to between 1,250 and 1,500 copies after 1587. For more information on print runs, see Joad Raymond, *Pamphlets and Pamphleteering in Early Modern Britain* (Cambridge: Cambridge University Press, 2003), 80; Mark Bland, "The London Book-Trade in 1600," in *A Companion to Shakespeare,* David Scott Kastan, ed. (Oxford: Blackwell, 1999), 450–63. See also Alan Farmer and Zachary Lesser, "The Popularity of Playbooks Revisited," *Shakespeare Quarterly* 56 (2005), 1–32, esp. 5–6 and 16–17. For a compilation of Renaissance print run statistics, see William St. Clair, *The Reading Nation in the Romantic Period* (Cambridge: Cambridge University Press, 2004), Appendix I.
42. In imitation of medieval romances and especially the Arthurian tradition, concealment, disguise, and lost heirs were common motifs in Spanish romance, such as, most famously in *Amadís de Gaula.* For a discussion of this disguise trope in translation in *The Mirrour of Knighthood,* see my article, "'De-Naturalizing' Rape in Translation: Margaret Tyler's *Mirrour of Princely Deedes and Knighthood* (1578)," *Modern Language Studies* 44 no. 2 (2015), 10–27.

of the Sun cast adrift to Persia where he becomes a ward of Prince Florion, while his brother is raised in the court of Hungary. As young men, the brothers separately embark to lands of exotic questing, while their unknown father engages in sensual delights as a prisoner to the mysterious enchantress, Princess Lindaraza. Elaborating the conventional appeals of eros, the romance compares Trebatio's erotic encounters with Lindaraza and her gentlewomen with those of Odysseus in the mysterious snare of the sirens: "Some [of the women] played on instruments, and other [sic.] sang sweetly to them. Such kind of mermaids would have beguiled a well-stayed Ulysses"[43] Meanwhile, for Trebatio's sons, the call to arms also incorporates the sensual delights, most famously through the Knight of the Sun's amours with the Amazonian princess, Claridiana of Trabisond (in northeast Turkey), daughter to the goddess-styled-as-Amazonian-empress, Diana, and her associated moon cult.

When the Spanish *Espejo* was published in 1555 (Zaragoza: Esteban de Nájera), Charles was already in the process of abdicating his throne; at the time, it was thought that perhaps the Holy Roman Empire would pass to his son, Philip, but in 1556, the crown was bestowed upon Charles's brother, Fernando/Ferdinand I (1503–1564; Holy Roman Emperor from 1556–64), while his Spanish empire was left to Philip. (It is said that upon his abdication, which devotees might have compared to Lisuarte's relinquishing his kingdom of England to Amadís, Charles retired to the monastery of Yuste, where he spent his remaining days reading his favorite books of chivalry and divine philosophy.) Perhaps hoping to capitalize upon the enormous success of the *Amadís* cycle, so beloved of Charles and Philip, Ortúñez imbued his *Espejo* with elements corresponding with the Holy Roman Emperor's self-fashioning as universal monarch, particularly in the form of the Knight of the Sun's solar aspect,[44] which aligned with the sun's growing signification within European scientific, political, and religious thought. During the sixteenth century, with the publication of major scientific treatises by Nicolaus Copernicus, Johannes Kepler, and Galileo Galilei, overturning the dominant geocentricism advocated by Ptolemy, "the Sun acquired a new dimension in symbology," and this "is precisely when a modern solar iconography was conceived and developed, when the major books of emblems and impresas were published, along with a majority of mirror-for-princes books" (my translation).[45] The sun also offered theological illumination by the common equation of Christ with the light of divine truth, and with the Holy Roman Emperor's

---

43. Margaret Tyler, trans., *Mirror of Princely Deeds and Knighthood* [*The Mirrour of Knighthood*], Joyce Boro, ed. Modern Humanities Research Association, Tudor & Stuart Translations, Andrew Hadfield and Neil Rhodes, eds., vol. 11 (London: MHRA, 2014), 200.
44. This solar attribute of the birthmark is repeatedly highlighted in the work by Ortúñez and in the translation by Tyler, who describes the detail of his naming "as [after] the sun in his left side named him the Gentleman of the Sun when he was first found in the sea by [the heroic Saracen named] Florion" (113). The translation narrates that the Knight of the Sun received his name for a sun-shaped birthmark located "in his left side near upon his heart" (75), a location specified by Tyler. Boro points out that Ortúñez had the mark simply between his breasts, as upon his heart (note 281).
45. Víctor Mínguez, *Los reyes solares: iconografía astral de la monarquía hispánica* (Publicacions de la Universitat Jaume I, 2001), 46.

self-fashioned role in dispensing true faith to this colonial subjects. Ortúñez dedicated the work to Martín Cortés. Popularly called El Mestizo, Martín was the firstborn son of the conquistador, Hernán Cortés, and the indigenous interpreter known as La Malinche, who aided in the conquest of Aztec México (see Chapter 2). Raised in the royal court in Spain, Martín was by then in residence in England, having traveled with Prince Philip's retinue upon the occasion of his marriage to Mary Tudor in 1554.

A symbolic heliocenter, Charles V was popularly depicted as towering over the earth in oversight of history's first global empire. In fact, long before France's King Louis XIV (1638–1715), Charles was in his own right a "Sun King," for his vast dominium was famously known as the "empire on which the sun never sets."[46] Although the 1521 conquest of México was a veritable launching point for the sun's evangelical association to America, Charles's solar iconography did not gain full traction until after 1533. This year marked Francisco Pizarro's subduing of the gold-rich city of Cusco, Perú, capital of the largest pre-Columbian civilization, and the subsequent demise of the sun-worshiping Inca people, following the seizure and execution of their final emperor, Atawallpa (Atahualpa) (died 1533). The full conquest of Perú would not be completed until 1572, but victory was proclaimed with the City of Gold. Charles could now well boast that he was the Sun King, that his pagan subjects were his adopted Children of the Sun, and that the next era in Spanish exploration was to be a Siglo de Oro.

The association of "Sun King" took on additional currency with the ascendance of Philip to the Spanish throne, appearing in the young prince's royal impresa from about the 1550s.[47] One prominent example was his personal motto, "Iam illustrabit omnia" (He shall illuminate everything), most likely coined in commemoration of his 1554 marriage to Mary Tudor, which referred to his mission to spread the light of Christian truth across the globe.[48] This typically featured Apollo in his carriage of four white horses, wielding a lit torch that resembled a whip, a visible reminder of the power and fury of Philip's theology of conquest.

Apollo's Challenger

Any European monarch could draw comparisons with Apollo, and the literature of moment predominated with ubiquitous solar metaphors, but during the Age of

---

46. The expression was a rephrasing of Virgil's expression for Augustus's empire "A SOLIS ORTU AD OCASSUM" (From sun rise to sun set (from east to west, that is, the whole world)). Translation by Andrea Kouklanakis.
47. This impresa first appeared in print in Girolamo Ruscelli's *Le Imprese Illustri con espositioni, et discorsi* (Venice: Franciscus Rampazetto, 1566), 233. It must have come into being sometime prior to this, most logically around the time of Charles's abdication. For a reading of Philip's solar emblem, with images, see Laura Fernández-González, "Negotiating Terms: King Philip I of Portugal and the Ceremonial Entry of 1581 into Lisbon," in Fernando Checa Cremades and Laura Fernández-González, eds. *Festival Culture in the World of the Spanish Habsburgs* (Farnham: Ashgate Publishing, 2015), 87–113.
48. This image and the evangelical massage are found on a medal by Jacopo da Trezzo (1555), which is traceable to the royal marriage festivities. Mínguez, *Los reyes solares*, 94.

Conquest, there was undeniably no Sun King so famous as Philip. As the English biographer, William Camden, remarked of the king of Spain, "beyond all the Emperours [...] he might truely say in his Motto, *Sol mihi semper lucet*."[49] Nevertheless, since state propaganda generally works to celebrate the local while demonizing the foreign, the cultic traditions of England and Spain would have worked together only very rarely. All modern fancies aside, there was by the late 1500s, following the death of Mary and ascendance of Elizabeth, little interest in supporting an Anglo-Spanish marriage.[50] Thus, there would have been little reason to entertain Philip's aggrandizing pretensions, if not to lampoon him. England sought to suppress this identification, to negate it, or otherwise to appropriate it for the country's deified queen, particularly by the late 1500s, when the queen's advanced age brought increased anxiety about the succession, as I further discuss in Chapter 3.

In fact, Philip's cosmic pretensions as a self-fashioned world emperor informed Elizabeth's own royal iconography as a virgin empress of Europe and the New World, now further styled as Apollo's challenger. For instance, her Armada portraits directly challenged Philip's identification with Phoebus leading his cart across his vast global empire. This collection of near-identical portraits depicts Elizabeth in a resplendent dress, ruff, and headdress. She is seated between two windows depicting dichotomous scenes of the famous naval episode, one upon a calm sea (at left) and the other upon a stormy sea (at right). These cast Elizabeth as the source of divine radiance, gazing toward the daylight scene with a radiant tranquility that contrasts with the background stormy scene at night to the right.[51] The message is that Phoebus has been supplanted by Phoebe,

---

49. William Camden, *The historie of the life and reigne of that famous princesse Elizabeth containing a briefe memoriall of the chiefest affaires of state that haue passed in these kingdomes of England, Scotland, France or Ireland since the yeare of the fatall Spanish invasion to that of her sad and ever to be deplored dissolution* (London: William Webbe, 1634), sig. Ff1r.
50. In fact, English opposition to the marriage of Philip and Mary was so great that in 1553 Parliament had prohibited Englishmen from publishing any books that disparaged the Spanish marriage or slandered "the King or Queen," under the penalty of loss of the right hand. Stationers' Company, *A Transcript of the Registers of the Company of Stationers of London, 1554–1640 AD, vol. 5*, Edward Arber, ed. (Birmingham: Priv. print, 1896), xl.
51. See, e.g., James Aske's *Elizabetha triumphans* (London: Thomas Gubbin, 1588). The following verse is worthy of inclusion:

> But England ioy, O England thankefull be,
> The Night is gone, and now the Day appeares:
> The God of heauen, who knoweth euery thought,
> And ruleth them by his eternall power:
> The God of Gods, who is the morning Starre,
> Which giueth light in euery creatures heart,
> That God (I say) did see his [Philip's] wickednesse,
> And seeing, would not let it longer last,
> For by the Sunne, Elizabeth our Queene,
> Whose vertues shine as bright as Sol it selfe,
> By that same Sunne the Wolfe is put to flight,
> And by that Sunne Gods flocke doth liue in rest.
> From that bright Sunne, Religion hath her beames,

Figure 1 George Gower (attr.), Armada Portrait, oil on canvas, (ca. 1588), Woburn Abbey Collection (George Gower, ca. 1588), Bedfordshire, UK, © The Duke of Bedford and the Trustees of the Bedford Estates.

who now commands the gendered forces of day and night and the clime. In two extant versions, that by George Gower (Figure 1) and that by an unknown artist (held at the National Portrait Gallery),[52] the daylight scene of England's approaching ships is flanked by two marble columns, which recall Philip's motto, "plus ultra" (go beyond), represented by the Pillars of Hercules.[53] This detail rebukes Philip's venturing to conquer England, for Elizabeth would not suffer her people to be colonized.

> Which lightens those who did in darkenesse sit:
> By that same Sunne, Sinceritie is plast,
> Where heeretofore false Error ruled Lord,
> Through that same Sunne Gods word is truly preacht,
> And by that Sunne all Popish reliques burnt. (sig. B2r)

52. The version in the National Portrait Gallery (NPG 541) was cut down at some point, so only one column shows. It is speculated that the two portraits bearing the columns may have come from the same workshop.
53. The expression had particular relevancy to the port and city of Cádiz, with its mythos of the Pillars of Hercules displaying the dictum, "Ne plus ultra." As a late-seventeenth-century work explained: "Insula nunc Cadiz vocata, in litore Hispanico sita, ultra fretum olim

Elizabeth's skirt and sleeves are decorated with numerous golden suns, while her voluminous appearance, from her oversized ruff to her golden headdress, gives the impression of a towering stature relative to the modest globe poised below her hand, tilted so as to reveal the Western Hemisphere. This is a reference to Philip's additional motto, "Non sufficit orbis" (The world is not enough), first appearing on a 1583 medal, and also in Spain's royal arms. Sir Francis Drake related that when he and his soldiers stormed the governor's palace during the 1586 raid of Santo Domingo, they found a "Scutchion" of Spain's royal arms featuring the globular motto, which he called "a very notable marke and token of the vnsatiable ambition of the Spanish King and his nation."[54] He added, "in the lower part of said Scutchion, there is likewise described a globe, containing in it the whole circuite of the sea and the earth, whereupon is a horse standing on his hinder part within the globe, and the other fore part without the globe, lifted vp as it were to leape, with a scrolle painted on his mouth, wherein was written these words in Latin NON SVIFFICIT ORBIS."[55] Referencing Philip's cosmic ambitions, Elizabeth in the Armada portrait seems to stroke the globe, her long elegant fingers straddling the expanse of America, also encoded by the countless pearls (recalling Virginia, the Land of Pearls) that decorate her attire. Lying in the foreground of the sunlit Armada episode, flanked by the marble columns, the globe links both hemispheres in the Anglo-Spanish contest. It reminds the viewer of England's fledgling colonial project in America, more a symbol of England's rising star than a tangible reality. The portrait therefore also elaborates Elizabeth's new self-identification as world empress, captor of Philip's *plus ultra*.[56]

When the *Mirrour of Knighthood* debuted more than a decade earlier in 1578, English readers were confronted with a host of heliotypic symbols corresponding with Spain and Spanish Catholicism. Ortúñez had characterized the Knight of the Sun's superior chivalry as an illumination of Christian truth, particularly by his uncommon beauty in connection

---

Herculeum dictum, hodie angustiae de Gibralter; hic Poetae Herculem duas Columnas statuisse volunt: Extremum occidentem credebant antiqui unde Elogium Herculis Columnis inscriptum. NE PLUS ULTRA" (The island now called Cadiz, situated on the Hispanic shore, beyond the strait once called Herculean, today there are narrow paths down from Gibraltar; here the poets want to believe that Hercules set up two columns: the ancients used to believe that this place was the farthermost/farthest region on the occident farthest point of the setting sun, whence Hercules' inscription was written on the columns: 'No more beyond here'). Henry Higden, *A modern essay on the tenth satyr of Juvenal* (London: T. Milbourn, 1687) (annotation, n.n.). Translation by Andrea Kouklanakis.

54. Sir Francis Drake, *Sir Francis Drake's West Indian Voyage, 1585–86* (Kiribati: Hakluyt Society, 1981), 245.
55. Drake, *Sir Francis Drake's West Indian Voyage*, 245. All of these images of the king as world emperor featured in the designs for Philip's mausoleum. For a reading with images, see John A. Marino, "City Solidarities and Nodes of Power," in *Becoming Neapolitan: Citizen Culture in Baroque Naples* (Johns Hopkins University Press, 2011), 119–68, esp. 154–64.
56. Held by the Royal Collection Trust, an engraving attributed to Crispin van de Passe the Elder (1564–1637), "ELIZABETHA D.G. ANGLIAE, FRANCIAE, HIBERNIAE, ET VERGINIAE REGINA CHRISTIANAE FIDEI VNICVM PROPVGANCVLVM" (1596), also depicts Elizabeth flanked by two pillars, and wielding the traditional props of power, the scepter and the orb.

to his solar aspect. These details were further elaborated by translator, Margaret Tyler, as in the following passage:

> There was none which had had but a blush of him within his tender years but took him rather to be a celestial seraphim than a human creature and believed that this might not be done without some great mystery, as if the young gentleman showing in his infancy the *comeliness of stature and other excellent qualities wherewith he was endowed, besides the strange finding of him alone in the rage of the tempest,* did well foreshow his nobility in time to come (my emphasis).[57]

The italicized passage pertaining to the Knight of the Sun's comeliness of stature, added by Tyler, provided a somewhat unctuous image of the knight's symbolic tutelary, King Philip, who was not himself of great height, though he seemed to tower above the earth as universal monarch. Tyler also elaborated the description of his identifying solar birthmark, further associating the beauty of the sun with the imperial prowess of his classical inspiration: "The first born of them (the Knight of the Sun) hath the form of a face very beautiful and so bright that I dare liken it to the sun, which overshadoweth the earth."[58] In contradistinction with Ortúñez's "illuminates," which conveyed Philip's evangelical motto of messianic conquest, *Iam illustrabit omnia,* Tyler's "overshadoweth" further conveyed the classical sense of Apollo towering over the earth.[59]

For English readers, this latent imperial iconography also would have informed their impression of the Knight of the Sun's courtship by Princess Claridiana. Though she hails from the classical East, Claridiana also represents the European imperial fantasy that was projected unto the mysterious West. She comes to this role as imperial Princess of the Amazons, a classical race of warrior women who were believed to have been found in America, as Chapter 5 discusses.[60] Claridiana is an uncanny hybrid of what Michel de Certeau has provocatively called "the Indian 'America'[…] an unnamed presence of difference, a body which awakens a space of exotic fauna and flora […] a historicized body—a blazon—of [the conqueror's] labors and phantasms. She will be 'Latin America.'"[61] In her first appearance in the story, Claridiana seems alone, invoking

---

57. Tyler, *The Mirrour of Knighthood*, 89.
58. Tyler, *The Mirrour of Knighthood*, 78.
59. In the scene of the discovery of the knight's resplendent portrait, the work notes that "when they saw him naked and the portraiture of the Sun, with the brightness that it gave to the beholders, it was so strange that they called to mind Phaeton's fall out of heaven, comparing this young gentleman with Phaeton as if he had been Phoebus's son, like as Phaeton was." Tyler, *The Mirrour Knighthood*, 89. As Boro explains, the comparison attempts to "reconcile classical narrative to Christian doctrine." "Introduction," in Tyler, *The Mirrour of Knighthood*, 1–36 (16).
60. Amazons were frequently mentioned in sixteenth-century colonial and historical tracts dealing with America. One example was the *Decades de Orbe Novo,* published in 1516 by the Lombard humanist Peter Martyr, who had incorporated material directly supplied by Christopher Columbus.
61. Michel de Certeau, *Writing of History,* Tom Conley, trans. (New York: Columbia University Press, 1988), xxv. For a reading of America as a woman, and as an Amazon, see Louis Montrose, "The Work of Gender in the Discourse of Discovery," *Representations* no. 33 (1991), 1–41.

the Amazon woman's traditional individuality, but it is revealed that Claridiana also commands an integrated hunting party, "which concomitantly serves to neutralize the feminist, separatist Amazonian ideology since Claridiana's entourage is comprised of equal numbers of male and female knights."[62] This integration indicates Claridiana's acceptance of masculine rule in the tradition of her conquered Amazonian mother, as she explains:

> I am called Claridiana, the daughter of Theodoro, lord of this empire, and to the Empress Diana, Queen of the Amazons, which two having been mortal enemies as by long wars appeareth, continued hotly on either part, they were after great friends, meeting in a pitched field, either being then young and unmarried. I am promised to be made knight, for my mother, being but young, achieved such enterprises that in her time there was no knight more famous. And I am desirous to be somewhat like unto her, especially in that point.[63]

This battle of passions between Claridiana's parents, Theodoro and Diana, consummated "in a pitched field" and solemnized in marriage, defuses the formerly autonomous gynocracy of Diana's Amazonian domain, aligning love to empire as a gendered conquest.[64] Along this theme, Claridiana's amorous pursuit of the Christian Knight of the Sun represents an allegory for the pagan world's desire to be conquered and converted to Christianity in accordance with natural, patriarchal law. She specifically recalls the marital practices of conquistadors like Hernán Cortés and his men, who married Aztec princesses and noblewomen (love) to concretize their military conquest of México (arms), as the Spanish work's dedication to Martín Cortés "El Mestizo" further underscores.

This representation also accords with Diana's deferential role in Philip's royal iconography. For example, in commemoration of the 1580 founding of the Iberian Union under Philip, a ceremonial pageant took place in 1581 in Lisbon featuring a series of 15 triumphal arches. One of these, the German Merchants' Arch, was decorated with paintings imitating bronze bas-reliefs, and a statue of Philip with engravings that exalted the king's messianic mission through his imperial identification with the sun: "TV SOL SPLENDENS SEMPER VIGILANS ABSQVE OCASSV" (You are the luminous sun, that always guards without setting).[65] Coupled with this, a panel on the right-hand entrance depicted Diana offering her empire to Philip. She was represented as a three-headed figure, associating the Greek goddess Hecate, with bow and arrows dominating three lions, with the inscription beneath: '"TVO ILLVSTRATA LUMINE PONAM TOLLAMQUE. OCEANVM QVUOCVMQVE JUSSERIS" (Enlightened with your luminosity, I will calm and shake the ocean if you so command).[66] Embodying the lawless seas at last bowed to Spain's tutelage, as in this new Union of Iberia, this representation

---

62. Boro, "Introduction," *The Mirrour of Knighthood*, 17.
63. Tyler, *The Mirrour of Knighthood*, 207.
64. The reference to the scene "in pitched field" may also be a callback to the first congress between Oriana and Amadís, also in open field.
65. Translations and readings derived from Fernández-González, "Negotiating Terms," 99–101.
66. Fernández González, "Negotiating Terms," 100.

also signified a fantasy of agreement between the Old and New Worlds under one universal Catholic monarchy, crucially embodied by a woman.

In England, however, Queen Elizabeth's separate association with the cult of Diana, which could be read into the figure of Claridiana, necessitated a "careful sorting out of allusions," as Joyce Boro notes.[67] This "woman knight of whom this story specially entreateth"[68] was integral to the English reception of *The Mirrour of Knighthood*, serving as a crucible of meaning and of conflict. Claridiana's composite signification incorporated not only the gendered logics of romance, intertwined with the operative discourses of the New World and the contemporary eroticizing of Amazons, but also the gynocratic politics of Elizabethan England by her association to Diana's moon cult (see Chapters 3 and 5). Perhaps sensitive to these resonances, Tyler was careful with rendering the Spanish symbology in reference to Claridiana. While she highlighted the Amazonian princess's association to hunting, and thus to Diana, she suppressed certain references to the moon; this decision was more noteworthy given that erasure of classical references was "atypical of Tyler's methodology."[69] Her precautions notwithstanding, Tyler was apparently brought before the state on charge of recusancy, according to archival evidence uncovered by Louise Schleiner.[70] It could not have helped that her work had highlighted Philip's Apollo cult, at points indulging the king's cosmic pretensions. Though perhaps innocuous for an uninitiated reader, this heliotypic imagery could easily have drawn the attention of an agent of the state, who might have connected it with crypto-Catholic communities in England.[71]

Tyler was a servant in the household of Thomas Howard, Fourth Duke of Norfolk. The elder Thomas Howard was executed in 1572 for supporting Mary, Queen of Scots in the Ridolfi plot. Clearly sensitive to her own vulnerable position in the midst of the family's shifting fortunes, Tyler dedicated the work to Howard's younger son, Thomas, noting that by "your honour's protection I shall less fear the assault of the envious."[72] The dedication encoded Tyler's intimacy with the masculine subject matter, which

---

67. Boro, "Introduction," in *The Mirrour of Knighthood*, 17.
68. Tyler, *The Mirrour of Knighthood*, 237.
69. Boro, "Introduction," *The Mirrour of Knighthood*, 16.
70. Louise Schleiner, "Margaret Tyler, Translator, and Waiting Woman," *English Language Notes* 29 (1992), 1–9 (5).
71. For discussion of *The Mirrour of Knighthood*'s connection to English Catholics, see Donna Hamilton, *Anthony Munday and the Catholics, 1560–1633*, second edition (New York: Routledge, 2016), esp. 80–81; and Deborah Uman and Belén Bistué, "Translation as Collaborative Authorship: Margaret Tyler's *The Mirrour of Princely Deedes and Knighthood*," *Comparative Literature Studies* 44, no. 3 (2007), 298–323. As Boro notes, the work's treatment of Catholicism is inconsistent. For example, it omits a reference to the Catholic prayer sequence called the *novena* and the practice of rising to hear Catholic mass. Nevertheless, it also adds some references, such as in Princess Briana's secluding herself in her room (she believes her husband to be dead), which is likened to her becoming an anchoress (72). For a list of Tyler's treatments to Catholic references, see Boro, "Introduction," in *The Mirrour of Knighthood*, esp. 1–2 and 10–15.
72. Tyler, *The Mirrour of Knighthood*, 48.

she described as "mine old reading."[73] The work preceded the forthcoming military career of Howard himself, who was at the time in the prime of his "noble youth."[74] Thomas had not yet earned the title of First Earl of Suffolk (granted 1603), nor was he yet the captain of the Golden Lion who would join in England's defeat of the Spanish Armada in 1588 and in the English capture of Cádiz in 1596. But the call to war was nigh. Tyler noted the romance's suitability "to set on fire the lusty courages of young gentlemen to the advancement of their line by ensuing such like steps. The first tongue wherein it was penned was Spanish, in which nation, by common report, the inheritance of all warlike commendation hath to this day rested."[75] And it may well be that Thomas found his courage to confront the Spanish, turning against the treasons of his father and the disgrace of his house, by reading works written by Spanish authors, including this one. In time it would become one of the era's most formidable *books of the brave* English.

In fact, the work was in such demand that printer/publisher Thomas East hastened to license the sequel by Pedro de la Sierra, Part I, Book 2 (I.2) within two years of I.1. This book deals explicitly with the Knight of the Sun's betrothal to Lindabrides, the Tartarian imperial princess and presumptive heir to all "within the Orient all regions."[76] By winning in a test of arms against her brother, the aptly named Prince Meridian, and vowing to defend her beauty for a period of three months (the length of a season), the Knight of the Sun wins her hand in marriage, so earning the crown to a vast eastern empire. In Chapter 31, the enamored Knight of the Sun fights bravely in defense of Lindabrides's beauty in a tournament under the apt pseudonym of the Knight of the Chariot. He defends Lindabrides against the claims of another disguised knight who brings boast of a beautiful lady "very strange & far from this country, that if you did see hir, doubtlesse she would seeme vnto you to be of no lesse beauty, then the princes."[77] It is none other than Claridiana, who has been questing to find the knight after espying his portrait in the castle of the enchantress, Lindaraza. In Spenser's *Faerie Queene*, the sequence informs Britomart's pursuit of Artegall, Knight of Justice, whom she first espies in Merlin's mirror, and later defeats in a battle for another's beauty, both knights appearing in disguise in Book IV. As I further discuss in Chapter 3, Britomart and Artegall's virtuous ultimate union will bring forth the Tudor dynasty.

The battle between Claridiana and the Knight of the Sun is described with references to the sun and the moon as they respectively make their passages across the sky, one always chasing the other. After a long skirmish, bravely fought on both sides, the two knights strike each other simultaneously, both falling backward:

---

73. Tyler, *The Mirrour of Knighthood*, 48.
74. Tyler, *The Mirrour of Knighthood*, 48.
75. Tyler, *The Mirrour of Knighthood*, 49.
76. Robert Parry, trans., *The second part of the first booke of the Myrrour of knighthood in which is prosecuted the illustrious deedes of the knight of the Sunne, and his brother Rosicleer, sonnes vnto the Emperour Trebatio of Greece: With the valiant deedes of armes of sundry worthie knights, very delightfull to bee read, and nothing hurtfull to bee regarded* (London: Thomas Este, 1599), sig. Liiir. The first publication was in 1585.
77. Parry, *The second part of the first booke of the myrrour of knighthood*, sig. Pir.

> But straight way they setled themselues vpright againe, & as you see that shining Sun & the faire Diana, when they doe appeare: euen so séemed the faces of these two knights, for that the knight of the Sun did shew that perfect & seuere countenance, which vntill that time not one that was in all that place had seene. And of the other part, the strange knight did séeme to be the soueraine, & without comparison in beauty, that faire, Claridiana, whose Rubicomde haire which séemed to bée of fine gold fell loose & spred about hir eares, & hanged ouer all hir backe, parted in the midst, as though it had ben don by a compasse, showing hir celestiall face, which seemed vnto all people, to be some diuine creature.[78]

This scene registers with the new cosmic vantage point of the sixteenth century, recalling "that shining Sun & the faire Diana, when they doe appeare" as they meet briefly in the sky upon their respective westward journeys. In this respect, this "faire Diana," arriving from a "very strange & far country," is an allegorized America, emblazoned with "celestial face" and golden hair, parted as though by a "compasse." Her arresting beauty splits the Sun Knight's focus between an allegorized east and west. As he burns with love for both ladies, his heart, upon which he bears his famous solar birthmark, is "clouen asonder in the midst,"[79] literalizing this division of east and west.

For reasons that are unclear, I.2 did not appear in print until 1585. East did, however, publish II.1 and II.2 by Pedro de la Sierra in 1583 (seemingly without license). Thus, in the epistle to the reader of the first edition of II.1 (STC 18866) he apologized for the delay in translation of I.2, and he begged that readers entertain themselves with this later book in the saga in the meantime:

> Moreover (curteous Reader) I request thee to note, that whereas the beginning of this part followeth not consequently upon the same booke which was published in the name of the first part, it is not to be imputed to any errour committed in the translation of this second part: for that it is verely the selfe same, that beareth the title of the second part in the Spanish tongue, but the booke that lacketh, is the seconde booke of the first part, which with as much spéede as may be, shall be joyned thereunto. In the meane time, accept this in good parte, which I now present: wherein thou shalt finde the strange and wonderfull prowesse of the worthy *Trebatio*, and his sonnes, nephewes, kinsmen, and sundry other couragious knights, mixed with many lamentable and sorrowfull histories, together with the redresse of the wronged innocents.[80]

Perhaps the sequel translator, Robert Parry, had translated the wrong "second part,"[81] or more likely, the work was delayed by the stationers. Donna Hamilton surmises that

---

78. Parry, *The second part of the first booke of the myrrour of knighthood*, sig. Piv.
79. Parry, *The second part of the first booke of the myrrour of knighthood*, sig. Piiir.
80. Thomas East, "To the Reader," in Robert Parry, trans., *The second part of the Myrror of knighthood Containing two seuerall bookes, wherein is intreated the valiant deedes of armes of sundrie worthie knightes, verie delightfull to be read, and nothing hurtfull to bee regarded. Now newly translated out of Spanish into our vulgar tongue by R[obert] P[arry]* (London: Thomas East, 1583), sigs. A3r–A3v, sig. A3v.
81. In fact, the titles of romance sequels were commonly irregular, constantly using *book* and *part* interchangeably from one edition or volume to another (such as in STC 18862 and STC 18866).

there may have been a dispute with Christopher Barker and Francis Coldock, who had licensed the book on condition that it should be brought to them for final perusal, "and yf any thinge be amisse therein to be amended."[82] This delay resulted that readers were instead first introduced to the love triangle's resolution, which involves the Knight of the Sun, tormented by his split affections for Lindabrides and Claridiana, banishing himself to a wilderness on the Solitarie Iland, where he inadvertently drinks the water of a magic fountain that causes him to forget his beloved Lindabrides. Purged of his affections, he condemns his former folly in loving a non-Christian: "Tel me thou lost man, who hath bene affectioned vnto a Moore without faith, but onely thy selfe? Who would haue left his naturall wife, for to loue a stranger & Barbarian, but thou? Who would giue so many sighes in vaine, but I most miserable, giuing occasion of euerlasting death and damnation vnto my soule."[83] Thus, having forgotten his contrary desire, the Knight of the Sun is after some adventures joyfully reunited with his Christian bride, the Empress Claridiana. Apart from appealing to the conventional fear of Islam that was communicated to English readers through romance's Orientalized depictions of the eastern Other, this plot also resonated with the literary Maurophilia that was intimately associated with Spain by the late 1500s.[84]

Perhaps owing to *The Mirrour of Knighthood*'s strong resemblance to the *Orlando* epics, upon which it was loosely based, coupled with its poignant allegories to American and global conquest, translations of all three parts of *The Mirrour of Knighthood* (comprising nine books) were printed by 1601, perhaps making it England's most read Spanish romance series of the 1580s and 1590s. Comparable rates of turnover were also witnessed by the books of *Amadís*, *Palmerín*, and *Primaleón*, spurred by the translations of Anthony Munday. But *The Mirrour of Knighthood* was unique in that its enormous growth on the English print market contrasted with the work's reception on the Iberian Peninsula, where, in comparison to those other more prominent cycles, the multi-volume cycle was a relatively

---

82. Qtd. in Hamilton, *Anthony Munday and the Catholics*, 80.
83. Parry, *The Second Part of the Myrror of Knighthood Containing Two Seuerall Bookes*, sig. Svr. This recalls a scene from Matteo Boiardo's *Orlando innamorato*, first published in 1483, upon which the cycle is based, in which Rinaldo forgets his love Angelica by drinking from a magic fountain.
84. For a discussion of "literary Maurophilia," see Barbara Fuchs in *Exotic Nation: Maurophilia and the Construction of Early Modern Spain* (Philadelphia: University of Pennsylvania Press, 2009). The book observes that "conceptual models based on the distance between West and East miss the more interesting and paradoxical connections of the Spanish case, and, moreover, that from the fall of Granada, if not earlier, Spain itself is often orientalized in the European imagination." Fuchs, *Exotic Nation*, 4. Boro further notes that "portrayal of Saracens in English romance […] is illustrative of Edward Said's conceptualization of Orientalism, which predicates difference at the root of the construction of European superiority. In contrast, stemming from the extensive Spanish co-habitation of Spaniards and Moors, their cultural relationship is characterized by proximity and intimacy; there is a shared material cultural rather than a dominating binary." "Introduction," *The Mirrour of Knighthood*, 12–13.

minor success. It was only in Spanish colonial America where this cycle enjoyed a comparably strong following.[85]

Perhaps by its cosmographical metaphors for global conquest and exploration, the work struck a chord with English readers, who further associated it with England's transatlantic ventures in global exploration, navigation, and sea piracy. In William Shakespeare's history play, *1 Henry IV* (ca. 1596–97),[86] for example, the playwright referenced the work in relation to the competing energies of the sun and the moon, which he further imagined as a gendered struggle for transatlantic domination. In Act 1, scene 2, for example, Falstaff defends his profession as a night highway robber against Hal's charges of idleness, remarking:

> FALSTAFF. Indeed, you come near me now, Hal, for we that take purses go by the moon and the seven stars, and not by Phoebus, he, "that wandering knight, so fair".
>
> [...]
>
> Marry, then, sweet wag, when thou art king, let not us that are squires of the night's body be called thieves of the day's beauty. Let us be Diana's foresters, gentlemen of the shade, minions of the moon; and let men say we be men of good government, being governed, as the sea is, by our noble and chaste mistress the moon, under whose countenance we steal. (1.2.12–28)[87]

While "Phoebus, he, that wandering knight so fair" refers to the Caballero del Febo, "Diana's foresters," refers to Claridiana and her "gentlemen of the shade," or rather her integrated train of woodland knights.[88] Classically depicted as rival siblings, and transformed by Spanish romance into star-crossed lovers, here Phoebus and Diana represent rivaling forces of nature, with the sun representing the Spanish empire of the sun; the moon, by contrast, represents the new female upheaval of the conventional world order, embodied by this chaste Diana of the moonlight who gives her loyal servants license to steal.

As a defense of theft, the duality of day and night also encodes the Janus-faced character of Elizabethan foreign policy toward Spain, which officially courted peace and diplomacy by light of day, while simultaneously financing English privateers from the shadows. Diana's thieving squires, or "minions of the moon" therefore refer to Elizabeth's numerous court favorites involved in the profession of privateering. These were men

---

85. Leonard notes that Ortúñez's *Mirrour of Knighthood*, along with the imitation, Esteban Corbera's *Caballero del Febo*, ranked "high on the [Spanish] ship registers, though usually in small quantities on individual orders, which fact indicates, perhaps, a fairly steady demand." Leonard, *Books of the Brave*, 107–8.
86. Unless otherwise indicated, all dates for English plays are performance dates derived from *DEEP: Database of Early English Playbooks*. Alan B. Farmer and Zachary Lesser, eds. Created 2007. http://deep.sas.upenn.edu.
87. William Shakespeare, *Henry IV, Part I*, David Bevington, ed. Oxford World Classics Edition, Stanley Wells, ed. (Oxford: Oxford University Press, 2008).
88. Though less likely, the reference could also be to Esteban Corbera's *El caballero Febo el Troyano* [*Knight of Phoebus*] (1576), which was based on the work by Ortúñez. The work relates Febo's later knightly exploits as intermingled with episodes pertaining to his beloved Diana.

like Sir Francis Drake, Sir John Hawkins, Sir Martin Frobisher, and Sir Walter Raleigh, Elizabeth's famous Sea Dogs who had made "good government" by pirating Spanish ships and performing other extralegal aggressions on Spanish territories. Although they were essentially contracted thieves, they were also heralded as great English heroes, "governed, as the sea is, by our noble and chaste mistress the moon." Falstaff, who is believed to have been one of Elizabeth's favorite Shakespearean characters, especially embodies the contradictory ethos of the Elizabethan privateer, who belied the time-honored medieval codes of warfare.[89] Since it was relatively common for such thievery to be honored with an induction to the Order of the Garter, there is an ironic aptness to Falstaff's jesting suggestion that he and his thieving confederates be called "gentlemen of the shade."[90]

This contradiction is ironized by Falstaff's famous love of Spanish *sack*, a fortified Spanish wine that was stolen in large quantities during the English *sack* of Cádiz from 1596. In his account of his military service in Spain, the pirate and explorer Sir Richard Hawkins described sack as a biological weapon: "The enemy [Spain] I feared not so much as the wine; which […] overthrew my people […] Since the Spanish sacks have been common in our taverns […] our nation complaineth of calenturas, of the stone, the dropsie, or infinite other diseases, not heard of before this wine came in frequent use, or but very seldom."[91] These documented side effects of Spanish sack may be connected to the perceived dangers of Spanish romance. Whereas Falstaff's references to *The Mirrour of Knighthood* identify him as an avid Spanish romance reader (also in 3.3.25–26 when he calls Bardolph "Knight of the Burning Lamp"), his over two-dozen references to sack imply a connection to literal and symbolic piracy.[92] As a commonly pirated Spanish

---

89. For instance, Elizabethan favorite Sir Robert Dudley, Earl of Leicester, had commanded several famous acts of heroism in defense of England, such as his having commanded the land forces against the Spanish Armada, but he was also notorious for having allegedly committed many crimes, including the suspected murder of his wife, Amy Robsart. A libelous tract accused Dudley of "spoyling and oppressing almost infinite private men: but also whole Towns, Villages, Corporations, and Countries, by robbing the Realme with inordinate licences, by deceiving the Crown with racking, changing and imbezeling the Lands, by abusing his Prince and Soveraigne in selling his favour both at home and a[b]road […] In which sort of traffick he commit[e]th more theft oftentimes in one day than all the way-keepers, cut-purses, conseners, pirates, burglares, or other of that art in a whole yeare, within the Realme." *Leycesters Common-Wealth Conceived, Spoken and Published with most Earnest Protestation of all Dutifull Good Will and Affection Towards this Realme, for Whose Good Onely, it is made Common to Many* (London: s. n., 1641), sig. M3v. For a discussion of Falstaff and Dudley, see Jacqueline Vanhoutte, *Age in Love: Shakespeare and the Elizabethan Court* (Lincoln: University of Nebraska Press, 2019), 77–120.
90. Recall that in Spanish *gentleman* was *caballero*.
91. Richard Hawkins, *The Observations of Sir Richard Hawkins, Knt. in His Voyage into The South Sea in the Year 1593, reprinted from the edition of 1622*, C. R. Drinkwater Bethune, ed. (London: Hakluyt Society, 1847), 153–54.
92. Like other Spanish supplies and goods headed for the New World, the *books of the brave* were carried on the same merchant ships that brought sack and other spirits from the major port of origin in Sevilla (Seville), all of this organized by the Casa de Contratación or House of Trade, and passing off the coast of Africa, usually stopping at Islas Canarias (the Canary Islands) on

good, which he also ties to English wit,[93] and so, to English letters, sack provided a tangible metaphor for the real and symbolic corruptions that the English felt they faced as a result of their hyper-consumption of Spanish culture.

The discovery of the bottle of sack in Falstaff's sword case during the battle at Shrewsbury further points to the role of this beverage in England's various competitive relations, both cultural and military, as the exchange between Hal and Falstaff underscores:

> PRINCE. Give it me: what, is it in the case?
> FALSTAFF. Ay, Hal, 'tis hot, 'tis hot; there's that will sack a city.
> *The Prince draws it out, and finds it to be a bottle of sack.*
> PRINCE. What, is it a time to jest and dally now?
> *He throws the bottle at him.* Exit. (5.3.52–54)

There is an implied wordplay here between Falstaff's absent sword "that will sack a city" and the bottle of Spanish *sack* that has caused him to neglect his duty. This exchange is doubly ironic in light of Falstaff's comment that "a coward is worse than a cup of sack with lime in it" (2.4.114–115).[94] For the English nation, currently submerged in a protracted military and ideological war with Spain, sack's symbolic transformation into a sword could point to the sociopolitical contexts of trade and piracy in which the English were actively engaged during the period.[95] The play's conflation of Spanish products, from the literary to the gustatory, underscores a developing sense among many thinkers of the period that the English strategy of pirating Spain may have been doing more harm than good to the English masculine spirit. That the angered Hal literally "*throws the bottle at him*" is therefore a sign of a crucial conflict at work. The bottle is "a symbol of the tavern world,"[96] as Derek Peat remarks. "That it is offered instead of the sword,

---

their common trajectory to the New World. This created a key opportunity for piracy. In 1577, for example, when Sir Francis Drake undertook his voyage to the South Sea, he took two ships off the coast of Africa, taking their entire cargo. So grave was the problem of piracy that by the end of the late sixteenth century, the final South American port for imported books (and of the Spanish Treasure Fleet returning to Spain) had to be changed from Nombre de Dios to Puertobelo, Panama, due to the frequency of raids, particularly those of Drake (1572, 1595). It is also worth noting that books were exempted from all export taxes except for the *avería*, a convoy tax of between 1 and 7 percent necessary to equip merchant fleets with an armed guard to protect against pirate attacks. For more information on the Seville-based shipping of Spanish books, including threats of piracy, see Leonard, *Books of the Brave*, esp. 124–39 and 270–89.

93. Falstaff notes that "A good sherry-sack…becomes excellent wit" (4.2.93–98). William Shakespeare, *Henry IV, Part 2*, René Weis, ed. Oxford World's Classics Edition, Stanley Wells, ed. (Oxford: Oxford University Press, 1997).
94. Lime was a common fortifying ingredient.
95. See Barbara Sebek, "'More natural to the nation': Situating Shakespeare in the "Querelle de Canary" in *Shakespeare Studies*, vol. 42, James R. Siemon and Diana E. Henderson, eds. (Madison: Farleigh Dickinson University Press, 2014), 106–21.
96. Derek Peat, "Falstaff Gets the Sack," *Shakespeare Quarterly* 53, no. 3 (2002), 379–85 (380).

the symbol of the world of chivalry, is also significant. In a play that pits the tavern against the court, the balance appears to swing toward chivalry and honor and away from Falstaff's questioning of them."[97] But the tension here is not just between the tavern world and the chivalric world, but between rhetoric (love) and deeds (arms), and between romance's mediating of the two. Hal's throwing the bottle of sack at Falstaff in anger thus constitutes a masculine call to arms in defense of the nation.

This conclusion was altogether fitting for the late 1590s, when Spanish invasion attempts had become a nearly seasonal threat. In fact, during the summer of 1599, when the sequel, *Henry V*, first debuted, London was in the grip of a new Armada scare. James Shapiro aptly summarizes the Armada incident of 1599 as "at once a voice from the past and a current threat, a restaging of an old and familiar plot."[98] This revival of an old plot would have made the repeating of England's glory at Agincort a timely and visceral experience intended to serve the heroic spirit of English triumph that had become national manifesto in 1588. Correspondingly, the play witnesses an older, more mature Henry leading the charge of England's troops, having finally abandoned the petty mischiefs of the past. Perhaps this was the character of severity that Shakespeare sought to find in his aged sovereign as she turned away from the double-dealing courtiers and thieving sycophants of previous years to lead the charge against this imminent threat. Correspondingly, in the play, the fat drunken Falstaff remains tucked safely out of sight, dying offstage of venereal disease, though "They say he cried out of sack" (2.3.25). Tinged with both pathos and irony—"He's in Arthur's bosom, if ever man went to Arthur's bosom" (2.3.9–10)—the account of Falstaff's death, glutted on Spanish excess,[99] provides a final remonstrance of the man's character, and of Spain, well befitting the sobriety of the national moment.

---

97. Peat, "Falstaff Gets the Sack," 380.
98. James Shapiro, "Revisiting Tamburlaine: *Henry V* as Shakespeare's Belated Armada Play," *Criticism* 31, no. 4 (1989), 351–66 (356–57).
99. A known usage of the word *sack* was as a signifier for excess, or "a proverbial type of flagrant disproportion," such as in the line from *1 Henry IV*: "O monstrous! But one half-pennyworth of bread to this intolerable deal of sack?" (3.1.521–522). "sack, n.3." OED Online. Oxford University Press. https://www.oed.com.

CHAPTER 2

DREAM VISIONS AND COMPETING DREAMS: REWRITING THE SPANISH MODEL IN AMERICA

On November 8, 1519, a small retinue of Spanish soldiers and native Tlaxcalan warriors led by Hernán Cortés entered the Aztec[1] capital city, Tenochtitlán. The foreigners had been searching for this wondrous city since Don Diego de Ordaz and his companions had a glimpse of it a month earlier after enduring the volcanic ascent of Popocatépetl. From this brave summit, the conquerors first beheld the incomparably rich valley of México, intersected by a vast lake system, and at the center, the famed Aztec capital, with its white towers and pyramidal teocalli rising from their walled enclosures, reflecting the rays of the sun on their stucco walls. To the European observers, the sight seemed analogous to that beheld by eleventh-century Christian Crusaders who marched on Jerusalem. The truth of the event was far different. Cortés brokered a fateful agreement with the Mexica Emperor Moctezuma II, who later found himself hostage to the Spanish soldiers and was killed in the ensuing conflicts (June 29, 1520). Moctezuma's attitude toward the white men[2] had initially been guided by the fact that their ships appeared in the year in which the Aztec god, Topiltzin-Quetzalcoatl, was supposed to make his appearance. Initially, at least, Moctezuma was unsure as to who these men were.[3]

Less than two years later, Cortés and his compatriots had defeated Moctezuma's son-in-law, the final Emperor Cuauhtémoc (ruled 1520–1521), and with him, the Aztec Empire fell. Accounts differ wildly on the facts of the conquest, with some expressing sympathy for the late Moctezuma, apparently double-crossed by Cortés, and others

---

1. For connotative effect, I intermittently use the term *Aztec* (not popularized until the nineteenth century) to refer to the pre-Hispanic Nahua indigenous peoples of the central valley of México, who called themselves *Mēxihcah* or *Mexica*.
2. I use *white* as a collective term to describe the European colonizers, though men like the West African-born Juan Garrido counteract the stereotype of the conquest of America as an exclusively white European endeavor. For more information, see Matthew Restall, *Seven Myths of the Spanish Conquest* (Oxford: Oxford University Press, 2003), esp. 44–63.
3. The Mexica people initially believed that the Spaniards were "*hombre-dioses*" (man-gods), co-essences of Aztec gods appearing in human form, though extended contact disabused them of this belief. For a concise summary of these first contacts, see Davíd Carrasco, "Spaniards as Gods," in Bernal Díaz del Castillo, et al., *The History of the Conquest of New Spain, Translated with, with an Introduction and Notes, by Janet Burke and Ted Humphrey* (Albuquerque: University of New Mexico Press, 2008), 466–73.

vilifying him as a traitor to his own people.⁴ The net result was the destruction of the Mexica civilization, which became famous in Europe for both its incredible richness and its tragic demise. This chapter tracks that powerful legacy through Spanish histories and romances and into English drama, where it served to rationalize England's own colonial interventions in America.

México in the Renaissance Imagination

In his correspondence with Holy Roman Emperor Charles V, Cortés emphasized the supreme cultural and economic wealth of the Aztec Empire, particularly observing México's great causeways and modern aqueducts—easily comparable to those of ancient Rome—and its bustling marketplace and trade economy—not unlike contemporary Venice. These letters conveyed the simultaneous cultural richness and pagan Otherness of the Mexica peoples. For instance, in his second letter to Charles, dated October 30, 1520, Cortés described Tenochtitlán's religious sector as follows:

> This great city contains many mosques, or houses for idols, very beautiful edifices situated in the different precincts of it [...] Amongst these mosques, there is one principal one, and no human tongue is able to describe its greatness and details, because it is so large that within its circuit, which is surrounded by a high wall, a village of five hundred houses could easily be built."⁵

The sense of wonder is paramount to this account, as is the implied Orientalism of the Mexica culture. Note the emphasis on idol worship as both underscored and confused by the Arabic-derived "mosques" (mezquitas) in the place of the Latin-derived "temples" (templos) to describe the Mexica places of worship.⁶ This linguistic lapse points to Europeans' classic fear of Islam, which is wrongly interpreted here in Native American practices. It also demonstrates the reassertive ethos of white superiority over non-Europeans, which Edward Said forcefully demonstrates as historically propelling European imperialism. Said observes that "the major component in European culture

---

4. This polarizing characterization of the emperor's surrender is different from the attitude that predominates today. For instance, in the *Plaza de las Tres Culturas* (Square of the Three Cultures) in the main square within the Tlatelolco neighborhood of Mexico City, hangs a placard that reads "El 13 de agosto de 1521 heroicamente defendido por Cuauhtémoc, cayó Tlatelolco en poder de Hernán Cortés. No fue triunfo ni derrota, fue el doloroso nacimiento del pueblo mestizo, que es el México de hoy" (On August 13, 1521, heroically defended by Cuauhtémoc, Tlatelolco fell to the power of Hernán Cortés. This was neither a triumph nor a defeat; this was a painful birth of the mestizo nation, which is the Mexico of today).
5. Hernán Cortés, *Letters of Cortes: The Five Letters of Relation from Fernando Cortes to the Emperor Charles V*, vol. I, Francis Augustus MacNutt, ed. (New York: G. P. Putnam's Sons, 1908), 259–60. I have omitted many details, including the description of many businesses and marketplaces, the description of the city priests who live in its largest teocalli, and the lengthy description of pagan religious practice.
6. Cortés used the terms *templo* and *mezquita* interchangeably.

is precisely what made that culture hegemonic both in and outside Europe: the idea of European identity as a superior one in comparison with all the non-European peoples and cultures. There is in addition the hegemony of European ideas about the Orient, themselves reiterating European superiority over Oriental backwardness"[7] In the context of early travel narratives, the Orientalist characterization of Native Americans as Moor-like in both their cultural richness and their religious backwardness further underscores colonization's continuance of the holy mission of the Crusades and, by extension, the early European politic of interventionism. This ethnographical and theological argument undergirded the larger administrative project of imperial expansion as one designed to supplant more *primitive* non-Christian cultures, as suggested, for example, by Cortés's quickness in identifying the site of the principal "mosque" (Huey Teocalli), as a space where "a village of five hundred houses could easily be built."

Additionally, European writers' habits of comparison with the Moors also encoded language's failure to encompass the wonders that they encountered in this new continent and the foreign peoples who inhabited it. This struggle also emerged in the conclusion of the *Códice Mendoza* or *Codex Mendoza*, a major manuscript history of precolonial Mexica culture, commissioned by first viceroy of New Spain, Don António de Mendoza, and deeply inspirational to colonial enthusiasts like Samuel Purchas. The Castilian translator noted that "it was a mistake for the interpreter [of this work] to use the Moorish words *alfaqui mayor* and *alfaqui nouiçio*;[8] saçerdote *mayor* should be written for *alfaqui mayor*, and *saçerdote noviçio* for the novice. And where *mezquitas* is written, *templos* is to be understood."[9] This comment anticipated readerly objections over the translator's linguistic imprecision. Nevertheless, the writer's presentation of Christian and Moorish terms where Native American institutions and practices were "to be understood" evinces the problem, as Stephen Gilman put it, that the "New World must be given in translation; yet in the very act of translation there can be linguistic salvation, recreation of the old in such a way that it means more than it ever meant before."[10] Such comparisons, which reflected the enduring legacy of the Crusades, lent terror and furor to the experience of religious and cultural difference by Christian travelers to the New World, especially by the Spanish, who had finally defeated the Moors only decades before. This European imperial program, which imposed the representation of indigenous peoples as Other, casting them as both civilized and subhuman, was used to justify the conquest of America as a missionary project for the salvation of pagan souls that by nature required European involvement. This

---

7. Edward Said, *Orientalism* (New York: Vintage Books, 1979), 7.
8. These were Arabic terms for the hierarchical offices of legal scholars charged with interpreting Islamic law.
9. *Codex Mendoza*, Bodleian Library, Oxford University, MS Arch. Selden A. 1. (fol. 71v). Transcriptions and translations derive from the digital version on Codex Mendoza Online (INAH: National Institute of Anthropology and History): https://codicemendoza.inah.gob.mx/inicio.php?lang=english.
10. Stephen Gilman, "Bernal Díaz del Castillo and Amadís de Gaula," in *Studia Philologica: Homenaje ofrecido a Dámaso Alonso,* vol. II (Madrid: Gredos, 1960), 99–114 (112).

agenda was supported by the literature produced in Spain and England, the two countries privileged in this study (though they were certainly not alone), first emerging in the historical chronicles of México by Spanish historians and allegorical romance writers, and next reemerging in the romance adaptations produced in England.

All five of Cortés's letters were published in Latin in a work titled *Praeclara Ferdinandi. Cortesii de noua maris oceani Hyspania narratio sacratissimo* [...] published in Nuremberg in 1524 by Friedrich Peypus. This book also contained the first printed city plan of Tenochtitlán in a woodcut produced by the Nuremberg house, included as a foldout plate with Cortés's second letter. Throughout the sixteenth and seventeenth centuries, printing houses published versions of this map, such as in Giovanni Ramusio's *Terzo Volvme delle Navigationi et Viaggi* and Georg Braun and Franz Hogenberg's *Civitates Orbis Terrarum*.[11] It was distinctive for collapsing the distinct temporalities of the pre- and postcolonial eras with such features as a large Habsburg banner waving in the background, and a small cross affixed to the Templo Mayor, labeled "Templum ad Sacrificum" to highlight pagan practice. A full color version held in the Newberry Library in Chicago, U.S.A. also shows the fully painted houses with what look like terra cotta roofs (Figure 2).[12] Based on Cortés's own city plan, the woodcut is also remarkable for its great symmetry, featured as a series of concentric circles (evoking a globe) with a central square for the *Templo Mayor*, intersected by causeways that create four quadrants.[13] The city's planimetry mirrored the "horizontal cosmos of the four directions, assimilating the city to the form of the four quadrants that constituted the cosmos."[14] According to Davíd Carrasco, this "material expression of [Mexica] cosmovision"[15] captured the city's famous dreamlike quality, as also enhanced by the mixed pagan and Christian elements, particularly in the distinctly spherical shape, which disclosed the local understanding of the universe. Barbara Mundy has shown that this design was probably based on an "indigenous proptoype—a Culhua-Mexica map of the capital city," particularly tying the distinct globe-like dimensionality of the Nuremberg map to local "cosmic modeling" that was featured in the planimetry of Tenochtitlán.[16] Tenochtitlán features as "the cosmic center of a world that stretches from the distant horizons and is focused inward toward its ritual heart [...] Europeanized to fit the visual

---

11. For a full list, see Appendix I in Barbara Mundy, "Mapping the Aztec Capital: The 1524 Nuremberg Map of Tenochtitlan, Its Sources and Meanings," *Imago Mundi*, 50 (1998), 11–33 (32).
12. *Praeclara de noua maris Oceani Hyspania narratio* (Nuremberg: Friedrich Peypus, 1524). Edward E Ayer Collection, The Newberry Library.
13. The distinctive shape of this city plan, represented as a series of concentric circles, was also unusual for the reversed orientation of the paired coastal map, which featured the west lying to the south, charting the Gulf of Mexico from the Yucatán Peninsula to Florida.
14. Davíd Carrasco, "Tenochtitlan as a Political Capital and World Symbol," in Bernal Díaz del Castillo, *The History of the Conquest of New Spain*, Janet Burke and Ted Humphrey, trans., Davíd Carrasco, ed. (Albuquerque: University of New Mexico Press, 2009), 448–57 (454).
15. Carrasco, "Tenochtitlan as a Political Capital and World Symbol," 453.
16. Mundy, "Mapping the Aztec Capital," 13.

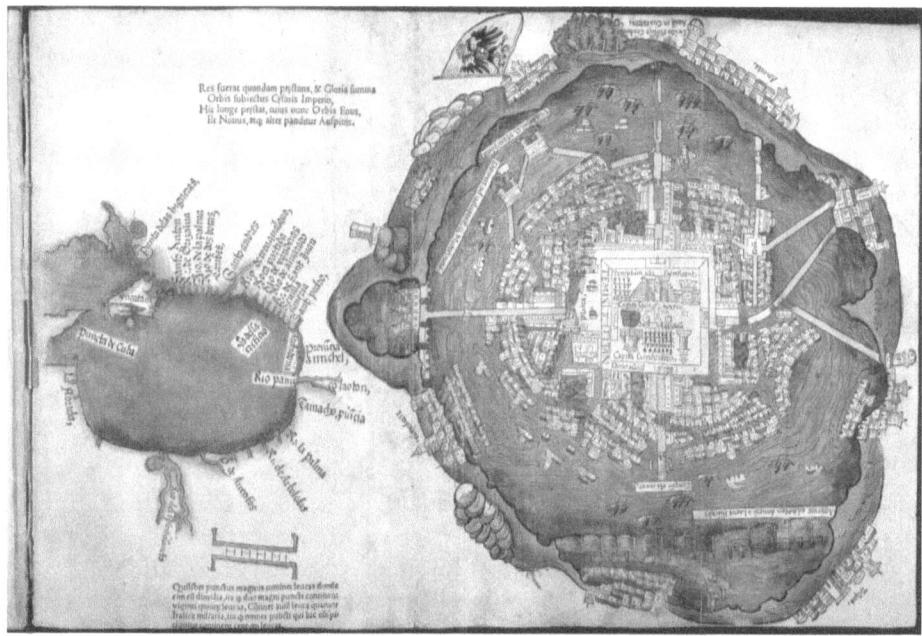

Figure 2 Woodcut map and plan of Tenochtitlán, in *Praeclara de Nova maris Oceani Hyspania Narratio* (Nuremberg, F. Peypus, 1524). Courtesy of Edward E. Ayer Collection, The Newberry Library.

codes that were accepted and understood by Europeans," as Elizabeth Hill Boone remarks.[17] This European fixation with translating the foreign into the familiar accounts for why the large buildings resemble structures of early modern Europe while the gleaming teocalli resemble medieval towers.[18]

Dream Visions

For a generation thoroughly fascinated with the New World conquest, the destruction of a marvelous pagan empire by Christian crusaders was thoroughly captivating subject matter, as were the imperial foot soldiers who had helped to make this project a reality. The contingent Spanish force of common infantrymen, minor hidalgos, and younger sons of the aristocracy were motivated by three goals: to amass a fortune deserving of a true knight; to serve their king and country; and to spread the Catholic faith into the Americas. "God, glory, and gold" was the guiding mantra of the age, echoed in countless

---

17. Elizabeth Hill Boone, "This New World Now Revealed: Hernán Cortés and the Presentation of Mexico to Europe," *Word & Image* 27, no. 1 (2011), 31–46 (38).
18. Boone, "This New World Now Revealed," 38.

travel narratives and accounts of these so-styled soldiers of Christ. One of these men was Bernal Díaz del Castillo,[19] who penned an authoritative account of the conquest of México based on his own recollections; his *Historia verdadera de la conquista de la Nueva España* (*The True History of the Conquest of New Spain*) was set down and revised from 1551 to 1568, decades after the fall of Tenochtitlán, arriving in Spain in manuscript in 1575, where it was revised by the Mercedarian friar and polemicist of colonialism, Alonso Remón.[20] Dubbed a *True History*, the work was designed to counteract other accounts that Díaz considered apocryphal, particularly those of Francisco López de Gómara and Bartolomé de Las Casas, which presented a decidedly *unromantic* picture of the conquest. Thus, Díaz found himself in the uncomfortable position of having to defend the position of the conquistadors against an onslaught of legal disputations and humanist attacks.[21]

A highly literary work,[22] the *True History* also adopted forms and styles of chivalric romance. One famous example is Díaz's description of the Spaniards' first encounter of Tenochtitlán, the extraordinary city on the lake, which uses comparison with the worlds of fiction to translate America's Otherness within the episteme of European civilization:

> During the morning, we arrived at a broad Causeway and continued our march towards Iztapalapa, and when we saw so many cities and villages built in the water and other great towns on dry land and that straight and level Causeway going towards Mexico, we were amazed and said that it was like the enchantments they tell of in the legend of Amadis, on

---

19. Born around 1495 in Medina del Campo, Díaz joined Pedrarias Dávila's expedition to Tierra Firme in 1513. He participated in the 1517–18 explorations of the Yucatán coast led by Francisco Hernández de Córdoba and Juan de Grijalva, respectively, and then he joined the 1519 expedition to México Central under Hernán Cortés. After partaking in Cortés's failed expedition to Hibueras (Honduras) in 1524–26, he spent the rest of his life in New Spain, settling in Guatemala, where he had an encomienda and held the office of regidor [governor] of Santiago de los Caballeros. In 1584 he died, the last remaining deponent to Cortés's conquest.
20. Prior to the institution of copyright laws, writings were commonly read and edited in manuscript form by diverse writers. Díaz composed and corrected his manuscript from the 1550s until his death. Yet, a copy of his original manuscript (which remained in Guatemala) arrived in Madrid in 1575. Chapter 212 attests that Díaz's work was also being read in manuscript. He relates that two university men requested to read his account of the conquest of México in order to determine how his testimony differed from those of Francisco López de Gómara and Bartolomé de Las Casas. He provided the men with his manuscript on the condition that they not alter it in any way. Unfortunately, his hopes for uncorrupted transmission were ultimately unfulfilled, as demonstrated by the separate revision by Remón. Remón added some fabricated sections and deleted others. This version was published in Spain in 1632 and was later translated into English in 1800 and 1844. German printings appeared in 1838 and 1844; the French appeared in 1876 and 1877; and the Hungarian in 1877, 1878, and 1899.
21. For more information on the legal challenges to Spanish conquest, see Rolena Adorno, "Bernal Díaz del Castillo: Soldier, Eyewitness, Polemicist," in Díaz, et al. *The History of the Conquest of New Spain*, 389–98.
22. Obviating his literary borrowings, chapter 210 was related as a dialogue with the allegorical figure of Fame, whose discursive interjections countermanded the vilified picture of conquest presented by Gómara and Las Casas.

account of the great towers and cues and buildings rising from the water, and all built of masonry. And some of our soldiers even asked whether the things that we saw were not a dream. It is not to be wondered at that I here write it down in this manner, for there is so much to think over that I do not know how to describe it, seeing things as we did that had never been heard of or seen before, not even dreamed about.[23]

Díaz's *Amadís* reference was probably not idiosyncratic; it was rather indicative of the common comparisons that America elicited with the worlds of romance. Published 11 years prior to Spaniards' first sights of Tenochtitlán, *Amadís* not only conditioned European expectations of the wonders and dangers that lie in the New World, but it also provided writers and readers with a convenient representational lens, as Gilman remarks:

> *Amadís* in those days was not, as it is for us, a more or less unread text, a mere title suggestive of chivalric ideals and hazy adventures. It was rather, as it was for its most celebrated reader [Díaz], intensely perused and intensely present, sharply visual. Hence, its suitability to this particular moment. The first long-awaited sight of lake, and city—after the unsatisfactory descriptions of the Tlaxcalans and the distant glimpse that Diego de Ordaz and his comrades had of it from the summit of Popocatepetl—is the apogee of marvel and so of memory, visual memory: "agora que lo estoy escribiendo se me representa todo delante de mis ojos como si fuera cuando esto pasó" [now that I am writing this, it represents everything before my eyes as if were now as before].[24]

But what precisely was Díaz's *Amadís* allusion, and how might México's "cities and villages built in the water and other great towns on dry land" have matched with "the enchantments they tell of" in those books? One possible referent, as Gilman notes, was the fortress of Bradoid of chapter 11 of I.1, which is described as follows:

> About five days after their departure, by good hap they came neere a very faire and strong Castle, named Bradoid, seated on the toppe of a mountaine, environed about with Fennes and Marishes, as also with a salt water, that ran before it wondrous swiftly, so that without a Barque it was impossible to get thither. And because the Marish was very long, there was to passe over it a faire long Causey, being so broad that two Chariots might well meet together on it: and at the entrance of the Causey was a draw-bridge where-under the water ran with such a violent fall, as no one was able to by any meanes passe it.[25]

Similarly, at the entry to Tenochtitlán, the Spanish explorers found, in the words of their commander Cortés: "two towers, surrounded by walls, twelve feet high with castellated tops. This commands the two roads, and has only two gates, by one of which they enter, and from the other they came out."[26] Cortés concluded: "The said city being built as

---

23. *The History of The Conquest of New Spain*, 156.
24. Gilman, "Bernal Díaz del Castillo and Amadís de Gaula," 112.
25. *Amadis de Gaule, translated by Anthony Munday,* Helen Moore, ed. (Aldershot: Ashgate, 2004), 82.
26. *Letters of Cortes*, 232.

I have described, they might, by raising the bridges at the exits and entrances, starve us without our being able to reach the land"[27]

Nevertheless, more iconic than Bradoid's elevated castle on the water, with its "Fennes and Marishes, as also with a salt water," and accessible by a "faire long Causey," is the romance's famous Ínsula Firme (Firm Island). Ínsula Firme derives its name from the slightness of the land, which is "no more then a bow shoot of firme ground, and all the rest was water."[28] Its entry is "only five leagues in breadth, and seven in length,"[29] similar to the Great Causeway, which extended seven miles to Iztapalapa.[30] Ínsula Firme is bounded by a fortified castle, which forces travelers through to the arch of the faithful lovers, a boundary that admits only a true knight. This double test of loving fealty and knightly prowess could be read as an analog for the New World sought by Christian conquerors. It was designed by the Greek prince Apolidon to grant lordship of the island to the worthy knight who successfully passes through the arch, proving himself "as good a Knight as he [Apolidon], and as true in love as hee was.[31]

Ínsula Firme is also famous for its indescribable wonders, which are alluded to several times before Amadís ever reaches the island. There he at last discovers, in the words of Munday, "such strange and marvailous things as are to be seene."[32] The work elaborates the city's wondrous towers, built in the water and made of precious metals, which bear some resemblance to Tenochtitlán's incomparable wonders, namely its royal palace: "[Apolidon] caused to be builded in that place, one of the fairest palaces that was to be found in all the Isles of the Ocian: the which he beautified so gorgeously, and furnished so richly that the greatest monarch of the earth would have found it a very difficult matter to have builded the like."[33] If Díaz had hoped to reconcile this fictional palace to the Huey Teocalli (Templo Mayor) that Spaniards later discovered in Tenochtitlán, then he must have also noted the stronghold's significance to the Christian conquest narrative that was writ large upon America. It was built by the city's founders when they settled the region. As the *Codex Mendoza* narrates, this was the culminating event of a long indigenous pilgrimage akin to that of the Israelites led by Moses, who wandered the desert for 40 years:

> In the year 1324, after the coming of our lord and savior Jesus Christ, the Mexicans arrived at the site of the city of Mexico, and since they liked the space and site after having wandered

---

27. *Letters of Cortes*, 257.
28. *Amadis de Gaule*, 313. This also corresponds with the South American region of Tierra Firme. Founded in 1510, Tierra Firme was a long way off from where Cortés and his men stood beholding Tenochtitlán, but Díaz's phrasing reminds us of the region's shared feature with the city of wonders from *Amadís*, which was likewise named after the smallness of land upon which it stood.
29. *Amadis de Gaule*, 308.
30. See Appendix II in *Letters of Cortes*, 330–35 (330). Ínsula Firme is at one point described as a peninsula, seven leagues long and five wide, connected to Britain by a narrow isthmus. Later in the story, the location moves to southern France.
31. *Amadis de Gaule*, 310.
32. *Amadís de Gaule*, 311.
33. *Amadis de Gaule*, 306–7.

for many years in their journey from place to place, in some of which they had stopped for some years, having left from a distant land [...] And with this determined, they strengthened their position using the waters for walls and fences, and reeds and marshes for ambuscades.³⁴

From this description of the fabled water paradise of Tenochtitlán, long sought by its first founders "who wandered for many years" the reader could also observe comparisons with Ínsula Firme, Amadís's long-sought destination on his mission to pass through the arch of faithful lovers. This symbolic journey realized a primal western boundary crossing described by the ancients, folding America into Europe's constructed teleology of the world (see Chapter 4).

Amadís was the pinnacle of Díaz's romanticism. The work helped to flesh out the Biblical progress of history, filling the gaps of language and of memory so that readers could see things that "had never been heard of or seen before, not even dreamed about." This explanation further aligned México to the Promised Land, drawing language indirectly from Paul's First Letter to the Corinthians: "Eye hath not seen, neither eare heard, neither haue entred into the heart of man, the things which God hath prepared for them that loue him" (2:9).³⁵ So ubiquitous was this romanticizing of an American Promised Land that a parallel observation also appears in William Shakespeare's English comedy play, *A Midsummer Night's Dream* (1595–96). In Act 4, Nick Bottom returns from his sensual romp through faery land (of which he was briefly king), and he remarks, "I have had a most rare vision. I have had a dream, past the wit of man to say what dream it was [...] The eye of man hath not heard, the ear of man hath not seen, man's hand is not able to taste, his tongue to conceive, nor his heart to report what my dream was!" (4.1.201–209).³⁶ The mocking reference to Corinthians, so central to the colonizer ethos, underscores America's allegorical presence in romance as a "most rare vision" of the Promised Land, a mystery so inscrutable as to seem a dream.

Competing Dreams

The marvelous, lake-bound capital city, Tenochtitlán, was fertile subject matter for romantic mythologizing—and for patriotic propagandizing. Chroniclers remarked upon "the causeway so straight and level,"³⁷ and "the towers and cues and buildings that are in the water,"³⁸ which seemed to extend seamlessly to the enclosing heavens. These three features (the causeways, the towers, and the temples) lent a distinctiveness to the island empire that sparked curiosity and wanderlust in generations of masculine readers. For Díaz, this city was like a fabled faerie land. Others, especially Gómara, would further

---

34. *Codex Mendoza,* fol. 1r.
35. *The Holy Bible* (King James Bible) (London: Robert Barker, 1611).
36. William Shakespeare, *A Midsummer Night's Dream,* Peter Holland, ed. (Oxford: Oxford University Press, 1994).
37. *The History of The Conquest of New Spain,* 156.
38. *The History of The Conquest of New Spain,* 156.

posit that it was the lost city of Atlantis.[39] In his dialogues *Timaeus* (especially 24–25) and *Critias*, Plato had described Atlantis as a wealthy and powerful city founded by Phoenician seafarers. It was located somewhere beyond the westernmost limit at the Pillars of Hercules, within a huge archipelago in the Atlantic Ocean, which served as gateway to a vast continent. The rulers of this wealthy and powerful city-state attempted to conquer the surrounding Mediterranean, but they were defeated by the neighboring Athenians. A volcanic cataclysm ensued, and Atlantis purportedly disappeared beneath the sea as a result of earthquakes and floods, while the survivors were driven elsewhere.

The connection to Atlantis was fostered by the proliferation of pre-Columbian Mexica history in works like *Praeclara Ferdinandi* and the *Códice Mendoza*. In a speech later cited as proof of his empire's destined decline, Emperor Moctezuma had reportedly revealed that:

> I, nor those who inhabit this country, are descendants from the aborigines of it, but from strangers who came to it from very distant parts; and we also hold, that our race was brought to these parts by a lord, whose vassals they all were, and who returned to his native country [...] And we have always held that those who descended from him would come to subjugate this country and us, as his vassals; and according to the direction from which you say you come, which is where the sun rises, and from what you tell us of your great lord, or king, who has sent you here, we believe, and hold for certain, that he is our rightful sovereign[40]

As by this reported assertion of European supremacy, a genealogy of Atlantis could be reconstructed: a lost island empire, partially descended into the water; a great and powerful people arrived from the east; and an incomparable political power suddenly reduced to ruins. For a determined reader, the *Amadís* sequel, *Sergas de Esplandián*, might also have advanced a new mythology of Atlantis in America. At the conclusion of this famous *book of the brave*, Urganda the Enchantress gathers together the mortally wounded heroes on Ínsula Firme. After healing the heroes with magical herbs, she commands that Ínsula Firme will magically disappear into the depths of the earth, only to return in the days of Arthur, thus also linking with the myth of Avalon, Island of Glass Towers, Ynys-vitrius, or the British Atlantis. As Simone Pinet summarizes, "With this sunken Atlantis [Ínsula Firme] as a legacy, books of chivalry [would] multiply archipelagoes, their characters hoping for the reappearance of Ínsula Firme, reenacting forms of fiction (and politics) in their itineraries."[41]

---

39. Others suggested that it was merely the new land sought by Atlantis's survivors. Imperial polemicist, Nathaniel Crouch disputed this notion: "Plato's *Atlantis*, cannot intend this Countrey, because he placeth it at the mouth of the Streights or *Mediterranean* Sea, which is separated from *America* by a vast Ocean, and saies it is not now in being, but was by an earthquake sunk and overwhelmed in the Sea," sig. A3v. R[obert] B[urton], *The English Empire in America by R.B.* (London: Nath: Crouch, 1685), sig. A3v. Robert Burton was Crouch's pseudonym.
40. *Letters of Cortes*, 234–35.
41. Simone Pinet, *Archipelagoes: Insular Fictions from Chivalric Romance to the Novel* (Minneapolis: University of Minnesota Press, 2011), 137.

Perhaps Tenochtitlán's most significant legacy was not the watery site itself, but its relevance to Spain's narrative of itself as world savior. In Spanish recollection, Emperor Moctezuma appeared as a symbolic mouthpiece for pre-Columbian Mesoamerica's seemingly destined decline. He was commonly depicted as an impressive but flawed ruler, proud of his pagan beliefs and unwilling to convert to Christianity, who fatefully succumbed to the combined pressures of Mexica prophecy and his imprisonment by Cortés. Correspondingly, Emperor Moctezuma's conciliation to Charles could be read as an admission of the fated decline of premodern pagan empires, which was underscored by México's perceived parity with Atlantis.[42] For the Spanish, therefore, Moctezuma's story heralded the rise of the Habsburg dynasty in the West.

For the English, by contrast, his story most forcefully instantiated the rising hubris of the new Rome,[43] which signaled the destined return of King Arthur to lead a new Roman conquest (see Chapter 3). From at least as early as the first Latin printing of Cortés's letters, the cruel fate of Moctezuma, and of the Aztec Empire more generally, became an English household legend. Shortly after their European publication, copies in Latin and Italian of the second letter (quoted here throughout) and the third letter arrived at the Cambridge University Library, Clare College, and Trinity College.[44] Most of the relevant details also appeared in Peter Martyr's *Decades of the Newe Worlde or West India* (1555), based on diverse sources, and an appended chapter from Francisco López de Gómara's *Historia general de las Indias*, translated by Richard Eden; the earliest English map of Tenochtitlán dates to 1572.[45] As evidenced in Ireland, England's first plantation colony, the English had been closely studying the Spanish colonial exploits in America, particularly modeling its forced labor economy after the Spanish encomienda. Nevertheless, the English were also forced to contend with the two competing visions of colonization: the negative, Catholic model, denoting abuses of power and excess cruelty, as so thoroughly instantiated by the devastations of México and Perú, and the positive, Protestant model, which proponents associated with the divine will of God and of the restored Church of the forefathers, which was to be realized in the West. Writers such as William Shakespeare and John Dryden would therefore use Emperor

---

42. Plato had used Atlantis as an illustrative example to condemn hubris and luxuriance.
43. For instance, in William Lightfoot's 1587 *The Complaint of England*, which included a loose translation of Las Casas, the English translator highlighted the Spaniards' treachery in arresting Moctezuma on the same day he had welcomed them with gifts and hospitality. This work also alleged further Spanish atrocities, such that they "deuoured" an infant, and of a "tender child," "cut off firste his armes, then his legs, casting them to his dogs for liuerie." *The Complaint of England, Wherein it is clearely prooued that the practices of Traitrous Papists against the state of this Realme, and the person of her Maiestie, are in Diuinitie vnlawfull, odious in Nature, and ridiculous in pollicie* [...] *later by the Spaniards outrages, in his exactions raised vpon Naples, and his tyrannies executed in the Indies* (London: John Wolfe, 1587), sig. H2r.
44. H. M. Adams, *Catalogue of Books Printed on the Continent of Europe 1501–1600 in Cambridge Libraries* (Cambridge: Cambridge University Press, 1967), 316.
45. For more information on the English profusion of Mexica history and depictions of Tenochtitlán, with images, see María Fernanda Valencia-Suárez, "Tenochtitlán and the Aztecs in the English Atlantic World, 1500–1563," *Atlantic Studies*, 6 no. 3 (2009) 277–301.

Moctezuma's fate as a crystalline example of the impermanence of power, which ebbs and flows with the changing of the seas, ironically denoting the predestined end of the pre-Columbian empires of Mesoamerica, and the first chapter to the divinely ordained arrival of Europeans: translatio imperii.

And yet, there was no avoiding the obvious fact that the sudden disappearance of these illustrious civilizations, which should spell doom for the Spaniards, likewise boded ill for England. Thus, it became necessary to simultaneously underscore Spaniards' faults as imperial overlords and highlight the uncommon virtues of the English, in order to defend the country's imperial aspirations as divinely willed. For instance, those familiar with Tenochtitlán, known for "the great towers and cues and buildings that are in the water," so incredible as to seem "a dream," and closely associated with the famous pagan man who had once ruled over it, might perceive something tragically related—and foreshadowed—in the following speech by magician and exiled Duke of Milan, Prospero, in Shakespeare's staged romance, *The Tempest* (circa 1610):

> Our revels now are ended. These our actors,
> As I foretold you, were all spirits, and
> Are melted into air, into thin air,
> And, like the baseless fabric of this vision,
> The cloud-capped towers, the gorgeous palaces,
> The solemn temples, the great globe itself,
> Yea, all which it inherit, shall dissolve,
> And, like this insubstantial pageant faded,
> Leave not a rack behind. We are such stuff
> As dreams are made on, and our little life
> Is rounded with a sleep. (4.1.148–158)[46]

For a colonial enthusiast, "The baseless fabric of this vision," denoting a "structure without foundation [...] an edifice without a base,"[47] and the "cloud-capped towers, the gorgeous palaces, / The solemn temples, the great globe itself," could be compared with Tenochtitlán's famously spherical shape (as in the Nuremberg woodcut), and the towering teocalli,[48] jutting out from the water, as if without foundation, and stretching forward to the heavens. The line also implies the tragic irony of a great civilization now utterly extinguished by European conquerors. I am particularly reminded of Díaz, who said of Tenochtitlán: "I stood looking at it and thought that never in the world would there be discovered other lands such as these, for at that time there was no Peru, nor any

---

46. William Shakespeare, *The Tempest*, Stephen Orgel, ed. (Oxford: Oxford University Press, 1987).
47. Stephen Orgel, ed. *The Tempest* (note to 4.1.151).
48. For instance, Gómara reported that the holy Mexica city Chololla "sheweth outwardes verye beautifull, and full of towers, for there are as manye temples as dayes in the yeare, & euery temple hath his tower. Our men counted foure hundred towers," sig. Xiiiv.

thought of it. Of all these wonders that I then beheld today all is overthrown and lost, nothing left standing."⁴⁹

The English fixation with Spanish-American conquest is also encoded by the substance of the vision itself. This speech occurs immediately after the masque of Ceres, Iris, and Juno, who with their nymphs perform a harvest dance in celebration of Miranda and Ferdinand's marriage. The dance is a callback to Gonzalo's "had I plantation of this isle" speech from Act 2, while the crops listed by Ceres at 4.1.61—wheat, rye, barley, vetches, oats, and peas—were common English staples planned for cultivation in overseas colonies.⁵⁰ The pairing of this vision of "cloud-capped towers, the gorgeous palaces / The solemn temples, the great globe itself," which resonates with this famously extinguished city that left "not a rack behind,"⁵¹ also accords with the new era of the encomienda that this destruction marshaled forward. The image of destruction highlights empire's limited lifecycle, for "our little life / Is rounded with a sleep."

This speech also corresponds with the larger English milieu of eager romance reading that produced *The Tempest*. Frederick de Armas has noted that Prospero's speech fits the description of Ínsula Firme from *Amadís*, suggesting that Shakespeare probed the work

---

49. *The History of the Conquest of New Spain*, 157.
50. Consider, for example, this comment of a region of Newfoundland from 1622: "the leuell lying of many hundred acres in large valleyes of good deepe earth, open and cleane, without rocks and trees, which (questionlesse) is fit for Wheat, Rye, Barley, and other graine [...] also for Flax, Hempe, Woad, Tobacco, and many other purposes." Richard Whitbourne, *A Discourse Containing a Louing Inuitation both Honourable, and Profitable to all such as Shall be Aduenturers, either in Person, Or Purse, for the Aduancement of His Maiesties most Hopeful Plantation in the Nevv-found-Land, Lately Vndertaken. Written by Captaine Richard Whitbourne of Exmouth, in the County of Deuon* (London: Felix Kyngston, 1622), sig B3r.
51. Perhaps a clue to the cartographical inclinations of Shakespeare's audience may be found in the variant inscription of Prospero's speech on the monument to Shakespeare in the Poet's Corner in Westminster Abbey (erected in 1741):

> The Cloud capt Tow'rs,
> The Gorgeous Palaces,
> The Solemn Temples,
> The Great Globe itself,
> Yea all which it Inherit,
> Shall Dissolve;
> And like the baseless Fabrick of a Vision
> Leave not a wreck behind.

The change presents the image of a world in ruin, also suggested by the substitution of "rack" (a wisp of cloud) with "wreck," a ruin. There has been much speculation over the meaning of Shakespeare's "rack." Contentions vacillate over whether Shakespeare meant "rack" as in the uppermost coverings used in masque scenes, as in Ben Jonson's *Hymenaei* ("Here the upper part of the scene, which was all of clouds, and made artificially to swell, and ride like the rack, began to open"), or "rack/wrack" as a variant of "wreck," as in John Fletcher's *Wife for a Month* ("You may snatch him up by parcels, like a Sea Rack"). *Wreck* better fits with the theme of imperial decline.

for the plot of his play.⁵² This hypothesis carries weight, for Prospero's appearance on the Summer Isle also generally accords with the origins of Ínsula Firme. The work relates that the book-loving Apilodon arrived on the island in flight from his brother, who was chosen by their father to rule Greece. This can be compared to Prospero's absconding to the Summer Isle as a result of Antonio's usurpation of Milan. One difference, however, is that Apolidon's companion, Grimanesa, is not his daughter but his lady. For her sake, Apolidon battles the fierce ruling Giant (a prototypical Caliban), who threatens to rape Grimanesa. Beheading the Giant, Apolidon leaves him dead in a field, a detail that is perhaps comically recalled by Shakespeare in the form of Caliban's being mistaken for dead by Trinculo and Stefano in Act 2, scene 2.

Although *Amadís* is probably a common ancestor for *The Tempest*, the play also has unique correspondences with another Spanish source, the fourth chapter of Antonio de Eslava's *Noches de invierno* (Winter Nights) (1609).⁵³ In this work, the exiled magician King Dárdano flees with his daughter Serafina to the bottom of the sea where he fashions for himself an extravagant undersea palace "fabricated out of those deep abysses."⁵⁴ This is very close to not only the water-bound palace of Ínsula Firme, but also Tenochtitlán's construction "using the waters for walls and fences."⁵⁵ The Mexica people regarded the lake's waters as *inhuica atl* (celestial water), which is why the indigenous and European maps depicted Tenochtitlán's edifices seemingly floating in water, extending from the land-edge to merge with the sky.⁵⁶ In *Noches*, the water is also what comprises the palace's *"cuatro altísimas torres"* (extremely tall towers), bedecked with "crystalline windows, golden balconies,"⁵⁷ while its interiors boast artwork depicting Apollo's zodiac.⁵⁸ Don Fabricio,

---

52. See Frederick de Armas, "Galeotto Fu '1 Libro: Don Quixote, Amadis, and *The Tempest*," *Cervantes: Bulletin of the Cervantes Society of America* 37, no. 2 (2017), 9–34, esp. 22–30.
53. For further discussion of this possible source, see Edmund Dorer, *Das Magazin für die Litteratur des In- und Auslandes*, January 31, 1885; Richard Garnett and Edmund Gosse, *English Literature: From the Age of Henry VIII to the Age of Milton* (New York: Grosset and Dunlap, 1904), 251; Marcelino Menéndez Pelayo, *Orígenes de la novela*, vol. II (Madrid, Consejo Superior de Investigaciones Científicas, 1943), 120–38; Julia Barella Vigal, *"Antonio de Eslava y William Shakespeare: historia de una coincidencia," El Crotalón: Anuario de Filología Española*, vol. 2, 1985, 489–501.
54. Antonio de Eslava, *Noches de invierno*, Julia Barrella, ed. (Zaragoza: Iberoamericana, 2013), 109. All translations are my own. Dárdano cedes his Bulgarian crown to the Greek emperor Nicíforo, who passes rule on to his greedy younger son, Juliano, displacing his virtuous elder son, Valentiniano. For more information, see note 64.
55. *Codex Mendoza*, fol. 1r.
56. In chapter 220 of his *Historia general*, Gómara had suggested that the Nahua term, *"atl"* meaning "water," further pointed to Plato's Atl-antis.
57. Eslava, *Noches de invierno*, 109.
58. As Fabricio relates

> Its strong walls were lined inside and outside with polished silver, and within them were reliefs depicting the Pharsalian Wars. The antechamber was wrought with so much care and artifice that the architecture could not further proceed within the realm of the imaginary: friezes and obelisks and labors exceeding the works of Phidias; terraces made of Porphyry; pavement squares made of the finest stone that swirled together delightfully in certain places; Corinthian columns with admirable bases and capitals; the vaulted ceilings, rooftops and coffers elaborated with gold, ivory and mother of pearl; hanging from them were large clusters of gold and in the main vault was a relief of the celestial sphere with great delicacy and peregrine trace, which was a thing to see: the zodiac

who is narrating the story, aptly remarks that "so excellent and sumptuous a palace neither king nor prince had ever had in this world."[59]

In flight from Greece, Valentiniano boards a boat in the Adriatic gulf that is captained by the exiled king Dárdano. He transports Valentiniano to his undersea palace; there the prince falls instantly in love with princess Serafina. Rather than condemn his capture, Valentiniano "count[s] his blessings for having descended those profound depths of the sea" (111). Compare this to *The Tempest* with Ferdinand's conclusion, welcoming his servitude to Prospero, "Might I but through my prison once a day / Behold this maid [Miranda]. All corners else o'th'earth / Let liberty make use of—space enough / Have I in such a prison" (1.2.491–94). The lovers marry; as Juliano's fleet passes overhead on return from Juliano's wedding, a great tempest ensues, conjuring an image of divine justice: "A furious Nor'easter […] contrary winds were battling each other, so forcefully that the thick ship masts and ropes began to squeak; the bows rose to the heavens; the sterns dropped within; the riggings all broke; the clouds rained down fire, thunderbolts and lightning; the hungry waves swallowed the larger part of [Juliano's] ships."[60] Intervening for the god Neptune, Dárdano ascends the sea to condemn Juliano's tyranny and prophesize death. Shortly after, Juliano and his empress both die, and just as the imperial denizens begin to despair for their lost heir, Valentiniano and his new wife Serafina emerge to assume their rightful rule, and Dárdano retires, having founded a new dynasty. Eslava relates that "with a *prosperous wind* they went navigating to the port and city of Delcia where with great joy they were received by the people of Greece" (my emphasis).[61] Following his resolution of the play's conflicts through Miranda and Ferdinand's union, Prospero similarly declares: "I'll deliver all, / And promise you calm seas, auspicious gales, / And sail so expeditious that shall catch / your royal fleet far off" (5.1.311–14). His declaration marks Prospero as the source of the "prosperous wind" or "*viento próspero*" (Shakespeare's "auspicious gales") that carries the imperial couple home. While the Spanish version favors the native understanding of *prosperidad* as when events conspire together favorably, as if by divine will, Shakespeare's version, by contrast, entrusts that role to Prospero, whose name in Spanish means "I prosper." This feature of naming places further weight on Prospero's character as an agent of resolution.

---

        of Apollo and the twelve signs and seven planets, who conducted his office with rashness. No less admirable was Ursa major, whom the vulgar call Carro; and Ursa minor, whom they call Bocina, and the blade of Perseus, northern figure of twenty-six stars; and the Corona Australis composed of thirteen stars; and the guardian of Ursa Minor, which is called Beotes. (109)

    These details emulate the constellation of luxuriance, from friezes of the cosmos to columns of gold and precious stone, described in elaborate detail by Montalvo in Book 4, chapter 2 (745–52). Nicholas de Herberay des Essarts elaborated these in the French version, also used by Munday.

59. Eslava, *Noches de invierno*, 109.
60. Eslava, Noches de invierno, 111.
61. Eslava, Noches, 113.

And yet, the informing tale by Eslava, which sheds light upon Prospero's exceptionalism, has largely been dismissed by scholars because the story lacks, in the words of de Armas, a "rivalry between brothers and instead of a mysterious island, we encounter a palace under the sea."[62] This comment echoes earlier reservations expressed by Frank Kermode, who particularly noted that the story by Eslava has "not even an island to recommend it" as Shakespeare's source.[63] The charge that the *Noches* chapter lacks a fraternal rivalry is simply incorrect as the subplot of Valentiano and Juliano proves.[64] As for the story's purported lack of an island, Eslava's water palace is close enough, especially since this magical realm is located in the same Mediterranean zone (from Naples to Tunis along the Adriatic Sea) as Shakespeare's Summer Isle. It is also worth noting that the island that Prospero discovers (or rather, that he steals from Caliban) is called such in order to denote a land unknown to Europeans.[65] Moreover, Eslava obviously based his work on *Amadís*. So, what makes *Noches* a better candidate for *The Tempest* is not that it is independent of the textual traditions that precede it—recall that Montalvo himself was inspired by America, writing imagined New World wonders into his romance—but that all the details of the fabled island city have been translated from their original form (spanning several books) into a single chapter,[66] making it far more suitable for (and more similar to) Shakespeare's dramatic plot, which takes place in a single day. I do agree with de Armas, however, that Shakespeare must have read *Amadís*; maybe he selected the Eslava chapter because he recognized its general details and plots from Montalvo's books as well as other Spanish romances.[67]

---

62. De Armas, "*Galeotto fu 'l libro*," 23.
63. Frank Kermode, ed. "Introduction," in *William Shakespeare's The Tempest*, reprint (London: Routledge, 1994), lxiv–lxvi (lxvi).
64. Modeled closely after the story from *Amadís*, the *Noches* chapter relates that Valentiniano (the Ferdinand character) is forced to flee his imperial seat in Greece because his younger brother Juliano is preferred for rule by their tyrannical father. This is reflected in *The Tempest* with the plot of Sebastian to murder Alonso and take his throne. Valentiniano flees, hoping to one day recover his empire from his brother.
65. In naval cartography, any newly discovered region would likewise be called an island. For a discussion of literary representations of "island" seeking, see Pinet, *Archipelagos*, esp. 114–41.
66. *Winter Nights* is a collection of short stories told in the form of a dialogue, closely following the tradition of Boccaccio's *Decameron* (ca. 1353) and Castiglione's *Book of the Courtier* (1528). Produced during an era of Spanish experimentation with exemplary novels, which would later include those of Miguel de Cervantes and María de Zayas, *Winter Nights* combines elements of Moorish novellas, with Spanish and continental romances of chivalry, pastoral romances, and Byzantine novels. These include Esteban Corbera's *Caballero del Febo* (1576); Jerónimo Fernández's third and fourth parts of *Belianís de Grecia* (1579); Pedro de la Sierra's second part of *Espejo* (1580); Marcos Martínez's third and fourth parts of *Espejo* (1587); Miguel de Cervantes's *Galatea* (1585), and the *Diana* cycle of Jorge de Montemayor and Gaspar Gil Polo; the anonymous *Lazarillo de Tormes* (1554) and Mateo Alemán's *Guzman de Alfarache* (1599); and Jerónimo de Contreras's Byzantine novel, *Selva de aventuras* (*Forest of Adventures*) (1565). Eslava's work also echoes a rich tradition of humanistic paratexts and dialectical influences that were shared with the many romance works informing the basic story of *The Tempest*.
67. Joseph de Perott identified connections between *The Tempest* and *The Mirrour of Knighthood*, especially the lovestruck Lindaraza's plot to lure the Emperor Trebatio to her island abode. See Joseph de Perott, *The Probable Source of the Plot of Shakespeare's* The Tempest (Worcester: Clark University Press, 1905).

Both works translated the wonders of Tenochtitlán, which had come to embody the dream visions and competing dreams of Europe's imperial fantasies.[68] This connection is explicit in Miranda, whose name is typically associated with the Latin word *mirari*, which means "to be amazed, surprised, bewildered and/or to look at in wonder, awe, or admiration," but is often translated simply as "to wonder." This association emerges in Act 1, scene 2, when Ferdinand remarks upon encountering Miranda, "My prime request, / Which I do last pronounce, is—O you wonder!— / If you be maid or no" (424–26). As a proper name, Miranda has been conventionally understood as Shakespeare's original invention, though this is obviously wrong given that Miranda was a common Spanish surname (as in nobility from the Spanish region of Miranda).[69] In Spanish, the Latin-derived *miranda* specifically refers to "a high place from which a great extension of land may be discovered."[70] In other words, a *miranda* is a discovery observed from a high elevation, such as the wondrous valley of México, first observed by Diego de Ordaz and his companions from the peak of Popocatépetl or the Holy Land observed by Moses from the summit of Mount Nebo.

This terministic valence is also conveyed in Prospero's instruction to Miranda as she first espies Ferdinand: "The fringed curtains of thine eye advance / And say what thou seest yond" (1.2.407–8). Miranda is immediately enamored with Ferdinand, son of Alonso, who embodies Spanishness by his eponymous equation with Spanish Naples: "Myself am Naples" (1.2.521).[71] This revelation reinscribes the paradigm of transatlantic discovery onto the idealized framework of the romance story. Resembling a naïve indigene, Miranda regards the foreign Prince Ferdinand, with his European refinement and trappings of civilization, as a godlike spirit, or an *hombre-dios*. She proclaims, "'tis a spirit!" (1.2.490), but Prospero immediately corrects her: "No, wench, it eats and sleeps and hath such senses / As we have" (1.2.491–2). For love of Miranda, Ferdinand

---

68. In keeping with the theme of imperial destruction and Spanish decimation of New World wonders, Eslava noted that when Dárdano and the young lovers prepared their triumphant return to Delcia, "with new contentment was divested the royal palace, taking the greatest richness of it [with them]" (113).
69. The Spanish regions of Miranda de Douro and Miranda de Ebro, respectively found along the Douro and Ebro rivers, were widely demarcated on contemporary maps, including Gerard Mercator's *Historia Mundi: or Mercator's Atlas* (1631) and Abraham Ortelius's highly acclaimed *Teatrum Orbis Terrarum* (*Theater of the Orb of the World*), a presentation copy of which was commissioned by John Norton (1556/7–1612), printer to King James I.
70. "miranda, n." *Diccionario de la lengua española,* Real Academia Española, Online (accessed September 28, 2020). https://www.rae.es/.
71. The first Aragonés king of Naples (from the House of Trastámara, the Spanish ancestral line common to the sixteenth century Habsburgs) was Alfonso I (ruled 1442–1458), who was succeeded by his son, Fernando/Ferdinand I (ruled 1458–1494). He was succeeded by his son Alfonso II (ruled 1494–1495), who was succeeded by his son Ferdinand II (ruled 1495–1496). Ferdinand II was succeeded by his son, Frederick I, whole ruled until the French conquest in 1501. Ferdinand III (Philip II of Spain's great-grandfather) reconquered Naples in 1504, initiating a period of over a century of sustained Spanish rule of Naples.

endures the humiliation of forced labor, specifically by carrying logs, just as the slave Caliban is commanded to do in Act 1, scene 2. He remarks:

FERDINAND. I am in my condition
  A prince, Miranda; I do think, a king;
  I would, not so!—and would no more endure
  This wooden slavery than to suffer
  The flesh-fly blow my mouth. Hear my soul speak:
  The very instant that I saw you, did
  My heart fly to your service; there resides,
  To make me slave to it; and for your sake
  Am I this patient log-man. (3.1.59–67)

Ferdinand's speech introduces the "traditional amatory trope of the lover as a slave, which carries local and topical implications"[72] with the Triangular Trade of New World goods and African lives. A representation of European power and civility, lovelorn Ferdinand is a clear foil to the earthly Caliban, who plays the role of the unrequited lover, romantic rival, and rightful heir to the pagan land. In his attempt to physically coerce Miranda into sexual congress, Caliban also represents the constructed character of the wild and carnal king of the pagans: "Would't had been done! / Thou didst prevent me. I had peopled else / This isle with Calibans" (1.2.348–50).[73]

Miranda's further use as a term that demarcates contested regions, such as between Portugal and León,[74] therefore illustrates what the abstract reading of Miranda as embodied wonder tends to neglect: her relation to Prospero's imperial gaze. This imperialism is most clearly suggested by Miranda's first encounter with the Neapolitans, in which she famously remarks, "Oh wonder! / [...] / O brave new world / That has such people in't" (5.1.181–4). It is further suggested by Miranda's function as an intermediary (or interpreter) between Prospero and Caliban, whose words of resistance ironically

---

72. Roland Greene, *Unrequited Conquests: Love and Empire in the Colonial Americas* (Chicago: University of Chicago Press, 1999), 28.
73. Miranda's conclusion, "Abhorred slave, / [...] / But thy vile race, / Though thou didst learn, had that in't which good natures / Could not abide to be with" (1.2.350–59) expresses the English and European horror at the *mestizaje* (mixed race), which was cropping up in México, Perú, and other Spanish viceroyalties. The rape trope also evinces the play's ties to romance where threatening violence against a defenseless woman is a signifier of villainy. Shakespeare's language has echoes with Munday's description of Apolidon's first arrival upon Ínsula Firme in *Amadis*, such as the following speech by the Giant ruling Ínsula Firme, who threatens to rape Grimanesa if Apolidon should lose their battle: "Base slave, although I am not accustomed to be kind unto any, yet I am content for this once, to suffer thee to fight against me alone, on this condition, that if thou be overcome, this faire Lady shall be mine" (307).
74. For example, Edmund Bohun's *Geographical Dictionary* (1693) described Miranda de Douro as a "city in Portugal, upon the North side of the River Douro [...] Being a frontier town against the Kingdom of Leon." Edmund Bohun, *A Geographical Dictionary* (London: Charles Brome, 1693), sig. Mm3r.

originate with Miranda's lessons. In fact, as a foreigner raised in this strange land, as a translator, and as a wild woman in love with a European, Miranda is strongly reminiscent of La Malinche, or Doña Marina, a former pagan princess, born outside of the Aztec Empire, and sold to Mexica merchants as a slave, who later served as interpreter and coconspirator with the Spanish invaders in México, and personal mistress to Cortés, bearing him their natural son, Martín. A key difference here is that while La Malinche's given Christian name, Marina, means "borne of the sea,"[75] Miranda's means *wonder of the land*—a continental discovery. The name is even a close anagram of Marina, as Caliban's is an anagram of Michel de Montaigne's *canibal*, described in his most famous *Essai* asserting the inherent nobility of the so-called *savage*.[76]

As *The Tempest* drew broadly from both the romances and travel narratives that mythologized Tenochtitlán, Caliban originated with the pagan emperor who had once ruled there. Inhabiting the symbolic role of Moctezuma as written into European accounts, Caliban is both noble and childlike, civilized and subhuman. As in the case of Moctezuma, Caliban's resistance is conveyed in European language,[77] while the drama transforms his rebelliousness into subservience. Nevertheless, in contradistinction to Moctezuma, who had only to choose between resistance and acceptance of a foreign sovereign in Charles V, the key dilemma for Caliban is to choose from among foreign rulers. He must determine to trade his false gods, Stephano and Trinculo, who represent the greedy Spanish, for the righteous and mild-mannered Prospero, who represents England's King James I (1566–1625; ruled 1603–25). Mirroring the journey of Moctezuma, Caliban comes to accept his colonial overlord in a comic subplot that underscores the play's larger examination of competing models of governance, from the utopian idealism of Gonzalo, to the single-minded opportunism of Stephano and Trinculo, to the cunning brutality of Sebastian and Antonio. With the exception of Gonzalo's utopian platitudes,[78] all these models come down to a ceaseless pursuit of

---

75. The name also appears in *Pericles, Prince of Tyre* (1608). The lovely and virtuous Marina explains that she is called such "for I was born at sea."
76. "Of the Caniballes," appeared in print in 1603, translated by John Florio.
77. Caliban's understanding of European language gives him a voice with which to curse the common European justifications for conquest: "You taught me language, and my profit on't / Is, I know how to curse. The red plague rid you / For learning me your language!" (1.2.427–29). Later, when Stephano is force-feeding Caliban with liquor, the instrument of his manipulation, he sarcastically remarks, "Here is that which will give language to you, cat" (2.2.82–83). The drug is intended to return Caliban to a more childlike state as a subdued slave, as clued by accounts like the Codex Mendoza, which reported that "the Indians generally are much inclined to drinking," fol. 8v.
78. Drawing language from Florio's translation, the speech echoes Montaigne's idealistic praise of the polity of Brasil, especially by Gonzalo's telling proposition, "Had I plantation of this isle, my lord—" (2.1.141). Gonzalo's naïveté in imagining an abundant utopia fatally ignores the tangible realities of governing, including, most tellingly, the invisible class of slaves—such as the Indians forced into labor by the encomienda, and the Africans now being transported to the continent—who would be needed to realize his vision of a plantation island without sweat or toil. The play pushes back against such empty-minded rhetoric.

profit, which is further revealed by the Europeans' immediate recourse to the slave trade. There is Trinculo's first remark: "Were I in England now, as once I was, and had but this fish [Caliban] painted, not a holiday fool there but would give a piece of silver" (2.2.29–30), which is followed by Stephano's comment: "If I can […] get to Naples with him, he's a present for any emperor" (2.2.77). And finally, there is Antonio's observation, "Is a plain fish, and, no doubt, marketable" (5.1.299–300).[79] The ruthless self-serving of these Spanish Italians implies the danger of *de-civilization* by Spanish conquest, as in medieval Napoli, where the Català presence had reportedly introduced depravity among the conquered Italians, as Chapter 6 discusses.[80] In this way, the play finds the old world reproducing itself in the new; it alludes to the need for English intervention to prevent the same vices from playing out in America, where Spanish activities had already brought many signs of cruelty.

By comparison with these other Italians, Stefano and Trinculo and Sebastian and Antonio, the play thus introduces the virtue ethic of England's supreme civility, as embodied in Prospero/King James. Given the growing ubiquity of English slave trade,[81] Prospero's civility less corresponds with an outright rejection of imperial conquest than with a recognition of the paternal responsibility that this project entails. In Act 1, scene 2, Prospero explains that he enslaved Caliban not for his own profit but for fear of his native simplicity ("thy vile race, / […] had that in 't which good natures / Could not abide to be with"). Though punctuated by threatened violence, Prospero's (constructed) care for Caliban reflects the Christian European view of pagans as spiritual children, for which a paternal model of colonial rule forms the crux of natural law. This view also informs Prospero's liberal transmission of language to Caliban, and his having "lodged thee / In mine own cell" (1.2.346–47), though he revoked the policy after Caliban attempted to rape Miranda. Prospero's stewardship thus represents the only and best moderation between kindness and severity in ruling over these pagan children, as Caliban's final conversion implies:

---

79. These statements reflect real-world practices of presenting Native Americans as slaves in the courts of Europe.
80. Prospero's deriving from landlocked Milano makes little sense for the play's seafaring plot. Prospero would have needed to navigate from the port of Darsena all along the Po just to reach the sea. If Shakespeare wanted for the story to take place on an island, he could have made Prospero the ruler of a sea-region, such as the duchy of Urbino, which lies on Mare Adriatico (Adriatic Sea). A semiautonomous state loosely tied to Florencia, Urbino would have registered with ideas of negotiated republicanism, Brutus's Roma; by contrast, the Spanish seigniories, Napoli and Milano, would have brought to mind republicanism's converse, the seat of Caesar.
81. Although the English played a more limited role in the Triangular Trade until around the 1640s, the practice nonetheless represented an important tactic against Spanish imperial hegemony. On August 20, 1619, about 20 Angolans, kidnapped by the Portuguese, arrived in the British colony of Virginia, where they were purchased by English colonists. This event is usually cited as the official beginning of the slave trade in British North America, though the practice obviously predated the Virginia incident. For instance, Sir Francis Drake and Sir John Hawkins had kidnapped Africans as part of their privateering practice, beginning about 1562.

CALIBAN.   I'll be wise hereafter
              And seek for grace. What a thrice-double ass
              Was I to take this drunkard [Stephano] for a god
              And worship this dull fool. (5.1.296–99)

By trading his false Spanish gods for a singular English ruler (*converting*) this symbolic Moctezuma has once again ceded his empire. By the logic of the play, Caliban has traded a false Spanish god for a righteous English prince, garbed in signs of *civility*. This choice transforms the tragedy of Spanish conquest into a comedy of English salvation. Caliban's renewed fealty to Prospero, spoken in English language and invoking English religion (i.e., "seek[ing] for grace"), therefore publicly reinscribes Prospero's rightful dominium over the Summer Isle. Once Caliban has performed this key function, Prospero dismisses him to his cell, and Caliban disappears from the story, as "such stuff / As dreams are made on."

"Empires fall and rise"

In the later seventeenth century, the enduring legacy of *The Tempest* was notably instantiated by such works as John Fletcher's *The Sea Voyage* (1622), and William Davenant and John Dryden's operatic comedy, *The Tempest, or The Enchanted Island*, first performed in 1667, as well as Thomas Duffet's *The Mock Tempest, or the Enchanted Castle*, first performed in 1674. Rather than tracking the Mexica tragedy in this more diffuse dramatic afterlife, which departed from Shakespeare's quasi-noble construction of Caliban as Moctezuma,[82] this chapter instead turns to Dryden's heroic play, *The Indian Emperour, or the Conquest of Mexico by the Spaniards* (1665). This celebrated Restoration-era play more clearly evinces Moctezuma's use as a symbolic mouthpiece for the necessity of English conquest. A sequel to Dryden's *The Indian Queene*, coauthored with Robert Howard, Dryden's *Conquest of Mexico* was also inspired by William Davenant's *The Cruelty of the Spaniards in Peru* (1658), which recounted in the form of static dumb shows set to music "the Spaniards Conquest of that Incan Empire, and [...] the cruelty of the Spaniards over the Indians, and over all Christians [...] And towards the conclusion, it infers the Voyages of the English thither, and the amity of the Natives towards them, under whose

---

82. Following Ben Jonson in the Induction to *Bartholomew Fair* (1614), and other critics of his age, Dryden expressed apprehension over Shakespeare's endowing civilizing language to Caliban: "He seems there to have created a person which was not in Nature, a boldness which, at first sight, would appear intolerable; for he makes him a species of himself, begotten by an incubus on a witch; but this, as I have elsewhere proved, is not wholly beyond the bounds of credibility, at least the vulgar still believe it." Dryden, preface to *Troilus and Cressida* (London: Able Swall and Jacob Tonson, 1679), sig. B1r. His biographer, Nicholas Rowe, also expressed incredulity at Shakespeare's novel characterization in that "extravagant character of Caliban" in whom he "devised and adapted in new manner of language for that character." Rowe, *Some Account of the Life of Mr. William Shakespeare* (Ann Arbor: Augustan Reprint Society, 1948), xxiv. For a reading of the neoclassical dispute over Caliban, see Kevin Pask, "Caliban's Masque," *English Literary History* 70, no. 3 (2003), 739–56.

Ensigns (encourag'd by a Prophecy of their chief Priest) they hope to be made Victorious, and to be freed from the Yoke of the Spaniard."[83]

The premise of Dryden's Mexico play is much the same: to provide evidence of Spain's inordinate cruelty in America so to "infer" England's destined arrival as a salvation from Spanish tyranny. *The Indian Emperour* also highlights the tragic defeat of Moctezuma, the most recognizable icon of Aztec Mexico,[84] "who in the Truth of the History, was a great and glorious Prince; and in whose time happened the Discovery and Invasion of Mexico by the Spaniards; under the conduct of Hernando Cortez, who, joyning with the Taxallan-Indians, the inveterate Enemies of Montezuma, wholly Subverted that flourishing Empire; the Conquest of which, is the Subject of this Dramatique Poem" (28).[85] Reflecting a version of the poet himself, Dryden's Montezuma is presented in the dedication as a courtier to Ann Scott, Duchess of Monmouth and Buccleuch, under whose patronage Moctezuma/Dryden "hopes he is more safe than in his Native Indies: and therefore comes to throw himself at your Graces feet; paying that homage to your Beauty, which he refus'd to the violence of his Conquerours" (25). He adds, "[Montezuma] begs only that when he shall relate his sufferings, you will consider he is an Indian Prince, and not expect any other Eloquence from his simplicity, then that, with which his griefs have furnished him. His story is, perhaps the greatest, which was ever represented in a Poem of this nature" (25). Like Davenant's *The Cruelty of the Spaniards in Peru*, Dryden's *Conquest of Mexico* begins with the first impression of a wondrous pagan empire as viewed through European eyes. The Spaniards receive directions to the hidden city from an Indian, who remarks: "Your eyes can scarce so far a prospect make, / As to discern the City on the Lake. / But that broad Caus-way will direct your way, / And you may reach the Town by noon of day" (l.1.45–48). The Spaniards' first impression is related by Commander Vasquez, who remarks, associating the works of Edmund Spenser and William Shakespeare, "Methinks we walk in dreams of fairy Land, / Where golden Ore lies mixt with common sand; / Each downfal a flood the Mountains pour, / From their rich bowels rolls a silver shower" (1.1.27–30).

So close are these details to the many Spanish descriptions of Tenochtitlán and pre-Columbian Mesoamerica already discussed[86] that they hardly require further commentary, other than to note that the references to "golden Ore [...] mixt with common sand" and "each downfall [...] a silver shower" further reflect the common rumor, propelled

---

83. Sir William Davenant, *The Cruelty of the Spaniards in Peru* (London: Henry Herringman, 1658), sig. A2r.
84. Although the last Mexica emperor was actually Cuauhtémoc, Moctezuma was by far better known to Europeans. This probably had to do with the ubiquity of Cortés's first account, which included Moctezuma's conciliatory speeches to Charles.
85. John Dryden, "*The Indian Emperour, or The Conquest of Mexico by the Spaniards* (1665): Connexion of the Indian Emperour, to the Indian Queen," in *The Works of John Dryden*, Vol. 9: Plays; *The Indian Emperour; Secret Love; Sir Martin Mar-all*, John Loftis and Vinton A. Dearing, eds. (Berkeley: University of California Press, 1996), Oxford Scholarly Editions Online (2015).
86. Dryden's assumed sources include *Purchas his Pilgrimes* (based on the Codex Mendoza and other Spanish chronicles), as well as the accounts of Bartolomé de las Casas and of Francisco López de Gómara, or, more likely, Montaigne's *Essais*.

by romance conflations and Spanish boasts, that Tenochtitlán was built entirely of crystal and precious metal. It also associates the myth of El Dorado, which originated with the 1531 voyage of Diego de Ordaz to the Orinoco region, spurring a common European supposition that gold deposits were ubiquitous in the soils of Central and South America.[87] The play highlights the infamous gold-lust that motivated Spaniards' conquest of the Americas and that served as key evidence of their unfitness for colonial rule. This is suggested, for example, by the earthly spirit conjured to proclaim Mexico's doom, remarking "A Nation loving Gold must rule this place, / Our Temples Ruine, and our Rites Deface" (2.1.35–36).

With strong ties to epic and romance,[88] *The Indian Emperour* nods toward the many mythologies of America that circulated in European literature and history, as in the following exchange from the Spaniards' first conversation with the Indians:

> Mont[ezuma]. Whence or from whom dost thou these offers bring?
> Cort[ez]. From Charles the Fifth, the Worlds most Potent King.
> Mont[ezuma]. Some petty Prince, and one of little fame,
> For to this hour I never heard his name:
> The two great Empires of the World I know,
> That of Peru, and this of Mexico;
> And since the earth none larger does afford,
> This Charles is some poor Tributary Lord.
> Cort[ez]. You speak of that small part of earth you know,
> But betwixt us and you wide Oceans flow,
> And watry desarts of so vast extent,
> That passing hither, four Full Moons we spent. (1.2.252–63)

This passage is riddled with allusions, especially to Spenser and Shakespeare.[89] Nevertheless, as a play about first contacts, *The Indian Emperor* most importantly invokes

---

87. Rumors circulated of a lake (the legendary Lake Parima) rich in gold deposits, having been the fabled site where a pagan chief (the original Golden One or El Dorado) of the Muisca people would submerge himself in gold and then wash himself in the water as an initiation rite.
88. Additionally, there was French drama (particularly by Pierre Corneille) and English romantic drama of the Caroline and Commonwealth periods; these also corresponded with mid-seventeenth-century theoretical developments that closely tied epic and tragedy. There are also some affinities with Calderòn de la Barca's *El Principe Constante* (1628/29), though it was not previously translated into English. See N. D. Shergold and Peter Ure, "Dryden and Calderón: A New Spanish Source for *The Indian Emperour*," *Modern Language Review*, 61 (1966), 369–83.
89. Reflecting common knowledge derived from Spanish accounts, Montezuma's "The two great Empires of the World I know, / That of Peru, and this of Mexico," which is but "that small part of earth I know," can be compared, for example, to Díaz's "I...thought that never in the world would there be discovered other lands such as these, for at that time there was no Peru, nor any thought of it" (157). It is also a reversal of the proem to Book II of Spenser's *Faerie Queene*, which asks, "But let that man with better sence aduize, / That of the world least part to vs is red: / [...] / Who euer heard of th'Indian *Peru*?" (2). For further discussion of this verse by Spenser, see Chapter 5.

Shakespeare's *The Tempest*, especially by Montezuma's outspoken resistance to Charles's rule, which may be compared to similar speeches, resisting Prospero's European supremacy, that are voiced by the native Caliban. In fact, *The Tempest* was so influential that in the manuscript version of this play, Dryden had even named the Indian High Priest Calliban; though this was later changed, one lingering "Callib." accidentally slipped into the first edition.[90] These allusions establish a narrative through line by canonical English authors, from Spenser to Shakespeare to Dryden, of simultaneously erasing Spain's presence in America, alluding to it only as a corrupted model to avoid, while justifying England's own colonial aspirations.[91] The English bias becomes explicit later in the play when Spanish commanders, Vazquez and Pizarro, who have entered into a revenge plot with Prince Odmar, respectively demand as payment for their services a beautiful Indian woman (Princess Alibech) and "the gold" (4.3.77). Capitalizing upon the operative themes of European travel narratives and contemporary books of chivalry, the play romanticizes the conquest of America via several rivalries of love, also calling back to those of the prequel, *The Indian Queen*.

The primary love conflict pertains to Cortez's lovelorn pursuit of Princess Cydaria, Montezuma's daughter, who embodies the exotic Aztec land he seeks to conquer.[92] In the midst of battles and negotiations with the Christians, the princesses Almeria and Cydaria transform into jealous rivals vying for the love of Cortez. This plot coheres with

---

90. John Dryden, *The Indian emperour, or, The Conquest of Mexico by the Spaniards Being the Sequel of The Indian Queen* (London: H. Herringman, 1667), sig. B2r.
91. Playing carefully with the controversies of conquest, Dryden also used Montezuma to voice the conventional English complaint against Spain, as in the following exchange:

> MONT[EZUMA]. You speak your Prince [Charles V] a mighty Emperour,
> But his demands have spoke him Proud, and Poor;
> He proudly at my free-born Scepter flies,
> Yet poorly begs a mettal I despise.
> Gold thou may'st take, what-ever thou canst find,
> Save what for sacred uses is design'd:
> But, by what right pretends your King to be
> This Sovereign Lord of all the World, and me?
> PIZ[ARRO]: The Soveraign Priest,—
> Who represents on Earth the pow'r of Heaven,
> Has this your Empire to our Monarch given.
> MONT[EZUMA]. Ill does he represent the powers above,
> Who nourishes debate not Preaches love;
> Besides what greater folly can be shown?
> He gives another what is not his own. (1.2.274–86)

> Montezuma expresses objection with the papal bull *Inter caetera* (1493) of Pope Alexander VI (ruled 1492–1503), for which he claims the Roman vicar "Ill does […] represent the powers above, / […] / He gives another what is not his own." The additional charge of Charles's petty preoccupation with gold, "a metal I despise," associates the stereotype of Spanish boastfulness and greed, as widely communicated in the romantic mythologies of America.

92. She also represents Doña Isabel Moctezuma (born Tecuichpoch Ixcaxochitzin), Moctezuma's daughter and widow to Cuauhtémoc. Upon the emperor's death, she was forced to become Cortés's mistress, and she bore him a daughter.

romance conventions. In *Esplandián,* for example, pagan women *convert* into viable partners for European conquerors, betraying their own loyalties for love of Christian men, as Chapter 5 discusses.[93] The conclusion finds the rejected Almeria stabbing Cydaria, and then herself, thus following the tragic fate of her mother, Zempoalla, the late Indian queen from the prequel. This plot also intertwines General Cortez's passions with those of Montezuma's sons, Odmar and Guyomar, who compete for the hand of Princess Alibech in increasingly hyperbolic love proclamations.[94] Also sought by commander Vazquez, who plots with Odmar, not knowing that they both pursue the same woman, Alibech has promised to marry whichever of the two brothers defeats the Spaniards, thus literalizing the competition for America as a test of love and arms.

The first skirmish between the two armies finds Cortez victorious and Prince Guyomar in bonds; in his conduct as victor, Cortez demonstrates his civility, first by advocating for peace, and second, by freeing Guyomar in a gesture of goodwill (and love for Cydaria). This act transforms Guyomar into a lifelong ally, who vacillates pointedly over his sympathy with the colonizer: "this *Spaniard* is our Nations foe, / I wish him dead—but cannot wish it so; / Either my Country never must be freed, / Or I consenting to so black a deed. / [...] / Now if he dyes I Murther him, not they" (3.1.107–12). Both parties are

---

93. As a traitor to her people, Almeria inhabits a similar role to that historically occupied by La Malinche. According to the accounts of Cortés, Gómara, and Díaz, La Malinche was a key informant in the conquest, even participating in events that led to a famous massacre of Cholulans. She was later married to a Spanish captain, Juan Jaramillo. For a reading of the historical representations of La Malinche by Díaz and others, see Sandra Messinger Cypess, "La Malinche as Palimpsest II," in Díaz, et al., *The History of the Conquest of New Spain,* 418–38.
94. For instance, marveling at Alibech's beauty, Odmar remarks, "I watcht the early glories of her Eyes, / As men for day break watch the eastern Skies." This is a reference to Shakespeare's *Romeo and Juliet* (1595), in the famous balcony scene:

> JULIET.
>   By whose direction found'st thou out this place?
> ROMEO.
>   By love, that first did propel me to inquire.
>   He lent me counsel and I lent him eyes.
>   I am no pilot; yet, wert thou as far
>   As that vast shore wash'd with the farthest sea,
>   I would adventure for such merchandise. (2.2.85–90)

Presented in the form of a negation ("I am no pilot"), Romeo's comparison recalls bold Tiphys, first navigator, captain of the Argonauts who accompanied Jason on his voyage for the golden fleece, only here that navigational role is performed by love. It is love that first sends Romeo adventuring for Juliet, who lives in the same city as Romeo, and yet is as remote as farthest Thule, "that vast shore wash'd with the farthest sea." Nevertheless, the scene's correspondence with India (clued by "such merchandise") also confuses the directionality of Romeo's reference, which serves Shakespeare's metaphor for global travel. Romeo's earlier comment, spotting the light through Juliet's window, "it is the east, and Juliet is the sun / *Arise, fair sun, and kill the envious moon*" (2.2.3–4) reveals that he is gazing eastward, but his command to Juliet, "kill the envious moon," likens her diurnal motion to the celestial navigation of Columbus, whose experiments following the light of the sun led him to a new world in the west. For more information about the Jason myth and America, see Chapter 4.

unhappy enemies, forced to make war by the imperial foe to the east and mutinies on both sides. The play's central tension, played out in pits for love, thus concerns the competing ethics of Montezuma/Guyomar/Cortez and the other Spaniards, Vazquez and Pizarro, who, like Stephano, Trinculo, Antonio, and Sebastian, represent the historical Spaniards, whose underscored lusts must be checked by English civility.

The Indians' respect and love for Cortez also serves to demonize the rival Spaniards while moralizing England's own vexed position vis-à-vis the American conquest. Himself a Spaniard, Cortez is nevertheless so unlike his men that he is also apprehensive of their treachery, or "the insolence of Spaniards," as Prince Orbellan calls it at 3.2.19. As Ayanna Thompson remarks, Cortez "inscribes the English into the conquest narrative,"[95] likewise evincing the play's ambiguity on the subject of colonization. Dryden's dramatic retelling of history transforms the conquering Spaniards into foils and forebears for the English. For instance, when hesitating to kill Cortez, the lovelorn Almeria muses to herself that Cortez bears "some Charm," though the conqueror is "Thy Country's Foe" (4.1.29). This *Faerie Queene* allusion anachronistically treats Dryden's Cortez as precursor to Spenser's Redcrosse Knight, "Saint George of mery England," who will become "thine owne nations frend" by his destined conquest of America (see Chapter 4).[96] Incapable of stabbing Cortez, Almeria turns the blade on herself.

In the midst of the siege of Tenochtitlán of Act 4, scene 2, during which Montezuma and his men lament the people's starvation, "gap[ing] for food which they must never find" (line 43), scene 3 opens in "a pleasant grotto" where the commanders Vasquez and Pizarro "and other Spaniards" entertain themselves with music, dancing, and cavorting among the native women. Guyomar and his men surprise the unarmed Spaniards, taking them into custody, and prompting Vasquez and Pizarro to lament their misfortune:

> Piz[arro]. *Vasquez*, what now remains in these extreams?
> Vasq[uez]. Only to wake us from our Golden Dreams.
> Piz[arro]. Since by our shameful conduct, we have lost
> Freedom, Wealth, Honour, which we value most,
> I wish they would our Lives a Period give:
> They Live too long who Happiness out-live. (4.3.19–24)

Preferring death over ignominious capture, Vasquez and Pizarro acknowledge their suffering as a divine punishment for their "shameful conduct," which has cost them "Freedom, Wealth, Honour, which we value most." Given honor's common appearance in Spanish romances, this squandered virtue particularly suggests a divine covenant for America that the Spaniards broke with their "shameful conduct." The specificity of this critique, as a uniquely Spanish problem, simultaneously demonizes Spanish imperialism while reserving that "honor" for the English.

---

95. Ayanna Thompson, *Performing Race and Torture* (New York: Routledge, 2008), 88.
96. Edmund Spenser, *The Faerie Queene*, second edition, A. C. Hamilton, ed. (London: Routledge, 2007).

Moreover, as the shared civility of Cortez and Montezuma, which tragically links them on opposing polarities, is implicitly likened to Dryden's self-construction via the dedication to Princess Anne, these characters also take on the heroic role traditionally reserved for the English, though the plot events predate England's arrival in America. Invoking Aristotle's conception of poetry as aspiring to higher truths, Dryden explained in the dedication that: "I have neither wholly follow'd the truth of the History, nor altogether left it: but have taken all the liberty of a Poet, to adde, alter, or diminish, as I thought might best conduce to the beautifying of my work. It being not the business of a Poet to represent Historical truth, but probability."[97] The play's commixture of historical details and romance strategies correspondingly interprets the Spanish problem as a mandate for English involvement, affirming the "probability" of England's imperial rise. Here the play draws from several of the most famous constructions of English civility, namely Spenser's *Faerie Queene*, Shakespeare *Midsummer* and *The Tempest*, and William Davenant's 1658 operas, *The Cruelty of the Spaniards in Peru* and *The History of Sir Francis Drake*. The latter works by Davenant were most forceful in advancing the "racialization of civility" as Thompson has put it,[98] though the same essentialist argument plays out in the English romances of Spenser and Shakespeare, as Chapters 4 and 5 discuss.

The play's conclusion offers one more commentary upon the brutality of Spanish conquest, as expressed in the titular character's plain "Eloquence" "furnished" by "grief." In Act 5, Moctezuma is being tortured by a Christian priest who is in search of gold. This torture scene parallels the opening, which depicts the Indians "at Temple" making a human sacrifice of "Five hundred captives." Although the blood sacrifice serves the internal logic of the play,[99] the motif also heralds a destined imperial transfer through final revelation of the "uncanny familiarity"[100] between Spaniards and Indians. By presenting the Spaniards as the "embodiment of savagery,"[101] cruelty defines the deterministic logic of translatio imperii.[102] When the priest compels Montezuma to convert to Christianity or face damnation in Hell, Montezuma responds: "Thou art deceiv'd: for whensoe're I Dye, / The Sun my Father bears my Soul on high: / [...] / I in the Eastern parts, and rising Sky, / You in Heaven's downfal, and the West must

---

97. Dryden, *The Indian Emperour*, 25. Aristotle noted that history-writing is naturally opposed to poetry, for, "poetry unifies more, whereas history agglomerates." Aristotle, *On the Art of Fiction: An English Translation of Aristotle's Poetics*, L. J. Potts, trans. (Cambridge: Cambridge University Press, 1968), 29.
98. Thompson, *Performing Race and Torture*, 88.
99. Thompson argues that the torture scene serves to "locate heroism outside of the play precisely because of [Dryden's] fissured construction of racial differences [within the play]," 77.
100. Joseph Roach, *Cities of the Dead: Circum-Atlantic Performance* (New York: Columbia University Press, 1996), 148; also discussed in Thompson, *Performing Race and Torture*, 91.
101. Thompson, *Performing Race and Torture*, 91.
102. Even Cortez's sympathetic portrayal is marred by Spanish cruelty. Although he frees Montezuma, Montezuma's refusal to rule under Spanish dominium exposes Cortez's "mistaken Clemency" (lines 228–37), which enables Spanish tyranny. Thompson also notes that the rack's generally remaining onstage in performance implicates this brutality in the success of Cortez's conquest. See *Performing Race and Torture*, 91–93.

lye" (5.2.43–8). A reference to Cydaria's earlier supposition that Cortez's native Europe, "is then the same [place] / That souls must go to when the body dies" (1.2.367–8), the passage highlights Moctezuma's glorious legacy in England. It also signals the Spanish Monarchy's decline in "Heaven's downfall."[103] The prophecy rounds out the play's many historical callbacks, particularly the observation by the pagan High Priest, at the start of the play, that the pursuing moon's walks "see Empires fall and rise" (2.1.16). Certainly, an observer around 1665 would not fail to note that the formerly vast Spanish empire, upon which the sun famously never set, had been significantly eroded, while the star of England had begun to rise.

---

103. The decline of the Spanish empire involved many factors. In spite of the heavy galleons that yearly arrived from the Americas, many were raided by pirates or wrecked by storms. Frequent insurrections in the colonies likewise depleted the exchequer of money and resources. Above all, the strain of the Thirty Years' War (1618–1648) and the recent losses of the Low Countries and Portugal most poignantly denoted an empire in decline.

CHAPTER 3

SUN KINGS AND MOON QUEENS: THE COURTING AND UNCOURTING OF SPAIN

From *Diana* and *Amadís* to *Orlando* and *Espejo*, love stories precipitated Spain's rise to global supremacy,[1] especially by the king's "preferred strategy of matrimonial imperialism."[2] But as stories of love and arms were incorporated into the cultural and political diet of the Elizabethan court, carrying over discourses of Spanish conquest, an English politic of *virtuous imperialism* emerged as a distinct wartime strategy to combat the ambitions of the Spanish king, bent on global conquest. This ethic transformed romance's conventional love discourse into a mirrour for Spanish lust, mobilizing Elizabethan chastity as an imperial antidote.

Embodied in Elizabeth's faerie analogs, Gloriana, Belphoebe, and Britomart, female virtue became an overarching trait of England's self-fashioned civility. Drawn in imitation of Spanish and Italian romance heroines, these Elizabethan characters were central to Spenser's *poetics of piracy*. Figures that had once brought dishonor upon the queen now denoted England's cosmic empire of virtue. The altering event was the publication of Spenser's 1590 *Faerie Queene*, which transformed Oriana into Gloriana, and Claridiana into Belphoebe and Britomart, *glorious* harbingers of England's destined supremacy in the project of global conquest.[3]

Gloriana Triumphs

That Spenser chose to adapt Oriana into Gloriana is somewhat surprising, especially for the first edition of *The Faerie Queene* of 1590, when he lacked assurance of royal patronage. Spenser must have known that his queen would immediately catch the reference; the Ambassador de Spes controversy was, after all, a "well-documented diplomatic

---

1. "How did [Spain's] unprecedented dominance rise?" Geoffrey Parker asks, "First, matrimony—or, in the aphorism of the time, *Bella gerant alii. Tu, felix Austria, nube* ('Others make war. You, happy Habsburgs, marry.')." *The World Is Not Enough: The Imperial Vision of Philip II of Spain*, The Twenty-Second Charles Edmondson Historical Lectures (Waco: Baylor University, 2000), 10.
2. Parker, *The World Is Not Enough*, 12.
3. Spenser told Raleigh, "In that Faery Queene I meane glory in my generall intention, but in my particular I conceive the most excellent and glorious person of our soveraine the Queene, and her kingdome in Faery Land." Spenser, Letter to Raleigh, in *The Faerie Queene*, second edition, A. C. Hamilton, ed. (London: Routledge, 2007), 713–18 (716). All quotations from the poem also derive from this edition.

incident"[4] and international scandal. But whereas Spes had cited *Amadís* to forecast Spain's happy ending by imperial matrimony, Spenser used the same work to forecast England's triumph in virtue. Gloriana was a superlative improvement upon her Spanish romantic forebear; she cited the Second Coming in relation to Elizabeth's destined ascendance as world savior.[5] This technique drew out Oriana's eponymous equation with the sun, capping Elizabeth's imagined rise to world empress.[6] To drive home his point, Spenser created Archimago, a high sorcerer in his poem, in parallel to *Amadís*'s infamous necromancer, Arcaláus, whom Spes had earlier compared to Cecil. Archimago was designed to mock the Spanish king as an "architect of false images" through the etymology of his name.[7]

But if Gloriana and Archimago analogized to characters in Spanish romance, what of the hero, *Amadís*? Expectedly, he was not rewritten but replaced by King Arthur, the archetypical hero, father of the Matter of Britain cycle, an English Christ, he who was first beloved of God. By a historical genealogy linked to Brutus, Arthur makes a Second Coming in the poem. The most outstanding representative of "Britons moniments," he is destined to wed the queen's *virtuous imperialism*.

Symbolically wedded to Arthur/Christ, Gloriana therefore represents England's triumph over the tyranny of Spanish imperialism and its chief liberation: the Lamb's wife described in Revelations 21 (see Chapter 4). By her relation to Una (Christian Truth), who also aids Arthur in his rescue of the English hero, Redcrosse, Elizabeth further inhabits the poem as a harbinger of England's role in the Messianic kingdom, which was to span the globe in one universal monarchy. Indeed, Una/Elizabeth is "pure and innocent, as that same lambe / […] / And by descent from Royall lynage came / Of ancient Kinges and Queenes, that had of yore / Their scepters stretch from East to Westerne shore" (I.i.5.1-5).

To reconcile that innocence to the notion of virtuous conquest, the Spanish romance's famous eroticisms between Amadís and Oriana only manifest between Gloriana and Arthur in the form of Gloriana's dream visitation, which prompts Arthur to his questing:

---

4. Tim Crowley, "Contingencies of Literary Censorship: Anglo-Spanish Diplomacy and *Amadís de Gaula* in January 1569," *Sixteenth Century Journal* (2015), 891–926 (894).
5. For a discussion of Elizabeth and divine justice, see Donald Stump, "A Slow Return to Eden: Spenser on Women's Rule," *English Literary Renaissance* 29, no. 3 (1999), 401–21, esp. 415–21.
6. Spenser, "Letter to Raleigh," 716. The prefix "Ori-" referred to rising or ascendance, as in the sunrise.
7. Hamilton, ed. *The Faerie Queene* (note to I.1.43). Arcaláus's name derives from the Latin root *arc(h)-* meaning "high" and the noun *laus* meaning "fame." Archimago's name derives from the same Latin root *archi-* and the noun *magus* meaning "magician." Another possible inspiration is *Amadís*'s horrific giant, Endriago, a scaley monster born of incest who exhales a poisonous reek; the dominant features of this monster of idolatry compare with Spenser's beast of Errour, a half-serpent woman who spews a vomit of Catholic books and papers, and consumes her own offspring.

From loftie steed, and downe to sleepe me layd;
The verdant gras my couch did goodly dight,
And pillow was my helmett fayre displayd:
Whiles euery sence the humour sweet embayd,
And slombring soft my hart did steale away
Me seemed, by my side a royall Mayd
Her daintie limbes full softly down did lay:
So fayre a creature yet saw neuer sunny day.

Most goodly glee and louely blandishment
She to me made, and badd me loue her deare;
For dearly sure her loue was to me bent,
As when iust time expired should appeare.
But whether dreames delude, or true it were,
Was neuer hart so rauisht with delight,
Ne liuing man like wordes did euer heare,
As she to me deliuered all that night;
And at her parting said, she Queene of Faries hight.

When I awoke, and found her place deuoyd,
And nought but pressed gras where she had lyen,
I sorrowed all so much, as earst I ioyd,
And washed all her place with watry eyen.
From that day forth I lou'd that face diuyne;
From that day forth I cast in carefull mynd,
To seeke her out with labour, and long tyne,
And never vowd to rest, till her I fynd,
Nyne monethes I seek in vain yet ni'll that vow vnbynd. (I.ix.13–15)

Cast in gendered, romantic terms, this brief scene titillates with the Spanish romance's carnal delights, evoking the pleasures of Eden.[8] But the dream vision sufficiently muddles the events described so as to discourage charges of excess "levity" toward Elizabeth, for which Ambassador de Spes had famously been condemned. Like other dream-lovers—Chaucer's Sir Topas or Shakespeare's Bottom—Arthur can hardly trust the truth of his experience. Still, the "pressed gras where she had lyen" does encourage him that "true it were." Propelled by this small proof, Arthur vows "never […] to rest, till her I fynd."

Through Arthur's pilgrimage to Gloriana, Spenser favored "the presaged union of Gloriana-Elizabeth with a British Protestant bridegroom."[9] In Arthur, Spenser offered Elizabeth "the only marriage she could possibly have accepted, a marriage with

---

8. The vision specifically references the scene of first congress between Amadís and Oriana, which takes place in open field.
9. Daniel Vitkus, "The Unfulfilled Form of *The Faerie Queene*: Spenser's Frustrated Fore-Conceit," *Renaissance and Reformation* 35, no. 2 (2012), 83–112 (84).

Prince Arthur as a synecdoche for Britain's Celtic past."[10] Arthur's "magnificence" in the poem is portrayed as a masculine reflection of the Virgin Queen's own regal divinity, thus casting chastity (i.e., temperance) as a prime determinant of the empire of Christ. Arthur's symbolic quest for Elizabeth justifies her largely honorary title as "THE MOST HIGH, MIGHTIE AND MAGNIFICENT EMPRESS [...] OF ENGLAND, FRAVNCE AND IRELAND AND OF VIRGINIA" as expressed in the dedication of the 1590/96 editions.[11]

Spenser's adaptation of Oriana into Gloriana marked his *poetics of piracy* as an imperial strategy designed to deprive Spain of its symbolic nodes of power, specifically the Spanish romance heroine who had been repeatedly called upon to serve as an idealized object to Philip's imperialist designs. The Anglo-Spanish borrowings were so ubiquitous and so obvious, in fact, that in 1601, Thomas Morley printed a songbook titled, the *Triumphes of Oriana* (hereafter *Triumphes*), boasting a collection of 25 patriotic madrigals, most linked by the common expression, "Long live fair Oriana."[12] Published in 1603 after the queen's death, the work struck a timeless, eternal image of the queen in her divine magnificence, atop her "Charret," surrounded by gods and goddesses who "in reuels do accord"[13] her brilliance.[14] The work also identified Oriana as "that maiden Queene of the Fayrie Land, with scepter in her hand?"[15]

Spenser and Morley's Anglicized vision of Spanish romance, marking the genre's submission to Elizabethan magnificence, also incorporated the beloved pastoral, the *Diana*

---

10. Laurie Finke, "Spenser For Hire," *Culture and the King: the Social Implications of the Arthurian Legend*, Martin B. Shichtman and James P. Carley, eds. (New York: University of New York Press, 1994), 211–33 (225).
11. In Spenser's letter to Raleigh, he explained that "in the person of Prince Arthure I sette forth magnificence in particular, which vertue, for that (according to Aristotle and the rest) it is the perfection of all the rest, and conteineth in it them all" (716).
12. *Madrigales, The Triumphes of Oriana, to 5. and 6. Voices: Composed by Diuers Severall Aucthors, Newly Published by Thomas Morley...* (London: Thomas Este [East], 1601), reprinted ca. 1605–6.
13. Ellis Gibbons, "Round about her Charret &c. XIX," in *Triumphes*, sig. B4r.
14. Iohn Lisley, "Faire Citharea Presents Her Doues &c. XXII," in *Triumphes*, sig. C1v.
15. Daniel Norcome, "With Angels face and brightnesse. I," in *Madrigales the triumphes of Oriana, to 5 and 6 voices: composed by divers severall aucthors*, STC 18130 (London: Thomas Morley, 1601), sig. B1r. In "Music and Late Elizabethan Politics," Jeremy Smith notes that a song containing the *Faerie Queene* reference was also added to the edition of 1604 in place of one that supposedly alluded to the coronation of the new queen, Anne of Denmark (1574–1619), thus "keeping Oriana safely under the guise of the dead monarch Elizabeth" (547). But Norcome's song containing the line "queen of fairy land" was also published in the edition of 1601, so Smith's supposition that the association with Elizabeth was forged posthumously does not add up. I am more inclined to agree with Roy Strong, who places the work in context of the late-sixteenth- and early-seventeenth-century madrigal culture, showing that the Elizabeth–Oriana equation was part of a commonplace English tradition. This tradition simply evolved during the Jacobean period, with Oriana's name only slightly adapted to suit Anne, who adopted Ori-Anna as another royal avatar. See Strong, "Queen Elizabeth I as Oriana."

of Jorge de Montemayor.[16] In fact, those who sang in refrain, "Long live Oriana," were "the shepherds and Nimphs of Diana." Elizabeth's many Diana avatars were, in other words, versions of the Diana represented in contemporary romance, with Montalvo's creation pointing reflexively to Montemayor's.[17] The two avatars denote Elizabeth's symbolic control over the forces of day and night, the sun and the moon.[18] They strike an image of global harmony under the virginal queen's tutelage, and they superimpose the false Apollo cult of King Philip.

As we have already seen, *The Mirrour of Knighthood* further shaped the Elizabethan tradition of Diana. The characterization of Elizabeth as eternally virginal, or Diana-like, dates back as early as the 1560s.[19] Nevertheless, John King argues that the Diana image specifically associated with the queen's virginal "moon cult" did not take root until the 1580s and 1590s, "after the failure of [Elizabeth's] last effort at marriage," this time to François, duc Alençon (later duc d'Anjou).[20] He uses Spenser's *April Eclogue*, printed in 1579, one year after *The Mirrour of Knighthood*, as "a borderline text that enhances the queen's standing as a princess eligible for marriage at the same time that it praises her in a manner that may be read as an appeal to remain unmarried. When the poet came to portray Elizabeth in *The Faerie Queene* [...] however, Belphoebe personified her virginity as a permanent state."[21] If King's supposition is correct, this means that the Elizabethan Diana was on the horizon at the precise moment that *The Mirrour of Knighthood* was

---

16. Elizabeth's poetic cult of Diana bore strong ties to the *Diana* of Montemayor. For instance, Raleigh's poem, "Prais'd be Diana's fair and harmless light" was first published in *England's Helicon* (1600), which also contained two dozen poems from Montemayor's *Diana*.
17. Montemayor expressly praised Diana's virgin cult over the lusty cult of Apollo in the verse Dardanea composes in response to the love letters of Disteus, also printed in Yong's translation. Bartholomew Yong, *Diana of George of Montemayor: translated out of Spanish into English* (London: G[eorge] B[ishop], 1598), Hh1v–Hh3r. Reflecting the influence of Montemayor's opus, another song in Morley's collection went, "With Angels face & brightnesse, & orient hew, faire Oriana [...] faire Oriana shining, O're hills & mountaines, o're hills & mountaines, At last in dale she rested, hard by *Dianaes* fountaines, *Dianaes* fountaines, With septer in her hand, with septer in her hand…" George Kyrbie, "With Angells face and brightnesse. XX," in *The Triumphs of Oriana*, sig. D4v. The line, "hard by *Dianaes* fountaines," comes from the work's inspiration, the 1592 Italian madrigal collection, *Il trionfo di Dori*, specifically the madrigal, "Ove tra l'herb' e i fiori," by Venetian composer, Giovanni Croce. A fountain also provides a central meeting point for the lovers in Montemayor's pastoral romance; one famous scene depicts Diana weeping crocodile tears into the fountain when pledging love for her shepherd. In 1595, a fountain in West Cheap was restored with a statue of Diana.
18. The overlapping Elizabethan cults of Diana and Oriana were linked by the Latinate "ana" suffix, typically used to convert single nouns into collective nouns. The prefix "Di-" referred to "duo," as well as "dī-," deriving from dies (day), as in the reflected source of daylight. Diana, the force of the moon, was Oriana's complement.
19. For a reading, see, e.g., Susan Doran, "Juno versus Diana: The Treatment of Elizabeth I's Marriage in Plays and Entertainments, 1561–1581," *The Historical Journal* 38, no. 2 (1995), 257–74, esp. 264.
20. See King, "Queen Elizabeth I: Representations of the Virgin Queen," *Renaissance Quarterly* 43 (1990), 30–74 (43).
21. King, "Queen Elizabeth I," 32.

rising on the print market, and around the same time that Giordano Bruno directly compared Elizabeth to Diana in his panegyrics of 1584–85.[22] It seems almost impossible that initiated readers should not have made the connection between Belphoebe and the *The Mirrour of Knighthood*'s famously amorous princess Claridiana. In fact, this *virgo bellatrix* provided a model for Spenser's warlike women, Belphoebe and Britomart, as we shall see.

Anglo-Spanish Contests

> Madame, you may very well leaue this name of Domina Beatrix,[23] and bee called hereafter *Imperatrix,* or Empresse Queene, Princesse, Marchionesse, Countesse, Lady, and Gentlewoman, since that these two pillars of Hercules, which underprop all the world, are so much at your seruice, I would say this Castilianoes body, filled with abundance of courageous soldiers, which are this breast and this arm, stronger than the tower of Babylon, & especially when it is aided with my redoubted sword: because that the fire of the edge of it penetrates and surmounteth in splendor the glittering beames of the Sunne.
>
> —*Miles Gloriosus, the Spanish Braggadocio* (1630)

Part patron and part muse, Elizabeth presides over faerieland with the "blazing brightnesse" of the sun,[24] while Philip symbolically tyrannizes with his false fiery torch of Apollo. For example, in the House of Pride of Book I, there presides over a devilish edifice of Catholic falsehoods, the satanical Lucifera on her chariot. She is followed by a train of deadly sins, the last of which is Wrath. Wrath rides upon a lion with a "burning brond" (I.iv.33.3) in hand, recalling the ferocity of the new Hispano-Roman regime.[25] This figure corresponds with the well-formed view of Spanish–Habsburg tyranny, a mixture of masculine fury and lust for power. The stereotype was famously embodied by Philip II, Europa rex, as in the above-quoted anti-Spanish satire, *Miles Gloriosus, the Spanish Braggadocio, the Humour of the Spaniard* (1630). In this bilingual edition of a late sixteenth-century satire of French origin, the Spaniard (both a common soldier and mirror for Philip), who is scurrilously named "Martin Alfonsus of Galeon shite-fire" remarks, "what things are there created in the world, which doe not honour and obey me, if I with my mighty strength doe make the earth to tremble"[26] Later, he adds, "With this most

---

22. For a discussion of Bruno's reference, see Roy Strong, *Gloriana: The Portraits of Queen Elizabeth I* (New York: Thames and Hudson, 1987), 125–26.
23. A reference to Beatrice de Luna, born Gracia Mendes Nasi (1510–69), a Portuguese-Aragonese *conversa*, who with her family, fled to Venice, and became one of the wealthiest women in Europe.
24. "Blazing brightness" is used to refer to both Una (I.xii.23.1) and Arthur's uncovered shield (I.viii.19.4). Both are mirrors for Elizabeth's reign.
25. The lion is a common symbol for Spain, also the symbol for the Spanish crown of León. See Fernández-González, "Negotiating Terms," esp. 100 and 104.
26. *Miles Gloriosus, the Spanish Braggadocio, Or, the Humour of the Spaniard Lately Written in French, and Newly Translated into English, with the French Annexed*, I.W. trans. (London: I.E., 1630), sig. B1v.

redoubtable sword, I ruinate, I burne, and set all on fire, breaking inexpugnable armies, Cities, Castles, Trenches, Towers, Walles and Fortresses."[27]

Such stereotypical boasts, mingled with phallic references, mockeries of Spanish chivalry, and profligate womanizing,[28] also find expression in Book V of the 1596 *The Faerie Queene* in Braggadocchio, the Spanish braggart, miles gloriosus. Braggadocchio vainly dons the solar emblem on his shield, ironically calling the braggart's chivalry into question.[29] His humiliation by Talus, who with Artegall and Guyon, exposes Braggadocchio's falsehood, is marked by the solar arms being "blotted out" (V.iii.37.7). Meanwhile, Arthur's "sunlike shield" (V.viii.41.2) marks him a *true* Sun Knight, and a magnificent embodiment of the order of chivalry, which defends the divine truth of English Protestantism.

By its use of Spanish sources and royal iconography to ridicule and coopt the empire on grounds of Spaniards' delegitimizing cruelty, Book V provides "Spenser's most thoroughgoing fictional exploration of geopolitics from an English standpoint."[30] Recent scholarly interest has concentrated on the sequence in which Arthur and his half-brother Artegall liberate the lady Samient from the clutches of the vicious Souldan (Philip II) and his wife Adicia (injustice).[31] This sequence provides an elaborated Armada episode, with the Souldan's great chariot recalling Spain's mighty galleons dashed and scattered in the naval battle. But just as in Elizabeth's Armada portraits, which ridiculed Philip's Apollo cult in response to the recent English victory, here solar metaphors lampoon the Spanish king for his oversized ambitions, with the "embatteld cart" (V.viii.34.3) of the heretical Souldan casting Philip in the oppositional role of a "Paynim king," reviving the Crusades with a conspicuous layering of Orientalist references and symbols upon the banner of Roman Catholicism. The Souldan's embattled cart simultaneously underscores the

---

27. *Miles Gloriosus, the Spanish Braggadocio*, sigs. B2v–B3v.
28. Another example: "This sword hath fed mee this twenty yeeres. By it I am feared of men, and loued of women," in *Miles gloriousus, the Spanish Graggadocio*, sig. A6v.
29. For example, in *Miles Gloriosus, the Spanish Braggadocio*: "I am King of the Paladines, the terrour of the world, the flower of the nobility of the Rodomontes, Rowlands and Renalds, endued with infinite graces, beautifull as an Angel, courageous as Lucifer, a seruant to Ladies, and souereigne Prince of the company of Murderers," sigs. A4r–A4v.
30. Roland Greene, "The 'Scriene' and the Channel: England and Spain in Book V of *The Faerie Queene*," *Journal of Medieval and Early Modern Studies* 39, no. 1 (2009), 43–64 (46). Book 5 also recalls the Dutch Revolt against Spain with the Belge episode of cantos ix and x, where Belge's 17 murdered sons represent the 17 provinces decimated by Spanish cruelty. The triple-bodied tyrant Gerioneo also alludes to Philip II, ruler of the three nations of Spain, Portugal, and the Low Countries, currently bearing the "yoke of inquisition" (V.x.27.2). These Philip analogs are counterbalanced by multiple figures for Elizabeth, especially Mercilla, whose "*Mercie*, […] of Iustice part" in her conviction of Duessa (here most forcefully representing Mary, Queen of Scots), "distinguishes [Elizabeth's] administration of English law from her dispensation of justice to 'nations farre." Greene, "The 'Scriene' and the Channel," 57.
31. See Chris Highley, *Shakespeare, Spenser, and the Crisis in Ireland* (Cambridge: Cambridge University Press, 1997), esp. 124–31 (146); Roland Greene, "The 'Scriene' and the Channel"; Barbara Fuchs, "Spanish Lessons: Spenser and the Irish Moriscos," *SEL: Studies in English Literature, 1500–1900* 42 no. 1 (2002), 43–62.

failure of Philip's invasion of England, lampooning his self-identification with Phoebus and his cart, and furthermore mocking, in the words of René Graziani, "Philip's claim to dispense the divine light of the True Faith."[32] This Catholic heresy is further despoiled by comparisons to Phaeton (V.viii.40.2), whose prideful attempt to steer Phoebus's cart leads to a great fall. The scene evinces Spenser's characteristic impulse "to protect the fundamental symbols of good from such fraudulent encroachments."[33]

Philip's boastful self-identification with Apollo is defused by his identification with Paynims, Saracens, and devilish avatars: Archimago, Orgoglio, Gerioneo, Braggadocchio, and the Souldan. Still, Spenser's most forceful challenge to Philip's pretensions appears in the poet's contrasting representation of Elizabeth as a virtuous, militantly chaste sovereign, the *true* leader of Christendom, beginning with Gloriana's solar aspect, and continuing through her lunar counterparts, Cynthia, Belphoebe, and Britomart, all figures for Diana, the moon goddess. As Spenser remarked to Elizabeth in the proem to Book III:

> But if in liuing colours, and right hew,
>   Thy selfe thou couet to see pictured,
>   Who can it doe more liuely, or more trew,
>   Then that sweet verse, with *Nectar* sprinckeled,
>   In which a gracious seruaunt pictured
>   His *Cynthia*, his heauens fayrest light?
>   That with his melting sweetnes rauished,
>   And with the wonder of her beames bright,
> My senses lulled are in slomber of delight.
>
> But let that same delitious Poet lend
>   A little leaue vnto a rusticke Muse
>   To sing his mistresse prayse, and let him mend,
>   If ought amis her liking may abuse:
>   Ne let his fairest *Cynthia* refuse,
>   In mirrours more then one her selfe to see,
>   But either *Gloriana* let her chuse,
>   Or in *Belphoebe* fashioned to bee:
> In th'one her rule, in th'other her rare chastitee. (4–5)

As these verses suggest, Cynthia "with the wonder of her beames bright" is indebted to Elizabeth's familiar construction as Diana, such as in Raleigh's elegy, "The Ocean to Cynthia," yet unpublished.[34] But in case one should think that Spenser failed to

---

32. René Graziani, "Philip II's *Impresa* and Spenser's Souldan," *Journal of the Warburg and Courtald Institutes* 27 (1964), 322–24 (323); for further discussion, see Jane Aptekar, *Icons of Justice: Iconography and Thematic Imagery in Book V of* The Faerie Queene (New York: Columbia University Press, 1969), 82–83 and 218–19.
33. Graziani, "Philip II's *Impresa* and Spenser's Souldan," 324.
34. Only a fragment of the 22nd book, "entreating of sorrow," has survived. Spenser described Raleigh as "The Shepheard of the Ocean," who had written of the "usage hard, / Of

discover his own Diana of "heauens fairest light," with "mirrours more," this "rusticke Muse" supplies the reader with her Amazonian reflections, Gloriana/Tanaquill, and the huntress Belphoebe, famed for her "rare chastitee." Metamorphosed from classical prototypes, these English faerie analogs encode the gendered and sexualized politics of imperial conquest, transformed into a righteous Protestant program through strategies of comparatio and antithesis that cast the fair feminine form of Elizabeth, the Virgin Queen, as a desirable alternative to the so-styled libertine, King Philip.

It must be remembered that the Moon was also a classical site of imperial conflict, as in Lucian of Samasota's second century satire, *The True History*. This conflict was resolved by an androcratic marriage alliance between Phaeton and Endymion's princes.[35] But, against the force of Philip's matrimonial imperialism, the Elizabethan cult of Diana insisted (much out of necessity) that restoration and imperial triumph could be achieved through the moon's implied gynocratic separation, independence, and matriarchy, or in other words, *virtuous imperialism*. Although the Elizabethan cult of Diana richly incorporated diverse sources, those which spoke to Spanish cultural and imperial dominance most directly revealed England's anxieties and aspirations over the consolidation of European power. This anxiety mobilized the chastity thesis in redress to the popular *romanticizing* of Spanish empire, especially its celebration of Philip's *matrimonial imperialism*.

The weaponizing of *virtuous imperialism* begins with Belphoebe's characterization in conversation with Spanish romance. The character incorporates a number of literary antecedents, including the description of Aeneas's encounter with his mother, Venus, disguised as Diana, from the *Aeneid* (1.314–24), and the emblazoned description of the lady, Alcina, in her first appearance to Ruggiero in *Orlando furioso* (7.9–16).[36] But Spenser's quirk of compound naming also announces Belphoebe's kinship with the Amazonian princess Claridiana of *The Mirrour of Knighthood* cycle, with Belphoebe's name representing a direct synonym for Claridiana. The poem plays with this compound eponymity, proclaiming Belphoebe's "face so faire as flesh it seemed not, / But heuenly portraict of Bright Angels hew, / Cleare as the skye, withouten blame or blot, / Through goodly mixture of complexions dew" (II.iii.22.1-4).[37]

Cynthia, the Ladie of the Sea" in *Colin Clout* (inscribed to Raleigh, 1591). These lines also call to mind Raleigh's "Prais'd be Diana's fair and harmless light," especially because, in his sonnet to Raleigh, printed with the first three books of *The Faerie Queene*, Spenser suggested that his work was to replace Raleigh's "till that thou thy poem wilt make known / Let thy fair Cynthia's *praises* be thus rudely shewn" (my emphasis; lines 11–12).

35. These communities were described as all-male.
36. The first encounter of Belphoebe, in which Timias cries, "Angell, or Goddesse do I call thee right?" (III.v.35.5), recalls Book I of the *Aeneid*, in which Aeneas discovers his mother in disguise as a huntress in the forests of Carthage, exclaiming "O dea certe" (O surely you are a goddess).
37. Phoebe is equivalent to Diana. The Latin root *bel-* means beautiful, as in *bella*, while the Latin root *clarus* means clear, bright, gleaming; both senses are used synonymously in Spenser's poem with cosmic brightness typically referenced as a metaphor for Elizabeth's beauty. "Goodly mixture," notes Belphoebe's hybridity, while "clear as the skye" refers to the Latin *clarus* (bright or clear), in reference to Claridiana. The rest of the stanza corresponds with Alcina and Venus.

This wordplay is further reinforced by textual correspondences between Claridiana's first appearance in *The Mirrour of Knighthood* and Spenser's description of Belphoebe in her first entrance into the poem. In the words of translator, Margaret Tyler: "Out of the *thickest of the wood*, they [the assembled princes] saw a wild boar, driving so fast as possibly it might, and in the pursuit thereof, a young gentlewoman upon a mighty courser and *a boar spear in her right hand*; her *hunter's weed was all of green velvet*; *her tresses hanging down, in colour like the gold of Araby*" (my emphasis).[38] Comparably, of Belphoebe, Spenser wrote: "Eft through the thicke they heard one rudely rush; / […] / […] Eftsoone there stepped foorth / A goodly Ladie, clad in hunters weed," (II.iii.21.1-7). The poem notes that, "in her hand a sharpe bore-speare she held" (II.iii.29.1). It further describes her "yellow lockes crisped, like golden wyre" (II.iii.30.1). These descriptive elements, the distinctive "hunters weed" and "bore-speare she held" and her "yellow lockes crisped, like golden wyre" encode a conspicuous evolution of aspects of Belphoebe's character from the best-selling Spanish romance, with the boar-spear specifically representing the masculine optics of the hunt invaded and transformed in the hand of a virtuous woman. Belphoebe is, in other words, an improvement of Claridiana, just as Gloriana is a superlative figure for Oriana. The poem replaces these characters' famous decadence and sexual liaisons with Christian knights with a steadfast chastity that magnifies Elizabeth's deified beauty: "So faire, and thousand thousand times more faire" (II.iii.26.1); and "glorious mirrhour of celestiall grace / And soueraine monument of mortall vowes" (II.iii.25.6–7).[39]

While this representation lightly accorded with the developing representation of Elizabeth as an Amazon (in the aftermath of the Armada), it highlighted that her warlike identity developed in conversation with Spain and Spanishness. In other words, by answering the call to arms to defend her embattled country, Elizabeth justified her failure to marry as a Reformed ethic that was naturally opposed to Philip's unnatural desires, specifically his excess ambition to conquer England. In *The Faerie Queene*, this message is carried out through Belphoebe's formidable defense against the rape attempt by the false Sun Knight Braggadochio—a threatened imperial conquest.[40] The event reinterprets

---

38. Tyler, *The Mirrour of Knighthood*, 206.
39. A conversant Spanish romance reader might also have recalled Claridiana by the comments comparing Belphoebe to "Such as *Diana*" (II.iii.31.1) and "that famous Queene / Of Amazons" (II.iii.31.6) though the literal referent is the Amazonian Queen Penthesilea. Louis Montrose notes that Spenser found Penthesilea particularly apt as an exception to the warlike and anti-masculine representation of Amazons, "acceptable and appropriate precisely because she sacrificed herself not for the Amazonian cause but for the cause of patriarchal Troy, the mythical place of origin of the Britons." "The Work of Gender in the Discourse of Discovery," 27.
40. See, for example, *Miles Gloriosus, or the Spanish Braggadocio*: "Only with my voice, I will penetrate hell, and only with my presence, I will bring all the world into subiection, euen from the East vnto the West, that I may pillage, spoile and cut in pieces all the men which are borne in it. Then it shall be knowne of all, what a man I am." The braggart proceeds to elaborate how his mansion is constructed of the dismembered parts of the people's of the world, including his lodging walls which are built of "peeces as well of Caskets as head peeces, of the Ancient bearers of the Queene of England, which I haue cut off with this feareful and dreadfull sword…" sig. A7r–A7v.

The Mirrour of Knighthood's famous amours between the Christian Knight of the Sun (a figure for Philip) and the Amazonian princess Claridiana (turned avatar for Elizabeth) into a vile sexual conquest thwarted by Elizabeth's militant chastity. Prompted by "Prouidence heuenly" (III.v.27.1), and reflecting the queen's "souerain mercy" (III.v.45.2) for suffering innocents, Belphoebe represents the self-fashioned English ethos of a righteous alternative to Spanish imperialism: "Wee mortall wights, whose liues and fortunes bee / To commun accidents stil open layd / Are bownd with commun bond of frailtee, / To succor wretched wights, whom we captiued see" (III.v.36.6–9).[41] She notes that "Abroad in armes, at home in studious kynd / Who seekes with painfull toile, shal honor soonest fynd" (II.iii.40.8–9).[42] As the poem thus relates of the heroic Belphoebe/Elizabeth, "In woods, in waues, in warres she wonts to dwell, / And wilbe found with perill and with paine" (II.iii.41.1–2).[43]

Empire of Lust

Belphoebe's militant resistance of the allegorized lusts that Protestant Europe had attributed to (Spanish) Catholicism forms a strong contrast to the erotic torments of her long-suffering twin sister, Amoret, who seems to invite such abuse by her allegorized representation of matrimony. Raised by the love goddess Venus (while Belphoebe was raised by the virgin goddess Diana),[44] Amoret is the ultimate representation of courtly love's eroticized destruction of the beloved female object. She represents just one of the many "wretched wights" that comprise the body politic of Philip's allegorized empire of lust. Amoret also manifests the Spanish–Habsburg policy of *matrimonial imperialism,* specifically by her embodiment of married love as naturally constrained by lust. Thus, Amoret must be rescued by Britomart, another figure for Elizabethan chastity, from the pleasure-house of Busirane (as in Philip's "busy reign"), associated with what Belphoebe calls

---

41. According to Sir Walter Raleigh in his account of the *Discovery of Guiana*: "I made them [the Indians] understand that I was the servant of a *Queene,* was with the great *Cassique* of the *North,* and a virgin [...] that she was an enemy to the *Castilians* in respect of their tyrannie and oppression, and that she delivered them all such na*ci*ons about her, as were by them oppressed, and having freed all the coast of the northern world from their servitude had sent me to free them also, and withal to defend the cuntry of *Guiana* from their invasion and conquest," *Sir Walter Raleigh's Discovery of Guiana,* Joyce Lorimer, ed. (London: The Hakluyt Society, 2006) (Lambeth Palace MS 250).
42. This is comparable to the exchange between Redcrosse and Contemplation (I.x.60–64) over the active life versus the contemplative life, which culminates with Contemplation's revelation of deeds that Redcrosse must perform for the honor of his country. Just as this revelation rationalizes Redcrosse's departure from Una, Belphoebe's call to find "honoor" "Abroad in armes" serves to defend her steadfast chastity. In other words, Elizabeth cannot marry because she has a greater duty to defend the world against Spain.
43. Instead of the pain that is typically associated with womanhood, the shedding of virginal blood and the pain of childbirth Belphoebe is meant for the "pain" (labor) of transatlantic conquest.
44. Note that Diana symbolically serves as Belphoebe's mother; Diana was literally Claridiana's mother.

"pleasures pallace" (II.iii.41.8) and "Princes court" (II.iii.42.1) where "where happy blis / And all delight does raigne" (II.iii.39.4–5). *The Faerie Queene*'s militant virgins therefore celebrate Elizabeth's wisdom in choosing virginity, so that her sovereign person could never be conquered.[45]

For Belphoebe, love and honor (or lust and fortitude) cannot be present simultaneously, even in marriage. Therefore, chastity is the purest virtue, as signaled by the various torments vaulted upon the lady Amoret in the House of Busirane. The most significant moment in his pleasure-house is when Busirane ties Amoret to a pillar and pierces her chest with a spear-like pen, removing her heart and using her blood for ink. The pen most accords with Petrarchan love poetry, specifically the blazoning of the female body, *"writing that conquers."*[46] The shifting focus on Amoret's suffering emphasizes her absorption of masculine power discourse and of masculine violence (i.e., rape) as a function of the period's insistent reading of the female body as object of conquest.[47] Amoret's blood turned to ink further underscores poetry's idealizing of masculine lust, and the corresponding eroticism of imperial lust, such as in the tapestries that Britomart encounters in the House of Busirane, depicting:

> Many faire pourtraicts, and many a faire feate,
> And all of loue, and all of lusty-hed,
> As seemed by their semblaunt did entreat;
> And eke all *Cupids* warres they did repeate,
> And cruell battailes, which he whilome fought
> Gainst all the Gods, to make his empire great (xi.29.2–9)

In the second room, she also finds tapestries depicting the results of "false love" (III. xi.51.8):

> And all about the glistring walles were hong
> With warlike spoiles, and victorious prayses,
> Of mightie Conquerours and Captaines strong,
> Which were whilome captived in their dayes

---

45. Indeed, Amoret's later rape by Lust, "The shame of men, and plague of womankind" (IV. vii.18.5), emphasizes the horrors of men's vicious entitlements that can only be resisted by militant chastity. There is also the sad story of Aemylia, a high lord's daughter whose love to a "Squire of low degree," and plan to run away from him causes her to become a sexual slave to Lust, who did "ouerthrow my state and dignitie," IV.vii.15.7, 5.
46. Michel de Certeau, *The Writing of History*, Tom Conley, trans. (New York: Columbia University Press, 1988), xxv.
47. This episode of Amoret's torment may have been inspired by a similar episode of an enchanted lady named Mirabella who bleeds continually from a sword wound, from the *Amadís* cycle. See Helen Moore, *Amadís in English: A Study in the Reading of Romance* (Oxford: Oxford University Press, 2020), 80–81.

> To cruell loue, and wrought their own decayes:
> Their swerds and speres were broke, and hauberques rent;
> And their proud girlonds of tryumphant bayes
> Troden in dust with fury insolent,
> To shew the victors might and mercilesse intent. (III.xi.52)

This theme of conquerors and captains falling victim to love (lust) recurs in the poem, such as in Book IV, Canto vii, which deals of Amoret's torments by Lust, beginning with the following verse:

> GReat God of loue, that with thy cruell dart
>   Doest conquer greatest conquerors on ground,
>   And sets thy kingdome in the captiue harts
>   Of Kings and Keasars, to thy seruice bound,
>   What glorie, or what guerdon has thou found
>   In feeble Ladies tyrann[iz]ing so sore;
>   And adding anguish to the bitter wound,
>   With which their liues thou lanchedst long afore,
> By heaping stormes of trouble on them daily more? (IV.vii.1)

The direct address to Cupid, and the talk of love conquering conquerors, sets the expectation that this canto will concern the suffering of mournful male lovers (such as Timias's melancholic response to Belphoebe's departure), but the verse turns surprisingly to a lament of Cupid's "tyrann[iz]ing" of women by "heaping stormes of trouble on them daily more." In other words, in defending women, the verse indirectly attacks the "Kings and Keasars, to thy [Cupid's] seruice bound" just like the tapestries in the House of Busirane, depicting "mighty Conquerours and Captaines strong, / Which were whilome captived in their dayes / To cruell love." The poem thus casts men's capture by Cupid as not only emasculating, but also tyrannizing, for those who fall victim to their own desires are most often those who neglect or abuse their sovereign power, especially through rape. Spain is indirectly implicated. For instance, the satirical *Miles Gloriosus, or the Spanish Braggadocio* includes numerous aphorisms equating imperial conquest with rape, such as the following:

> As the world is diuided into foure parts, whereof 3 are Africa, Asia, and Europe, and these three are compassed and enuironed with the Sea; so my heart is diuided into three other parts, of a nature affable, terrible, and cruel; and these three parts are enuironed not with water, but with the liuing flames of ardent fire […] I would lay al mankind on the ground, making riuers of bloud longer than Ganges, broader than Po, and more terrible then Nilus, […] and this because of the supertranscendent affection whith I beare vnto my Mistresse.[48]

---

48. *Miles Gloriosus, or the Spanish Braggadocio*, sigs. B1v–B2v.

In this Black Legend tract, the Braggadoccio's mistress is alternatively specified and unspecified; she indicates no woman in particular, and all women together. The Spaniard's (Philip's) violent pursuit of her ("lay[ing] al mankind on the ground, making riuers of bloud") associates the stereotyped carnal lusts of his people with the compulsion to conquest (rape), embodying the free world as a woman who is used to sate the tyrant's insatiable desires. Courtship and reproduction therefore specifically tie to the imperial prerogative.[49]

While admitting the natural compulsion to inordinate passion (lust) as a conventional masculine struggle, English writers had long used the Spanish model as a warning to urge English imperialists to turn away from lust and to develop fortitude (to borrow Llull's construction from *Book of the Order of Chivalry*). Consider the following verse by Sir Thomas Wyatt published in *Tottel's Miscellany* (1557):

> If thou wilt mighty be, flee from the rage
> Of cruell wyll, and see thou kepe thee free
> From the foule yoke of sensuall bondage,
> For though thy empire stretche to Indian sea,
> And for thy feare trembleth the fardest Thylee,
> If thy desire haue ouer and thee the power,
> Subiect then art thou and no gouernour.[50]

Based on Boethius's *De consolatione philosophae* (ca. 524), the poem uses lust to mean both carnal delights and imperialist sentiment.[51] As Roland Greene puts it, this poem was "likely Wyatt's reflection on the ethics of conquest, and in thinking about love he crosses into empire or vice versa—it is perhaps impossible to say whether these seven lines are 'about' one or the other."[52] Especially by Tottel's title, "He ruleth not though he raigne

---

49. In another instance: "Doe not troub'e your selfe, Mistresse, and Lady of my life, be not angry if I be sought for so much and loued of Ladyes, and Princesses, who liue being abused, and lose their loues in vaine. For I haue not, nor beare affection vnto any other, but to your Ladyship (Mistresse) since that you are more beautifull then Diana, endued with excellent graces, of a more pleasant carriage then Pallas, more sweet then Venus. All these three soueraigne Goddesses and you are mine owne, vnto whom I giue my heart. Consider then that I loue you, and let me goe for another, since that I am more then a Gentleman. If you wil be vnto me, I sweare by the faith of a Captaine, and by the life of the King my father (for I neuer knew him by any other name) to beget you the first night, a regiment of souldiers, which shall conquer all the world." *Miles Gloriosus, or the Spanish Braggadocio*, sigs. C8r–C8v.
50. Sir Thomas Wyatt, "122. He ruleth not though he raigne over realms that is subject to his own lustes," *Tottel's Miscellany: Songs and Sonnets of Henry Howard, Earl of Surrey, Sir Thomas Wyatt and Others*, Amanda Holton, ed. (New York: Penguin Books, 2012). I use the numeration of this edition.
51. The first stanza is from 3.5, and the second is from 3.6, and the third is from 3.3. Wyatt probably used Chaucer's *Boece* as his source.
52. Roland Greene, *Unrequited Conquests: Love and Empire in the Colonial Americas* (Chicago: University of Chicago Press, 1999), 23.

over realms that is subject to his own lustes," some have interpreted the ballad as a warning and indictment of England's King Henry VIII (1491–1547; ruled 1509–47),[53] but Wyatt's qualification that "thy empire stretche to Indian sea, / And for thy feare trembleth the fardest Thylee" (or in other words, *farthest Thule*) more directly corresponds with Holy Roman Emperor Charles V, who prided himself as the world's first universal monarch. So, to put it differently, in thinking about lust, Wyatt crossed into Spanish empire, and vice versa.[54] In effect, the poem uses the infamous case of Charles of the House of Habsburg to diagnose the tyrannical lusts of Henry of the House of Tudor, citing the infamous Spanish lusts (e.g., gold-lust) as a lesson for Henry to curb his own vicious appetites.

In Henry's daughter, Elizabeth, who had officially forsworn all carnal delights through her characteristic ethos of chastity, there was reasonable justification for claiming that English conquerors would, by the virtuous direction of their sovereign, not succumb to Spain's notorious excesses. Elizabeth's private conduct with favorites like Sir Walter Raleigh and Sir Robert Devereux was of course another matter, and so it was probably no coincidence that Belphoebe represents Elizabeth's private virtue as militantly chaste.[55] *The Faerie Queene* extolls female virtue as a way of diagnosing the destructive aspects of male psychology, particularly as it concerns all manner of unnatural desire. The poem's verses about "conquerors" falling victim to Cupid's thrall thus inveigh against courtly love as a topos that romanticizes conquest (arms), citing as proof Spain's moral fall from grace in the New World. The discovery of America had brought accounts of a paradise of women and gold, spurring the appetites of would-be English colonizers. But while the desire for a golden paradise of women motivated new expeditions, there was always the comingled recognition that inordinate greed or *desire* had also been the undoing of the Iberian conquerors, whose unnatural lusts brought out the most perverse cruelties. Hernán Cortés and Francisco Pizarro were just some of the first men to penetrate this virgin paradise, conquering the space, despoiling the land, capturing the gold, taking native princesses for mistresses and common-law wives, and siring by them some of the first *mestizo* children born on the continent.[56] These were the stories driving men like

---

53. See Holton, ed. *Tottel's Miscellany*, note to poem 122.
54. Wyatt was English ambassador to Charles's court, which featured regularly in his poems. There was, for example, Wyatt's "130. Of disappointed Purpose," which concerns his 1537 embassy to Charles's court, where he had fruitlessly attempted to prevent Catholic powers from leaguing against England.
55. In his letter to Raleigh, Spenser explained: "For considering she [Elizabeth] beareth two persons, the one of a most royall queene or empresse, the other of a most vertuous and beautiful lady, this latter part in some places I doe expresse in Belphœbe, fashioning her name according your owne excellent conceipt of Cynthia (Phœbe and Cynthia being both names of Diana)," 716.
56. Cortés bedded a number of native Mexica women, along with the former slave woman, Doña Marina (La Malinche), who bore him Martín. Doña Marina later married a Spanish hidalgo. Pizarro married Inés Huaylas Yupanqui, daughter to the Sapa Inca emperor, Wayna Qhapaq (Huayna Capa) (ruled 1493–1524). Inés bore her foreign husband two children: Francisca Pizarro Yupanqui and Gonzalo Pizarro Yupanqui.

Drake and Raleigh, the brave English whose explorations and conquests could be the making of a new empire, though it's hard to tell which desire drove them most: God, glory, gold—or *girls*.[57]

Spenser well knew that colonial projects must be carefully managed, and that success was often measured by the conduct of the men entrusted with this great duty. A veteran of the recent wars in Ireland, where the colonial model was being tested, Spenser conceived *The Faerie Queene* while serving as secretary to Lord Deputy Arthur Grey, 14th Baron Grey de Wilton. Recent atrocities in Ireland, especially the 1580 Siege of Smerwick, after which Grey executed 600 Spanish and Italian surrendering forces, also necessitated a careful exploration of the ideal ethos of an English colonizer, though Spenser's own bias dictated that he elaborately defend those actions as justified cruelty against Catholic aggressors.[58] In his letter to Sir Walter Raleigh, the *Faerie Queene*'s patron, dedicatee, and allegorized hero, who had led the mass execution at Smerwick, Spenser explained the poem's purpose as "to fashion a gentleman or noble person in vertuous and gentle discipline."[59] Akin to Llull's opus, the epic romance was intended as an English *book of the order of chivalry*, a narrative allegory and guidebook for knighthood's inductees, which further sought to reconcile medieval practices of chivalry to the new global imperial perspective of the sixteenth century. Spenser also allegorized Raleigh himself in Arthur's squire, Timias, whose characteristic frailty is probably the poem's best example of the aspiring conqueror too easily swayed by carnal impulses. This masculine weakness must be corrected by forceful example: Belphoebe's/Elizabeth's militant chastity, which produces the central tension underlying Timias's courtship of the virgin huntress.

The sequence begins with Timias's wounding by a group of men attempting to rape Florimell. Belphoebe encounters the unconscious knight, and in tending to his wound, she ultimately "makes another wound" (III.v.42.2), evoking Cupid's wounding arrow of love, by the beautiful woman's enflaming Timias's passions. Belphoebe's damsels lead Timias deeper into the wood "Where was their dwelling, in a pleasant glade, / With mountaines rownd about enuironed, / And mightie woodes, which did the valley shade," and "in the midst a little riuer plaide" (III.v.39.2–4, 7). The scene provides a vision of "earthly Paradize" (III.v.40.5), which is occupied by the women. There Timias develops

---

57. Although the term *girls* is used to denote unmarried virgins, *girl* carried different associations during the Renaissance. As Jennifer Higginbotham points out, the term was "part of a rich vocabulary of female youth that was multiple, complex and multivalent." *The Girlhood of Shakespeare's Sisters: Gender, Transgression, Adolescence* (Edinburgh: Edinburgh University Press, 2013), 7.
58. There is some debate about whether Spenser personally penned Grey's letter of November 12, 1580, which endeavored to justify the Smerwick massacre to the Queen. See H. R. Plomer, "Edmund Spenser's Handwriting," *MP,* XXI (1923–1924), 201–7; R. Jenkins, "Spenser with Lord Grey in Ireland," *PMLA,* 52 (1937), 338–53, especially the notes. Whatever the case, the event was well received by Elizabeth, who sent Grey a letter thanking him for his conduct. Although we do not know whether Spenser personally witnessed the massacre, in *A View of the Present State of Ireland,* Spenser had the character Irenius defend the mass execution.
59. Spenser, Letter to Raleigh, 714.

an ardent passion for Belphoebe, vacillating between the desire to possess her and the contrary duty to respect her honor (III.v.44).

Timias's tumultuous affections represent a kind of masculine violence (unruly desire), as revealed in Canto vii, which relates Timias's betrayal of Belphoebe in his carnal embrace with Amoret (akin to the Knight of the Sun's torn affections for Claridiana and Lindabrides). Belphoebe's offense structures the poem's polemical defense of chastity as an imperial argument. In rebuking Timias, Belphoebe reverses the conventional lament of the Petrarchan plaintiff, who inveighs against cruel fortune for turning his lady's affections against him. Perhaps the most famous of these, particularly for the 1590s, is the speech of tormented Amadís, who has been rejected by Princess Oriana following a false report of the knight's inconstancy. Spenser would have known the speech from the *Treasurie of Amadis* and from Munday's translation of Book II (published in 1595). The speech proceeds as follows:

> Alas fortune, too inconstant and fickle, why hast thou aduaunced me, and afterwards ouerthrowne me [...] Because thou knowest that if heretofore thou didst bestow upon me any cōtent, yet was it euermore mingled with great sorrow. In like sort shouldst thou reserue for mee some sparke of hope with this crueltie wherewith thou now tormentest me, executing upon me an incomprehensible thing, in the thought of those whom thou fauorest: who because they feele not this mischief, do think those riches, glories, and honours which unto them thou lendest, to be euerlasting. But they forget, that besides the troublesome trauels which their bodies do suffer for the keeping thereof, how their souls are in danger to perils therefore. For by thy flatteries and wanton entisements, thou utterly ouerthrowest them, and in the end compellest them to enter into the labyrinth of all desolation, from whence they are neuer able to depart. And quite contrarie are thy aduersities, for so much as if a man doe resist them patiently, flieng [sic.] greedie couetousnesse, and disordinate ambition, he is lifted out of this wild place into perpetuall glorie. Notwithstanding I being most unfortunate, could not chuse this good, seeing that if al the world were mine, and should be taken from me by thee, yet hauing only the good grace of my mistris, it should be sufficient to make me as mightie as the greatest monarke, the which I also lacking, how is it possible for me in any sort to liue? Therefore in fauour and recompense of my loialtie, I beseech thee not to giue me a languishing death: but if thou art appointed to end my daies, doe it whout delay, taking compassion of him, whose longer life thou art ignorant how irksome it is [...] Then within a while after he cried, Ah louely Oriana, you have wounded me deadly, in banishing me discourteously, for I wil neuer transgresse your commandementi, what danger soeuer may happen me, seeing that if therein I failed, my life also were thereby finished: notwithstanding for as much as I wrongfully receaue my death, the most extreme is my dolour.[60]

As represented in this English translation, the famous speech is addressed to the goddess of Fortune, whom Amadis accuses of having tormented him by the sudden turn of Oriana's disfavor, which Amadis would not trade even "if all the worlde were mine."

---

60. *The Second Booke of Amadis De Gaule Contaning the Description, Wonders, and Conquest of the Firme-Island. the Triumphs and Troubles of Amadis. His Manifold Victories...* L[azarus] P[iot] (Anthony Munday), trans. (London: C. Burbie, 1595), sigs. E2v–E3r.

The lady's love is akin to a global empire, the possession of which would make Amadís "as mightie as the greatest monarke." Although Amadís is wholly innocent of the inconstancy of which Oriana accuses him, his disregard for his holy mission makes him an apostate, for as he explains, "if a man doe resist [aduersities] patiently, flieng [sic.] greedie couetousnesse, and disordinate ambition, he is lifted out of this wild place into perpetuall glorie." Conversely, if he forsakes Christian fortitude for love, he outcasts himself from the Kingdom. Unable to bear Oriana's banishment, Amadís renounces the company of women, abandons his knighthood, and vows to commit suicide. The Hermit whom he encounters (Andahod) persuades him against self-slaughter, further urging him "henceforth to be more virtuous and constant: and seeing you are borne a kings son, and likely to gouerne a kingdome, return to the world, for it should be a great hurt to loose you in this sort […] seeing that although she were a woman so excuisit as she could not be equalled, yet for her should not such a man as you are be cast away."[61]

Countless works, from the Bible to ancient myths, unpack the dangerous implications that result when lust detracts from duty; this theme naturally informs the structuring principle of the erotic delay, so integral to chivalric romance's didacticism. Perhaps it would suffice to quote the romance, which explains that "the displeasure of a weake woman had brought him [Amadis] to this extremity: he would haue tried to colour his fault by the examples of the strong and valiant Hercules, Samson, the wise Salomon, Virgill, and an infinit number of other great and vertuous personages which haue all fallen into the like miserie"[62] Nevertheless, the work also rebukes men for their inconstancy to their station. For instance, when the page, Durin, first arrives on the Firme Island (Ínsula Firme) bearing Oriana's letter of banishment, we are told that "Gandalin entreated him to stay until he [Amadis] had tried the peril of the forbidden chamber, being assured that he brought letters from Oriana, the which perchaunce might haue bene a meane (as he thought) to cause [Amadis] either to forslow or to faile in the achieuing of so great an enterprise: for Amadis was so subiect to the princesse, as he would not only haue left off the conquest of the Firme Island, but also of the whole world beside, if she had commaunded."[63] The knight's apprehensions turn out to be correct. Under the name of the "Fair Forlorne" (Beltenebros), the rejected Amadís escapes to the "wild place" Peña Pobre where he is consumed by fits of mad melancholy.

In its reproduction of the familiar romance trope, *The Faerie Queene* also interprets Timias's supreme melancholy in response to Belphoebe's rejection as a crisis of faith, which is represented by the metaphorical wilderness in which he also finds himself:

> His wonted warlike weapons all he broke,
>   And threw away, with vow to vse no more,
>   Ne thenceforth euer strike in battell stroke,
>   Ne euer word to speake to woman more;

---

61. *The Second Booke of Amadis De Gaule*, sig. E3v.
62. *The Second Booke of Amadis De Gaule*, sig. H1r.
63. *The Second Booke of Amadis De Gaule*, sig. D3r.

> But in that wildernesse, of men forlore,
> And of the wicked world forgotten quight,
> His hard mishap in dolor to deplore,
> And wast his wretched daies in wofull plight;
> So on him selfe to wreake his follies owne despight. (IV.vii.39)

Referencing the romantic understanding of love/eroticism as a function of moral errantry, this fair "forlore" revives the famous torments of great lovers like Lancelot, Amadís, and Orlando.[64] In this respect, Timias is also very much like the Knight of the Sun, who flees to the Solitary Island in Part II of *The Mirrour of Knighthood,* also for his impossible love of two women, Claridiana and Lindabrides.

By casting aside his weapons, Timias enacts a symbolic castration, denoting his deviance from the proper path of masculine chivalry insofar as he has abandoned the holy mission appropriate to his station. This anticipates Artegall's later disarming by Radigund, again for masculine desire, which causes his arms to be hung as a trophy of the Amazon woman's conquest of a Christian man. But, more than his sources, Spenser was apt to condemn such men, especially Timias, for "his follies owne despight." Timias's psychological torture is one of his own making, a fit of madness provoked by his frailty

---

64. The episode has obvious parities with the furious madness of Orlando, as inspired by the frenzy of Amadís, which author Ludovico Ariosto had pulled from the Spanish romance, along with the famous torments of lovelorn Lancelot from the Lancelot–Graal cycle, another source for *Orlando furioso.* Timias's outcasting himself from society and later accompaniment by Arthur more closely resembles the inward torment of Amadís than the ferocity of Orlando, who after learning of Angelica's secret marriage, rampages the countryside, "with hate, with fury, with revenge and rage" (23.103.8; Oxford World's Classics edition, Guido Waldman, trans.). There are numerous textual correspondences between the narration of Timias's madness and that of Amadís. For instance, after Amadís delivers his famous speech to the goddess Fortune, decrying Oriana's rejection, which he experiences as "languishing death," the narrator relates, in Munday's translation, "This sayd, he fell down backward upon the grasse, and was as silent as if he had bene in a swound," sig. E2v. This corresponds with Spenser's narration that Timias "to [Arthur's] speech aunswered no whit, / But stood still mute, as if he had been dum, / Ne signe of sence did shew, ne common wit, / As one with grief and anguish ouercum" (IV.vii.1–4). It suits that Spenser would here more closely follow the version from *Amadís,* which depicts the melancholy lover driven mad for love of the worthy Oriana than the version from *Orlando,* which pertains to the hero's madness for love of unworthy Angelica. In other words, Timias is more "forlore" (IV.vii.39.5) than furious. Nevertheless, Ariosto's version is clearly imbricated with Spenser's account, especially the moment when Arthur discovers that Timias has engraven the name "BELPHOEBE" on every tree (IV.vii.46), which recalls Orlando's seeing the lovers' names carved on every trunk. Since this episode was inspired by Raleigh's secret marriage to Elizabeth Throgmorton, as later discussed, it is worth noting that in 1592, a relative of Raleigh, Sir Arthur Gorges, wrote a letter to William Cecil describing how the spurned favorite, held in custody, caught sight of the queen's royal barge on the Thames, and started brawling with his jailor to be released to find his queen. Gorges concluded, "I fear Sir. W. Rawly; will shortly growe to be Orlando furioso; if the bright Angelyca persever against hyme a little longer." Qtd. in Stephen Greenblatt, *Sir Walter Ralegh: The Renaissance Man and His Roles* (New Haven: Yale University Press, 1973), 77.

in succumbing to masculine lust; it is Timias's actions that revoke him from Belphoebe's favor, and so, symbolically, he is an apostate from the empire of Christ: "like outcast thrall." He only reclaims his arms by prostrate reconciliation to Belphoebe, who, occupying a role akin to Andahod's, lectures him about his indulgent grief, noting, "The grace of his Creator doth despise, / That will not vse his gifts for thanklesse nigardise" (IV.viii.15.8–9).

Conquering Lust

> *Riches*, and *Conquest*, and *Renowne* I sing,
> *Riches* with honour, *Conquest* without bloud,
> Enough to seat the Monarchie of earth,
> Like to *Ioues* Eagle, on *Elizas* hand.
> —George Chapman, *De Guiana, Carmen Epicum* (1596)

By casting out the characteristic excesses of the common conquistador for a male reading public eager to follow in his example, the 1596 *Faerie Queene* endeavored to inculcate Elizabeth's governors and generals into a polity of virtuous imperialism that would lead to the founding of the Messianic kingdom. Correspondingly, the incident of Amoret and Timias has often been read as a political allegory pertaining to Raleigh's secret marriage to Elizabeth Throgmorton in 1591, following her advanced pregnancy. This betrayal greatly angered Queen Elizabeth, who discovered it in 1592. By secretly pursuing Throgmorton (Amoret), Raleigh (Timias) had not only provoked the personal displeasure of Elizabeth (Belphoebe), but he had also put the fledging colonial project in jeopardy. Already the appetite for American colonization was waning, since conflicts with Spain kept the queen's attention (and royal exchequer) fully occupied. Native insurrections in Virginia and the perdition of Roanoke in the 1580s were also casting doubt upon the futurity of American conquest under Raleigh's direction.[65] An anonymous letter written by sometime following Raleigh's disgrace in 1592 therefore dubbed the marriage scandal "the end of [Raleigh's] speedy rising […] All is alarm and

---

65. In his account of colonial Virginia, Thomas Hariot reported an incident in which some stolen goods led to a massacre of Algonquins. Hariot attempted to reassure the queen that "although some of our company towards the end of the year showed themselves too fierce in slaying some of the people in some towns, upon causes that our part might easily enough have been borne withal, yet notwithstanding, because it was on their part justly deserved, the alteration of their opinions generally and for the most part concerning us is the less to be doubted." *A briefe and true report of the new found land of Virginia … at the speciall charge and direction of the Honourable Sir Walter Raleigh Knight, Lord Warden of the stanneries; who therein hath been fauored and authorised by her Maiestie and her letters patents: directed to the aduenturers, fauourers, and welwillers of the action, for the inhabiting and planting there: by Thomas Hariot; seruant to the abouenamed Sir Walter, a member of the Colony, and there imployed in discouering* (London: R. Robinson, 1588), sig. F2v.

confusion at this discovery of the discoverer, and not indeed of a new continent, but of a new incontinent."⁶⁶

Virginia's conquest had been despoiled by the very man who first understood *her* promise. This "new incontinent" of Raleigh specifically cast aspersion upon the Reformist narrative that Spanish conquistadors were disproportionately susceptible to their baser lusts, and that under the English, things would be different. As Charles Nicoll reflects, "one of the curiosities of the new English interest in America […] is that it entailed a curious rapprochement with the idea of 'Spanishness'—a sense that the Spaniards were the only role models for American exploration, and that Englishmen bound for America must emulate them, must in a sense *become* Spanish."⁶⁷ By giving into lust, Raleigh had seemed to become like the worst of Spain, and this disgrace inspired Raleigh's undertaking his 1595 voyage to Guiana, as Jeffrey Knapp notes:

> The man who debased himself through the "brutish offence" of impregnating a surrogate Elizabeth decides he cannot remedy that error by way of the figurative surrogate Elizabeth had originally granted him, Virginia; to honor the ideal of virginity he seems to have repudiated, Raleigh must instead journey to a land over which the queen has no title, risk the slander that intends once again to replace her in his affections […] and then show himself to have forgone, for Elizabeth's sake, all material satisfaction. It is to point this allegory of a voluntary restraint correcting the excesses responsible for his disgrace that Raleigh famously concludes, "Guiana is a Country that yet hath her Maidenhead."⁶⁸

In Guiana, it was hoped, Raleigh's lusts would finally be conquered through a new "*Conquest* without blood," as the opening passage from George Chapman's *De Guiana, carmen Epicum* (1596) suggests. Chapman sought to reconcile Raleigh's vicious past in this maiden voyage. He poetically imagined, in "Thespiads bright prophetic font" (line 148)⁶⁹ that Elizabeth would bless the disgraced knight's fateful voyage, heaping her approval upon a new American enterprise that would realize England's destiny in the West:

> Methinks I see our liege rise from her throne,
> Her ears and thoughts in steep amaze erect,
> At the most rare endeavor of her power.
> And now she blesses with her wonted graces
> Th'industrious knight, the soul of this exploit,
> Dismissing him to convoy of his stars.

---

66. Qtd. in J. Collier, "Continuation of New Materials for a Life of Sir Walter Raleigh," *Archaeologica* 34 (1852), (161). For a reading, see Louis Montrose, "The Work of Gender in the Discourse of Discovery," *Representations*, no. 33 (1991), 1–41 (10).
67. Charles Nicholl, *The Creature in the Map: A Journey to El Dorado* (New York: Morrow, 1995), 38.
68. Jeffrey Knapp, *An Empire Nowhere: England, America, and Literature from Utopia to The Tempest* (Berkeley: University of California Press, 1992), 191.
69. George Chapman, "De Guiana carmen Epicum," in Richard Hakluyt, *The Principal Navigations Voyages Traffiques and Discoveries of the English Nation In Twelve Volumes*, vol. X, reprinted from the 1600 edition (Glasgow: James MacLehose and Sons, 1904), 446–50.

And now for love and honour of his worth
Our twice-born nobles bring him bridegroom-like,
That is espoused for virtue to his love,
With feats and music, ravishing the air,
To his Argolian fleet… (lines 148–58)

Having abandoned his former lusts, Raleigh is now presented as a bridegroom "espoused for virtue" to his true love. The English Argonaut is brought to his "Argolian fleet," destined to follow in Columbus's footsteps in the discovery of a new Promised Land (see Chapter 4). Capitalizing upon the thesis of English bravery, as by its references to classical mythology and Christian eschatology, the poem revealed the great significance of Raleigh's voyage to England's grand narrative of conquest and conversion as one predicated upon English saviorism: "A world of Savadges fall tame before them" (line 166). In *The Faerie Queene*, this voyage also allegorically manifested in the form of Artegall's voyage to the Amazonian realm of Radegone and Britomart's subsequent reformation of the pagan warrior women, as we shall see.

Empire of Virtue

The second edition of the *Faerie Queene* of 1596 emphasizes that America was not sullied by England's recent scandals and disappointments, for it was Elizabeth, not Raleigh, who ultimately led the charge of this "rare endeavor." Elizabeth's exceptionalism is best captured by Britomart, the exemplary *virgo bellatrix* whose characteristic chastity uniquely suits her to the project of global conquest. With Britomart, the poem insists, almost self-consciously, that the English colonial program will be different because England's virgin queen is fundamentally different from, and far superior to, Spain's lustful king. Indeed, unlike Columbus and his successors, who had pursued Spain's perverse desires in the West, English explorers would follow their own moral lodestar in Elizabeth, who would lead them in a reconquest of America from the Spanish tyrant, subjecting millions to the kingdom of Christ.[70]

Britomart's relationship with Artegall, the Knight of Justice, forms a main focus of *The Faerie Queene*. It is destined to bring forth a line of kings, and so, it has sometimes been read as Spenser's subtle rebuke of Elizabeth for her separatist gynocratic politics, specifically her refusal to marry. For example, Andrew Hadfield claims that Spenser used Britomart "to attack Elizabeth for what she had not done, marry and have children, in showing the female knight on a quest for her husband, Artegall, the Knight of Justice,

---

70. Of course, this argument about righteous holy conquest was a version of the same argument that Spanish and Portuguese colonizers had made by applying the doctrine of natural law to justify their conquest, enslavement, and forced conversion of Native Americans because they reportedly practiced cannibalism, sodomy, idolatry, and human sacrifice. See Anthony Pagden, "Dispossessing the Barbarian: The Language of Spanish Thomism and the Debate over Property Rights of the American Indians," in *The Languages of Political Theory in Early Modern Europe*, Anthony Pagden, ed. (New York: Cambridge University Press, 1987), 79–98.

to secure the future of her dynasty."[71] He adds that had "Elizabeth been chaste—rather than simply virginal (temperate)—like Britomart, Spenser argues, the future would probably look bright."[72] This interpretation of Britomart would perhaps make sense if *The Faerie Queene* were written two decades earlier, but it makes little sense for the political moment of the 1590s, when there was absolutely no possibility that the almost sexagenarian queen (by the first edition) could physically produce an heir. This fact no *mask of youth* could possibly obscure and so there would have been no incentive for the poet to risk the queen's displeasure with such a pointless criticism. While the poem certainly can be read as urging the queen to choose her successor, the love plot pertaining to Britomart and Artegall cannot be meant to simply rebuke the queen. Instead, it urges the queen to recommit her "enthusiasm or material support for the various colonizing ventures that ignited the energy, imagination, and desire of many of her restive masculine subjects."[73] To move the queen to support this brave endeavor, *The Faerie Queene* therefore attempts to discover a vision for English futurity in the new global paradigm of transatlantic empire by Elizabeth's determined chastity.

Britomart, as we know, is the Knight of Chastity, and is destined for marriage. But her marriage is primarily allegorical, designed to signal the union of chastity to justice, the basis for righteous English empire ruled by Elizabeth, born through a virtuous monarchal line. In *Orlando*, which provides a basis for Britomart in the form of Bradamante, *virgo bellatrix*, Bradamante's marriage to the convert Ruggiero is foretold as the founding of the Este dynasty. In *The Mirrour of Knighthood*, which supplied another forebear in the form of Claridiana, Claridiana's union with the Knight of the Sun also founds a line of male Christian heroes starting with their son, Claridiano. But Britomart's union with Artegall founds a dynasty of a different kind:

> Renowned Kings, and sacred Emperours,
>   Thy fruitfull Ofspring, shall from thee descend;
>   Braue Captaines, and most mighty warriours,
>   That shall their conquests through all Lands extend,
>   And their decayed kingdomes shall amend:
>   The feeble Britons, broken with long warre,
>   They shall vpreare, and mightily defend
>   Against their forren foe, that commes from farre,
> Till vniversall peace compound all ciuill iarre. (III.iii.23)

Embedded in a vision of Britain's ancient past, casting Artegall and Britomart as forebears to a line of ancient kings sprung "out of the aunciente Troian blood" (III.iii.22.6), Merlin's prophecy, which is quoted above, provides a vision of royal succession that leads to the "sacred Peace" (III.iii.49.3) of Elizabeth's reign. (It invokes the post-Armada

---

71. Andrew Hadfield, *Edmund Spenser: A Life* (Oxford: Oxford University Press, 2012), 261.
72. Hadfield, *Edmund Spenser: A Life*, 261.
73. Montrose, "The Work of Gender in the Discourse of Discovery," 8.

representation of *Eliza Trimphans,* as in the 1589 engraving by William Rogers depicting the world empress holding an olive branch.[74] As a figure for Elizabeth herself, Britomart therefore celebrates the contradictory fruitfulness of female chastity, which, wed to justice in "eternall vnion" (III.iii.49.1), produces a "famous Progenee" (III.iii.22.5) not in the biological sense, but in the humanistic sense of a universal Christian polity.

Thus Merlin specifies that the progeny of Britomart and Artegall will not derive from lust: "It was not, Britomart, thy wandring eye, / […] / But the streight course of heauenly destiny, / Led with eternall prouidence, that has / Guyded thy glaunce, to bring his will to pass" (III.iii.24.1–5). The nurse Glauce asks for clarification:

> How shall she know, how shall she finde the man?
>   Or what needes her to toyle, since fates can make
>   Way for themselues, their purpose to partake?"
>   Then *Merlin* thus: "Indeede the fates are firme,
>   And may not shrinck, though all the world do shake:
>   Yet ought men's good endeauours them confirme,
> And guyde the heauenly causes to their constant terme. (III.iii.25.3–9)

This is no regular courtship ritual; it is Virgin conception—a lineage of "Renowned Kings, and sacred Emperours" who will descend from this divine herald of Christian temperance, one who is also able to "withstand / The powre of forreine Paynims, which invade thy land" (III.iii.27.8–9). This fortitude will equip Elizabeth's line to resist the tyranny of Spanish imperialism, in lands distant and far, on behalf of Old and New Christians. The marriage will therefore be the catalyst for the foundation of an earthly empire of Christ, a union of disparate nations leagued by love for their God who has chosen a virgin as His holy harbinger. And if she should set events in motion by sanctioning a conquest of Guiana, Elizabeth by her status as a virgin, "sacred Peace shall louingly persuade / The warlike minds, to learne her goodly lore" (III.iii.49.1–4).

This also explains the urgency with which Spenser allegorizes the reformation of the Amazonian realm of Radegone in reference to Guiana, the continued independence of which represents an imminent threat to not only English masculinity but also the natural order that Elizabeth had committed to protect. As the poem reflects:

> Ioy on those warlike women, which so long
>   Can from all men so rich a kingdome hold;
>   And shame on you, ô men, which boast your strong
>   And valiant hearts, in thoughts less hard and bold,
>   Yet quaile in conquest of that land of gold.
>   But this to you, ô Britons, most pertaines,
>   To whom the right hereof it selfe hath sold;

---

74. In Morley's *Triumphes,* the nymphs of Oriana, later described as Diana's huntresses (sig. D1r) bestow Oriana (Elizabeth) with an olive garland.

> The which for sparing little cost or paines,
> Loose so immortall glory, and so endlesse gaines. (IV.xi.22)

This verse attempts to reconcile the masculine focus of contemporary romance, with its masculine rhetoric of conquest grafted on symbolically female lands, to the new paradigm created by Elizabeth's female sovereignty. As Montrose notes, "Implicit in this conceptual shift from *the land as woman* to *a land of women* is the possibility of representing women as collective social agents […] Unlike the other indigenous societies described by Raleigh, in the case of the Amazons it is the women who are synonymous with the political nation."[75] That Britomart (Elizabeth) subdues this political nation not by full-scale war but by one-to-one face-off with Radigund is indicative of carnal lust being overcome by Christian love. It is not a rebuke of Elizabethan chastity, but a celebration of her just, righteous administration, tending to recover the deficit created by the fall from grace of men like Raleigh, or Raleigh himself. By appealing to Elizabethan justice, embodied in the queen's dual masculine and feminine functions, the poem also reconciles colonization's dual exigencies toward love and arms. Through Britomart's pursuit of Artegall, which brings her to Radegone, the poem constitutes the standard romance trope of the love-quest as a first chapter of Elizabeth's *virtuous imperialism* overturning the dominant force of Philip's *matrimonial imperialism*, which for love of pagan subjects, brings her as a protector to foreign shores.

In condemnation of masculine lust, symbolized by Artegall's distraction with and conquest by Radigund, Britomart finally triumphs over the Amazonian queen, Radigund, and she reforms the Amazonian nation in accordance with natural (patriarchal) law:

> During which space she there as Princess rained,
> And changing all that forme of common weale,
> The liberty of women did repeale,
> Which they had long vsurpt; and them restoring
> To mens subiection, did true Iustice deale. (V.vii.42.3–7)

This passage has been typically read as rebuking Elizabeth for refusing to marry and conform to masculine rule. Brian Lockey suggests, for example, that the episode reflects "how difficult it was for English Protestant writers, during this period, to imagine an imperial identity based on the prior traditions of natural law, because such traditions directly conflicted with the religious and legal traditions of England as well as with the gender identity of its sovereign. Spenser himself obviously understood how potentially dangerous the putting to paper such imaginings could be."[76] But when we consider that this trope of reverting to masculine rule was standard for the genre, as in the case of Claridiana's mother, the empress Diana, Spenser's inclusion of it in *The Faerie Queene*

---

75. Montrose, "The Work of Gender in the Discourse of Discovery," 25.
76. Brian Lockey, *Early Modern Catholics, Royalists, and Cosmopolitans: English Transnationalism and the Christian Commonwealth* (London: Routledge, 2016), 183.

seems far less politically charged in reference to Elizabeth's chastity. In fact, Britomart's precedence over Radegone's reformation reveals that she, like Claridiana, has not simply surrendered all forms of female power but only that power which is deemed corrosive to the political state: lust.

Recall that since women are generally the distraction from arms, Artegall's arms "hang'd on high, that mote his shame bewray" (V.v.21.7) represents a trophy of Radigund's sexual conquest, and this, as we have seen, constitutes a threat to both Christian empire and Christian justice. Her dressing Artegall in women's attire, a nod to a familiar romance trope from such works as Sidney's *Arcadia* and Montemayor's *Diana*, both of which feature men posing as Amazons, reflects the contemporary view of love-in-excess (and the lengths to which men go for desire) as not only anti-masculine, but also anti-virtuous.[77] Radigund essentially embodies the masculine abuse of imperial power that results from an unbridled desire for possession. Her allures dissuade Artegall from pursuing his battle, giving her the upper hand to overpower him, and so, his arms are hung in witness to this miscarriage of justice. The lustful Amazon Radigund therefore represents the affront to natural law comprised by this militant empire of women insofar as they are ruled by lust, and this, precisely, is the power that they must surrender in order to be reconciled with the empire of Christ.

Joan Curbet suggests that the poem separates out Claridiana's dichotomous identity as the amorous virgin (single-minded in her pursuit of the Knight of the Sun), into Britomart and Radigund. This divorcement of the *virgo bellatrix* from her lustful counterpart deriving from contemporary romance casts the poem in the positive Reformed tradition embodied by the chaste Britomart, who forms a foil to the negative, anti-masculine tradition embodied by the Amazonian queen Radigund, both composite in Claridiana. Therefore, Radigund's abuses of men, forcing them to don women's clothes, also correspond with the threatening, "repressed" Amazonian dimension of Claridiana that forms a basis of Elizabeth's virginal Diana cult:

> The distance between Tyler's translation and Spenser's epic is the difference between a wish-fulfilling fantasy that voices a desire for gender equality and a political allegory that excludes that possibility. It was inevitable that this difference should have been so profound in a historical moment when the Head of State could only guarantee her continuity through the explicit acknowledgement of her exceptionality as a female ruler: a moment when, to become a military leader, the Queen had to turn, figuratively, into a man, acquiring her legitimacy as a leader of the Army by guaranteeing the continuity of the patriarchal state.[78]

---

77. In Sidney's *Old Arcadia,* Pyrocles reveals to his friend Musidorus that he plans to dress as an Amazonian woman in order gain access to his beloved Philoclea. Musidorus argues that this behavior amounts to an effeminate wordliness, or love of the world. In other words, Musidorus associates the love of woman with lust, turning men away from virtue. For a reading, see Amy Greenstadt, *Rape and the Rise of the Author: Gendering Intention in Early Modern England*, reprint (Abingdon, Routledge, 2016), 29–56.
78. Joan Curbet, "Repressing the Amazon: Cross-Dressing and Militarism in Edmund Spenser's *The Faerie Queene,*" in *Dressing Up for War: Transformations of Gender and Genre in the Discourse and Literature of War,* A. Usandizaga and A. Monnickendam, eds. (Amsterdam: Rodopi Press, 2001), 157–72 (171–72).

This is why Britomart must overcome Radigund, not because Radigund is female, but because she is the wrong kind of female. What Britomart feels for Artegall is love, guised as Christian justice, while what Radigund feels for Artegall is lust, guided by the pleasures of the body. As Simon Shepherd observes, Amazons like Radigund use their fortitude "for non-virtuous, specifically lustful ends,"[79] while warrior women like Britomart "are armed with the strength of their moral views."[80] So, the task of reformation passes to Britomart, the paragon of chastity, a character who provides both literal and figurative restoration to the narrative's celebration of holy English conquest. In other words, as the poem suggests, the male spirit, though compelled to sovereignty by force of natural law, is also weakened by the inordinate desires innate to the sex; women, by contrast, "were borne to base humilities," but upon great occasion, "the heauens them lift to lawfull souereigntie" (V.v.25.10).

---

79. Simon Shepherd, *Amazons and Warrior Women: Varieties of Feminism in Seventeenth-Century Drama* (Sussex: Harvester Press, 1981), 1.
80. Shepherd, *Amazons and Warrior Women*, 2.

CHAPTER 4

SIGNS OF ENGLAND: REDCROSSE CROSSES THE ANCIENT BOUNDARY

The fictional space of Spenser's faerieland represented a version of what the ancients imagined to lie beyond Thule: a space of boundless possibility and a mirror for civilization. The challenge for Spenser was to replace the historical feats of the Spanish and Portuguese in America, the world beyond the world limit, with those of the English privateers and early colonizers who were attempting to *circumnavigate* and *circumvent* the Habsburg control of these regions; this poetic politicizing of faerieland performed a Herculean labor in challenging the dominant narrative of Spain as God's chosen empire.

In Book I of *The Faerie Queene*, Spenser's characterization of the Red Cross Knight as an English Saint George prefigures the character's holy discipleship to King Arthur, a Christ figure who would assuredly "wynne the holy crosse" for England.[1] Spenser's reclaiming the heraldic symbol of the red cross for England served this teleological narrative of the Second Coming, which cast the English as the protagonists in a divine doctrine of universal monarchy and Christian salvation. This process began with divorcing the red cross's contentious signification with Habsburg supremacy and the veritable confusion of crosses that had characterized the political iconography of early modern Europe. Spenser constructed a fictional mythology of England in faerieland, casting the English as the major protagonists of New World conquest and its chosen saviors. Mobilizing the red cross of Saint George as a sign of divine favor, he argued that the civilized British were destined to complete what the cruel Iberians had begun and that their final struggle for America would bring about the New Jerusalem in America.

Beyond Thule

> venient annis saecula seris,
> quibus Oceanus vincula rerum
> laxet et ingens pateat tellus
> Tethysque novos detegat orbes
> nec sit terries ultima Thule.
>
> —Lucius Annaeus Seneca, *Medea*

---

1. Thomas Malory, *Le morte darthur, Emprynted and fynysshed in thabbey Westmestre* (London: Caxton, 1485), sig. Cc1v.

>   -time shall in fine out breake
> When Ocean waue shall open euery Realme.
> The wandring World at will shall open lye.
> And TYPHIS will some newe founde Land suruay
> Some travelers shall the Countreys farre escrye,
> Beyond small Thule, known farthest at this day.
> —*Medea,* translation by John Studley (1581)

Columbus was reportedly stirred to dreams of a westward voyage by the above passage from the first-century tragedy of *Medea* (lines 375–79) of the Hispano-Roman dramatist, Seneca.[2] The *Medea* passage was alluded to in one of Columbus's letters from Jamaica, dated July 7, 1503 and addressed to the Catholic monarchs, Isabel and Ferdinand.[3] The voyager reflected that during a night of particular distress, he heard a voice saying, "I gave you the key to free the timid inhabitants of the Ocean sea, who were restrained by such strong chains."[4] In his own hand, Columbus also transcribed the Latin passage from *Medea* followed by a translation in Castilian upon which he embellished: "Seneca in the seventh tragedy Medea in the chorus '*Audax nimium.*' In the end days certain times will come in which the Ocean will loosen the bonds of things and a great land will be opened; and a new mariner, like that one who was guide to Jason, who was named Tiphys, will discover a new world, and then the island of Thule will not be the last of the lands."[5] In adapting the *Medea* passage to his purposes, Columbus deployed two mistranslations: first, Seneca's "novos […] orbes" became "a new world." Second, based on a scribal error between manuscript copies,[6] the discoverer of novos orbes became Tiphys, the fabled helmsman of the Argo, instead of the Titan goddess Tethys, wife to the god Oceanus. These changes aggrandized the voyager's claim to *first* discovery of America. He, the purveyor of "un nuebo mundo," was the reincarnation of history's first

---

2. Lucius Annaeus Seneca, *Seneca His Tenne Traigedies, Translaited into Englysh,* John Studley, trans. (London: Thomas Marsh, 1581), sig S1v. Seneca was born in Córdoba, Hispania Baetica.
3. Christopher Columbus and Roberto Rusconi, *The Book of Prophecies edited by Christopher Columbus,* vol. III, Roberto Rusconi, ed., Blair Sullivan, trans. (Berkeley: University of California Press, 1997), 34.
4. Qtd. in *The Book of Prophecies edited by Christopher Columbus,* vol. III, 34.
5. Qtd. in James Romm, "'Novos Orbes' and Seneca in the Renaissance," in Wolfgang Haase and Meyer Reinhold, eds. *The Classical Tradition and the Americas, vol. 1: European Images of the Americas and the Classical Tradition* (Berlin: Walter de Gruyter, 1994), 77–116 (82). In agreement with the interpretation of James Romm, I have translated Columbus's "tardos años" (from Seneca's "annis seris") as "end days" to capture the implied Apocalypse, which was essential to Columbus's understanding of his role in hastening Scriptural prophecy. See Romm, "'Novos Orbes' and Seneca in the Renaissance," esp. 82–84.
6. Columbus was utilizing a coincidental corruption of the original text in Renaissance editions that generally substituted *Tiphisque* for *Tethysque*. Columbus possessed a manuscript of Seneca's tragedies, but he may have also followed the convention of the first printed edition of 1491 by the Italian humanist Bernardino Gellio Marmita, in which the *Medea* text formed part of an interpolated redaction where "Tiphisque" had replaced "Tethysque." *The Book of Prophecies edited by Christopher Columbus,* vol. III, 34.

sailor, Tiphys, who had guided Jason on his famous mission to recover the golden fleece, a symbol for kingly authority now associated with America.[7]

By this misreading, Columbus wedded the classical nodes of universal monarchy to the Spanish West Indies under Holy Roman Emperor Charles V, stretching from the Indian subcontinent to this new world beyond ultima Thule—or Thule itself, as America was frequently called. This interpretation ignored *Medea*'s highly negative portrait of Tiphys as one who brought an end to the classical Golden Age by his introduction of navigation (lines 318–34).[8] Underscoring the error was "*Audax nimium*" (too bold). These two words open the Chorus's main speech in Act II, which reflects on the distortion of nature that ensues from this voyage: "All boundaries have moved, cities / Have set their walls in new lands, / Nothing keeps its former place / In a world unclosed" (lines 368–71). *Audax* was the "quintessential epithet of the Argonauts," also used for Horace's first sailor, as in his ode to Virgil (*Odes* 1.3), which Seneca referenced.[9] This repeated phrase fused the "transgressions of the first sailor to those of Prometheus, placing the origins of navigation in the larger context of primal boundary violations and offences against the gods."[10]

This lesson was lost on Columbus in view of the adventurous spirit with which he personally identified. In Columbus's opinion, the *Medea* passage was prophetic and propitious: the ancients had promised that a new Tiphys would venture forth beyond the world limit and a new world would be revealed to him. Seneca may have cast Tiphys's death at sea as a punishment for impiety (lines 616–21), but Columbus had interpreted the New World as a reward for his boldness. Consequently, as Diskin Clay suggests, possibly "no classical text was as inspirational to the navigators in the age of discovery" than Seneca's *Medea*.[11]

Spain Founds the New Jerusalem

Columbus's letter and the famous passage from *Medea* appeared in Columbus's hand in his manuscript copy of *The Book of Prophecies*, a compilation of Columbus's own writings, and of biblical texts and writings of the early Church fathers and medieval theologians. Begun sometime around 1502, the work's purpose was to connect the discovery of the Indies to a teleological history of Christian doctrine and salvation, "presented as the first step toward the liberation of Jerusalem and the Holy Land from Muslim domination, and to assign a prominent role in these events to Christopher

---

7. For more information on the fleece's association to America, see Jean-Pierre Sánchez, "'El Dorado' and the Myth of the Golden Fleece," in *The Classical Tradition and the Americas, vol. I*. Haase and Reinhold, eds. (Berlin: Walter de Gruyter, 1994), 339–78 (361).
8. These lines were strongly influenced by the depiction of the Golden Age in Virgil's Fourth Eclogue.
9. A. J. Boyle, ed., *Seneca's Medea* (Oxford: Oxford University Press, 2014) (note to lines 301–8).
10. Boyle, ed. *Medea* (note to lines 301–8).
11. Diskin Clay, "Columbus' Senecan Prophecy," *The American Journal of Philology*, 113, no. 4 (1992), 617–20 (617).

Columbus."[12] When Ferdinand Columbus inherited the manuscript around 1526, he described the *Book of Prophecies* in his records as "Prophecies concerning the recovery of Jerusalem and the discoveries of the Indies, handwritten."[13] The work placed particular emphasis on the role that the American indigenes were to play in the New European Zionism. Revelations 21 describes a heavenly city come down to earth and guarded about the city gates by angelic hosts:

> And I John saw the holy city new Jerusalem come down from God out of heaven, prepared as a bride trimmed for her husband. And I heard a great voice out of heaven, saying, Behold, the Tabernacle of God is with men, and he will dwell with them: and they shall be his people, and God himself shall be their God with them [...] And he said unto me, It is done, I am Alpha and Omega, the beginning and the end: I will give to him that is athirst, of the well of the water of life freely [...] But the fearful and unbelieving, and the abominable and murderers, and whoremongers, and sorcerers, and idolaters, and all liars shall have their part in the lake which burneth with fire and brimstone, which is the second death [...] And had a great wall and high, and had twelve gates, and at the gates twelve Angels, and the names written which are the twelve tribes of the children of Israel [...] And the wall of the city had twelve foundations, and in them the names of the Lamb's twelve Apostles.[14]

A common belief was that the Native Americans descended from one of the 10 lost tribes of Israel (among the original 12) carried off into captivity in 721 BC by the order of the Assyrian king Shalmaneser. This notion was reinforced by the claims of the vanquished Emperor Moctezuma that the Mexica people had arrived at the site of Tenochtitlán from a far distant place and that their augurs prophesied that a foreigner would one day rule them. In his history of the Mexica people, the Dominican friar Diego Durán wrote of this hypothesis:

> The curious reader can find many proofs in the Scriptures [...] which tell of the rigorous punishment that God predicted would befall these ten tribes because of their wickedness and evil doings and infamous idolatries [...] it is told that, in return for such ingratitude, God promised a scourge and severe punishment. And it must be noted that it was prophesied that these people would lose their lands, homes, and treasures, their jewels and precious stones, their wives and children; and they would be taken to foreign lands, and be sold there, while others were to take possession of their estate. It seems to me that even without other explanation we have here sufficient proof that these Indians descend from the Hebrews [...] And after they had populated this vast world, God tired of tolerating their abominations and evil doings and idolatries, so He brought alien people. Like an eagle that comes from the end of the earth [...] without mercy He destroyed them. They were kept in hunger, in thirst, in nudity, and in perpetual exhaustion, until they were humbled, cowed, defeated.[15]

---

12. Roberto Rusconi, Introduction to *The Book of Prophecies edited by Christopher Columbus*, vol. III, Roberto Rusconi, ed., Blair Sullivan, trans. (Berkeley: University of California Press, 1997), 5.
13. *The Book of Prophecies edited by Christopher Columbus*, vol. III, 9.
14. Quotation derived from the 1599 Geneva Bible.
15. Diego Durán, *The History of the Indies of New Spain*, Doris Heyden, trans. (Norman: University of Oklahoma Press, 1994), 5.

As a converging zone for European and pre-Columbian beliefs, the New World came to represent the new garden of innocence where the new Zion would be established through fire and bloodshed in coherence with the Scriptures.

Columbus also saw the *Medea* prophecy as part of the same nexus of auguries that spoke of the end of days described in Revelations. In the letter to Isabel and Ferdinand, Columbus's marginal notes called for the *Medea* prophecy to be preceded with a paragraph, "inspired by these verses [...] inserted before the one identifying premonitory signs of the final days of the world found in the Bible."[16] The implication was that he, "nuebo marinero, como aquel que fue guia de Jasón" (new mariner, like he who had been guide to Jason) had come to liberate the peoples of the world, as Christ had liberated the Jews. In the words of James Romm, "the idea of COLUMBUS as a new Argonaut, a man of daring originality who was at the same time modelled after heroes of the ancient past, reinforced a classical view of history which was immensely important to the Christian myth of his voyage. As the 'second coming' of Tiphys, that is, COLUMBUS provided a powerful analogue for the Second Coming of Christ."[17]

According to Ferdinand's biography of his father, published in Venice in 1571, Columbus had himself voyaged to the island of Thule, which he believed to be Iceland, prior to his expedition to the Americas.[18] The story was that a new Argonaut had sailed to Thule, and then ventured beyond this limit to discover a new world to the west. In a copy of Seneca's tragedies, he wrote beside the *Medea* passage: "This prophecy was fulfilled by my father."[19]

Romancing Spanish Supremacy

With its wandering heroes and tragic loves, *Medea* shared common ground with the sixteenth-century romances that also originated from Greek epic and Ovidian myth. In these epic tales of love and arms, boundary crossings feature as transformative ventures into the worlds of magic; these wonderlands collectively reference the recent discoveries in America, especially the great civilizations of México and Perú. Perhaps most famous of these boundary crossings was the crossing of Amadís through the Arch of Faithful Lovers, which wins the hero a lordship: "Thus did he win the Signory of the firm Island, and al the inhabitants there-of haue already sworne unto him homage, and fealty, according to the custome of the Country, which is one of the fairest and strongest places in the world."[20] By crossing through this arch that none before transcended, Amadís proves himself worthy to rule a Christian colony; the test of the "faithful lover" transforms brutal conquest (arms) into rationalizing

---

16. *The Book of Prophecies edited by Christopher Columbus*, vol. III, 34.
17. Romm, "'Novos Orbes' and Seneca in the Renaissance," 84. "Columbus" is fully capitalized by Romm.
18. The report may have been fabricated by Ferdinand, or he may have misread his father's notes.
19. Qtd. in Clay, "Columbus' Senecan Prophecy," 617.
20. *Amadis de Gaule*, 347.

civility (love), equating the chivalric code with the requisite characteristics of a divine colonizer.[21]

In keeping with the classical concept of a boundary passage was Charles's other personal motto, *plus ultra*. Later adopted by his son Philip, the phrase referred to the imperial push to conquer lands beyond the world limit, inverting the *ne plus ultra* (go "no further") that was supposedly inscribed on the Pillars of Hercules by the hero himself to warn sailors against passing through the straits of Gibraltar to the Atlantic.[22] In 1516, Charles adopted the phrase *plus ultra*, and the image of the Pillars of Hercules, as his personal symbol; this remains an iconic feature of Spain's coat of arms.[23] The inspiration for the motto probably derived from the epic romance, *The Histories of Troy*, commissioned by Duke Philip III "the Good" of Burgundy.[24]

The *plus ultra* motto also informed Charles's promotion of the chivalric Order of the Golden Fleece, first founded in 1430 by Philip of Burgundy as an homage to the epic quest of Jason.[25] Geoffrey Parker reports that in March 1516, at the funeral mass for Ferdinand II of Aragón, a procession of Knights of the Order of the Golden Fleece preceded Charles into the Cathedral of St. Gudule, Brussels. A golden crown and sword were presented to Charles, who was proclaimed king with the words: "Here is the sword you will use to administer justice."[26] The same year, Charles's doctor and advisor Luigi Marliano featured the *plus ultra* in his speech to the chapter knights, "calling on the young king to be 'a new Hercules, a new Atlas.'" *Plus ultra* also appeared on the stall where Charles sat at the Golden Fleece chapter in Barcelona, "and later in a thousand other locations."[27] Inspired by a medieval romance, this elision of Jason's mission to recover

---

21. Amadís passes governorship to his squire Gandalín as a reward for his brave and honorable services. This is parodied in *Don Quixote de la Mancha*, with the island of Barataria that is mockingly granted to Sancho to govern as reward for his services to the deluded Don.
22. According to Strabo (3.5.5), Hercules raised the Pillars during one of his Twelve Labours to mark the western edge of the inhabited world. The most common referent was the Rock of Gibraltar; another was the "Pillars of Melqart" in the temple near Gades/Gádeira (in Cádiz).
23. Charles's self-fashioning in the tradition of Hercules drew support from the hero's travels in Spain in pursuit of the cattle of the three-bodied giant Geryon, whose Erytheian home was located across the Tartessos River (Guadalquivir). Note the correspondence with Spenser's triple-bodied giant Geryoneo, a figure for Philip II, ruler of the three nations of Spain, Portugal, and the Low Countries, currently bearing the "yoke of inquisition," V.x.27.2.
24. Geoffrey Parker, *Emperor: A New Life of Charles V* (New Haven: Yale University Press, 2019), 69. The Trojan myth was deeply concerned with the legitimacy and glorification of monarchs, and with the revival of the Crusades.
25. Parker, *Emperor*, 69. Upon his wedding to Isabella of Portugal in 1430, Philip the Good of Burgundy founded the order at Brugge (Bruges). Its first chapter was held at Lille in 1431, and its official seat was set in the Burgundian capital, Dijon, in 1432. Founded with the expressed purposes of defending Roman Catholicism, enhancing the doctrine of chivalry, and bringing honor to the Burgundian nobility, the order was also supposed to settle all disputes between its knights, whose actions were reviewed or tried at its chapters. In 1477, the marriage of Mary of Burgundy to the Austrian archduke Maximilian caused the grand mastership to pass to the house of Habsburg.
26. Parker, *Emperor*, 57.
27. Parker, *Emperor*, 69.

the golden fleece with the code of chivalry underscored the use of tales of love and arms to support the system of universal monarchy.[28] Under Charles V, the chivalric Order of the Golden Fleece became the highest order of Christianity. Designed to unify the principalities of the Holy Roman Empire under the expressed jurisdiction of the King of Spain, the Spanish branch of the Austro-Hungarian order also gave the inducted knights freedom to prosecute their own offenses. Charles granted the order jurisdiction over all crimes attributed to its members, and he gave the grand mastership to his son Philip.[29] This "ultimate reward of chivalric distinction" to the princely Order of the Golden Fleece "attempted to bring together the aristocrats of his far-flung empire in a single brotherhood."[30]

By Charles's concentrated efforts to support expeditions to the New World, the symbolic search for the golden fleece transferred to American soil, with many convinced that its true location lie in El Dorado. For a humanist reading public, "ultima Thule" represented a common marker of distance, either symbolic or literal, and a natural boundary to empire, such as in the hymn to Augustus in Virgil's Georgics 1.30: "Tibi serviat ultima Thule" (furthest Thule shall thy nod obey), and in Boethius's *De consolatione* (ca. 524): "Tellus tua jura tremiscat, et serviat ultima Thule" (Let earth shake before your oaths, and let farthermost Thule serve you) (3.5).[31] But Columbus's discovery extended the imperial boundaries beyond Thule to America, crafting the New World as a new world's limit, and pushing the bounds of human aspiration to the worlds beyond the ocean. As such, Virgil's "Tibi serviat ultima Thule" became an additional motto for Holy Roman Emperor Charles V in his efforts to conquer the New World.

For sixteenth-century readers, these colonial intersections provided proof of a manifest destiny for Europe's westward expansion, which was deemed necessary for reconstituting the New Jerusalem in America. Unifying all these prophecies was Canto 15 of Ariosto's *Orlando furioso* (1516; completed 1532), which featured the handmaiden, Andronica, delivering a prophecy of universal empire to the English duke, Astolfo, upon a voyage westward from India to Europe. Astolfo asks his guide about attempting the voyage in the eastward direction, and she confirms that the earth is made of islands surrounded by waters that feed into each other, carrying passage to lands unknown. This prompts a close retelling of the divine verse of the Medea:

---

28. Instrumental to the America myth associated with the golden fleece was Benoît de Saint-Maure's *Roman de Troie* (ca. 1160). The work was translated into several languages, especially Castilian and Galician. Jean-Pierre Sánchez, "'El Dorado' and the Myth of the Golden Fleece," in *The Classical Tradition and the Americas, vol. I*. Haase and Reinhold, ed. (Berlin: Walter de Gruyter, 1994), 339–78 (361).
29. In 1600, Pope Clement VIII granted grand mastership to all of Philip's successors. In 1700, the Bourbon kings of Spain and the Austrian Habsburgs vied for this honor. Following an order by emperor Charles VI in 1713, the Austrian and the Spanish sovereigns were awarded the Golden Fleece as their principal order of knighthood.
30. Jennifer R. Goodman, *Chivalry and Exploration: 1298–1630* (Woodbridge: The Boydell Press, 1998), 153. The order functioned as a high governing body for Spain's universal monarchy, charged with such responsibilities as approving the sovereign's appeal to go to war.
31. Translation by Andrea Kouklanakis.

Ma volgendosi gli anni, io veggio uscire
da l'estreme contrade di ponente
nuovi Argonauti e nuovi Tifi, e aprire
la strada ignota infin al dì presente…

[But with the passage of time I see new Argonauts, new Tiphyses hailing from lands which lie furthest to the West, who shall open routes unknown to this day.] (15.21.1–4)[32]

As these lines reveal, the New World provides the allusive background to the events of Ariosto's epic romance, which take place in Western Europe and the Eastern Mediterranean during the crusades of the Emperor Charlemagne (748–814; Emperor from 800–814), in his battles against the Muslim Saracens invading Europe. The America prophecy connects Charlemagne's Christian empire with that of Charles V. It also hints at the crucial role that the English duke, Astolfo, is to play by captaining a mythical journey to the moon to recover Orlando's wits.[33] In venturing beyond the earth to rediscover Orlando's sanity, Astolfo becomes a superlative figure for Tiphys—and for Columbus. He is "one who exceeds the boundaries of the known world, irrevocably changing its parameters, and as one who—as an almost paradoxical outcome of his lunar journey—reconstitutes the figure of the traditional hero by restoring the 'old' Orlando."[34]

This begins with a visit to a high hill that "toucht the circle of the Moone" (34.50).[35] Astolfo discovers that this hill bordering the celestial sphere is the Earthly Paradise, another America signaled by reference to precious stones: "The soyle thereof most fragrant floures did yield / Like Rubies, Gold, Pearles, Saphyrs, Topas stones, / Crisolits, Diamonds, Jacints for the nones" (34.50).[36] There he meets the prophet Elijah, a harbinger of the Messiah, and Saint John the Evangelist, who presages the Second Coming of Christ: "For he shall go before him in the spirit and power of Elijah, to turn the hearts of the fathers to the children, and the disobedient to the wisdom of the just men, to make

---

32. Translation and Italian verse derived from the Oxford World's Classics edition, Guido Waldman, trans. (Oxford: Oxford University Press, 2008). Tiphys is not directly mentioned in Canto 15 in the translation by John Harington.
33. For a reading, see Eric MacPhail, "Ariosto and the Prophetic Moment," *Modern Language Notes* 116, no. 1 (2001), 30–53.
34. Erin McCarthy-King, "The Voyage of Columbus as a 'Non Pensato Male,'" in *New Worlds and the Italian Renaissance: Contributions to the History of European Intellectual Culture*, Andrea Moudarres and Christiana Purdy Moudarres, eds. (Leiden: Brill, 2012), 25–44 (26).
35. John Harington, trans. *Ludovico Ariosto's Orlando Furioso: Translated into English heroical verse by Sir John Harington,* R. McNulty, ed. (Oxford: Oxford University Press, 1972), Oxford Scholarly Editions Online (2012).
36. See Revelations 21:19–21: "And the foundations of the wall of the city were garnished with all manner of precious stones: the first foundation was jasper: the second of Sapphire: the third of a Chalcedony: the fourth of an Emerald: The fifth of a Sardonyx: the sixth of a Sardius: the seventh of a Chrysolite: the eight of a Beryl: the ninth of a Topaz: the tenth of a Chrysoprase: the eleventh of a Jacinth: the twelfth an Amethyst. And the twelve gates were twelve pearls, and every gate is of one pearl, and the street of the city is pure gold, as shining glass."

ready a people prepared for the Lord" (Luke 1:17).[37] Astolfo converses with saints all day, "But when the Sunne began this earth to balke / And passe into the tother hemispheare, / [...] / [...] strait the firie charret that did beare / *Elyas* when he up to heav'n was caryd / Was readie in a trise and for them taryd" (34.68). Commanding Elijah's fiery chariot, Astolfo and Saint John cross over to the lunar sphere, which represents a mirror for human civilization—"like a glasse all voyd of spot / Or like a peece of purelie burnisht Steele" (34.70)—containing the props of past empires and a trove of lost things.

In Greek romance, the moon had represented an elusive world beyond the world limit and a mirror for civilization, such as in *The Wonders beyond Thule* of Antonius Diogenes, which formed the basis of the satirical *True History* of Lucian of Samosata. The work by Lucian was most famous for the narrator's undertaking a westward voyage beyond the Pillars of Hercules, which results in his aerial voyage to the moon. There, the travelers become intertwined in a war between the King of the Moon and the King of the Sun for lunar colonization, as I noted in the previous chapter. In Spain's Golden Age reinterpretations of this famous satire, the moon became an allusive setting for the European race to imaginatively colonize in the west.[38] This colonial subtext to the classical voyage to worlds unknown also informs Astolfo's lunar journey to reclaim Orlando's sanity, deemed crucial so "That *Charles* and holy Church may now at length / Be freed" (34.56). As Andronica's prophecy implies, however, this lunar voyage to recover the crusader Orlando is but the first chapter in the divine narrative of colonial conquest that would one day lead to a universal Christian empire under a second Charles, Charles V. And, to mark the phenomenal impact of the conquest of México to this conception of universal empire, in the third revised edition of *Orlando furioso* (Ferrara, Francesco Rosso da Valenza, 1532), Hernán Cortés is first among the prophesied conquerors whom Providence will supply to Charles: "He gives him Captaines both by sea and land / That shall win places never yet detected. / And none shall dare their forces to withstand: Cortese first, by whome shall be erected / The Emp'rors banner in the Indian sand" (15.19.1–4).[39] The succession of captains' accolades that follows this of Cortés does not, however, include any other conqueror of America. What follows is instead a celebration of four leading figures of the Italian wars.[40] México is thus, in the words of Antonio Río Torres-Murciano, "part of a whole that is not the New World [...] but instead the providential and eminently European empire of Charles V. The only sheepfold under a

---

37. This passage did not apply to John the Evangelist originally, though it has since become synonymous with him. For more information about John's role in bringing about the New Jerusalem, specifically in light of American conquest, see David A. Boruchoff, "New Spain, New England, and the New Jerusalem: The 'Translation' of Empire, Faith, and Learning (Translatio Imperii, Fidei Ac Scientiae) in the Colonial Missionary Project," *Early American Literature* 43, no. 1 (2008), 5–34, esp. 9–10.
38. For a reading, see Sònia Boadas. "Lucian of Samosata and Celestial Journeys in Spanish Golden Age Literature," *Dix-septième siècle*, 286, no. 1 (2020), 135–51.
39. In Robert Greene's play, *The Historie of Orlando Furioso*, printed in 1594, a Mexica king named Mandricard is also included among the many leaders of Africa and the Orient vying for Angelica's hand in marriage.
40. They are Prospero Colonna, the marquis of Pescara and Vasto, and Andrea Doria (15.28–35).

single shepherd in which the Catholic monarchy will have to become, in fulfillment of the prophecy of Christ 'there will be one flock and one shepherd'" (my translation).[41] This interpretation accorded with the special preference that was given to Cortés for his work in the spiritual crusade in America, considered the farthest western reach of Charles's Christian domain.[42]

Signs of England

Although Ariosto's intention was to glorify the conquest of America as divinely ordained for the Spanish Emperor Charles V, folding in the post-Columbian conception of America as the New Jerusalem, these prophetic passages also bore great personal significance for English readers. For instance, John Harington's 1591 translation of *Orlando furioso*, which has been quoted throughout, placed particular focus on Andronica's prophecy as pointing, somewhat additionally, to the victories of England:

> Yet I foresee, ere many ages passe,
> New mariners and masters new shall rise,
> That shall find out that erst so hidden was,
> And that discouer where the passage lies,
> And all the men that went before surpasse,
> To find new lands, new starres, new seas, new skies,
> And passe about the earth as doth the Sunne,
> To search what with Antipodes is done. (15.14–15)

In a marginal note to the Medea prophecy at stanza 14, line 2 ("New mariners"), he wrote: "Sir Francis Drake followed the sunne till he gained a day in account from sun rising to sun setting." As Frances Yates observes, this passage was "very freely translated" by Harington, "in order to make it fit Drake's exploit."[43] It not only omitted Ariosto's mention of Tiphys, synonymous with Columbus as by his own liberal translation of *Medea*, but it also omitted the subsequent lines that alluded to the feats of Ferdinand Magellan: "volteggiar l'Africa, e seguire / tanto la costa de la negra gente, / che passino

---

41. Antonio Río Torres-Murciano, "'Aquestos y Otros Triunfos'. Historia de Indias e Historia de Europa En La Épica Cortesiana," *Revista de Indias* 80, no. 278 (2020), 29–61 (31).
42. For Durán, Cortés's conquest demonstrated God's will that "the augury of the Sacred Scriptures be fulfilled and that three hundred men overcome so many people and that all those millions be possessed of such cowardly and frightened hearts that they would flee from the three hundred." *The Histories of the Indies of New Spain*, 6. Another chronicler remarked that God "by the very valorous captain D. Hernán Cortés did make the door to open, so that preachers of the Holy Gospel might enter to preach the Catholic faith to so miserable people […] so that now our Lord God may reap a great harvest of souls that they be saved" (my translation). Bernardino de Sahagún, *Conquest of New Spain: 1585 revision*, S. L. Cline, ed. (Salt Lake City: University of Utah Press, 1989), 248.
43. Frances A. Yates, *Astrea: The Imperial Theme in the Sixteenth Century*, second edition (London: Routledge, 1999), 55.

quel segno onde ritorno / fa il sole a noi, lasciando il Capricorno" (Others I see coast Afric, and pursue So far the negroes' burning shore, that they / Pass the far sign, from whence, on his return, / The sun moves hither, leaving Capricorn).[44] In his commentary on Canto 15, Harington furthermore praised England's own circumnavigators: "for the Indian voyages, we need not so much admire the captains of forren nations, hauing two of our owne nation that haue both as forwardly aduentured, and as fortunatly performed them, namely, sir Francis Drake, whom I touched before, and yong Master Ca[ve]ndish."[45]

In the voice of Andronica, Ariosto furthermore described the Spanish conquest of America as the divine mystery of God's will being realized in America and traceable through a succession of signs:

> Behold I see the signe of the holie crosse,
> A signe within these quarters seene but seeld;
> I see where ten a thousand put to losse
> And to th'imperiall banner all do yield;
> I see in spite of ev'rie thwart and crosse
> The house of Arragon still wins the feeld;
> I see that fortune is disposed to lift
> Up unto heav'n the name of Charles the fift.
>
> It pleaseth God to keepe the wayes unknowne
> Unto these parts as they have bene and are
> Untill seven hundred years be overblown,
> What time he meanes to raise an Emp'ror rare
> That shall both finde and make them all his owne,
> And one that shall most worthily compare
> In warre for courage and in peace for justice
> With Trajan, with Aurelius or Augustus. (15.15–16)

The agency that Ariosto had applied to Charles's royal iconography in the "signe of the holie crosse," a symbol of empire ("Veggio la santa croce, e veggio i segni imperial"), was also galvanizing for Edmund Spenser, inspiring his Redcrosse knight, a figure for Saint George. In *Orlando*'s Canto 15, Astolfo exchanges gifts with Sansonet, the Christian king of Jerusalem, receiving in his turn, the girdle and spurs of Saint George: "That for that knight were thought to haue bin made / That slue the Dragon with a deadly blow, / Which did the Ladie chast and faire inuade" (79). But whereas the original Italian romance related the recovery of Jerusalem by the cross of Spain, Spenser transferred that glory to England. He mobilized the Georgic red cross as a symbol for English victory in the New World, imagining English empire as the culminating *revelation* of his poetic passage through fairieland.

---

44. *Orlando furioso*, Oxford World's Classics edition, Guido Waldman, trans.
45. Harington, trans. *Ludovico Ariosto's Orlando Furioso*, 174.

Crossing into Faerieland

Faerieland was a space of endless possibility and wonder. It was a setting where the operative assumptions of the real world, dominated by Catholic Habsburg rule, could be interrogated and replaced. This was also the space where the most significant literary authoring of an English empire prophecy took place. In the poem Redcrosse is the allegorized New World adventurer who will cross the ancient boundary to found a New England in the West. This divine plan for Redcrosse is unfolded by the hermit Contemplation, who occupies the role of Saint John the Evangelist as a harbinger of the Messianic kingdom:

> That done, [Contemplation] leads [Redcrosse] to the highest mount;
>   Such one as the same mighty man of God,
>   Who blood-red billows, like a walled front,
>   On either side disported with his rod,
>   Till that his army passed through dry-shod
>   Dwelt forty days upon; where writt in stone,
>   With bloody letters by the hand of God,
>   The bitter doome of death and balefull mone
> He did receiue, whiles flashing fire about him shone:
>   […]
> From thence, far off, he vnto him did shew
>   *A little path that was both steepe and long,*
>   Which to a goodly Citty led his vew;
>   *Whose wals and towers were builded high and strong,*
>   *Of perle and precious stone, that earthly tongue*
>   *Cannot describe, nor wit of man can tell;*
>   Too high a ditty for my simple song:
>   The Citty of the greate king hight it well,
> Wherein eternal peace and happiness doth dwell.
>
> As he thereon stood gazing, he might see
>   The blessed angels to and fro descend
>   From highest heaven, in gladsome companee,
>   And with great ioy into that city wend,
>   As commonly as frend does with frend.
>   Whereat he wondred much, and gan enquere
>   *What stately building durst so high extend*
>   *Her lofty towres vnto the starry sphere,*
> *And what vnknowen nation there empeopled were.* (my emphasis; I.x.53–56)

This vision of the New Jerusalem is intervened by associations with the New World, a mystery "that earthly tongue / Cannot describe, nor wit of man can tell." A vision of Tenochtitlán is immediately suggested by the mount upon which Redcrosse first espies this wondrous city, invoking the first sight by Don Diego de Ordaz and his companions upon the dreaded volcano, Popocatepetl.⁴⁶ This vision, like *Orlando*'s Earthly Paradise, invites comparisons between the fabled American site and the volcanic Mount Sinai, whereupon Moses received "The holy law, / […] / […] while flashing fire about him shone," thereby linking both visions of Jerusalem as part of a single fabric of Christian Revelation.

Closely associating the wonder and grandeur of Aztec México, as described in recent accounts, are the "little path that was both steep and long" (i.e., the great causeway seven miles in length) and the "wall and towers [that] were builded high and strong, / Of pearl and precious stone" (i.e., the white stucco buildings and crystalline towers),⁴⁷ and likewise, the "stately building [that] dares so high extend," recalling Tenochtitlán's Huey Teocalli or Templo Mayor.⁴⁸ Redcrosse's impulse to question "what vnknown nation therein empeopled were" further encodes Europe's deep fascination with precolonial México, envisioned as a hidden society, primitive in religion and advanced in architecture and knowledge of the cosmos, that was believed to contain one of the lost tribes of Israel. Here, however, Spenser wrested the city from "her" negative Spanish Catholic cast, as in the prophetic verses of Columbus and gold-rich writings of Cortés, and he gilded her in the matter of England.

Drawing inspiration from the Spanish, whose literature proved prophetic, *The Faerie Queene* anachronistically anticipated the arrival of the English—especially their Reformed religion—long before they had actually made contact upon western shores. Thus the "City of the greate king" simultaneously accords with the earthly paradise of Christ and also the fabled pagan city ruled by Emperor Moctezuma, whose great empire had been transformed, as the next stanza alludes, into "The new [English] *Hierusalem,* that God has built, / For those to dwell in, that are chosen his; / His chosen people, purg'd from sinful guilt, / With pretious blood, which cruelly was spilt / On cursed tree, of that vnspotted lam" (I.x.57.2-6). By this comparison with the Passion, the poem justifies the ongoing Christianization of the Americas, and, the Native blood "cruelly" spilt by the Spaniards (likened to the imperial Romans who killed Christ) in order to realize this imagined destiny for England. It justifies that these innocents were given Christian salvation, such that "Now are they Saints all in that Citty sam / More dear vnto their God then younglings

---

46. The hybridity of the image was underscored by Spenser himself, who specified its parity with not just Mount Sinai, but also Mounts Parnassus and Olivet (I.x.54).
47. When describing Cortés's passage through a Mexican marketplace, Gómara remarked that the Spaniards "saw on their right hande, a great walled house made of lyme and stone, with loupe holes and towers, whited with playster that shined lyke siluer, being so well burnished and the sunne glistering vpon it. And that was the thing that the Spaniards thought had bene walles of siluer. I doe beléeue that with the imagination and great desire whiche they had of golde and siluer, all that shined they déemed to be the same mettall." Francisco López de Gómara, *The Pleasant Historie of the Conquest of VVeast India, now called new Spain, Atchieued by the vvorthy Prince Hernando Cortes Marques of the valley of Huaxacac, most delectable to Reade,* Thomas Nicholas, trans. (London: Henry Bynneman, 1578), 74–75. This section was quoted by Robert Southey in *Madoc* (1805, 1812).
48. Durán compared the great pyramid erected by Moctezuma to the "Temple of Jerusalem" built by King Solomon. Durán, *The Histories of the Indies of New Spain,* 130.

to their dam" (I.x.57.7-9). These references to election and predestination encode the early Christian Church's Restoration in America.[49] The comparison further reconstructs the New Jerusalem sought by Columbus and his predecessors into the New Albion—or New England—that was to be established in the site of Mesoamerica, first by Sir Francis Drake, and later by Sir Walter Raleigh "el Draque" and Sir Thomas Cavendish.

Reserving saviorhood for these English pirates and proud knights of the Garter, Spenser further associated Tenochtitlán's fabled grandeur to that of England, capitalizing upon the same rhetorical tactics that Cortés had employed decades earlier in likening Tenochtitlán to "Seville or Cordoba"[50] and Huey Teocalli to the great Cathedral in Seville.[51] According to the poem, "That great *Cleopolis*, where I haue beene, / In which that fairest *Fary Queene* doth dwell," formerly "The fairest Citty was, that might be seene; / And that bright towre all built of crystall clene, / *Panthea*, seemed the brightest thing, that was: / But now by proofe all otherwise I weene, / For this great Citty that does far surpas, / And this bright Angels towre quite dims that towre of glas" (I.x.58.2-9). Cleopolis stands for England, the seat of Elizabeth, "that fairest Fairy Queen," while Panthea denotes a great English palace (probably Westminster Abbey—or the mythical Glastonbury Castle upon Avalon, Ynys-vitrius) that serves as English analog for the Cathedral of Seville. But in presenting a vision of the past, of Tenochtitlán long ago destroyed and of ancient Jerusalem, it also provides a vision of the future, of the New Jersulem, the path to which was believed to pass through Guiana, site of the long-sought golden city, El Dorado. As the poet George Chapman remarked of El Dorado, "there do palaces and temples rise / Out of the earth, and kiss the enamour'd skies" (lines 180–81). Thus, when Raleigh first arrived on the Orinoco River's Caño Manamo in Guiana less than five years after *The Faerie Queene*'s first printing, he and his companions "called [it] the river of the *Red Crosse*, our selves being the first Christians that ever came therein."[52] This account gives witness to the galvanizing spirit of Spenser's literary divinations from *The Faerie Queene,* England's own *Book of Prophecies*.

Following the example of books of chivalry and other contemporary romances, *The Faerie Queene* used the imaginative space of faerieland as a symbolic world beyond the world limit, a space where allegorized English discoveries served to prophetically announce England's destined boundary passage into terra incognita. Correspondingly, Spenser created a fitting analogue for Astolfo/Columbus/Tiphys in the knight of the Red Crosse. This reincarnation of Saint George—a composite for England's great voyagers, Drake, Raleigh, and Cavendish—was to be the first of Arthur's 12 disciples, one who would serve God and country by reconstituting the Messianic kingdom in America. England's

---

49. In keeping with the vison's collapsed temporalities, "Saints" recalls the early Church fathers, while "younglings" recalls the Native Americans, who were regarded as Europe's spiritual children.
50. *Letters of Cortes*, 256.
51. *Letters of Cortes*, 260. For a discussion of Cortés's exaggerations regarding the *Templo Mayor*, see Appendix V, 345–48.
52. *Sir Walter Raleigh's Discovery of Guiana,* Joyce Lorimer, ed. (London: The Hakluyt Society, 2006) (Lambeth Palace MS 250).

American conquest was to be the final legend pertaining to Saint George, who, "sprong out from English race" (I.x.60.1), by his heroic deeds in "seruice, for her grace" (I.x.60) would become a "doughtie Conqueror" (I.xii.6.1) and found this fabled holy land, and after "famous victory" (I.x.60.5), "To yonder same *Hierusalem* [would] bend" (I.x.61.4) where for him was "ordaind a blessed end" (I.x.61.5), just like Moses, who died within sight of the Promised Land.[53]

Spenser Claims the Red Cross for England

For modern readers of *The Faerie Queene*, it is easy to take for granted the distinct Englishness of Spenser's Redcrosse, and, by extension, the essential Englishness of England's patron saint, following his election by King Edward III (1312–77). Yet, this perception of Saint George as a native English hero is in fact *The Faerie Queene*'s most successful fiction. In keeping with Elizabethan iconography, Spenser mobilized the heraldic symbol of Saint George—a red cross upon a white background—into a symbol of British national pride, and of the British monarchy. This martial representation directly informed Tudor image-making, such as in the family coat of arms, encircled by the blue garter of England's Georgic brotherhood, a sign of dynastic legitimacy. Though further developed during the later dynasty of the Stuarts, beginning with the iconography of James I, the cross of Saint George also took on additional ferocity for the English people united against a tyrant. Three days before the execution of King Charles I (1600–1649; ruled 1625–49) on January 30, 1649, the regicides reportedly replaced England's royal court of arms, which was displayed behind the judges' seats, with a cross of St. George.[54]

In Reformed England, Saint George was a figure of "deep cultural contradictions."[55] In the decades preceding Spenser's poem, George had become a beloved figure of English popular culture (as opposed to a purely aristocratic one), appearing in numerous contemporary performances, from pre-Reformation watches and ridings in urban centers such as Norwich and London, to the boisterous folk revelries in Wells and Chester in the early seventeenth century.[56] By the late 1500s, "he had become a complex cultural sign, whose various and contradictory meanings circulated in written works that continue to inform

---

53. Six years after the publication of Part I of *The Faerie Queene*, Drake died from fever, or possibly dysentery near Puertobelo, Panama. In an elegy to Drake, the poet Charles Fitzgeoffrey wrote: "Let famous REDCROSSE yield to famous DRAKE / And good Sir Guyon give to him his launce." Knapp, *Empire Nowhere*, 287.
54. Sean Kelsey, "Staging the Trial of Charles I," in *The Regicides and the Execution of Charles I* (Hampshire: Palgrave, 2001), 71–93 (84).
55. Mary Ellen Lamb, "The Red Crosse Knight, St. George, and the Appropriation of Popular Culture," *Spenser Studies* 18, no. 1 (2003), 185–208 (185).
56. Lamb, "The Red Crosse Knight, St. George, and the Appropriation of Popular Culture," 185. Saint George was also associated with the "George" of the tavern sign. See Beatrice Groves, "The Redcrosse Knight and 'The George,'" *Spenser Studies* 25 (2010), 371–76.

most critical understandings of his appearance in Book I as the Red Cross Knight."[57] Nevertheless, Spenser expected "at least some of his readers to recognize allusions to a conception of George quite different from the popular one."[58]

England's historical identification with Saint George formed part of a much larger European tradition devoted to the martyr, but that is not at all how he is remembered in English historiography. In the words of Harold Weatherby, "Spenser claim[ed] the true Saint George for England and transform[ed] her popular patron into a symbol of the ancient Christianity which she boasted of having restored."[59] Spenser may have described Redcrosse as having "sprong out from English race" (I.x.60.1), but as he was assuredly aware, George was heralded across the Byzantine and Roman Catholic worlds, including the Habsburg territories.[60] This global hero was also deeply interconnected with Catholic history and the iconography of the medieval Crusades. As the patron saint of Portugal, Saint George also became the patron saint of what would eventually become the Viceroyalty of Brasil, ported over by Portuguese settlers who constructed colonial Brasil as a New World locus of the slave trade; when Brasil became a Spanish territory after 1580 with the creation of the Iberian Union, George thereby also became the patron saint of the Spanish American plantation colony, hybridized by cultural contacts between Portuguese settlers who imagined themselves as New World crusaders, and enslaved West Africans, who incorporated the figure within the Afro-Brazilian religion, Condomblé.[61]

The cross was, of course, the dearest symbol of Christianity, and after the Protestant Reformation, a prime battleground for religious conviction. A flourished red cross with a fitchy point was the heraldic symbol of Saint James, patron saint of Castile and northern Spain, and of the Reconquest of northern Iberia from Moorish invaders. A red saltire cross was the symbol of Saint Patrick, patron of Spanish Burgundy and

---

57. Harold L. Weatherby, "The True Saint George," *English Literary Renaissance* 17, no. 2 (1987), 119–41 (140). Weatherby further notes George's connection to Byzantine liturgical practices and Greek paschal tradition.
58. Weatherby, "The True Saint George," 140.
59. Weatherby, "The True Saint George," 140.
60. During the Middle Ages, George was adopted as the patron to the kingdom of Magyarország (Hungary) as well as medieval Aragón and Catalunya. George was also the patron of medieval Genova (Genoa), a Habsburg satellite; the powerful maritime city was also known for its affluent and enormously influential Casa delle compere e dei banchi di San Giorgi, or Bank of Saint George, in which Isabel and Ferdinand maintained their personal accounts and to which Christopher Columbus, presumed native of Genova, donated a portion of his income from the discovery of the Americas for the relief of local taxes on food stuffs.
61. *São* Jorge was associated to the martial Yoruba Orisha, Ogum. He remains an unofficial patron saint of Rio de Janeiro (rival to Saint Sebastian), with enormous local significance in festivals and cultural events; the martial *São* Jorge also remains iconographic in the conflict site of Rio's urban flavelas, where both gangs and police herald the saint before entering into the fray. For more information, see Marta-Laura Suska, "Power Structures: Police and Traffickers in Symbiosis. Of Saints, Dragons, and Masculinities," in *Global Uniformities versus Local Complexities: A Comparative Ethnography of Two Policing Programs in Rio de Janeiro and Recife, Brazil*, Doctoral Dissertation, University of Wisconsin-Madison, 2018.

naval ensign of the Spanish Armada. Meanwhile, the Georgic red cross was the symbol of the Habsburg St. Georgs-Orden, the brotherhood immediately below the princely Order of the Golden Fleece, and a chief advisory body for the Holy Roman Emperor.[62] The holy cross was also the prime symbol of the missionary conquest of America by Iberian conquistadors, whose maps of México and Perú proudly displayed the signs of Habsburg rule.

Emerging from this discord of signs, the Redcrosse knight undergoes a journey of self-discovery in the form of his chivalric adventures through faerieland. This process begins with a series of misidentifications and self-ablutions to gradually purge the hero of his false Catholic heraldry, culminating with the discovery of his destiny to be sanctified as George, divine intercessor in the English battle for supremacy. As Jonathan Goldberg notes, Redcrosse "enters the poem clothed as another; the 'bloudie Crosse he bore' (2.1) names him only through a sign."[63] Åke Bergvall further suggests that in his self-discovery as Saint George, patron saint of England, "Redcrosse *forms* a sign."[64] This begins in Book I with Redcrosse's challenges and deceptions by "subtill Archimago," (I.ii.9.1), who at one point disguises himself as the clownish youth in order to trick Una into following him. This plot plays out the enemy's perceived corruption of fundamental Christian iconography as an ideological function of Europe's wars of religion, as the poem relates:

> But now seemde best, the person to put on
>   Of that good knight, his late beguiled guest:

---

62. The order dates back to King Rudolf I (1218–1291), the first Habsburg on the German throne, who is said to have established a Saint George knighthood as early as the year of his election, 1273. Emperor Friedrich III (1415–1493) established the imperial Order of St. George. It was confirmed in 1469 by Pope Paul II (1417–1471). Emperor Maximilian I subsequently founded the Grand Master's dignity of the Order of St. George or the Brotherhood of St. George Knights. It has remained a part of the Habsburg-Lorraine Archdiocese to this day. By the reign of Spain's king Philip II, and following a royal edict of 1572, the patronage of the Spanish orders of knighthood fell directly under the purview of the Monarchy, part of a hierarchy of knightly orders that ended with the imperial order of the Golden Fleece. The king argued that to protect the crown, it was necessary for knights to form guilds, each with the patronage of some saint. This royal proscription led to the establishment of new confraternities, mostly recomposed of earlier orders and all generally affiliated with the four main Spanish orders of knighthood: the Order of Santiago (dedicated to Saint James), the Order of Alcántara (dedicated to Saint Julián), the Order of Calatrava (dedicated to Saint George), and the Order of Montesa (also dedicated to Saint George). The Order of Calatrava and the Order of Montesa were directly affiliated with each other, both having originated from the defunct Order of the Temple, and established by Alfonso I of Aragón (1104–1134). Though generally secular and often more ceremonial (especially when they united with the Crown of Castile), these orders originally followed the Augustinian rule for canonical life, for which the iconic white habit of the Templar Knight was required. This is why, in the iconography of Saint George in Aragón, he appeared in the same costume of Spenser's Redcrosse.
63. Jonathan Goldberg, *Endlesse Worke: Spenser and the Structures of Discourse* (Baltimore: Johns Hopkins University Press, 1981), 7.
64. Åke Bergvall, "The Theology of the Sign: St. Augustine and Spenser's Legend of Holiness," *Studies in English Literature* 33 (1993), 21–42 (32).

> In mighty armes he was yclad anon:
> And siluer shield, vpon his coward brest
> A bloody crosse, and on his crauen crest
> A bounch of heares discoloured diuersly:
> Full iolly knight he seemde, and well addrest,
> And when he sate vppon his courser free,
> *Saint George* himself ye would haue deemed him to be.
>
> But he the knight, whose semblaunt he did beare,
> The true *Saint George* was wandred far away. (I.ii.11–12.1-2)

This devilish imposture is the first time in the poem that Redcrosse is explicitly identified as Saint George. This concealment underscores Spenser's technique of recovering English myths and legends from alternative accounts. Here, Redcrosse's identity is revealed through an instance of false identification with Archimago, who recalls Philip II as an oppositional foil to Elizabeth/Gloriana. And of course, we should not forget that both Charles V and Philip II had been inducted to the Order of the Garter.[65] Archimago's example is therefore one of false signification and false witness; he represents Catholicism obscuring Christian truth, and the Habsburgs falsely bearing witness to a "signe" that England associated with the Tudors.

The poem is replete with such false representations and oppositional pairings, such as between Redcrosse, the holy knight, and Sansfoy, the infidel, and between Caelia and Abessa, and Una and Duessa, and Fidessa and Duessa; these oppositional foils harangue the Catholic tactic of masquerading Christian truths, so accused. At the House of Pride, the red cross's many significations become distorted, such that by the start of Canto vii, Archimago's posing as Redcrosse is brought back to mind by Duessa's posing as Fidessa:

> What man so wise, what earthly witt so ware,
>   As to discry the crafty cunning traine,
>   By which deceipt doth maske in visour faire,
>   And cast her coulours dyed deepe in graine,
>   To seeme like truth, whose shape she well can faine,

---

65. During an earlier era of Anglo-Spanish cooperation during the early 1500s, King Henry VIII (1491–1547; ruled 1509–47) had conferred Charles into the English Order of the Garter, and after him, Mary I had also conferred her husband, Philip. When peaceable relations later deteriorated during the reign of Elizabeth, such chivalric gestures of good faith were rescinded: "*Philip* King of *Spaine,* beeing offended with Qu. *Elizabeth,* about the altering of Religion, and thereby alienated from the *English*: delivered backe to the Lord Vicount *Mountague*, the robes and habit of the Order, wherewith he was invested on his marriage with Qu. *Mary.* By which his Act, as the Historian hath observed, *Cum Anglis amicitiam visus est prorsus eiurare*: he seemed to breake off utterly, all amitie and friendship with the realme of *England*." Peter Heylyn, *The historie of that most famous saint and souldier of Christ Iesus; St. George of Cappadocia asserted from the fictions, in the middle ages of the Church; and opposition, of the present. The institution of the most noble Order of St. George, named the Garter. A catalogue of all the knights thereof untill this present* (London: Henry Seyle, 1631), sigs. X8v–Y1r.

And fitting gestures to her purpose frame,
The guiltlesse man with guile to entertaine?
Great maistresse of her art was that false Dame,
The false *Duessa*, cloked with *Fidessaes* name. (I.vii.1)

The romantic misrepresentation and hallmark Catholic deception mirrors Archimago's donning the costume of Redcrosse as "an earthly signifier 'conjoyned' to a heavenly Signified" who "becomes an easy prey to the wiles of the Roman Duessa" in the House of Pride.[66] The pivotal moment comes when Duessa is disrobed, and we are at once confronted with her "secret treasons" (I.xii.33.5). Fidessa reveals her plot—in consort with Archimago, "this false footman, clokt with simplenesse" (I.xii.34.6)—to have killed Redcrosse/George with "daily wretchednesse" (I.xii.33.10). An abandoned signifier, Redcrosse is contained in Orgoglio's prison house until Una and Arthur return the armor, exposing Archimago: "No magicke arts hereof had any might, / Nor bloudie words of bold Enchaunters call, / But all that was not such, as seemd in sight, / Before that shield did fade, and suddeine fall" (1.vii.35.1–4).[67]

Canto vii is also when we are first acquainted with Una's sad plight as the only daughter of Phison and Euphrates, beloved monarchs (named after the rivers of Paradise) whose kingdom has been plagued by a ferocious dragon. Redcrosse's final battle with the dragon forms the climax of Book I; the plot recalls the legend of Saint George, who defended a kingdom of Cappadocia from the attacks of an implacable dragon about to devour a maiden (usually, the king's daughter). This allegory represents Christianity's fight against the forces of evil: "Cappadocia is as much to meane, as the world: the Dragon is the Diuel, that deuoureth al that come to his hands, the kings daughter is the Church of God, saint George is Christ, who seing his church in peril, slayeth that Dragon, and deliuereth his most faire daughter."[68] Drawing on this chief allegorical function, the principalities of Europe also interpreted the legend of Saint George and the dragon as anticipating the chief martial struggles of the Crusades. In Zaragoza, Aragón, for example, the *Real Maestranza de Zaragoza* (Royal Order of Chivalry of Zaragoza) holds the legend of Saint George and the Dragon as a beloved origin story pertaining to its patron saint, one which also honors the order's foundation during the Reconquest of Zaragoza in 1118.[69] Still

---

66. Bergvall, "The Theology of the Sign," 37.
67. For a discussion of this process, see Bergvall, "The Theology of the Sign," 33–37.
68. Celio Secundo Curione, *Pasquine in a Traunce A Christian and learned Dialogue (contayning wonderfull and most strange newes out of Heauen, Purgatorie, and Hell) Wherein besydes Christes truth playnely set forth, ye shall also finde a numbre of pleasaunt hystories, discouering all the crafty conueyaunces of Antechrist* (London: William Seres, 1566), sig. M3r.
69. During the fifteenth century, the constitution of this confraternity of knights of Saint George was confirmed by King Ferdinand with the expressed directive to continue the kingdom's chivalric traditions in honor of Saint George and to organize religious rituals for the Church. After the uprising of Zaragoza in 1591, which was provoked by the incarceration of Antonio Pérez and his subsequent invocation of the fueros (rights) of Aragón, the order fell out of royal favor, not to fully recover until the mid-to-late seventeenth century. Real Maestranza de Caballería de Zaragoza, "Historia en Aragón," RMCZ.com, http://www.rmcz.com/historia1.htm.

Figure 3 Tapestry depicting *Saint George and the Dragon*, on canvas (artist unknown, Palacio de Don Lope, Zaragoza, Spain).

a visible presence in the city of Zaragoza, the extant Order boasts possession of several relics from its medieval history during and after the Reconquest, especially a sixteenth-century tapestry depicting the legend of Saint George and the dragon (Figure 3).[70] The vanquished dragon, no larger than a man, is being trampled by George's horse while the hero is poised in triumphant action. He raises his sword high above his head as if preparing to chop off the dragon's head in the familiar stance of a Moor-slayer.

Like the Archangel Raphael, who traveled to earth to put demons to flight, Saint George was the miraculous intercessor of the Crusades, and of the Catholic Reconquest of Iberia. Aragonés legend related that Saint George had aided Spanish Crusaders during the 1096 Battle of Alcoraz, which brought the kingdom of Aragón back under Christian tutelage. In commemoration of Aragón's prophesied victory on behalf of Christendom, King Pedro I (ruled 1094–1104) adopted to the Aragonés coat of arms the symbol of the red cross of Saint George surrounded by the heads of four Moorish generals whom Pedro had reportedly defeated in battle with George's miraculous appearance; this representation accorded with the parallel depiction of Santiago Matamoros [Moor-slayer]. George reportedly appeared again during the 1237 Battle of the Puig, reconquering Valencia for Aragón's King James I (1208–76; ruled 1213–76). "The Battle of the Puig de Santa

---

70. For more information pertaining to the artistic and iconographic tradition of Saint George in Spain, see Rosa Alcoy I Pedrós, *San Jorge y la princesa: diálogos de la pintura del siglo XV en Cataluña y Aragón* (Barcelona: Biblioteca de la Universitat de Barcelona, 2004).

Figure 4 1237 Battle of the Puig of Santa Maria (artist unknown, ca. 1410–20) temple and gilt on pine panel, © Victoria and Albert Museum, London.

Maria" by Andrés Marzal de Sas (Figure 4) depicts the martial Saint George, dressed in full heraldic regalia, and wearing a white tunic with a red cross across the chest, fighting directly alongside of the king. While James towers over a crouched Moor who holds his shield up in terror, the martial George is mid-action, fatally piercing through the head of a Moorish legionnaire.[71]

---

71. Aragón's identification with Saint George remained a significant component of Aragonés royal iconography. In 1444, for example, Alfonso I of Aragón made arrangements and investment for the transport from the port of Barcelona to his Spanish court in Naples, a now-lost panel painting by Jan Van Eyck, which depicted "Saint George and the Dragon." Perhaps Alfonso interpreted his resumption of his hereditary claim to Naples as an extension of God's will again favoring the Crown of Aragón, as had occurred during the Reconquest of the Spanish Mediterranean. I thank Sarah Kozlowski consulting on this citation.

In light of such common local legends in Habsburg territories, Archimago's posing as Redcrosse specifically casts doubt upon the Catholic Church's repurposing of the divine Saint George as a martial figure and battle intercessor, specifically by his description: "In mighty armes he was yclad anon." This common representation of the *martial* George emerged in the artistic iconography of the latter Crusades, providing a vision of George that aligned his profession of soldiery with his famous battle with the dragon and eventual martyrdom, thereby inspiring his role as adopted patron of Christian knights.

In *The Faerie Queene*, the false George's unfitness is laid bare by the haughty knight Sansloy, who nearly kills the red-cross-bearing Archimago because he has mistaken him for Redcrosse. By posing as Saint George, Archimago has also falsely donned Redcrosse's battered armor, the same armor that transforms the knight from a lusty and clownish youth into a holy saint. It is the symbol of Christian crusade, which Spenser claims for England in its righteous resistance of the Spanish invaders and New World decimators. Described by Spenser as *"the armour of a Christian man specified by St. Paul v. Ephes,"*[72] and providing key theological illumination, especially by the blood-red cross emblazoned shield, Redcrosse's armor "exposes false significations and establishes interpretive bearings."[73]

The Neapolitan annalist of the Catholic Church, Cardinal Caesar Baronius (1538–1607), once described the martial George as "the picture of some state or country petitioning (according to the custome of those times) the ayd and helping-hand of so great a Saint against the violence of the Devill."[74] The martial George embodied the saint's allegorical function in Crusades legends as a sign of God's ultimate preference for a people. In other words, the martial George helped to constitute the idea of *country* as a sense of belonging and shared cultural identity. In England, for example, the martial George was not only heralded as a chief battle intercessor of the Crusades but also a chief figure in the early history of its cultural formation, dating back to the reign of King Richard I "the Lionheart" (1157–1199; ruled 1189–99). According to some accounts, while Richard was warring against the Turks and Saracens in the Holy Land, George miraculously appeared:

> Upon a divine inspiration, by the comming in and apparition (as it was thought) of St. GEORGE, it came into his mind, to draw upon the legs of certain choyce Knights of his, a certain Garter or tacke of Leather, such onely as hee had then ready at hand. Whereby they being distinguished, and put in minde of future glory promised unto them, in case they wonne the victory; they might be stirred up and provoked to perform their service bravely, and fight more valiantly.[75]

English clergyman, geographer, and historian, Peter Heylyn (1599–1662), cited this event as the precedent for Edward III's later foundation of the Order of the Garter, "dedicated unto Saint *George* also: by which he came possessed alone of that special patronage, as

---

72. Spenser, "Letter to Raleigh," 717.
73. Bergvall, "The Theology of the Sign," 36.
74. Qtd. in Peter Heylyn, *The historie of … St. George of Cappadocia*, sig. H1v.
75. Heylyn, *The Historie of … St. George of Cappadocia*, sig. V6v.

the military Saint [...] the *tutelarie Saint* and *Patron* of his Soldierie."[76] As in Aragón, a cultural essentialism, if not proto-nationalism, was implicit to this martial representation, especially by Heylyn's conclusion: "henceforth therefore, we must not look upon St. GEORGE, as a Saint in generall; but as conceived, (such was the superstition of those times) the speciall Patron of the *English:* of which, [Spenser] the *Pilgrim in the Poet, thus prophecieth* unto his *Red-crosse Knight,* as he there calls him."[77]

The key term here is "*prophecieth*" for the informing contexts of *Orlando furioso* and of the *Medea* verse, and the destined Spanish supremacy these works purportedly discovered, are refuted by Spenser's so-styled prophetic romance, particularly at the moment when Redcrosse discovers his true identity as Saint George upon the hill of Contemplation, receiving the famous prophecy:

> Then seek this path, that I to thee presage,
>   Which after all to heauen shall thee send;
>   Then peaceably thy painefull pilgrimage
>   To yonder same *Hierusalem* doe bend,
>   Where is for thee ordaind a blessed end:
>   For thou emongst those Saints, whom thou doest see,
>   Shalt be a Saint and thine owne nations frend
>   And Patrone: thou Saint *George* shalt called bee,
> Saint George of mery England, the signe of victoree. (I.x.61)

Here, George, the embodiment of Virgilian poetics, intimately intertwines with Spenser's poetics of place.[78] George is the hero, the martyr, the pilgrim, the farmer, the English Everyman. A conflation of concepts and images, he will symbolically till the consecrated earth of God through holy, chivalric deeds and eventual martyrdom for England.

In light of the global and American contacts with Saint George, particularly as connected to the Habsburg dynasty and the Spanish Empire, of which Spenser was undoubtedly aware, Redcrosse's discovered identity as an English Saint George bears a distinctly competitive dimension. As Heylyn noted in his *Historie of that most famous saint and souldier of Christ Iesus; St. George of Cappadocia* (1631):

> looke into all parts of the world, and tell me which of all the three, hath not afforded honour to him, as an holy Martyr. His name commemorated in the Martyrologies of *Rome*, and *Greece*; his *Reliques* reverenced in *Spaine, Constantinople, France* and *Germany:* Temples erected to his honour, in *Rome, Constantinople, Ramula, Diospolis, Alexandria, Caire,* and *Aethiopia,* and in other places; by Prelates, Popes, and Emperours. Temples in *Asia, Europe,* and in *Africa.* And in the

---

76. Heylyn, *The Historie of ... St. George of Cappadocia*, sig. X2r.
77. Heylyn, *The Historie of ... St. George of Cappadocia*, sig. X2v.
78. This definition is also conveyed by Jacobus de Voragine, who in his *Golden Legend* defined *georgos* as "one who works the earth, namely, his own flesh." Jacobus de Voragine, *The Golden Legend: Readings on the Saints,* William Granger Ryan, ed. (Princeton: Princeton University Press, 2012), 238.

principall Cities also of the East, and West, and Southerne parts of the whole world. Then certainly we may affirme of our St. *George*, as the Historian did of *Pompey; Quot partes terrarum sunt, tot fecit monumenta victoriae suae* [His victories have created as many monuments as there are places of the earth.]⁷⁹

After surveying many of "the greatest *Princes* and *Republics* in the Christian world [...] [who have made] him the tutelarie Saint of their *Men of Warre* [...] and not so onely, but the *Guardian* of the distressed affairs of *Christianitie*," he nevertheless expounded upon George's particularity to England: "[Saint George] hath been reckoned as the especiall Patron of this Nation; and as particular to us, as is Saint ANTONIE to *Italie*, Saint DENIS unto *France,* or any of the other [sic.] to their proper places."⁸⁰

Heylyn also credited Spenser for popularizing the idea that Saint George was an Englishman descended of English blood:

> To this Relation, of his [Saint George's] being borne of *English* Parentage, our admir'd *Spenser*, although poëtically, doth seem to give some countenance: where he brings in his *holy Hermite, heavenly Contemplation,* thus laying to St. *George*, the *Red-crosse Knight*, his Parentage and Country.⁸¹

Through chronological placement of Spenser among the contemporary authorities on Saint George, the work bills *The Faerie Queene* as a precursor for writer Richard Johnson's *The most famous history of the seauen champions of Christendome*, first published in 1596. Here Saint George was England's native son, hailing not from Cappadocia, but rather from the English city of Coventry (and further elaborated in later editions). According to Heylyn:

> [Johnson] hath made [Saint George] to be borne of *English* Parentage, and of the *royall bloud* [...] his birth-place, *Coventrey* [...] for like a *Coventrey* man, hee did his best at first; in his so dangerous an encounter with a burning Dragon in the Land of *Egypt*.⁸²

Seventeenth-century folk ballads transplanted the event of George's defeat of the dragon from its original location near Libya to the English countryside. By the eighteenth century, the explanation by medieval hagiographer Jacobus de Voragine that George was "a native of Cappadocia"⁸³ had been replaced with a common myth that "in the City of Coventry was born champion, saint george."⁸⁴

---

79. Heylyn, *The Historie of … St. George of Cappadocia*, sig. R3r. Translation by Andrea Kouklanakis.
80. Heylyn, *The Historie of … St. George of Cappadocia*, sig. V4v.
81. Peter Heylyn, *The Historie of that most famous saint and souldier of Christ Jesus; St. George of Cappadocia,* sig. C8v.
82. Heylyn, *The Historie of … St. George of Cappadocia*, sigs. C8r–C8v.
83. De Voragine, *The Golden Legend*, 238.
84. *Life and Death of Saint George. To which is added, the Song of St. George and the Dragon* (Travelling Stationers, 1790), sig. A3r.

Through a pageantry of signs, from George's martial representation to his prophetic revelations, Spenser introduced a verve for weaponizing the red cross for England, as in the country's flag, deriving from the royal standards of English kings, which formed the basis for the English maritime flag, and later, the Union Jack.[85] The Georgic red cross also served Elizabeth's own royal iconography as patron of the Order of the Garter and leader of a rising maritime power. Gathering together these elements, was a famous engraving by Thomas Cecil from circa 1625, known as "Truth Presents the Queene with a Lance" (cover image). It depicts Elizabeth in the tradition of the martial George, dressed in a breastplate and Amazonian in her warlike ferocity, riding upon a horse with lance in her hand. A many-headed dragon of "Catholicism" lies trodden underfoot, while the defeated Armada appears in the background. The engraving's references to the martial George characterize Elizabeth as a "Matamoros," here specifically called upon to lead the vanguard against Spain and Roman Catholicism.

Thule Rewritten

The Anglicizing of Saint George as a prophetic sign of English conquest (attributing to Redcrosse the role claimed by Astolfo/Columbus/Typhis) took place alongside of an English and European humanist tradition of probing ancient writings in search of forgotten wisdom, for which Seneca's ultima Thule became a prime locus of scholarly interest. For instance, in his celebrated world atlas, *Theatrum Orbis Terrarum* (1570), Abraham Ortelius expressed incredulity at the possibility that the ancients had no knowledge of America because Plato's Atlantis myth and the *Medea* passage of Seneca suggested otherwise.[86]

The new relevance with Spanish imperialism later inflected into the genre by Columbus's misreading of *Medea* also gave a greater sense of urgency and timeliness to the reading of Senecan tragedy. For some, *Medea* provided confirmation that the divine

---

85. The Saint George flag had roots in the royal banners used at least as early as the fourteenth century, but during the era of King Henry VIII, this banner was used interchangeably with those of Saints Anne, Edward, Katherine, and Peter, along with the heraldic symbols of the dragon, greyhound, portcullis and red lion. By the end of Henry's reign, these banners disappeared permanently. The Georgic cross's adoption as national flag of England was thus tied to two specific sixteenth-century events: the Reformist abolition of all saints except Saint George and the expansion of transatlantic navigation, for which a standardized flag was necessary. Upon the accession of King James I, the St. George flag was joined with Scotland's St. Andrews Cross flag (a red saltire cross upon a blue background), forming the basis of the Union Jack, for maritime purposes. It was not officially adopted until 1801 with the union of Great Britain and Ireland. For more information, see William Gordon Perrin, *British flags, their early history and their development at sea: with an account of the origin of the flag as a national device*, Cambridge Naval and Military Series (Cambridge: Cambridge University Press, 1922), esp. 44–71.
86. In later editions, Ortelius reflected that ancients may have been hindered by lack of a compass, though this would not preclude accidental discovery. For a reading of Ortelius's comments, see Romm, "'Novos Orbes' and Seneca in the Renaissance," 104–7.

narrative of world salvation was being entrusted in Spanish hands. In Chapter X of *The History of the Indies* (1542), for instance, Fray Bartolomé de las Casas interpreted the *Medea* passage as "profecía," further praising "the dignity and specialty of wisdom and grace that God was to infuse for this in Christopher Columbus, as would be called, the excellent and noted sailor and none other like him, as the inventor of noted and admirable novelty in things belonging to sailing as was that Tiphis" (my translation).[87] Tomasso Campanella, in his *Discourse touching the Spanish monarchy* (ca. 1600), also remarked upon the "Admirable Discovery of the New World [...] expressely foretold by Seneca, in his Medea, and there lively set forth in its proper Colours and Names, according as he had received the same from one of the Sibylls."[88]

Francisco López de Gómara, however, was not as convinced that Seneca's words constituted a genuine prophecy. He summarized his opinion with a famous Spanish proverb, "he that speaketh much shall sumtimes stumble on the truth."[89] In his essay "Of Prophecies" (1620), Sir Francis Bacon cited the Medea passage as evidence that "probable conjectures [...] being infinite in number, have been impostures, and by idle and crafty brains merely contrived and feigned, after the event past."[90] Nevertheless, since Columbus's writings were vital to Spain's American dominium, the so-called *Medea* prophecy featured heavily in the seventeenth-century disputations and histories of America written by the English. Building on Elizabethan premises, writers gathered together several patriotic myths and legends pertaining to the country's own destined role in America under the Stuarts. Although the Anglo-Spanish peace of 1605 allowed for unmolested English colonial access to North America as one of its key terms, relations with Spain remained tense into the early 1620s, when negotiations for a Spanish royal marriage between Prince Charles (later Charles I) and the Spanish Infanta María Ana (1606–1646; later Holy Roman Empress 1637–46) had stalled, leading to renewed conflict with the onset of the Thirty Years' War, and a trade dispute that produced the second Anglo-Spanish War of 1654–60.

As tensions came to a head, *Medea* once again turned her vengeful head with a new body of English patriotic literature dedicated to American colonization. There was, for instance, *An Encouragement to Colonies* (1624) by Sir William Alexander, Earl of Stirling, a work dedicated to Prince Charles. Alexander urged the future king "to purchase fame by the Plantation of a New World, nor as many Princes haue done by the desolation of

---

87. Fray Bartolome de las Casas, *Historia de las Indias*, tomo I, segunda edición (México: Fondo de Cultura Económica, 1965), 59.
88. Thommaso Campanella, *A Discourse Touching The Spanish Monarchy. Wherein We have a Political Glasse, representing each particular Country, Province, Kingdome, and Empire of the World, with wayes of Government by which they may be kept in Obedience. As also, The Causes of the Rise and Fall of each Kingdom and Empire* (London: Philemon Stephens, 1653), sig. Ee2r.
89. The passage appeared in Peter Martyr of Angleria's *The Decades of the newe worlde or west India* ..., Rychard Eden, trans. (London: Guilhelmi Powell, 1555), sig. JJjiv.
90. Lord Francis Bacon, *Lord Bacon's Essays with an introductory dissertation and notes*, Joseph Devey, ed. (London: George Bell and Sons, 1888), 104.

this."[91] The title page included a quotation from Virgil's *Eclogues* (4): "*Alter erit tum Tiphys, et altera quae vehat Argo Delectos Heroas*" (Then there will be another Tiphys, and another Argo to carry chosen heroes),[92] presumably equating Charles with the "new Tiphys" who would replace Columbus, discoverer of a New World, "by the Plantation of a New World" in America. Touching on the *Medea*, he wrote:

> [America] neuer came to the knowledge of any Hebrew, Greeke, or Roman, who had the most able mindes to haue found out such a mystery: and howsoeuer some would glose vpon that Fable of *Platoes* Atlantick Iland, I haue neuer obserued any thing amongst the Ancient Writers tending to such a purpose, if it be not these lines of *Seneca* the Tragedian, whereby hee might (if not with a prophetick, yet with a poetick rapture) deliuer that which he had a mind to make the posteritie expect, and was in possibilitie to happen.

In the proceeding lines, however, the work devalued Spain's claim to the discovery:

> If the *Spaniards* would sincerely, and gratefully haue bestowed the benefits whereby God did allure them to possesse this Land for the planting of it with Christians enclined to ciuilitie, and religion, it had at this day considering the excellency of the soyle, for all the perfections that nature could afford; beene the most singularly accomplished place of the world, but it hath infortunatly fallen out farre otherwise.[93]

These comments accorded with the Black Legend arguments against Spain's conduct in the Americas, suggesting that the *Medea* prophecy, if indeed a prophecy, was not commensurate to a divine mandate. Remarking that "the easiness of the prey hath blunted the appetite," Alexander condemned brutality toward the Native Americans, thereby implying a divine covenant for Spanish dominium of America that was broken by Spaniards' arrogance, brutality, and lack of care for their colonial subjects.[94] It was a thoroughly Senecan reading.

For Renaissance readers, *Medea* had endowed Thule with a new sense destined to supplant its earlier association as the northern limit of the Roman Empire (Virgil's "utmost Thule"), but the minor verse historian, Charles Aleyn emphasized the Virgilian sense of an imperial limit, indirectly indicting Spain's conduct in America:

> The prophecie of Seneca did make
> Small way to this discov'rie; it exprest
> Rather a flash of poetry, and spake

---

91. Sir William Alexander, *An Encouragement to Colonies* (London: William Stansby, 1624), sig. A3v.
92. Translation by Andrea Kouklanakis.
93. Alexander, *An Encouragement to Colonies*, sig. F4v.
94. The work next discusses Spain's poor enterprise of plantation colonies (owing to the poor Spanish work ethic), which must be supplied with "Negroes from Angola, and other parts, which being but an vnnaturall merchandise, are bought at a deare rate" for they are always "plotting" for their liberty (sig. B2v). The work next commends England's acumen for plantation colonies, "considering seriously of that which is lately done in Ireland" (sig. B2v). The book underwent two reprints in 1625 and 1630 (STC 341a and STC 342).

> Of Islands in the North, not in the West,
> It is said, that Thule should no longer be
> The boundarie of the Roman Monarchie.[95]

Aleyn traced the discovery of America to the Welsh prince Madoc, as first recounted by Welsh Anglican clergyman and historian, David Powel, in *The Historie of Cambria, now called Wales* (1584). The legend had it that Madoc had discovered America around the year 1170, and so works like Richard Hakluyt's *Discourse on Western Planting* (1584) used Madoc to justify English intrusions upon Spanish American territories. In the *Cosmographie* (1652), further discussed in the next chapter, Peter Heylyn also gave this argument some entertainment, preferring it over the prophetic reading of Seneca:

> But this Argument can bring no necessary, nor so much as a probable inference of any such Continent as this [America], then known to Seneca: *the Poet in that Chorus shewing as well the continual dangers, as the possible effects of Navigation*; that there might be, not that there were more Lands discovered, then those formerly known [...] Madoc the son of Owen Gwinedth Prince of Wales, of purpose to decline ingaging in a Civil war raised in that Estate, in the year 1170. put himself to Sea, and after a long course of Navigation came into this Country [...] And though I needs must say for the honour of Wales, that they have more grounds for what they say, then those which look for this New World in the Atlantis of Plato, the Atlantick Ilands of Aristotle and Plutarch, or the Discoveries of Hanno the Carthaginian: yet am I not so far convinced of the truth thereof, the use of the Mariners Compass being not so antient (without which such a Voyage could not be performed) but that I may conclude with more satisfaction, that this Country was unknown to the former Ages. (my emphasis)[96]

Citing Ortelius, Heylyn accepted the *Medea* passage only as a statement of ancient knowledge—mere inference, not prophecy—also underscoring the Chorus's offense as evidence of Columbus's misreading. He transcribed the *Medea* passage, retaining the erroneous "Tiphys," in place of "Tethys," though he also made another key departure:

> In the last dayes an Age shall come,
> Wherein the all-devouring Fome
> Shall lose its former bounds, and shew
> Another Continent to view.
> New-Worlds, which Night doth now conceal,
> A second Typhis shall reveal;

---

95. Charles Aleyn, *The Historie of That wise and Fortunate Prince, Henrie of that Name the Seventh, King of England. With that famed Battaile, fought between the sayd King Henry and Richard the third named Crookbacke, upon Redmoore neere Bosworth* (London: Willime Cooke, 1638), sig. I8r. See also Romm, "'Novos Orbes' and Seneca in the Renaissance," 98–99.
96. Peter Heylyn, *Cosmographie in Four Bookes: Containing the Chorographie and Historie of the Whole Vvorld, and all the Principall Kingdomes, Provinces, Seas and Isles Thereof* (London: Henry Seile, 1652), sig. Nnnn1v.

And frozen Thule shall no more
Be of the Earth the furthest Shore.[97]

Studley's "small Thule" was now "frozen Thule." It denoted a northern limit (i.e., Iceland), not a western limit. Heylyn further remarked that, "God remembering the promise of his Son, that his Gospel should before the end of the World be preached to all Nations, stirred up one *Christopher Colon* or *Columbus*, born at *Nervy*, in the Signeury of *Genoa*, to be the instrument for finding out those parts of the World, to which the sound of the Gospel had not yet arrived."[98] This explanation accorded with Columbus's own interpretation of his discovery of America as divinely ordained, intended to bring about the New Jerusalem in America. For Heylyn, therefore, the point was not to diminish Columbus's feat, but to amputate the New World from its Spanish imperial body.[99]

Translator Edward Sherburne also used his 1648 edition of *Medea* to challenge, by way of exclusion, the grand narrative of Spain's stylized supremacy. Described by the translator as "not [...] a Translation, but a Paraphrase,"[100] Sherburne's *Medea* altogether omitted the Tethys/Typhis reference from the second Chorus, rendering the famous passage as follows: "The'Age shall come, in fine of many years, wherein the Maine / M'unclose the universall Chaine; / More land may, and new worlds be found, / Nor Thule be Earths farthest Bound."[101] A subsequent annotation remarked that:

> Not a little doe the Spaniards glory in this Prophecy of Seneca; as pointing forth the discovery of America by them first found out. *Sanè non vana, si de Hispanis Hispanus,* sayes Delrius

---

97. Heylyn, *Cosmographie*, sig. Nnnn1v.
98. Heylyn, *Cosmographie*, sig. Nnnn2r.
99. The work narrates that Columbus had sent his brother Bartholomew to request funds for his fated voyage from England's King Henry VII (1457–1509; ruled 1485–1509), but Bartholomew was detained by pirates. He arrived too late, "[for] Christopher [...] not hearing any tidings from him, conceived the offer of his service to have been neglected; and thereupon made his Desires known at the Court of Castile." Heylyn, *Cosmographie*, sig. Nnnn2r. Upon this basis, the English claimed that Spain falsely aggrandized its American entitlements, a charge that also inspired a common stereotype regarding Spanish boastfulness. For example, in his biography of Elizabeth, William Camden wrote, "in the first Session of the Councell of *Trent*, vnder Pope Paul the third, when there was one and the same Embassadour of *Charles* the fifth, Emperour, who was also King of *Spaine*, and that that Embassadour tooke place of the French, by reason of the Emperors right; that, since the Spaniards haue arrogated to themselues the prioritie, not onely by the vertue of the Emperour, but as they are Kings of *Spaine*, because none euer contradicted it." See *The historie of the life and reigne of that famous princesse Elizabeth containing a briefe memoriall of the chiefest affaires of state that haue passed in these kingdomes of England, Scotland, France or Ireland since the yeare of the fatall Spanish invasion to that of her sad and ever to be deplored dissolution : wherevnto also is annexed an appendix of animadversions vpon severall passages, corrections of sundry errours, and additions of some remarkable matters of this history never before imprinted* (London: Thomas Harper, 1629), sig. Kk4v.
100. *Medea: A Tragedie. Written in Latine by Lucius Annaeus Seneca. Englished by E. S. Esq with annotations*, Edward Sherburne, trans. (London: Humphrey Moseley, 1648), sig. A2v.
101. *Medea a tragedie*, sigs. C3r–C3v.

[...] Concerning Thule there is no small difference among Authors. The Poets generally in their Expressions us'd it for a place farre remote, and beyond which there was no knowne land. Pliny makes it to bee an Island six dayes saile from Britaine Northward [in the region of Norway]; some have made it to be an Island in Britaine, and others Britaine it selfe so called.[102]

Accepting the *Medea* passage as "Prophecy," Sherburne then found Thule in the British isles, or even "Britaine it selfe so called." Although he acknowledged theories by geographers Gerard Mercator and Abraham Ortelius that together painted Thule as a "tract of Norway,"[103] he favored the conclusion of "Our English Pausanias (the learned [William] Cambden)"[104] that Thule was located in "Shetland or Hethland, an Island in the Scottish Seas, lying between Norway and Scotland, and under the Dominion of the latter."[105] To this patriotic reading, he added, "the name of this Island Suidas derives [...] some from the Saxon Word Tell, which signifies a Limit, as if it were a Bound of the North and West."[106]

Chief among English efforts to discount Columbus's prophetic reading was this equation of ultima Thule with the classical topos of ultima Britannia, a mass of remote coastlines that preceded ultima Thule. In the *Eclogues*, Virgil described Britannia's whole and complete separation: "Et penitus toto divisos orbe Britannias" (I.66).[107] These words produced a host of assertions by the English of Thule's equation with the British Isles, which could also imply England's destiny in America through the same *Medea* verse that Columbus had made a Spanish prophecy. Camden's *Britannia*, referenced by Sherburne, provided a catalogue of references that appeared to confirm the marginal note (in the English translation), "Thule for Britain,"[108] which Camden supposed to mean the Orkney Islands in Scotland or otherwise the Shetland Islands. First in his list were the lines from Virgil and Seneca.[109] In Edmund Gibson's largely expanded 1695 edition of Camden's *Britannia*, a further case was made for Thule in the Orkney Islands by an appended essay, "Thule of the Ancients," by Sir Robert Sibbald.[110] In Sibbald's essay, *Medea* is skipped, but Seneca is cited among the classical writers who purportedly

---

102. *Medea a tragedie*, sig. G2v.
103. *Medea a tragedie*, sig. G2v.
104. *Medea a tragedie*, sig. G2v.
105. *Medea a tragedie*, sig. G2v.
106. *Medea a tragedie*, sig. G2v.
107. Virgil, *The Eclogues and Georgics*, R.D. Williams, ed. (New York: St. Martin's Press, 1979).
108. I quote the 1610 edition, which contains the English translation by Philémon Holland: William Camden, *Britain, or A Chorographicall Description of the Most flourishing Kingdomes, England, Scotland, and Ireland, and the Ilands adioyning, out of the depth of Antiquitie: Beautified with Mappes of the several Shires of England: Written first in Latine by William Camden*, Philémon Holland, trans. (London: George Bishop, 1610), sig. T3v.
109. Camden, *Britain*, sig. T3v.
110. The essay was also published in James Wallace's *An Account of the Islands of Orkney* (London: Jacob Tonson, 1700).

affirmed Thule's location in Scotland.[111] Thinking diverged on Thule's signification, but as the perceived site of Thule moved farther northward to the British isles and beyond, its association was sufficiently diluted by other significations, such that Spain's former equations could seem a distant memory.

As Thule's presumed location moved farther northward, it also intertwined with an emerging English imperialism. One such rationalization appeared in Nathaniel Crouch's *The English Empire in America* (1685). The work traced the origins of English settlements in America, focusing on the exploits of English heroes, or "our brave English spirits,"[112] who led to the establishment of all 19 colonies since "the first discovery of the New World

---

111. In *Camden's Britannia, Newly Translated into English: With Large Additions and Improvements* (Oxford: Edmund Gibson, 1695), further information is given regarding the naming of certain Tribes of the Scots in Seneca's *Ludus de morte Claudii* (also called the *Apocolocyntnosis*), in the following verses:

    He to submit the *Britains* did compel,
    Beyond the utmost Ocean's bounds who dwell:
    The *Irish Scots* who painted are with blew,
    He forced to the Roman yoke to bow. (sig. L3v).

    This capitalized upon another scribal error (or ambiguity) in the phrase "Scoto Brigantes" (originally Scuta Brigantes, or shielded Brigantes). The translation "*Irish Scots*" apparently originated with French theologian and scholar, Joseph Scaliger, though Camden was dubious of the former's supposition:

    Concerning the time when the name of *Scots* was first broached in the world, there is some dispute; and upon this very point *Humfrey Lhuid* (the best of Antiquaries by the best of Poets) is quarrelied by [Scottish historian George] Buchanan; For *Lhuid* having said that the name of *Scoti* was not to be found in Authors before *Constantine* the Great, Buchanan flies upon him, catches him fast, and with two petty arguments thinks to dispatch him; the one drawn from the Panegyrist, and the other from his own conjecture [...] As for the conjecture, it is not his own, but that of the most learned *Joseph Scaliger*. For in his notes to Propertius, while by the by he restores that verse of Seneca's to the true Reading [...] He puts it *Scotobrigantes;* and forthwith cries out, that the Scots are indebted to him for the discovery of their original; for my part, I am sorry I cannot second this opinion, having ever honour'd him upon many accounts, and much admir'd his learning. For this conjecture is not the product of Copies, but of his own ingenuity and parts and the sense will bear either Reading, *caerules scuta Brigantes* as all the Books have it, or *Caeruleos cute Brigantes*, as the most learned *Hadr. Junius* reads it. Yet Buchanan, (chusing rather to play the fool with his own Wit and that of another, than to close with the common and true Reading) cries up this conjecture to the skies (sig. I2v).

    In Camden's section on Romans in Britain, the Seneca passage is again quoted with the original "Scuta Brigantes" retained.

112. R[obert] B[urton] (Nathaniel Crouch), *The English Empire in America, Or, A Prospect of His Majesties Dominions in the West-Indies [...] with an Account of the Discovery, Scituation, Product, and Other Excellencies of these Countries: To which is Prefixed a Relation of the First Discovery of the New World Called America, by the Spaniards, and of the Remarkable Voyages of several Englishmen to Divers Places Therein : Illustrated with Maps and Pictures by R.B., Author of Englands Monarchs, &c., Admirable Curiosities in England, &c., Historical Remarks of London, &c., the Late Wars in England, &c., and the History of Scotland and Ireland* (London, Printed for Nath. Crouch, 1685), B4r.

called America, by the Spaniards."¹¹³ Correspondingly, on the subject of Thule, Crouch wrote, "The next inquiry may be, whether the Ancient[s] had any knowledge of these Regions [of America], which many incline to think they had not; for though Seneca says in his *Msdea* [sic.], That new Worlds shall be discovered in the last Ages of the World, and Thule in Norway, shall be no longer the utmost Nation of the World, yet this seems only to intimate the common effects and discoveries of Navigation."¹¹⁴

In the words of Nicholas Canny, Crouch's work reflected the view that by the late seventeenth century, "an Empire of trade and dominion had been established [...] and that it was in the national interest to cherish and defend it."¹¹⁵ To glorify this vision of English America, Crouch included the famous quotation from Dryden's *The Indian Emperour, or the Conquest of Mexico by the Spaniards* (1665), "Methinks we walk in dreams of fairy Land," which served as proof of "so happy a climate" of the English empire in America "as our *English* Laureat sings."¹¹⁶ The reference illustrates how deeply these contested meanings of Thule intersected with the divine etiology of America. In the same opening section that discusses the *Medea*, Crouch wrote the following:

> Yet is it not incredible but that in former Ages, some Ships might by Tempest or other Casualties be driven to these parts, whereby some parts of America were peopled [...] The most probable Relation of this kind is that of Madoc ap Owen Gwyneth, who upon the Civil dissentions in his own Countrey of Wales, adventured to Sea, and leaving Ireland on the North, came to a Land unknown, where he saw many very wonderful things, which by Dr. Dowel and Mr. Humfrey Lloyd is judged to be the main Land of America, being confirmed therein, as well by the saying of Montezuma Emperor of Mexico, who declared that his Progenitors were Strangers as well as the rest of the Mexicans, as by the use of divers Welch words amongst them observed by Travellers; the story adds, that Madoc left several of his People there, and coming home, returned back with ten sail full of Welchmen, yet it is certain there are now left very few footsteps of this Brittish expedition, and no signs thereof were found at the Spaniards Arrival.¹¹⁷

Once again, the Welsh knight Madoc served to refute Columbus's *first* discovery, in essence suggesting that Seneca's prophecy instead pointed to the feat of a Briton, as further supported by the Mexica prophecy for foreign rule that was reportedly supplied by Emperor Moctezuma.

These ideas coalesced together in an appended poem by Edmund Waller, "our English Virgill," that was titled "Of a war with Spain, and fight at Sea" (dated to 1656, barely two years into the Second Anglo-Spanish War). The poem weaves together so

---

113. *The English Empire in America*, title page.
114. *The English Empire in America by R.B.*, sig. A3v.
115. Nicholas Canny, "The Origins of Empire," in Nicholas Canny, ed. *The Oxford History of the British Empire, Vol. I: The Origins of Empire* (Oxford: Oxford University Press, 1–33 (22–23).
116. *The English Empire in America*, sig. A2r.
117. *The English Empire in America*, sigs. A3v–A4r.

many Black Legend threads forged in Tudor and Stuart England, that it merits reproduction in full:

> For divers Ages had the Pride of Spain
> Made the Sun Shine on half the World in vain,
> While she bid War to all that durst supply
> The place of those her cruelty made dye.
> Of Natures Bounty men forbore to tast,
> And the best Portion of the Earth lay wast.
> From the New World her Silver and her Gold,
> Came like a Tempest to confound the Old.
> Feeding with these the brib'd Electors hopes,
> Alone she gave us Emperors and Popes,
> With those accomplishing her vast designs
> Europe was shaken with her Indian Mines.
> When Brittain looking with a just disdain
> Upon this gilded Majesty of Spain,
> And knowing well that Empire must decline
> Whose chief support and sinews are of Coin.
> Our Nations solid virtue did oppose
> To the rich Troublers of the Worlds repose,
> They that the whole Worlds Monarchy design'd
> Are to their Ports by our bold Fleet confin'd,
> From whence our Redcross they Triumphant see
> Riding without a Rival on the Sea;
> Others may use the Ocean as their Road.
> Only the English make it there aboad,
> Whose ready Sails with every wind can fly,
> And make a Cov'nant with the inconsistant Sky.
> Our Oaks secure as if there took root,
> We tread on Billows which a steady foot.
> Bold were the men which on the Ocean first
> Spread their new Sails when shipwrack was the worst.
> More danger from the English Spain doth find,
> Than from the Rocks the Billows or the Wind,
> Some Ships are Prize, while others burnt and rent
> With their rich lading to the bottom went
> Down sinks at once (so Fortune with us Sports)
> The pay of Armies and the pride of Courts.
> Vain man! Whose Rage buries as low that store
> As Avarice had digg'd for it before,
> What Earth in her dark bowels could not keep,

128 SPANISH ROMANCE IN THE BATTLE FOR GLOBAL SUPREMACY

> From greedy hands lies safer in the deep.
> Where th' Ocean kindly does from Mortals hide
> Those seeds of Luxury, Debate, and Pride.
> And thus into our hands the richest Prize,
> Falls with the noblest of our Enemies, &c.[118]

Here it all was: the imperial sun of Spain had scorched the earth with war and corruption, but the virtuous English "did Oppose / [...] the rich Troublers of the Worlds repose." This brave stand constituted a "Cov'nant" with the divine, which secured England's naval endeavors and privateering missions, while *almighty* tempests cast Spanish ships into the deep. The brave actions of England's explorers and privateers initiated a new age of Argonauts ("Bold were the men") who would carry the sign of the "Redcross" overseas as an emblem of hope and salvation to places far unknown. Thus, as the poem contends, with Spain's downfall goes to England "the richest Prize."

Coda

In 1875 the Victorian writer Richard Burton published *Ultima Thule; or, A Summer in Iceland*. The work's purpose was: "to clear up the darkness which has been heaped by a host of writers upon 'Thule.'"[119] Burton explained that Thule "applied to Iceland, and to Iceland only, from the earliest ages of its exploration."[120] Regarding the term's classical usage, Burton explained that "when imperial Rome extended her sceptre to the north of 'the Britains;' it was given to the outlying parts, Ireland, Scotland, the Orkneys, the Shetlands, and features known only to fabulous geography."[121] "Between the establishment of Christianity in England," he added, "the official or modern rediscovery, the term Thule was once more, as of old, limited to Iceland."[122] Of the *Medea* verse, Burton wrote only that, "L. Anneaus Seneca [...] first re-echoes Virgil in the celebrated 'prophetic verses,' whose sense has been extended to the New World."[123] The proceeding

---

118. *The English Empire in America*, sigs. I9v–I10r.
119. Richard Burton, *Ultima Thule: or, A Summer in Iceland*, vol. 1 (London: William P. Nimmo, 1875), 1.
120. Burton, *Ultima Thule*, 1.
121. Burton, *Ultima Thule*, 2. The work frequently alludes to Icelandic independence from Danish rule, which may lie behind the Roman equation. The work also corresponds with contemporary interest in travel and exploration in Iceland, which had produced "scenes of thrilling horror, of majestic grandeur, and of heavenly beauty, where our more critical, perhaps more cultivated, taste finds very humble features" (ix–x). Critical of such fantastical accounts, Burton traveled to Iceland "feeling by instinct that many travellers had prodigiously exaggerated their descriptions" (x). Burton's more "matter-of-fact" (xi) account was rather intended to "advocate the development of the island" (xiii).
122. Burton, *Ultima Thule*, 2.
123. Burton, *Ultima Thule*, 3.

30-odd pages of etymological and historiographical research, drawing heavily from the classics (e.g., Virgil, Pliny, Tacitus, etc.), concentrate solely on the classical precedents and passages that, to Burton, clearly pointed northward to the British Isles and then beyond to Iceland, in the process obscuring Thule's perceived connection to the New World, including the pro-Habsburg divinations of Columbus. The Old Enemy is nevertheless heavily present in the work as the implied "darkness which has been heaped by a host of writers upon 'Thule.'"

Burton was resting on the laurels of British writers who had been endeavoring to divorce Thule from its constructed Spanish mythology since the sixteenth century, in the process injecting the myth with England's own nationalist falsehoods. Such references hint at why Thule became an enduring fixture in the English imaginary: this fabled locus and terminus of the known world, denoting the boundaries of Roman imperial expansion, was perceived as a key to global westward expansion with Spain cast at the center. To dismantle the romantic Spanish narrative of the New World was to challenge Spanish supremacy itself. Correspondingly, when English writers turned self-reflexively to the classics in search of "ultima Thule," a "second Tiphys," and even an English Saint George, they were seeking to discover their own argonauts, their own prophetic verses, and their own divine mandate to America.

CHAPTER 5

BELIEVING BOTTOM'S DREAM: RATIONALIZING EXPLORATION FROM AMERICA TO AUSTRALIA

Sir Francis Bacon regarded Spain's progressive decline in the seventeenth century as divine retribution for the country's cruelty and hubris. He noted that there was not one

> of the first Conquerors, but died a violent Death himselfe, And was well followed by the Deaths of many more. Of Examples Enough: Except we should adde the Labours of Hercules: An Example, which though it be flourished with much Fabulous Matter, yet so much it hath, that it doth notably set forth, the Consent of all Nations, and Ages, in the Approbation, of the Extirpating, and Debellating of Gyants, Monsters, and Forreaine Tyrants, not onely as lawfull, but as Meritorious, euen of Diuine Honour.[1]

Invoking translatio imperii, the Pillars of Hercules, so symbolic for Philip, appeared on the title page of Bacon's unfinished work, *Instauratio Magna* (Great Renewal), published in 1620. The work included his famous treatise of empiricism, *Novum Organum, sive Indicia Vera de Interpretatione Naturae* (New organum, or true directions concerning the interpretation of nature) which advocated a scientific method that was inspired by such luminaries as Leonardo da Vinci and Galileo Galilei. The pillars bore the following inscription: "Multi pertransibunt et augebitur Scientia" (Many will pass through and knowledge will be the greater). The frontispiece featured a Stuart vessel passing beyond the Pillars on voyage to America. The message, "many will pass," constituted Bacon's "call to expand English science," in order to "curtail Spanish dominance of overseas expansion."[2]

Nevertheless, while the Age of Exploration widened England's knowledge of the world, planting the seeds of an Age of Reason, it simultaneously prompted belief in the fabulous and improbable, including the exotic faerielands of contemporary romance. This chapter associates the return to faerieland with both the dominant reason (logic) and unreason (rumors, as propagated in poetry, romance, and ancient writings) that informed the geographical heurism of the seventeenth century, as evidenced by the 1652 *Cosmographie in four bookes* of Peter Heylyn. Reviving tales of classical warrior women and

---

1. *Certaine miscellany works of the Right Honourable Francis Lo. Verulam, Viscount S. Alban.* (London: William Rawley, 1629), sig S3v.
2. James Ellison, *George Sandys: Travel, Colonialism, and Tolerance in the Seventeenth Century*, Studies in Renaissance Literature, 8 (Rochester: D. S. Brewer, 2002), 91.

of dubious quests, from *Amadís* and *Espejo* to *The Faerie Queene* and *Midsummer*, Heylyn appealed to poetry's universality, using romance maxims in order to call upon England to expand its exploratory ventures in the project of global conquest.

Of Poets, Lovers, and Madmen

During the first Anglo-Spanish War of 1585 to 1604, there was a real and present need for madmen willing to dream of America. These travelers faced not only the rugged terrain of an unknown continent, replete with mysterious dangers, but also an arduous roundtrip voyage in the path of enemy ships. Upon their return, they faced the stubborn (dis)belief of an English intellectual community in the early throes of a scientific revolution. For a creative mind like William Shakespeare's, "cool reason" must have seemed a most foolish dogma of the age. This concern emerges in the conclusion to *A Midsummer Night's Dream* in the form of Theseus, Duke of Athens, who expresses skepticism over the young lovers' wild tales of the Athenian wood. Their stories all concur, but Theseus declares, "More strange than true. I never may believe / These antique fables nor these fairy toys" (5.1.2–3).[3] "Strange" was a common descriptor for America as deployed by European explorers and colonial enthusiasts. Cortés repeatedly used the word to describe Tenochtitlán, such as in his famous second letter to Charles V, which told of: "la grandeza, extrañas y maravillosas cosas de esta gran ciudad" (the grandeur, strange and marvelous things of this great city).[4] *Strange* was also a preferred term to describe the colonial promised lands of contemporary romance, such as in *Amadís*, which acquainted readers, with "such strange and marvailous things as are to be seene" on Ínsula Firme.[5] The term was later used by John Dryden, who called back to the above speech by Theseus in his play, *The Indian Emperour*.[6]

---

3. All quotations derived from the Oxford edition, Peter Holland, ed. (Oxford: Oxford University Press, 1994).
4. Hernán Cortés, *Cartas y relaciónes de Hernan Cortés al emperador Carlos V*, Pascual de Gayangos, ed. (Paris: A. Chaix y Ca., 1866), 101-102. According to the *Oxford English Dictionary*, "strange" described "persons, language, customs, etc.: Of or belonging to another country; foreign, alien." Alternatively, "Of a country or other geographical feature: Situated outside one's own land." "strange, adj. and n." OED Online. Oxford University Press. https://www-oed-com.
5. *Amadis de Gaule, translated by Anthony Munday*, Helen Moore, ed. (Aldershot: Ashgate, 2004), 311. "Strange" is repeated throughout the work in reference to Ínsula Firme.
6. In Act 1, scene 2 of *The Indian Emperour*, Montezuma's son Guyomar has returned from spying on the approaching Spanish ships, which prompts the following exchange:

> MONT[EZUMA]. What forms did these new wonders represent?
> GUY[OMAR]. More strange than what your wonder can invent.
> The object I could first distinctly view
> Was tall straight trees which on the waters flew,
> Wings on their sides instead of leaves did grow,
> Which gather'd all the breath the winds could blow.
> And at their roots grew floating Palaces,
> Whose out-bow'd bellies cut the yielding Seas.
> MONT[EZUMA]. What Divine Monsters, O ye gods, were these
> That float in air and flye upon the Seas!
> Came they alive or dead upon the shore? (1.2.105–12)

To a man of "cool reason" like Theseus,[7] however, "strange" only calls to mind the wild fantasies of poets, lovers, and madmen:

> Lovers and madmen have such seething brains,
> Such shaping fantasies, that apprehend
> More than cool reason ever comprehends.
> The lunatic, the lover, and the poet
> Are of imagination all compact.
> One sees more devils than vast hell can hold:
> That is the madman. The lover, all as frantic,
> Sees Helen's beauty in a brow of Egypt. (5.1.4–11)

Chief among these disparaged faerie-mongers is the poet, whose boundless imagination "bodies forth / The forms of things unknown and gives to airy nothing / A local habitation and a name" (5.1.16–17). As an allusion to exploration and cartography, this statement has echoes with Spenser's "famous antique history," *The Faerie Queene*. The proem to Book II defends the poem's fictional construction of faerieland as follows:

> RIght well I wote most mighty Soueraine,
>> That all this famous antique history,
>> Of some th'aboundance of an ydle braine
>> Will iudged be, and painted forgery,
>> Rather then matter of iust memory,
>> Sith none, that breatheth liuing aire, does know,
>> Where is that happy land of Faery,
>> Which I so much doe vaunt, yet no where show,
> But vouch antiquities, which no body can know.
>
> But let that man with better sence aduize,
>> That of the world least part to vs is red:

While Guyomar's "More strange than what your wonder can invent" refers to *Midsummer* in Theseus's "More strange than true" speech, the Spanish ships "Whose out-bow'd bellies cut the yielding Seas" also recall the European cargo ships that Titania and her pregnant maid observed from the Indian shore "grow big-bellied with the wanton wind; / Which she, with pretty and with swimming gait, / Following (her womb then rich with my young squire), / Would imitate and sail upon the land" (2.1.133–36). Montezuma's observation that the ships "float in air and flye upon the Seas!" also recalls Puck's "I'll put a girdle round about the Earth / In forty minutes" (2.1.182–83). For more information, see note 44.

7. *Midsummer* uses "cool reason" to mean dispassionate logic based on inference or experience, primarily as a contrast to the more freewheeling inventiveness of poetic imagination (or the purely theoretical branches of natural philosophy). Therefore, this study uses *unreason* to connect with poetry's appeal to the Aristotelian sense of universal truth, which is opposed to the dogmatic rationalism of men like Theseus.

> And daily how through hardy enterprize,
> Many great Regions are discouered,
> Which to late age were neuer mentioned.
> Who euer heard of th'Indian *Peru*?
> Or who in venturous vessell measured
> The *Amazons* huge riuer now found trew?
> Or fruitfullest *Virginia* who did euer vew? (1–2)

The poet's concern that his work would be interpreted as "th'aboundance of an ydle braine" finds realization in Theseus's complaint that poetic imagination "bodies forth / The forms of things unknown…" "[V]ouch[ing] antiquities," Spenser playfully challenged the historicizing of knowledge based solely on firsthand experience. In fact, as we have seen, ancient writers like Aristotle, Seneca, and Virgil had inferred America's existence long before it was first observed. Theseus's ignorance of the truth of the lovers' reports therefore proves that "of the world least part to vs is red" and that men of "better sence" did not "so much misweene / That nothing is, but that which [they] hath seene" (II.pr.3). Indeed, "th'Indian Peru," the "*Amazons* huge riuer now found trew" and "fruitfullest *Virginia*" had made skeptics into believers.

Literature had the power to imagine possibilities about the unknown world that were as yet unverifiable; therefore, any such "antique fables" should not be automatically discounted as purely fabulous. This is further proved in Act 4 of *Midsummer* when Nick Bottom emerges from his sensual romp with the faerie queen, Titania, in the Athenian wood. Proclaiming, "I have had a most rare / vision […] past the wit of man to say / what dream it was" (lines 214–16), he determines to convert his true testimony into delightful fiction:

> Man is but an ass if he go about
> to expound this dream. Methought I was—there
> is no man can tell what […] The eye of
> man hath not heard, the ear of man hath not seen,
> man's hand is not able to taste, his tongue to
> conceive, nor his heart to report what my dream
> *was*. I will get Peter Quince to write a ballad of this
> dream. It shall be called "Bottom's Dream" because
> it hath no bottom; and I will sing it in the
> latter end of a play, before the Duke. (4.2.214–29)

As I discussed in Chapter 2, this speech indirectly cites *Corinthians* in order to represent America's allegorical presence in romance as a "most rare vision" of the inexpressible wonders of the unknown continent. Simultaneously playing the lover, the poet, and the madman, Bottom naturally chooses a ballad to present his testimony to the disbelieving Duke, who "never may believe" such "fairy toys." Echoing faerieland's other famous dream travelers, namely Chaucer's Sir Thopas and Spenser's Arthur, Bottom unknowingly confirms things long suspected but widely disbelieved. The message is that although some dreams, be they the dream of American conquest, or of faeries, lie "past the wit of man," they likely contained a vital kernel of truth.

Once upon a time, the renowned Genoese voyager Christopher Columbus was also thought a madman for daring to undertake his westward voyage to India. In the Elizabethan era, loyal Englishmen like Sir Francis Drake and Sir Walter Raleigh had also traveled to America to "say what dream it was," to "expound" upon it, and to "report" back to England. While the *brave* ventured out in pursuit of this dream, giving to "airy nothing / A local habitation and a name," the curious could simply open a book.

In Search of Amazons

The classical Amazon woman experienced a lively afterlife in early modern romance literature. Her body came to stand in for the fertility and precious materials of America, while her independence and desirability eroticized conquest. This trend was catalyzed by Garci Rodríguez de Montalvo's *Amadís* sequel, *Las Sergas de Esplandián*. First published in 1510, *Esplandían* was a mainstay of the colonial diet, as indicated by its common appearance on the lists of books imported to the Spanish viceroyalties.[8] It first appeared in England in 1598 under the title, *The fift booke of the most pleasant and delectable historie of Amadis de Gaule*, bringing with it the famous tale of an Amazonian queen named Calafia, who rules in the island of California. In the romance, the Persian king Armato has assembled a pagan horde to capture Constantinople from the outnumbered Christians, including Amadís and Esplandián. Among Armato's legions are a tribe of Amazon women led by "Calafre [Calafia] Queene of Califorine, a countrey most rich and abundant in gold and precious stones."[9] With their powerful griffins, the intervening Amazons make a formidable attack upon the assembled knights of "great Brittaine."[10] Emboldened, Calafia challenges Amadís and Esplandián to combat. Ever a servant unto ladies, Amadís is reluctant to make battle with Calafia. Striking him forcefully, however, she declares: "You account mee [...] one of that number [of your helpless ladies]: but you shall presently feele that I am something more."[11] At last, Amadís deals her a decisive blow, and he takes her for his prisoner. Later, while obsequies are observed for the fallen warriors, the emperor of Constantinople offers his daughter Leonorine in marriage to Esplandián, to whom he has also relinquished his territories. This provokes Calafia to confess her own "frustrated"[12]

---

8. See Leonard, *Books of the Brave*, esp. 91–103.
9. *The Fift Booke of the most Pleasant and Delectable Historie of Amadis De Gaule. Containing the First Part of the most Strange Valiant and Worthy Actes of Esplandian Sonne to Amadis De Gaule as His Strange Sailing in the Great Serpent, the Winning of His Sword, Conquest of the Castle La Montaigne Defendu, His Warres with Armato King of Turkie, His Loue to Leonorine Daughter to the Emperour of Constantinople, with Diuers Seruices done in Her Behalfe: The besieging of Constantinople by the Turks and Pagans, with their Ouerthrow by the Christian Princes: His Marriage with Leonorine, His Investing in the Empire of Greece: And Lastly His Enchantment with Diuers Other Princes in the Pallace of Apollidon Deuised by Urganda* (hereafter *Esplandian*) (London: Hugh Iackson, 1598), sig. Kk4r.
10. *Esplandian*, sig. Kk4r.
11. *Esplandian*, sig. Ll4r.
12. *Esplandian*, sig. Mm4r.

plan to marry Esplandián, with whom she is deeply enamored, but as a consolation, Emperor Esplandián offers to marry Calafia to his cousin, Talanque.

Correspondent with the masculine fantasy of martial and marital conquest of pagan women, Calafia responds favorably, and "leauing my law to accept of yours [Esplandián's],"[13] she takes Talanque as husband. She also declares that "the Island wherin I and others my predecessors would not suffer a man to liue, shal from henceforth be gouerned by him as other countries are by their Kings and Princes."[14] Calafia's accession to male rule is significant for the cycle's crusading theme, whereby marriage and military surrender become interdependent conversions. This is further implied by the etymology of her name, which most likely derives from the Arabic caliph, a Muslim ruler. Reflecting the Orientalist projection of the eastern Other onto the unknown west, the conversion trope became ubiquitous in early modern romances. Helen Hackett explains that

> When Amazons feature primarily as warriors and separatist gynocrats, they are represented as fierce and unnatural, as in Book V of *Amadis* where they are savage enemies who ally with the Turks to besiege the Christian defenders of Constantinople. In order to be sympathetic figures, Amazons must be softened by love, and thereby become good breeding stock for future heroes.[15]

Thus, in the sequel, *Lisuarte de Grecia y Perión de Gaula*, by Feliciano de Silva, besieged holy knights in the regions of Constantinople receive aid from "Calafea *reigning in the Isles of Califurnus, where Gold and precious stones doe grow in abundance.*"[16]

For European explorers, especially the Iberian conquistadors, Calafia and her isle of "Gold and precious stones" was instrumental in reigniting interest in discovering the fabled nation of the Amazons, whose hidden abode was thought to be found, not in Africa and Asia Minor as earlier supposed, but in America. Irving Leonard specifically ties *Esplandián*'s account of the Amazonian queen Calafia to the "strong revival [of the Amazon legend] in the early sixteenth century, and the universal belief in its validity among the Spanish conquerors roaming the New World, suggest[ing] that some recent and particularly vivid reminder had brought the subject sharply to mind."[17] This

---

13. *Esplandian*, Mm4r.
14. *Esplandian*, Nn1r.
15. Helen Hackett, *Women and Romance Fiction in the English Renaissance* (Cambridge: Cambridge University Press, 2000), 69. Together, the Knight of the Sun and Claridiana produce an heir, Claridiano, signaling the transfer of female power to a male son. In the seventh book of the *Espejo* cycle, written by Marcos Martínez and published in England in 1598, another Amazonian queen, the lady Archisilora of the Kingdom of Lira (Lyra), is also provided as a love interest for Claridiano.
16. *The Famous and Renowned History of Amadis De Gaule Conteining the Heroick Deeds of Armes and Strange Adventures, Aswell [Sic] of Amadis Himself, as of Perion His Son, and Lisvart of Greece, Son to Esplandian, Emperor of Constantinople [...] Translated Out of French into English by Francis Kirkman* (London: Jane Bell, 1652), sig. Q4v. The switch to the Latin the masculine nominative ending of "Californus" in the 1652 sequel could represent a linguistic homage to Calafia's acceptance of masculine authority.
17. Leonard, *Books of the Brave*, 37.

influence is also suggested by the naming of the peninsular region of Baja California Sur, first charted in 1533, and believed to be a reference to the fabled island of California ruled by Queen Calafia and her gynocratic race of warrior women.[18] The name had been nothing new, for Montalvo had derived it from the all-female city described in *La Chanson de Roland* (Song of Roland), as the author himself attested: "Sabed—dice el poeta—que a la diestra mano de las Indias hubo una isla llamada California, muy llegada a la parte del Paraíso Terrenal, la cual fue poblada de mujeres negras" (Know that—so says the poet—that on the right hand of the Indies there was an island named California, very close to the earthly paradise, which was populated by black women).[19]

Montalvo wrote the books of *Amadís* at a time when it was commonly suspected that Columbus had found a new route to the Asiatic mainland. Whereas Amazons were traditionally reputed to originate in Africa and Asia Minor, Columbus claimed to have espied them in island caves along the Caribbean, to which he had also affixed the term *Indies*.[20] That Queen Calafia's realm of California was supposed to be composed of caves "a la diestra mano de las Indias [...] muy llegada a la parte del Paraíso Terrenal" is further evidence that Montalvo was inspired by the voyager's testimony.[21] As if to confirm the rumor spread by Columbus, in his fourth letter to Charles V, Hernán Cortés also reported that an expedition led by one of his men, Cristóbal de Olid, had discovered an island-dwelling all-female society in Zacatula and Colima:

> At certain times men come over from the mainland with whom the women have intercourse; and those who become pregnant if they bear female children are kept, but if men children they are cast forth from their company. The island, they say, is ten days' journey from this province and many have been and seen it. They report, moreover, that it is very rich in pearls and gold; of all of which I shall endeavor to learn the truth and give a full account of it to your Majesty.[22]

In 1524, Charles commissioned another expedition led by Hernán's nephew, Francisco Cortés de San Buenaventura, to ascertain the truth of these reports of Amazons; the voyage was inconclusive.[23]

Rumors of American Amazons persisted among the English, who were eager to probe this foreclosed continent in search of the earthly paradise. The most forceful evidence of this obsession was Sir Walter Raleigh's eager pursuit of Amazons in Guiana,

---

18. The first Spaniard to arrive on Baja California is believed to be Fortún Ximénez, who landed there in 1533. This was followed in 1535 by an expedition by Hernán Cortés.
19. Garci Ordóñez (Rodríguez) de Montalvo, *Las Sergas del virtuoso caballero Esplandián, hijo de Amadís de Gaula* (Sevilla, 1510), (Madrid: Biblioteca de Autores Españoles, 1857), 539.
20. Leonard, *Books of the Brave*, 37.
21. For further discussion, see Leonard, *Books of the Brave*, 40; Dora Polk, *The Island of California: A History of the Myth* (Lincoln: University of Nebraska Press, 1995), esp. 121–32.
22. Hernando Cortés, "The Fourth Letter," in *Five Letters: 1519–1626*, second edition (London: Routledge, 2014), 243–86 (253).
23. See Leonard, *Books of the Brave*, 48–51.

following in the footsteps of Diego de Ordaz from his first expedition to the region in 1531–32:

> I made inquirie amongst the most ancient and best traueled of the *Orenoqueponi*, & I had knowledge of all the riuers between *Oreneque* and *Amazones,* and was very desirous to vnderstand the truth of those warlike women, because of some it is beleeued, of others not […] The nations of these women are on the south side of the riuer in the Prouinces of *Topago,* and their chiefest strengths and retraicts are in the Ilands scituate on the south side of the entrance, some 60 leagues within the mouth of the said riuer. The memories of the like women are very ancient as well in *Africa* as in *Asia:* In *Africa* those that had *Medusa* for *Queene*: others in *Scithia* neere the riuers of *Tamais* and *Thermadon:* we find also that *Lampedo* and *Marthesia* were *Queens* of the *Amazones*: in many histories they are verified to haue been, and in diuers ages and Prouinces.[24]

Although Raleigh did not directly mention *Esplandián*, his acknowledgment of differing accounts is indicative of his wide study of both romances and the classics.[25] Of these women's reproductive habits, he further wrote:

> But they which are not far from *Guiana* do accompanie with men but once in a yeere, and for the time of one moneth, which I gather by their relation to be in Aprill […] This one moneth, they feast, daunce, & drinke of their wines in abundance, & the Moone being done, they all depart to their owne Prouinces. If they conceiue, and be deliuered of a sonne, they returne him to the father, if of a daughter they nourish it, and reteine it, and as many as haue daughters send vnto the begetters a present, all being desirous to increase their own sex and kind, but that the cut of the right dug of the brest I do not finde to be true.[26]

This passage suggests that Raleigh had studied the *Historia general de las Indias* of Francisco López de Gómara, who had also rejected the classical notion of breast mutilation.[27] A similar account of the Amazon women's reproductive habits was also provided by Fray Gaspar de Carvajal, who had traveled with Francisco de Orellana in an expedition to chart the Amazon basin in 1542. An interview with a native prisoner yielded testimony of an all-female society in the Amazon basin ruled by a formidable pagan queen.[28]

---

24. *Sir Walter Raleigh's Discovery of Guiana*, Joyce Lorimer, ed. (London: The Hakluyt Society, 2006), Lambeth Palace MS 250.
25. Raleigh's reference to *Thermadon* in Asia Minor invokes the Amazon capital of Themiscyra where Hercules captured the Amazon queen's sacred girdle. Herodotus wrote that some of the captured Amazons escaped into Scythia, and joined with local hunters, crossed the *Tainais* river Don. The references to *Lampedo* or Lampedona and *Marthesia,* or Mariñsa invoke the queens of the Amazons from Ordericus Vitalis's twelfth-century *Historica ecclesiastica* and Giovanni Boccaccio's *De Claris Mulieribus*, as well as *Orlando Furioso*.
26. *Sir Walter Raleigh's Discovery of Guiana*, Joyce Lorimer, ed. (London: The Hakluyt Society, 2006), Lambeth Palace MS 250.
27. Lorimer, ed., *Sir Walter Raleigh's Discovery of Guiana* (Lambeth Palace MS 250, note 2).
28. He remarked, "And the captain [Orellana] asked him whether these women gave birth; he said that yes, and the captain asked how […] the Indian responded that these women engage with men at certain times and that when they have that certain desire, from an adjoining province governed by a great lord, these men, white except without beards, would come to

Likewise, excerpts from Spanish accounts were to be found in Peter Martyr's *Decades of the New World*.

It is telling that Raleigh should have been seeking Amazons at all in *Guiana*, which was better known for its boasts pertaining to the fabled golden city of El Dorado.[29] For Raleigh, however, these were shared enterprises; he hoped to secure control of Guiana in order to gather an invasion of gold-rich Perú, and from there spread his conquest to other Spanish-American territories. Although gold was his chief concern, Raleigh recognized that any colonization attempt would result in armed confrontation with the Spanish in the New World. The best chances for success would be if the local Indian nations were to ally with the English against the Spanish, just as Cortés had allied with the Tlaxacalans to defeat the forces of Emperor Moctezuma or as Pizarro had organized oppressed Huancas, Chankas, Cañais, and Chachapoyas to mount his attack against the Inca hosts of Emperor Atawallpa. To defeat the Spanish, Raleigh would need an army, one ideally composed of the descendants of the fabled king of Manõa "El Dorado" and their allies, and of the much-feared nations of the Amazons.

El Dorado: Gilded for a Queen

> It was farther told me, that if in the wars they tooke any [men] Prisoners, that they used to accompany with those also at what tyme soever, but in the end for certein they putt them to death, for they are said to be very cruell and bloodthirsty, especiallie to such as offer to invade their terrytories.[30]
>
> —Sir Walter Raleigh, *The Discovery of Guiana* (1596)

With English observers closely following the colonial exploits of Spaniards and Portingales in the New World, rumors of fierce American Amazons dwelling in the region of Guiana, the suspected location of El Dorado, were galvanizing reminders of the formidable Spanish threat, "for whatsoever Prince shall possesse it [El Dorado], shalbe [the] greatest, and if the king of *Spayne* enjoy it, he will become unresistable."[31] Certainly, these powerful female warriors, if discovered, might represent real challenges to the English if they should attempt an invasion, but more so if they should league with

---

      make congress with these women for some time and later depart. The women who become pregnant, if they birth sons, they say that they kill them or send them to their fathers, and if a female that the women raise them with much joy, and they say that all these women have as their chief lady whom they obey one whom they call Coroni" (my translation). Fray Gaspar de Carvajal, O.P., *Relación del nuevo descubrimiento del Famoso rio grande de las Amazonas*, J. Hernández Millares, ed. (Mexico City: Fondo de Cultura Económica, 1955), 104–5.

29. Raleigh was actually chasing a legend of El Dorado that originated in Colombia, though he did not know this at the time, and so he instead found himself exploring the Amazonian basin between what are now the countries of Venezuela and Guyana, significantly farther south than where it originated.
30. *Sir Walter Raleigh's Discovery of Guiana* (Lambeth Palace MS 250).
31. *Sir Walter Raleigh's Discovery of Guiana* (Lambeth Palace MS 250).

the enemy cause, just as Queen Calafia's army had done by aiding the invading Persians in Constantinople. Raleigh's pursuit of these "warlike women" in Guiana was therefore suggestive of a desire to exploit the fabled female warrior population for English interests. He proposed that an alliance might be brokered between the separatist women and his sovereign queen, one that he hoped to broker with the native Inca population of El Dorado more generally:

> I am resolved that if there were but a small army afoot in Guiana, marching towards Manoa [Manõa] the chief city of Inca, he would yield to Her Majesty [...] and that he would besides pay a garrison of three or four thousand soldiers very royally to defend him against other nations. Her Majesty heereby shall confirme and strengthen the opinions of al nations, as touching her great and princely actions. And where the south border of Guiana reacheth to the Dominion and Empire of the Amazones, those women shall heereby heare the name of a virgin, which is not onely able to defend her own territories and her neighbors, but also to invade and conquer so great Empyres and so farre removed.[32]

This depiction of Elizabeth as a great conqueror, masculinely warlike—Amazonian—had its origins earlier in the Anglo-Spanish War, dating back to her personal appearance to the troops at Tilbury on the eve of the Armada. Elizabeth's oft-quoted speech to the troops particularly highlighted the commixture of the masculine and the feminine in her royal person, divinely ordained by the cause the virgo bellatrix was called to fight:

> come let us Fight the battell of the Lorde [...] It maybe that they will challenge my [sexe] For that I am a woman so may I charge [their] mo[uld] [f]or that they ar but [men] [...] if God doe not charge England with the sinnes of England we shall not neede to feare what Rome or Spayne can doe against us w: whom is but An ar[mi]e o[f] Flesh where as with us in the Lord our God to Fight our battells.[33]

In the years following this famous event, Elizabeth's Amazonian identification was greatly elaborated, with many accounts noting her divine appearance, supposedly upon a white horse, with "martiall staffe" in hand,[34] and, according to some accounts, wearing a breastplate.[35] Susan Frye observes that "Tilbury offered [...] the opportunity to allegorize the Queen's chastity not only as Amazonian or goddess-like, but as intimately connected with the natural order [...] Elizabeth's militancy is that of an empress who prefers peace to war."[36]

---

32. *Sir Walter Raleigh's Discovery of Guiana* (Lambeth Palace MS 250).
33. Qtd. in Susan Frye, "The Myth of Elizabeth at Tilbury," *Sixteenth Century Journal* 23, no. 1 (1992), 95–114 (102).
34. *A Joyful Song of the Royall receiuing of the Queenes most excellent Maiestie unto her...Campe at Tilburie* (London: Richard Jones, 1588).
35. Winfried Schleiner, "'Divina Virago': Queen Elizabeth as an Amazon" *Studies in Philology* 75, no. 2 (1978), 163–80. Schleiner notes that there is no reliable account for what Elizabeth wore that day, beyond that she rode on a horse and carried a truncheon in her hand. The image of the Amazonian Elizabeth was rather the product of historical memory.
36. Frye, "The Myth of Elizabeth at Tilbury," 108.

In keeping with this contrary image of Elizabeth as a pacifist Amazon (one who was nevertheless not pacified), George Chapman further elaborated the image of the New World as a female subject eager to be conquered by a righteous queen of peace:

> *Guiana*, whose rich feete are mines of golde,
> Whose forehead knockes against the roofe of Starres,
> Stands on her tip-toes at faire *England* looking,
> Kissing her hand, bowing her mightie breast,
> And every signe of all submission making,
> To be her sister, and the daughter both
> Of our most sacred Maide: whose barrennesse
> Is the true fruite of virtue, that may get,
> Beare and bring foorth anew in all perfection,
> What heretofore savage corruption held
> In barbarous *Chaos*; and in this affaire
> Become her father, mother, and her heire. (lines 14–29)[37]

This sorority of the maiden country and "sacred" England coopts the Habsburg fantasy of Europa regina.[38] It serves as a rationalization for England's desired conquest of America, to bring the pagan world out of the world of "savage corruption" and turn "barbarous *Chaos*" into holy order. In Morley's *Triumphes*, similarly, Guiana represents a mirror for the queen's "royall Maiden[head]." Here the Amazons are not conquered by forceful one-to-one conquest, as in Britomart's encounter with Radigund, but rather softened into graces through Elizabeth's virtuous example, as a song by John Wilbye suggests:

> The Lady Oriana
> Was dight all in the treasures of Guiana,
> And on her Grace a thousand Graces tended,
> a thousand Graces tended,
> And thus sang they,
> faire Queene of peace & plenty,
> The fairest queene of twentie,
> Then with an Oliue wreath for peace renowned,
> Her Virgins head they crowned;
> Which ceremony ended,

---

37. George Chapman, "De Guiana carmen Epicum," in Richard Hakluyt, *The Principal Navigations Voyages Traffiques and Discoveries of the English Nation In Twelve Volumes*, vol. X, reprinted from the 1600 edition (Glasgow: James MacLehose and Sons, 1904), 446–50.
38. Created in tribute to the Habsburg dynasty, *Europa regina* was a cartographical depiction of Europe with the countries and coastlines rearranged to form the figure of a comely woman. Popular during the 1500s, the map depicted Europe with the Iberian Peninsula comprising her crowned head, and Bohemia as her heart.

Which ceremony ended,
Unto her Grace the thousand Graces bended.
Then sang the shepherds & Nimphs of Diana,
Long live faire Oriana,
Long live faire Oriana,
faire Oriana.[39]

The opening line, "The lady Oriana was dight all in the treatures of Guiana," proclaims Elizabeth as an empress of "peace & plenty," following an imagined English conquest of Guiana.[40] Thus, the pacified Amazons are imagined to have here "bended" to Elizabeth, upon whose "Virgins head they crowned." The peaceful pageantry, inspired by Petrarch's *Trionfi*, strongly implies Elizabeth's right to rule.

Raleigh also cited Elizabeth's characteristic chastity and formidable military mind as meritorious of her accession in Guiana.[41] In witness to this grand design, he also reported of a native Inca prophecy, of dubious origin, that spoke of English salvation of the New World. It closely mirrored that reportedly spoken the by augers of Emperor Moctezuma, which Cortés had supplied to Charles in defense of his conquest of México:

> And I further remember that Berreo confessed to me and others, which I protest before the Majesty of God to be true, that there was found among the prophecies in Peru, at such time as the empire was reduced to the Spanish obedience, in their chiefest temples, amongst divers others which foreshadowed the loss of the said empire, that from Inglatierra those Ingas should be again in time to come restored, and delivered from the servitude of the said conquerors.[42]

Publishing his *Discovery of Guiana* in 1596, Raleigh was also conscious of the need to rouse Englishmen's desires in support of this new America enterprise.

---

39. Iohn Wilbye, "The lady Oriana. XV," in *Triumphs of Oriana*, sig. D1r. Line breaks indicate repeating refrains.
40. This image represented a fantasy of England surpassing the fabled riches won by Spain through its American conquests. For instance, Raleigh's *Discovery of Guiana* reported that when the Spanish weighed the treasures of Emperor Atawallpa, they "founde fiftie and two thousand markes of good siluer, and one million, and three hundred twentie and six thousand and fiue hundred pesos of golde. Nowe although these reports may seeme straunge, yet if wee consider the many millions which are daily brought out of *Peru* into Spaine, wee may easely beleeue the same, for we finde that by the abundant treasure of that country, the Spanish King vexeth all of the Princes of Europe, and is become in a fewe yeares from a poore king of *Castile* the greatest monarke of this part of the worlde, and likelie euery day to increase" (MS 250).
41. The title page of the fifth volume of Braun and Hogenberg's *Civitates Orbis Terrarum*, two female figures representing Peace and Justice embrace under the wings of a dove. The image was invoked in Elizabeth's so-called *Peace Portrait* (or Wanstead Portrait), a 1585 portrait by Marcus Gheeraerts the Elder that famously depicted the queen holding an olive branch and standing on the sword of justice. In Wilbye's madrigal, this ethos is further signaled by an "Oliue wreath for peace renowned."
42. *Sir Walter Raleigh's Discovery of Guiana* (Lambeth Palace MS 250).

As if a hidden paradise of exotic women weren't enticement enough, he assured that:

> Those commanders and chieftains that shoot at honour and abundance shall find there more rich and beautiful cities, more temples adorned with golden images, more sepulchres filled with treasure, than either Cortes found in Mexico or Pizarro in Peru. And the shining glory of this conquest will eclipse all those so far-extended beams of the Spanish nation.[43]

God, glory, and gold: the three desires motivating England's envies and conquests throughout the sixteenth century were now mobilized to discover an empire that promised to surpass the fabled riches of the Moctezumas and of the Children of the Sun. There can be no doubt as to the rationale for the ferocity of Raleigh's hopes. El Dorado promised riches and conquest, honour and plenty: an English empire upon which the sun never set. In Guiana Raleigh saw far more than an opportunity to rewrite his legacy; he saw eternity.

England "holds the chase"

With near-constant sea and land skirmishes in Europe and the New World, the Anglo-Spanish War plunged the transatlantic world into perpetual chaos and discord. And the imperial competition between Elizabeth and Philip, which began as a failed courtship and dynastic marriage, was dramatized most plainly in the contest for America. In *Midsummer,* this race for global supremacy is allegorized by the competition between Titania and Oberon, two monarchal pillars of Europe, who could "the globe […] compass soon, / Swifter than the wand'ring moon" (4.1.101–2).[44] Consequently, their quarrel for possession of the Indian boy has set the world in commotion. As Chapman related of Spain's transatlantic colonization, "Those Conquests […] like generall earthquakes shooke / The solid world, and made it fall before them" (lines 45–46). Supplicating with his queen to undertake the pagan world's salvation, he added, "such ascending Majestie as you: / Then be not like a rough and violent wind / […] / let thy sovereign empire be increased, / And with Iberian Neptune part the stake, / Whose trident he the triple world would make" (lines 51–65).[45] This Elizabethan stand against Spain manifests in

---

43. *Sir Walter Raleigh's Discovery of Guiana* (Lambeth Palace MS 250).
44. The "wand'ring moon" corresponds with Puck, who declares: "I'll put a girdle round about the Earth / In forty minutes" (2.1.182–83). Puck's "girdle" alludes to an aerial circumnavigation akin to Ferdinand Magellan's voyage by sea, of 1519–22 (completed by Magellan's associate, Juan Sebastián Elcano after his death). Abraham Ortelius's world map in *Teatrum Orbo* depicts, sailing westward across the Atlantic, Magellan's famous ship, the Victoria, with the following inscription: "Prima ego velivolis ambivi cursibus Orbem, Magellane novo te duce ducta freto. Ambivi, meritoque vocor Victoria: sunt mî Vela, alæ; precium, gloria: pugna mare de Magell navi" (I was the first to sail around the world by means of sails, and carried you, Magellan, leader, first through the straits. I sailed around the world, therefore I am justly called Victoria, my sails were my wings, my prize was glory, my fight was with the sea.)
45. Chapman, "De Guiana carmen Epicum." Medieval mapmakers divided the world in three parts: Asia, Europe, and Africa.

the play in the form of the environmental disruptions provoked by Oberon's possessive bid for the boy's loyalty and Titania's refusal to deliver the boy to him. As Titania relates:

> These are the forgeries of jealousy;
> And never, since the middle summer's spring,
> Met we on hill, in dale, forest, or mead,
> By pavèd fountain or by rushy brook,
> Or in the beachèd margent of the sea,
> To dance our ringlets to the whistling wind,
> But with thy brawls thou hast disturbed our sport.
> [...]
> Therefore the moon, the governess of floods,
> Pale in her anger, washes all the air,
> That rheumatic diseases do abound.
> And thorough this distemperature we see
> The seasons alter: hoary-headed frosts
> Fall in the fresh lap of the crimson rose,
> And on old Hiems' thin and icy crown
> An odorous chaplet of sweet summer buds
> Is, as in mockery, set. The spring, the summer,
> The childing autumn, angry winter, change
> Their wonted liveries, and the mazèd world
> By their increase now knows not which is which.
> And this same progeny of evils comes
> From our debate, from our dissension;
> We are their parents and original. (2.1.84–120)

The moon is "Pale in her anger" because Titania and her votaresses have been prevented from keeping their vigils by Oberon's quarrel over possession of the Indian boy, who presumably never appears onstage though he is ever-present as the cause of the current chaos.[46]

Since the prime imperative of nature is reproduction, Oberon's jealousy is conspicuously *unnatural*. So, too, is Titania's forswearing Oberon's "bed and company" (2.1.64), though it represents a virtuous stand against his overbearing need for power. As Titania's fairy servant explains to Puck in Act 2, scene 1:

> FAIRY
> I serve the Fairy Queen,
> To dew her orbs upon the green.
> The cowslips tall her pensioners be;

---

46. For a history of the Indian boy in performance, consult Margo Hendricks, "'Obscured by Dreams': Race, Empire, and Shakespeare's *A Midsummer Night's Dream*," *Shakespeare Quarterly* 47.1 (1996), 37–60.

In their gold coats spots you see;
Those be rubies, fairy favors;
In those freckles live their savors.
I must go seek some dewdrops here
And hang a pearl in every cowslip's ear. (2.1.8–32)

As Puck coyly alludes, by their quarrel over the Indian boy, Oberon and Titania no longer "meet in grove or green, / By fountain clear or spangled starlight sheen." Hence, Titania's fairy servant must adorn the landscape with "orbs upon the green," substituting her literal barrenness with symbols of monarchal potency.[47] We might compare this to the activities of pensioners and privateers like Drake and Raleigh, who conquered New Albion in Elizabeth's name. The cowslips specifically implicate Raleigh, who used to wear a pearl in his ear in homage to his queen's favorite accessory.[48]

Titania's bid for stewardship of the changeling boy against the tyranny of Oberon's demands, which has caused so much natural commotion, literalizes the salvation theme that had developed in romance's allegorical representation of America. Titania's chastity furthermore recalls the Elizabethan ethos that saw America as a natural "recompense for the queen's virginity."[49] This theme is supported by America's related fecundity, which also comes to the fore with Titania's relation of the boy's origin:

His mother was a vot'ress of my order,
And in the spicèd Indian air by night
Full often hath she gossiped by my side
And sat with me on Neptune's yellow sands,
Marking th' embarkèd traders on the flood,
When we have laughed to see the sails conceive
And grow big-bellied with the wanton wind;
Which she, with pretty and with swimming gait,
Following (her womb then rich with my young squire),
Would imitate and sail upon the land
To fetch me trifles and return again,

---

47. The "orb" is a prop of monarchal power. The pearls of dew that the faerie must hang "in every cowslip's ear" recall Virginia, "Land of Pearls," so-called for its very rich stores. Thomas Hariot wrote that one of his expedition companions, "a man of skill in such manners" had obtained about 5,000 pearls from some native Virginians and with them made a "fayre chaine, which for their likenesse and vniformitie in roundnesse, orientnesse, and pidenesse of many excellent colours, with equalitie in greatnesse, were verie fayre and rare; and had therefore beene presented to her Maiestie." See *A Briefe and True Report of the New Found Land of Virginia* (Frankfurt on the Main: 1590), sig. B2r.
48. James Nohrnberg, "Raleigh in Ruins, Raleigh on the Rocks," in *Literary and Visual Ralegh*, Christopher Armitage, ed. (Manchester, England: Manchester University Press, 2016), 31–88 (69).
49. Henry Buchanan, "'India' and the Golden Age *in A Midsummer Night's Dream*," *Shakespeare Survey* 65, no. 1 (2012): 58–68 (65).

As from a voyage, rich with merchandise.
But she, being mortal, of that boy did die,
And for her sake do I rear up her boy,
And for her sake I will not part with him. (2.1.127–42)

As the Indian boy associates merchandise, the locus of Philip's desire, so too, does the "spicèd Indian air" recall the environment of transatlantic traffic and piracy, which has resulted from the post-Columbian world's evolution of navigation and global commerce.[50] As Kim Hall observes, Titania's description of the Indian boy "mystif[ies] Indian plunder and, possibly, slavery, in aligning the young squire with new world merchandise and hinting at the process of colonial trade in the pregnancy."[51] Meanwhile, Titania's "female refusal to trade [with Oberon] also suggests that we should at that point place Titania in league with the unconquered Amazons (unlike Hyppolyta) who run throughout colonial tracts as obstacles to foreign conquest."[52] The play's exposition of Titania's maternal care furthermore imagines native Indian preferment of feminine (English) rule, thus conjuring the "colonial rhetoric that the American Indians under the Spanish yoke (and Papal decree) sought English love and vassalship instead."[53] This matches with Spenser's prophetic claim in *The Faerie Queene*, invoking the contemporary mystification of America as Thule, that the Faeries "all Nations did subdew" from India to "all that America men call" (II.x.72).

As a votaress to the moon, "governess of floods," Titania further aligns the faerie queen to Elizabeth, as well as her faerie avatars, Belphoebe and Cynthia, inspired by the moon-goddess Diana. As the moonlight is created by the reflected light of the sun,

---

50. These ventures are embodied in Shakespeare's vague allusions to India, which direct the audience circuitously through Asia Minor and back to the West Indies in a symbolic retracing of the confused trajectory of Columbus. This split focus has borne scholarly disagreement over the precise location of Shakespeare's India. For a discussion of the play's association of subcontinental India, see Imtiaz Habib. "Bengal as Shakespeare's India and the Stolen Indian Boy: The Historical Dark Matter of *A Midsummer Night's Dream*," *Early Modern Literary Studies* 20.1 (2018), 1–27; and Shankar Raman, *Framing "India": The Colonial Imaginary in Early Modern Culture* (Stanford: Stanford University Press, 2001), 22. For a reading of the play in relation to the eastern spice trade, see Gitanjali Shahani, "The Spiced Indian Air in Early Modern England," *Shakespeare Studies* 42 (2014), 122–40; and R. W. Desai, "England, The Indian Boy, and the Spice Trade in *A Midsummer Night's Dream*," in *India's Shakespeare: Translation, Interpretation, and Performance*, Poonam Trivedi and Dennis Bartholomeusz, eds. (Delhi: Pearson Education India, 2005), 127–41. For discussion of the play in relation to transatlantic colonialism, see, e.g., Ania Loomba, "The Great Indian Vanishing Trick: Colonialism, Property, and the Family in *A Midsummer Night's Dream*," in *A Feminist Companion to Shakespeare*, Dympna Callaghan, ed. (London: John Wiley and Sons, 2016), 181–205; Jyotsna Singh, *Colonial Narratives/Cultural Dialogues: "Discoveries" of India in the Language of Colonialism* (London: Routledge, 1996).
51. Kim F. Hall, *Things of Darkness: Economies of Race and Gender in Early Modern England* (Ithaca: Cornell University Press, 1995), 85.
52. Hall, *Things of Darkness*, 85.
53. Buchanan, "'India' and the Golden Age," 67.

so is the sun reflected by Diana, in the form of Oberon, faerieland's tyrant and chief antagonist. The setting during midsummer night marks the period of the sun's greatest encroachment upon the night, which is also when Oberon carries out his love plots. Himself a creature of the night, Oberon is nevertheless at odds with the other fairies, who "do run / By the triple Hecate's team / From the presence of the sun / Following darkness like a dream" (5.1.400–403). Appearing at the house of Theseus in Act 5, he commands, "through the house give glimmering light, / By the dead and drowsy fire. / Every elf and fairy sprite, / Hop as light as bird from brier, / And this ditty after me, / Sing and dance it trippingly" (5.1.408–13). As a harbinger of the light, Oberon is right that he and Puck are:

> …spirits of a different sort.
> I with the Morning's love have oft made sport
> And, like a forester, the groves may tread
> Even till the eastern gate, all fiery red,
> Opening on Neptune with fair blessèd beams,
> Turns into yellow gold his salt-green streams. (3.2.411–15)

Oberon's connection to Phoebus (and so, to Philip) is further reflected by his intermeddling in Helena's pursuit of the profligate lover, Demetrius, to which she remarks, "the story will be chang'd / Apollo flies, and Daphne holds the chase" (2.1.219–200).[54] His interference indicates a character who seeks to impose his dogma on others though he thinks that the rules do not apply to him. For instance, upon their first meeting, "Ill met by moonlight," "jealous Oberon" complains to "proud" and "wanton" Titania of her infidelity (alluding to her "love to Theseus"). In response, Titania complains of his love for Hippolyta:

> Why art thou here,
> Come from the farthest step of India,
> But that, forsooth, the bouncing Amazon,
> Your buskined mistress and your warrior love,
> To Theseus must be wedded, and you come
> To give their bed joy and prosperity? (2.1.70–75)

Oberon's intervention into the lovers' plot, which ends up causing more harm than good (as his servant, Puck, muddles things), therefore underscores the "barbarous *Chaos*" that

---

54. The reference is to the story of Apollo and Daphne from Ovid's *Metamorphoses* in which the lustful god (shot with Cupid's arrow of love) chases after the repulsed nymph, Daphne, who, taking after Apollo's sister, Diana, prefers woodland sports and perpetual virginity. Shot with a lead-tipped arrow of disgust, she flees from Apollo, and she is turned into a laurel tree in resistance of his conquest. The story is retold in verse in Montemayor's *Diana*.

Chapman had comparatively tied to Spain's unvirtuous conquests, and which arguably necessitated English intervention.

Taking up the subject of masculine tyranny as an excess of unnatural, possessive desire, capacious and profligate in its objects, the play's frustrated love plots also reproduce in comic form the arguments for and against perpetual virginity, alternating symbols of obeisance and insubordination as represented by Titania/Hippolyta and Hermia/Helena. The competing narratives of the Anglo-Spanish War had a similar funhouse-mirror effect. One spoke of a powerful Sun King, drenched in the *blessed beams* of Christian theology and ancient wisdom, seemingly destined to rule over a vast global empire and making a mockery of his English enemy's imperial barrenness. The other spoke of a formidable virgin monarch who had famously *singed the king's beard* by the conquests of her privateers and Sea Dogs.[55] Paralleling the theme of cosmic changeability related in Spenser's unfinished *Mutability Cantos*,[56] Shakespeare further characterized Elizabeth as Daphne turning the chase upon Apollo. Hence, "the story will be changed."

Comically challenging the common epithet for the Spanish king, who boasted that his rule extended from India to farthest Thule, is Titania's observation that Oberon has to the Athenian forest "Come from the farthest steep of India" (2.1.69). If India points eastward to "the farthest steep," then the Athenian forest directs the audience to the extreme west, to a *new world* cast in symbolic darkness, embodied by the faeries, who "run / By the triple Hecate's team / From the presence of the sun / Following darkness like a dream." As they bring forth the liberating impulse of the night and of the sovereign moon, honored and marked by virtually every character in the play, the faeries imply Elizabethan salvation of terra incognita. As Athens denotes the masculine civilized world, the forest denotes its female opposite: a place of infinite possibility and undefined futurity, whose limits are bounded only by the boundless travels of its mysterious inhabitants. In the tradition of Gloria Anzaldúa, Margo Hendricks calls this space a *borderland*, but whereas she is more concerned with how faerieland's "easy violation of borders—both speciegraphical and geographical—adumbrates an ontological engagement with the linguistic complexities of *mestizaje*,"[57] I am here concerned with how fairieland shapes the Anglo-Spanish conflict as fluid, natural, and *romantic*. Occupying the liminal space between the civilized and uncivilized worlds, and between the imperial nodes of day and night, the forest is itself an America, a world beyond the primal boundary. This space

---

55. Coined by Sir Francis Drake, this expression *singed the king's beard* referred to England's successful privateering raids of the 1580s, specifically the victory at Cádiz.
56. For example, from the *Mutability Cantos*: "each of you [gods or stars] / [...] / Is checkt and changed from his nature trew, / By others opposition or obliqued view" (VII.vii.54.6-9). Invoking the power that planets exercise upon one another in orbit, the lines also call back to the example of Venus eclipsing Phoebus in verse 51: "that goodly Paragone, / Though faire all night, yet is she darke all day; / And Phoebus self, who lightsome is alone, / Yet is he oft eclipsed by the way, / And fills the darkened world with terror and dismay" (lines 5-9). Venus was another avatar for Elizabeth.
57. Hendricks, "'Obscured by Dreams,'" 56.

flees the penetrative impulse of conquest, with its imported value systems and imposed order, and yet, by the unnatural, mediating presence of Oberon, faerieland mirrors the patriarchal totality (tyranny) of Athens, a world ruled by men.

In the unnatural conflict between Oberon and Titania, the play therefore realizes a patriarchal fantasy of control over love, the operative theme of romantic conquest, which could be read against the reality of Queen Elizabeth's never having married. In imagining this dysfunctional marriage, Shakespeare affirms the wisdom of the queen's de facto chastity.[58] Ironic given his earlier jealousy, Oberon becomes a willing cuckold in matching Titania to Bottom, who will replace the Indian boy in the fairy queen's dotage. This is the consequence of Titania's having "forsworn [Oberon's] bed and company" (2.1.62); she is twice barren, deprived of her beloved child and matched to a twisted beast of nature. Allegorically, this childlessness corresponds with the failed conquests of the 1590s, when much ventured in America led to little gain by way of a permanent colony. Save for Ireland, the barren monarchy was in fact no flourishing colonial empire.

That Titania is powerless to correct this *unnatural* order is purely the result of her distraction with Bottom, who represents Sir Walter Raleigh. Raleigh's vacillating roles from conqueror to courtier are of course played by Bottom, who, during the rehearsal of *Pyramus and Thisbe* is assigned to play the tragic lover, though he determines to be a tyrant: "I could play Ercles rarely" (1.2.26–27). This prompts Bottom to deliver a garbled speech from Seneca's *Hercules Octaeus*: *"The raging rocks, / And shivering shocks / Shall break the locks / Of prison gates. / And Phoebus' car / Shall shine from far / And make and mar / The foolish fates"* (1.2.29–36). The speech derives from the opening soliloquy by Hercules, who has undertaken a voyage to the underworld. Having survived this primal boundary crossing from which no mortal previously returned, he exclaims: "The roring rocks haue quaking sturd, & none thereat hath pusht. / Hell gloummy gates I have brast oape / Where grisly ghosts all husht / Have Stood…"[59] Bottom's misquote, however, inserting "Phoebus's car," crucially shifts the focus. No longer is the boundary crossing between the mortal world and the underworld, but between the known world and the world beyond, that which the bold sun transgresses beyond the extreme *verge* of land.[60]

---

58. Susan Doran has persuasively argued that Elizabeth's cult of virginity may have resulted from her own counselors' earlier reservations that any marriage might compromise England's independence, and so, they de facto forced her celibacy. See *Monarchy and Matrimony: The Courtships of Elizabeth I* (London: Routledge, 1996).
59. Lucius Annaeus Seneca, *Seneca His Tenne Tragedies, Translated into Englysh*, John Studley, trans. (London: Thomas Marsh, 1581), sig. CC5v. These words are spoken by Deianira's nurse who boasts about her magic powers. Bottom, like the nurse, is claiming power above his station: a "tyrant's vein." Seneca's authorship of this play has been doubted, though it was included as the tenth tragedy in the 1581 edition, and it continued to be attributed to him throughout the early modern period.
60. A 1692 operatic adaptation of *Midsummer,* published with the title *The Fairy-Queen* (London: Jacob Tonson) rendered Titania's line as "Why are you here / Come from the farthest Verge of India?" (sig. C1v). A verge was a boundary of dominium. "verge, n.3." OED Online. Oxford University Press. https://www-oed-com.

This implied contest with the sun emerges later in the speech. Hercules complains that while Phoebus rides his golden chariot across the sky, he is constrained to the mortal realm.[61] His fate is therefore made and marred by his obsession with solar flight:

> In euery coast O Titan where thou dost thy selfe reueale.
> How I haue met thee face to face, to thee I doe appeale.
> Aloofe beyonde the compasse of thy light I set my foote,
> And neuer coulde thy blaze so farre his glymsinge glory shoote.
> As I haue forst the honour of my triumphes for to streatch,
> The day it selfe hath had his stint, within my trauells reatch
> Dame Nature faylde, the worlde was shogd beside his center dew,
> And ougsome night in shimmering shade, from dungeon darck I drew.[62]

Only in gruesome death is Hercules finally granted his wish. In jealousy over his affection for Iole, Hercules's wife Deianira seeks revenge by bestowing upon him a poisoned robe.[63] This robe drives Hercules into "most intolerable tormentes."[64] For remedy he appeals to Apollo, who commands that "hee should bee caryed vnto Mounte Oetus, and there, that a greate fier shoulde bee made [...] HERCULES went up into it, & was there burned."[65] Bemoaning his tragic fate upon the pyre, he proclaims: "who is it that the heauens agaynst me sparres? / And am I thus O father myne brought downe againe from starres. / Euen now Appolloës sowtring car did fume about my face / So nie I past the pinch of Death, lo Thrachin top in place / Who brought me backe to ground agayne, beneath me earst it lay / And al the world was vnder me ..."[66] After his death, the observers find nothing

---

61. In John Studley's translation of *Hercules Octaeus*, Phoebus's car appears in the opening lines wherein Hercules addresses Jove: "O LORDE of Ghosts whose fyryre flash (that forth thy hand doth shake) / Doth cause *the trembling Lodges* twain of *Phoebus* car to quake / Raygne reachlesse nowe..." *Seneca His Tenne Tragedies*, sig. Bii6r. The "*Lodges twain*" are the east and the west, which Hercules has conquered in Jove's name: "in euery place / thy peace procurde I haue / Aloofe where Nereus lockes vp lande / Empalde in winding Waue. / ... / The rauening tyrauntes Scepterlesse, are pulled from their crowne." *Seneca His Tenne Tragedies*, sig. Bii6r. Still, heaven is denied to him. He exclaims, "what is it *Ioue* that thee so much detarres? / What may thee force keepe backe thy sonne from scaling of the Starres?" *Seneca His Tenne Tragedies*, sig. Bii6v.
62. *Seneca His Tenne Tragedies*, sig. Bii7r.
63. The plot closely mirrors that of *Medea*, in which Medea bestows a poisoned gown on Jason's betrothed out of revenge for his infidelity. Titania's speech on the disorder of nature echoes Medea's invocation of Hecate (lines 750–94). Oberon's speech on Cupid shooting at a "fair vestal" (2.1.155) recalls the *Hippolytus* (lines 192–203, 294–95, 331–37, and 351). Theseus and Hippolyta's exchange on hunting and hounds (4.1.100) also echoes Hippolytus's directions to his huntsmen in the opening of *Phaedra* (lines 1–43). Helena's obsessive and degrading pursuit of Demetrius also could be read against Phaedra's pursuit of Hippolytus (lines 233–41, 699–712), which was also modeled after Ovid's portrayal of Apollo and Daphne in the *Metamorphoses*.
64. *Seneca His Tenne Tragedies*, sig. Bii5r.
65. *Seneca His Tenne Tragedies*, sigs. Bii5r–Bii5v.
66. *Seneca His Tenne Tragedies*, sig. E4r.

remaining of his body, and so they are "fully perswaded that he was deified, & taken vp into Heauen."[67]

Tapping into this tragic irony, Bottom's "Ercles" performance comically foreshadows his later transformation into a minor tyrant over faerieland through his love tryst with Titania, who is swayed by the effects of Cupid's flower, the "love-in-idleness,"[68] and commands her fairy servants to give him all he desires. But in rejecting the role of a lover to play the famous tyrant, Bottom's fate provides ironic consummation to man's unbridled desires, as later applied to Spain in this chapter's opening quotation from Sir Francis Bacon. Seeking a "tyrant's vein" (empire), Bottom is Raleigh in pursuit of El Dorado.[69] He foolishly proclaims a golden conquest to rival that of the imperious sun, but with his romantic trysts and scandals, he becomes a petty tyrant of *unvirtuous conquest*. (He is aptly bestowed with the head of an ass.) By the time Bottom returns to civilization, his experience is practically forgotten, and so, the faeries remain tucked in obscurity, as distant and unapproachable as that great city of gold that had inspired Raleigh to his dreaming.

Reason and Unreason from El Dorado to Australia

> And therefore letting pass these dreams of an El Dorado, let us descend to places of less Magnificence, but of greater reality.
> —Peter Heylyn, *Cosmographie in Four Bookes* (1652)

Romance's nebulous connection to the New World was ironically underscored by Amazons' failure to appear as promised. So, too, was Guiana's unfruitfulness a final straw to Raleigh's already strained relationship with Elizabeth. The explorer's welfare little improved during the reign of James Stuart, though the king's strong advocacy of colonial expansion better corresponded with Raleigh's own interests. After more than a decade of imprisonment for his involvement in the Main Plot, during which he wrote *The History of the World* (first published in 1614), Raleigh was ultimately pardoned and granted permission for another Guiana voyage in 1617. It, too, failed to produce the fabled riches that

---

67. *Seneca His Tenne Tragedies*, sig. Bii5v.
68. In *Hercules Octaeus,* the device of a love poison is also used to sway Hercules's affections for Deianira, who prays to Cupid that with his bolt, he will conquer Hercules.
69. The references to *Hercules Octaeus* may also condemn Raleigh's role as a courtier. The play strongly indicts courtiers and sycophants, who "euery time the sunne at West goes downe, / They looke another man should clayme the Crowne" (sig. Cc7v). Moreover, a typical courtier "would his greedy hunger staunche / With gubbes of goulde, (and though hee it possest) / Rich Arabie serues not his pyning paunch, / Nor western *India* (a worlde for to beholde) / Where *Tagus* flowes with streames of glittering goulde" (sig. Cc7v). The latter two lines were added by Studley who referred to the *Siglo de Oro* as a product of Spanish greed and opportunism. So inspiring was this choral ode that Queen Elizabeth herself is supposed to have translated it around 1589, the year after the Armada, producing a single translation that survives in manuscript, retained at the Bodleian Library (MA w Museo 55, fols. 48r–49r).

he had promised. But the *Discovery of Guiana* was already more impactful than the voyages themselves; it further spurred his generation's robust belief in the wondrous, even against the increasing force of pre-Enlightenment reason, and so it cultivated a culture of stubborn unreason even while the tales of love and arms were also on the decline.

Published some decades later, Peter Heylyn's *The Cosmographie in four bookes* (1652) bore witness to this prevailing unreason that had endured into the seventeenth century, as spurred by English hopes in exploration. A chronicle history written in the high mimetic mode of national epic, *The Cosmographie* trafficked in both kinds of wonders, real and fabulous, and this generic hybridity may help to account for its enormous popularity on the print market. An expansion of the *Microcosmos: a Little Description of the Great World* (1621), which saw eight editions by 1638, the enlarged chronicle account of Europe, Asia, Africa, and America presented world history within the context of biblical narrative, championing the English as its great protagonists and saviors; it saw eight editions by 1700.[70]

The most visceral evidence of the *Cosmographie*'s hybridity was its new appendix on Australia. By the time of the book's printing, America was no longer a site of endless promise, but rather one of bureaucratic turmoil, particularly as England vied for unfettered trade with other European powers, especially the Dutch.[71] Australia, by contrast, was ripe for discovery. As Heylyn remarked: "I have oft marveled with my self, that no further progress hath been made in Discovery of it: considering chiefly by the size and position of the Countrey, especially in those parts which lye nearest Asia, that there is nothing to be looked for elsewhere, either of profit or of pleasures, but may there be found."[72] In 1652, with the outbreak of the Anglo-Dutch War, and still more by the outbreak of the second Anglo-Spanish War two years later, there was now, more than ever, a real and present need for madmen willing to dream of Australia. To drive home the point, Heylyn cast the American enticements of Drake and Raleigh as passé, faded dreams of an old New World, while he better encompassed these and more in the new, New World in Australia. He noted that this vast uncharted tract of land had

---

70. A clergyman affiliated with Bishop Laud, court chaplain under Charles I, Heylyn prepared the *Cosmographie* as an *apologia* for the recent calamity of the Royalists, alluding to recent events as a short-term setback in a larger narrative of Royalist triumph. See Craft, "Peter Heylyn's Seventeenth-Century World View," *Studies in Medieval and Renaissance History*, 3rd ser., 2 (2014), 325–44.
71. There were also competing Dutch and French interests in Australia. In an expedition from 1644, Abel Tasman had landed on the continent, applying the name *Hollanda Nova* to the western half. The name is notably absent from the *Cosmographie*, except for its application to the regions of the Philippines. A famous map of New Holland "Hollanda Nova, detecta 1644" was also published in Paris in the first volume of Melchisédech Thévenot's *Relations de divers voyages curieux* (Account of Diverse Curious Voyages), published in 1663. The widely circulated map featured Tasman's original survey, and it consigned the boundaries of Dutch territory to the western side of the continent, divided at eastern longitude 135, the traditional western limit of Spanish claims to the South Pacific resulting from the 1494 Treaty of Tordesillas.
72. Peter Heylyn, *Cosmographie in Four Bookes: Containing the Chorographie and Historie of the Whole Vvorld, and all the Principall Kingdomes, Provinces, Seas and Isles Thereof* (London: Henry Seile, 1652), sig. Bbbbb2r.

more than enough to "satisfie the greatest and most hungry appetite of Empire, Wealth, and Worldly pleasures; besides the *Gallantry* and Merit of so brave and [sic.] Action."[73] Therefore, he found the lack of the interest in Australia surprising; it was as if "some *Nil ultra*" had weakened English spirit to explore the region.[74] Or perhaps, he joked, Australia's indigenes were "not yet made ripe enough to receive the Gospel."[75]

To spur masculine spirits to exploration, his geographical index supplied all the fabulous lands from travel accounts, legends, folklore, and romance that might be found in Australia: the fictitious Fantasia of Joseph Hall's 1605 satirical romance, *An Old World and a New, The Discovery of a New World, and Another World and Yet the Same*; the Utopia of Thomas More's 1516 satire; the New Atlantis "discovered" by Francis Bacon's posthumous work of the same name (1626); the Painter's Wives Island of Walter Raleigh's *History of the World*; the New World Discovered in the Moon of Ben Jonson's 1607 eponymous masque, and of course, the faerielands of Spenser's *Faerie Queene* and Shakespeare's *Midsummer*. He joked, "I will try my fortune, and without troubling the Vice-Royes of Peru, and Mexico, or raking out Commission for a new Discovery, will make a search into this Terra Australes for some other Regions, which must be found either here or nowhere."[76]

A larger story was thus being written into the *Cosmographie*, one of readerly hopefulness feeding exploratory spirit. Now constrained mostly to Australia, Terra Incognita was a convenient site for depositing the fabulous conceptions of the poetic imaginary, which if not wholly factual, at least served a kind of spiritual truth pertaining to English conquest. Upon some lands, like More's Utopia and Bacon's New Atlantis, Heylyn confidently deemed them inventions of authors who had intended to critique their society; he recommended reading these works that well befit the English character. Of other lands, he was more critical. Upon the Painter's Wives Island, he remarked, for example, that it was a complete fabrication by a Spanish captive, further adding, "I fear the *Painters wife* hath many *Ilands* and some Countries too upon the *Continent*, in our common *Maps*, which are not really to be found on the strictest search."[77] Regarding Jonson's New World Discovered in the Moon, he vaulted upon the confused lunar arguments dating back to antiquity, as in the *True History* of Lucian, finally concluding, "there are stronger hopes of finding a *New World* in this *Terra Australis*, then in the Body of that Planet; and such perhaps as might exceed both in profit and pleasure the later *discoveries* of *America*."[78] But upon the existence of faerieland he notably demurred:

---

73. Heylyn, *Cosmographie*, sig. Bbbbb2r.
74. Heylyn, *Cosmographie*, sig. Bbbbb2r.
75. Heylyn, *Cosmographie*, sig. Bbbbb2r.
76. Heylyn, *Cosmographie*, sig. Bbbbb2r.
77. Heylyn, *Cosmographie*, sig. Hhhhh5v.
78. Heylyn, *Cosmographie*, sig. Bbbbb3v. Evidence for the existence of an earthlike community of Lunar birdmen could be found in the annals of recorded history, from the *True History* by Lucian of Samosata, to Ariosto's *Orlando Furioso*, to the *Pantagruel* of François Rabelais. They were also treated in serious scientific discourses, including *The Discovery of a World in the Moon* (1638) and *A Discourse Concerning a New Planet* (1640) by John Wilkins. In the proem to Book II of *The Faerie Queene*, Spenser likewise gave credence to such lunar curiosities to defend faerie land:

FAERIE LAND, is another part of this Terra Incognita; the habitation of the Faeries, a pretty kind of little fiends, or Pigmey devils, but more inclined to sport then mischief; of which old Women, who remember the times of Popery, tell us many fine stories. A cleanlyer and more innocent cheat was never put upon poor ignorant people, by the *Monks* and *Friers*. Their habitation here or no where; though sent occasionally by Oberon and their other Kings, to our parts of the World. For not being reckoned amongst the good Angels, nor having malice enough to make them Devils (but such a kind of midling Sprites, as the Latines call Lemures Larvae) we must find out some place for them, neither Heaven or Hell, and most likely this [Australia]. Their Country never more enobled, then by being made the Scene of that excellent Poem, called the Faerie Queen.[79]

While faulting the falsehoods perpetrated by Catholics, Heylyn commended the creations of Spenser and Shakespeare.[80] He especially recommended reading *The Faerie Queene* as a boon to virtue. Well short of denying faerieland's existence, he rather associated the work's fabled location to Australia, notably departing from the earlier hypothesis of America.

"The difference between the historian and the poet," Aristotle once remarked, "is that one tells what has happened, and the other the kind of things that would happen. It follows therefore that poetry is more philosophical and of higher value than history; for poetry unifies more, whereas history agglomerates."[81] Heylyn likewise approached his history of the world with a unifying program, exercising a degree of poetic license

---

> Why then should witlesse man so much misweene
> That nothing is, but that which he hath seene?
> What if within the Moones faire shining spheare?
> What if in euery other starre vnseene
> Of other worldes he happily should heare?
> He wonder would much more: yet such to some appeare. (3)

79. Heylyn, *Cosmographie*, sig. Hhhhh5v. Faeries were believed to be fallen angels.
80. Heylyn's reference to sending faeries "to our parts of the World" coincides with the opening of *Midsummer*, which finds Oberon, Titania, and the faeries in the forest of Athens for the occasion of the Duke's marriage to Hippolyta. A similar description appears in John Milton's *Paradise Lost* (London: Robert Boulter, 1667), in the description of the rebel angels' shrinking themselves together to enter the council chamber in Pandemonium:

> Behold a wonder! they but now who seemd
> In bigness to surpass Earths Giant Sons
> Now less then smallest Dwarfs, in narrow room
> Throng numberless, like that Pigmean Race
> Beyond the Indian Mount, or Faerie Elves,
> Whose midnight Revels, by a Forrest side
> Or Fountain some belated Peasant sees,
> Or dreams he sees, while over head the Moon
> Sits Arbitress, and neerer to the Earth
> Wheels her pale course, they on thir mirth & dance
> Intent, with jocond Music charm his ear;
> At once with joy and fear his heart rebounds. (sigs. D1r–D1v).

81. Aristotle, *On the Art of Fiction*, L. J. Potts, trans. (Cambridge: Cambridge University Press, 1953), 29.

to tell the narrative he wanted to tell. He subtly teased out Terra Incognita's national-ideological fault lines in order deploy both reason and unreason to inspire English exploration. This was further evident in his description of the lands of chivalry:

> The LANDS of CHIVALRY are such islands, Provinces, and Kingdoms, in the Books of Errantry, which have no being in any known part of the World, and therefore must be fought in this. A gross absurdity, but frequent in those kind of Writers, who in describing the Adventures of their Knights in despight of Geography, (with which indeed they had no acquaintance) have not only disjoined Countries which are near together, and laid together Countries which are far remote; but given us the description of many Islands, Provinces, and mighty Kingdoms, which as the ingenious Author of the History of *Don Quixot* merrily observeth, are not to be found in all the Map. Of this sort is the Isle of Adamants in *Sir Hon of Burdeaux*; the *Firm Island*, in the History of *Amadis de Gaul*; the *Hidden Island*, and that of the Sage *Aliart*, in *Sir Palmerin of England*; the Islands of *Lindaraza*, and the *Devilish Fauno*, with the Kingdom of *Lyra*, (of which the Amazonian Lady *Archisilora* was the rightful Queen) and many others of that kind, in the *Mirrour of Knighthood*; and divers of like nature in *Palmerin de Oliva, Primaleon, Belianis of Greece, Parismus,* the *Romance of Romances,* and indeed whom not of all that Rabble? Handsomely humoured by *Michael de Cervantes* in his *Island of Barutaria* [sic.], of which the famous Sancho Panca was sometime Governour, and the Kingdom of Micomicona.[82]

The large representation of Spanish titles in this entry of geographical embarrassments points to not only chivalric romance's general disrepute as "true history," but also to *Don Quixote*'s particular use as a satirical mouthpiece for expressing criticism against the falsehoods attributed by Spanish Catholicism. Although troubling for a factual historian, labeling these romances "true histories" gave weight to the actions described, and thus these works had the capacity to inspire readers to virtue, as Heylyn also affirmed:

> And yet I cannot but confess (for I have been a great Student in these Books of Chivalry) that they may be of very good use to Children or young Boys in their Adolescency. For besides that they divert the mind from worse cogitations, they perfect him that takes pleasure in them in the way of Reading, beget in him an habit of speaking, and animate him many times to such high conceptions as really may make him fit for great undertakings.[83]

These were key ingredients for spurring Englishmen to exploration and conquest, as we have seen, for example, in the case of Paynell's *Treasurie of Amadis*, which was used both as a rhetorical guidebook and unofficial guide to Spanish conquest. In effect, Spanish books of chivalry had endowed readers with what Heylyn elsewhere pejoratively called the "*Spanish* Rhetorick (that is, by the Sword and the Canon),"[84] and so it seems that the weapon was being turned upon the wielder.

---

82. Heylyn, *Cosmographie*, sig. Bbbbb3v.
83. Heylyn, *Cosmographie*, sigs. Bbbbb3v–Bbbbb4r.
84. Heylyn, *Cosmographie*, sig. CC4v. This was a direct carryover from the *Microcosmos*. Though perhaps adapted from a common saying, the source was Robert Ashley's translation of

Going to California

For those readers involved in the joint labors of exploration and conquest, romance's common geographical falsehoods (unreason) would have presented problems that no amount of "high conceptions" or "great undertakings" could reconcile. In fact, the problem whereby books of chivalry "disjoined Countries which are near together, and laid together Countries which are far remote" and "given us the description of many Islands, Provinces, and mighty Kingdoms, which [...] are not to be found in all the Map" also led to real errors in cartography. Such was the case of Baja California Sur, which had been first taken for an island, likely by the inferences drawn by the first Spanish explorers from their reading of romance, and later in their largely fruitless pursuit of Amazons. In fact, the application of the Castilian name popularized by Montalvo to the lower Western Coast of North America, usually credited to Hernán Cortés, also contributed to an unfortunate cartographical blunder (witnessing the collision of readerly expectations with real transatlantic explorations) in the earliest maps of Baja California Sur, which was incorrectly drawn as an island to the west of the coast of México.[85] Projecting the discoveries of romance onto to the face of California reflected a spirit of hopeful anticipation for the natural wonders and precious metals that America was expected to offer. From this rich conceptual font originated the European fixation with charting the entire region of Baja California Sur, which might be "abundant in gold and precious stones."[86]

A Comparison of the English and Spanish Nation (London: John Wolfe, 1589), attributed to a "Gentil-homme François" (Francois de la Noue?). It described Philip's dispatch of the Duke of Alba to deal with insurrection in the Low Countries: "But laying aside these colours of *Castillan* Rhetorick, I say roundly, that our French tongue is so bare, that it hath no other tearme fit enough to specifie the good dealing of the Duke of *Alua*, but theft and robberie" (sig. D3v). The rewrite by Heylyn was reprinted in *An history of the transactions betwixt the crown of England and the states of the Netherlands* (1664) and *The Dvtch vsurpation* (1672). These later works expressed admiration of Spaniards' expediency in dealing with the Low Countries, clearly expressing antipathies further developed during the Anglo-Dutch War. Perhaps Heylyn did not anticipate that the Royalist faction would ally with Spain against the Commonwealth in 1657, though he may have developed a sterner view during Oliver Cromwell's trade war. Heylyn had formerly supported the Spanish Match, as suggested by his having contributed verses to an Oxford volume applauding Charles's arrival in Madrid in 1623. Published anonymously, the poetry is attributed to Heylyn by its survival in manuscript. See Anthony Milton, *Laudian and Royalist Polemic in Seventeenth-Century England: The Career and Writings of Peter Heylyn* (Manchester: Manchester University Press, 2007), esp. 16–17.

85. Early cartographical depictions of Baja California as an island are included throughout Polk, *The Island of California*, and listed on pp. 9–11.
86. *Esplandian*, sig. Kk4r. Prior to Munday's printing of 1598, English readers would have had to rely on Nicolas de Herberay's French translation, first printed in 1540. This French edition is notable for several features: it makes no mention of Calafia's blackness, and it omits the part about Talanque's arranged marriage to the Amazonian queen. Most significant, it coins the term *Californiennes*, thus tying the cartographical error to its romantic origins. For a summary of the translational omissions, and a critical reading, see Helen Moore, "The Eastern

Ironically, Heylyn had also taken the California peninsula to be an island "environed on all parts by the Main Ocean,"[87] even though numerous peninsular depictions had been supplied by early European explorers and cartographers during the 1500s. These followed the 1539 voyage of Francisco de Ulloa, whose discovery of California's peninsularity was incorporated in Gerard Mercator's map from 1569, Abraham Ortelius's map of 1570, and Fernao Vaz Dourado's map of 1570. More recently, the peninsula's coast was elaborately detailed in a 1620s map by Johannes de Laet.[88] Passing over these details, Heylyn vaguely attributed the discovery of Baja California's insularity to "some Adventurers."[89] Correspondingly, in the opening map to the second part of the fourth Book of Heylyn's "Cosmography & History of America, And all the principal Kingdoms, Provinces, Seas, and Isles thereof,"[90] Baja California is depicted as an island off the coast of North America, its northern limit stretching to latitude 43.

This mistake was probably less than innocent. The depiction of Baja California as an island was a common strategy of English counterintelligence, traceable to Sir Francis

---

Mediterranean in the English *Amadis* Cycle, Book V," *The Yearbook of English Studies* 41, no. 1 (2011), 113–25, esp. 123–24.

87. Heylyn, *Cosmographie*, sig. Qqqq2r.
88. A director of the recently formed Dutch West India Company, Laet had compiled in his *Nieuwe wereldt ofte Beschrijvinghe van West-Indien* (1625), one of four American regional maps: "*Americae sive Indiae Occidentalis*," the best West Coast delineation to date. The book was republished in 1630 and a Latin edition was published in 1633. Heylyn had clearly consulted the Latin edition, though he cast doubt upon its authenticity. He wrote of Baja California: "Supposed informer times to have been joyned, in the North parts of it, above the Latitude of 27. To the rest of the Continent, and so described in most of our later Maps, till the year 1626 and after that in the Chart or Map of *John de Laet, An.* 1633. which I wonder at: himself affirming, that in many of the old Maps it was made an Iland; *l.6 cap.* 11. and that he had seen a fair Map in parchment, a very fair and ancient draught, *Quae Californiam in ingentis Insulae modum, a Continente divideret*, in which it was expressed for a spacious Iland, *lib. 6. cap. 17*" (sig. Qqqq2r). One of these explorers who formerly claimed Baja an island was Juan de Fuca, who claimed the region an island by his purported discovery in 1592 of the Northwest Passage, beginning at the fabled Strait of Anián, and terminating at latitude 48.
89. "The reason of the Errour [of peninsularity] was," Heylyn claimed, "that those who first endeavoured the Discovery of it, sayling up the Sea of *Mer Vermiglio*, found it to grow narrower and narrower towards the North; till it seemed to be no bigger then some mighty River; but that of such a violent current that no Boat was able to pass upwards with wind or Oar, unless haled up with Cords by the strength of men. And taking it to be a River, they gave it the name of *Rio de Bona Guia*; known by that name, and continued in the opinion of being a River till the year 1620 or thereabouts. At what time some Adventurers beating on these Coasts fell accidentally upon a strait but violent passage, on the North hereof, which brought them with a strong current into *Mer Vermiglio*: discovering by that Accident, that the waters falling into that Sea, was not a River, as formerly had been supposed; but a violent breaking in of the Northern Ocean; by consequence that this part of *Califormia* was not a Demi-Iland or Peninsula but a perfect Iland," *Cosmographie*, sig. Qqqq2r.
90. Heylyn, *Cosmographie*, sig. Mmmm4v.

Drake's first circumnavigation of the world from 1577 to 1580. This expedition initially brought records of a peninsular tract of land connecting from the region of central America to the northern mainland, which he supposed to be California, but as this explanation gradually disappeared from a bulk of records, an "island" myth reemerged.[91] For the Spaniards, the greatest interest lie in discovering the precise location of Drake's port, for which the island hypothesis may have served as a useful distraction. Drake's port was carefully obscured from the Spaniards, with late sixteenth-century accounts apparently tailored to this effect.[92] The shift had to do with the search for a Northwest Passage to the Pacific Ocean, which was believed to intersect through Baja California and lead to continental North America by a (nonexistent) Strait of Anián upon the Vermillion Sea.[93] In the seventeenth century, island fantasies persisted, fueled in part by continued pursuit of the Northwest Passage, and by England's vested interest in claiming Drake's landing as a separate discovery independent of other European encroachments.[94] This so-called California island was also desired as an English port for trade and exploration in the Pacific. For instance, it would be instrumental in the colonization of Australia if that were to get underway.

Heylyn's omitting the connective land between Baja California and the American mainland thus served as yet another obfuscation: one mythos of Spanish supremacy replaced with another of English discovery, claiming the whole of Baja California for

---

91. Polk emphasizes that Drake did not himself claim Baja California an island. Rather, it was the Spaniards who appear to have first perpetuated the myth in part because they wanted to press Cortés's claim over Drake's. The English likewise saw fit not to correct this misapprehension. Drake and others seem to have reapplied the "island" in later accounts. See Polk, *The Island of California*, esp. 231–40.
92. For instance, California's geography was vaguely handled in Richard Hakluyt's *Principall Navigations, Voiages, Traffiques and Discoueries of the English Nation* of 1589. Its marginal headings listed both an "isle of California" and the "isles of California." For an account of the suppression of Drake's narrative in relation to Elizabethan politics, see Willis Holmes Kerr, "The Treatment of Drake's Circumnavigation in Hakluyt's 'Voyages,' 1589," *The Papers of the Bibliographical Society of America* 34, no. 4 (1940), 281–302.
93. The name "Anián" may have derived from *The Travels of Marco Polo* (ca. 1300; Book 3, Chapter 5). Of the Strait, Heylyn wrote only that: "Opposite to Cape Blance, in the extreme North parts of America, the supposed Kingdome of *ANIAN*, from whence the Streits of *Anian* which are thought by some to part *America* from *Asia*, do derive their name; is conceived to lie. Supposed, and supposed only; for not certainly known: the very being of such a Kingdom, and such Streits, being much suspected" (Qqqq3r).
94. As Barbara Mundy notes, "maps were highly charged documents; their possession brought power over territory… Knowledge about sea routes, ports, shoals, coastlines that these maps contained was necessary to the continuance of imperial power, and the royal bureaucracy maintained a tight hold upon them. […] The Escorial atlas, a survey of Spain sponsored by Charles's son, Philip II, was guarded in his library and to this day has never been published." "Mapping the Aztec Capital: The 1524 Nuremberg Map of Tenochtitlan, Its Sources and Meanings," *Imago Mundi,* 50 (1998), 11–33 (28).

England.⁹⁵ Whether he earnestly believed the California island myth, or simply chose to ignore the peninsular evidence is perhaps debatable. But prevailing English opinion at the time was that California was an island, so Heylyn had no reason to suppose otherwise, particularly as this thesis better suited his country's interests. On this account, Heylyn certainly recognized the utility in aggrandizing Drake's Famous Voyage, specifically by reviving the voyager's appellation of New Albion to the Northwest coast of Baja. As he explained, "looking on it [Baja] as an Iland, we have divided it into *Nova Albion*, and *California* specially so called."⁹⁶ Of Nova Albion, he wrote:

> NOVA ALBION formerly conceived to be a part of the Continent, hath of late times been found to have taken up but some part of this Iland; lying about the 38 degree of Latitude, and so Northwards as far as to Cape Blanco, as they call it now. Discovered by Sir Francis Drake in his Circumnavigation of the World, An. 1577. and by him named Nova Albion, in honour of England, his own Country, which was once called Albion [...] but the Country lying so far off that no benefit could redound by it to the English Nation, but the honour of the first Discovery: the name of Nova Albion by little and little was forgotten, and at last quite left out of the Maps or Charts; only a Point or Promontory, by the name of Po de [Port of] Francisco Draco, being left unto us to preserve his memory. And though we have caused the name of Nova Albion to be restored unto the Maps, as it was before: yet we must let the Reader know, that the name of New Albion hath been given lately with as much propriety, but more hopes of profit and advantage, to that part of Virginia which lieth betwixt Mary Land and New England, as before was noted.⁹⁷

Writing during the early 1650s, when The Old Dominion was undergoing a period of economic growth, Heylyn had every reason to conclude that Virginia would better constitute the New Albion. As he explained, however, the later application of Nova Albion to Virginia with "as much propriety, but more hopes of profit and advantage" was a deliberate and purposeful deviation designed to underscore England's right to its eastern colonies. To reapply the name to Lower California in the seventeenth century would have been to simultaneously underscore that primal claim to North America by separately pressing for California's insularity. As Polk observes, "'New Albion' even more than New England would have evoked in Spanish minds the concept of an island."⁹⁸ Perhaps the strong appeal of this legend was best summarized by the Jesuit missionary and cartographer, Eusebio Kino, who explored the region in the 1680s: "California is the first and principal island of the entire world and also the largest. It is separated from New Mexico by the narrow Red Sea [...] The renowned English captain Francis Drake [...] also touched at this island, calling it New Albion, that is New England, inasmuch as

---

95. Heylyn's map also cohered with Thomas Cavendish's purported island discovery from his Circumnavigation of 1587. The reader is directed to "the Cape of S. Lucas, [in the south of Baja California] remarkable for the great prize there taken from the Spaniards by Captain Cavendish in his Circumnavigation of the World," sig. Qqqq2r.
96. Heylyn, *Cosmographie*, sig. Qqqq2r.
97. Heylyn, *Cosmographie*, sigs. Qqqq2v–Qqqq3r.
98. Polk, *The Island of California*, 234.

England of old was called Albion. Thus, as far as is known, Drake was the first to go to California."[99]

Two possibilities could explain Heylyn's depiction of Baja California as an island: Heylyn's island hypothesis was completely earnest, based on a combination of presupposition and hopeful desire for an original English discovery; or the presumption of an island was no presumption at all, but rather a convenient pretense that could press England's claim while obscuring the Northwest Passage. If the former explanation is correct, and this is certainly possible, then we can take this as an ironic instantiation of Heylyn's complaint over the geographical falsehoods perpetuated by books of chivalry, for when Spanish explorers first arrived in the region, they translated their literary explorations to their encounters in the real world, either believing earnestly that the newly discovered land was that of Queen Calafia, or by drawing a symbolic comparison. The English, reading these accounts and arriving somewhat later in a period of heightened Anglo-Spanish aggression, would likewise make the same mistake. The problem would be perpetuated by a number of complicating factors, from the natural tendency to claim all discoveries as islands until unequivocally proven otherwise, to the English desire to claim an original discovery, to the publication of false maps, to the ongoing competition for a Northwest Passage, to romance literature's continued exoticizing of hidden isles and pagan women. As European conquerors continued to read, translate, and rewrite the myths of *Amadís* and other tales, translating the quest for the hidden lair of the Amazons from the page to the exploratory stage, they perpetuated insular myths, confirming their biases over and again, and stubbornly holding on to their assumptions against other reports that seemed to confirm the region's peninsularity.

If the latter explanation is correct, as Heylyn's distinction between California and Nova Albion certainly suggests, then Heylyn could also be blamed for perpetuating the very kind of geographical truism, derived from romance, that he claimed to despise. And if so, then California further belies the *Cosmographie*'s professed divorcement from the romance tradition. On the subject of Amazons, for instance, Heylyn revealed his deep personal interest. He included an entire section on the famous Amazonian queens of antiquity, and he mentioned virtually every place in the known world, from Ethiopia to Tartary to America, where Amazon-like women were reputed to have lived. He also offered this comment in the section on the viceroyalty of Nova Galicia:

> *COVLIACAN, or CVLVCAN*, lieth on the South of *Cinaloa*, coasting along the Bay of *California*, which it hath on the West; and part of *New Biscay* on the East. The Country well provided of fruits, inferiour unto none for all sorts of Provisions; and not without some Mines of *Silver* found out by the *Spaniards*. The chief Rivers of it, 1 *Rio de Macheras* or the River of *Women*, in

---

99. Qtd. in Polk, *The Island of California*, 236. Kino had originally accepted the insularity of California, but he made a series of overland expeditions from in 1698–1706, in part to settle the question. He gradually became convinced that a land connection must exist. The first report of Kino's discovery and his peninsular map from 1701 were circulated in Europe during the early 1700s, but cartographical opinion remained divided for some decades.

the North part of the Province; so called because the *Spaniards* found there more women then men; occasioning the opinion that it was inhabited by Amazons.[100]

Although this passage makes no reference to Queen Calafia, it points toward the Spaniards' supposition that the region of California was rich in precious metals and dominated by women, which originally drove the quest for Amazons in America. Since Heylyn also acknowledged the presence of Amazons in the lands of chivalry, he most certainly should have given some thought to California's fabled Amazonian queen.

Perhaps he regarded California as confirmation of a rare veracity in the books of unreason, but if so, then it also stands to reason that he should have mentioned it in his voluminous entry on California, particularly when discussing Baja's insularity. This inference makes sense if Heylyn was himself aware of the island of Queen Calafia from *Esplandián*, and of course he must have known about it. The first English reference to Queen Calafia and her realm of California dated back almost a century to Paynell's *Treasurie of Amadis*. It included the following letters:

1. Letters from Rodrigue Soudan of Liquie, and Calafia Queene of Californie, to Amadis of Fraunce, and his sonne Esplandian, to accepte the combat and fyghte, to knowe the vertue and strength of the best combattant. In the fifth Booke the 52. Chapter.
    ROdrigue Souden of Liquie the mortall enimie of the enimyes of our gods, and Calasia Quéene of Californie, a region ritch of golde and precious stones more than any other.[101]
2. Letters from the Queene Pintiquinestra to the Queene Calafie, admonishing hir that she wil fight with hir. In the .6. boke the .22. Chapter.
    Pintiquinestra Quéene of the people that haue no heades, to thée Calafie, that dost commaund the strong Iles of Californie.[102]
3. The Emperoure of Trebisondes letter, answering togither Armato, Grisilant and Pintiquinestra, to aduertise them, that they accept the combat, being assured to obtayne the victorie, considering the iust quarell of the Christians. In the .6. booke the .22. Chapter.
    WE, by the grace of God, Emperoure of Trebisond, Amadis king of France and of England, and Califie, ye Lord & ruler of the Iles of Californie, wher gold and very precious stones do grow in greate abundaunce."[103]

One must suppose that this "great student in the Books of Chivalrie" must have studied this volume of letters in his youth, particularly if he read chivalric romances as rhetorical guidebooks, as he claimed.

---

100. Heylyn, *Cosmographie*, sig. Qqqq4r.
101. Paynell, *The moste excellent and pleasaunt booke, entituled: The treasurie of Amadis of Fraunce* (London: Thomas Hacket, 1572), sig. K3v.
102. Paynell, *Treasurie of Amadis*, sig. S3v.
103. Paynell, *Treasurie of Amadis*, sig. S4r.

If California's romantic origins were mostly likely familiar to Heylyn, as they were also familiar to his readers, then why wasn't California's romantic persona discussed anywhere in the *Cosmographie*, at least as a possible reason for why the island was "specially so called?"[104] Perhaps it was because Heylyn was inclined to doubt *Amadís*'s historicity. He directly attacked its Ínsula Firme as fictitious, and elsewhere, when debating a historian's account of Alexander the Great's conquest of India, he remarked that "I give little or no credence to this story, ranging it in the same Catalogue of truth with the Adventures of Donzel del Febo, Rosicleer, Belianis, Amadis, and the rest of the rabble of Knights Errant."[105] Nevertheless, even if he personally placed no stock in the possible connection, he should probably have anticipated that readers might do so. The work had been widely read since its first Castilian printing in 1510, and in England, there was not only the *Treasurie of Amadis*, but also the first edition of *Esplandián* of 1598,[106] as well as the sequel, *Lisuarte de Grecia*, published in the same year, 1652. All of these contained references to California. There was also the 1540 French translation by Nicolas de Herberay, which was more widely read than even the Spanish original. This version was also notable for the first usage of "Californiennes," and for locating Calafia's island abode in Tartary.[107] For a bilingual reader, the change would have further cast doubt upon the idea that Baja California's earliest explorers had in fact found the hidden lair of Queen Calafia.

With such contradictions being magnified by California's real location on the maps, this heavily romanticized tract of land ought to have been just the example Heylyn needed to prove that books of chivalry communicated false geographies, and yet, Heylyn had nothing specific to say about it. This problem was further underscored by California's additional appearance in the 1640 translation of the *Romance of Romances* (a sequel to the *Belianís*, *Amadís*, and *Espejo* cycles), which brought account of "the fair Amazon, *Alteria* the Queen of California's Daughter."[108] Heylyn cited the work in connection to "many Islands, Provinces, and mighty Kingdoms, which […] are not to be found in all the Map. Of this sort is […] the Kingdom of Lyra, (of which the Amazonian Lady Archisilora was the rightful Queen) and many others of that kind, in the *Mirrour of Knighthood*; and divers

---

104. Heylyn, *Cosmographie*, sig. Qqqq1v.
105. Heylyn, *Cosmographie*, sig. Eeee6v. We must place such comments in the context of Europeans' deep fascination with Alexander the Great as a universal sovereign whose conquests spanned the known world. In Renaissance Istanbul, moreover, as Giancarlo Casale has shown, there was a robust debate over whether Alexander had first discovered America. See Casale, "Did Alexander the Great Discover America? Debating Space and Time in Renaissance Istanbul," *Renaissance Quarterly* 72, no 3 (2019), 863–909.
106. A reprint was also published 12 years later in 1664.
107. Although the *Roland* author had Africa in mind, Montalvo capitalized upon the new sense of the "earthly paradise" as located in America. In the account of his third voyage of 1498, Columbus concluded that the terrestrial paradise was to be found at the delta of the Orinoco. This claim further spurred European interest in Guiana.
108. Gilbert Saulnier Duverdier, *The love and armes of the Greeke princes. Or, The romant of the romants. Written in French by Monsieur Verdere, and translated for the Right Honourable, Philip, Earle of Pembroke and Montgomery, Lord Chamberlaine to his Majesty*, n. n., trans. (London: Thomas Walkley, 1640), sig. I2r.

of like nature in [...] *the Romance of Romances.*" If this was a veiled reference to California, however, it was cagey indeed, buried in a trove of titles and coordinating clauses, separating the *Romance of Romances* from Amazons and fictional islands by several degrees.

Willful deception, earnest ignorance, affectionate homage, or inside jest—any of these could explain the reasons of the Spanish explorers for settling on the name *California*. The same could be said for Heylyn's motivations in omitting the California of sixteenth- and seventeenth-century romance among those incorrectly charted or completely false lands of chivalry. If Heylyn had been so smart as to disbelieve the faerie tales promulgated in "times of Popery" and the "gross absurdit[ies]" published by romance writers, and likewise in the now dubious existence of El Dorado (as in the passage earlier quoted), then his silence on California's contemporary romanticism could have been deliberate. Certainly, if he had read *Don Quixote*, as he proudly claimed, then he should have known that *Esplandián* is the first book condemned to the fire for its paramount falsehoods.

Given the high likelihood of readerly associations between Baja California and the Amazons, it is logical that Heylyn failed to mention the island ruled by Queen Calafia in his diatribe on romance's prevailing unreason. To do so would have undermined the California island myth, and by extension, England's claims to North America and the Pacific. If his supposition of California's insularity was earnest, propelled by his country's great desire for the myth to be true, then discussing California's romantic origins would have been unwise, for the prevailing impression derived from these books was that California was an island. In this case, quarreling with the fictional histories of California would not have served Heylyn's loyalist patriotism. Even if there was no official dictum to censor such references—after all, they were printed—the geographer would not have been much compelled to cite Queen Calafia's island among those that were wholly fabricated or incorrectly charted by books of chivalry. To do so might have invited uncomfortable questions regarding Baja California's insularity. And what kind of patriot would Heylyn be if he didn't help to guard the essential sources of English pride from Spanish intrusions? In his preface to the reader he explained that "AS an *English-man* I have been mindfull upon all occasions to commit to memory the noble actions of my Countrey; exploited both by Sea and Land, in most parts of the World, and represented on the same *Theaters* [...] and filing on the Registers of perpetuall Fame the Gallantrie and brave Atchievements of the People of *England*."[109] This was clearly not a man who would dare to diminish Drake's historic feat in California, especially when he was so concerned to corner Pacific exploration that he included in his own purportedly *true history* an appendix of all the fictional faerielands that might inspire English dreams of Australia.

Silence at times reverberates more loudly than words. The myth of Baja California's insularity endured into the late eighteenth century.[110] Meanwhile, California's romantic origins remained undetected by the English-speaking world until the nineteenth century

---

109. Heylyn, *Cosmographie*, sig. D2r.
110. The matter was finally settled beyond doubt by Juan Bautista de Anza, who made expeditions between Sonora, México, and California's west coast from 1774 to 1776.

when they were purportedly *rediscovered* by an American scholar.[111] California is proof of the widespread unreason that resulted from the conventional enmity between England and Spain. Its obscurement underscores that early modern romance reading went hand-in-hand with counterintelligence and countermyth, requiring endless justifications and concealments. This was a natural response for England and Spain, longstanding contenders for imperial supremacy. As Heylyn himself remarked when defending an imprecise intelligence that the native Inca gave to the Spanish explorers searching for El Dorado, "Who sheweth his Treasure to a thief, doth deserve to lose it."[112]

---

111. Edward Everett Hale, "The Queen of California," *Atlantic Monthly*, March 1864, 265–78, rpt. in *The Queen of California: The Origin of the Name of California* (San Francisco: Colt, 1945), 1–47.
112. Heylyn, *Cosmographie*, Yyyy3r.

CHAPTER 6

UNRULY READERS: ANTI-SPANISH SENTIMENT AND THE FEMINIZING OF ROMANCE

Spain's perceived dominance over the sixteenth- and early seventeenth-century market for secular fiction seemed to corroborate the notion that the country was largely responsible for romance's corruption of the humanist program. This prevailing perception complicated the simultaneous transformation of romance during the seventeenth century into a genre primarily associated with women.[1] The perception of Spain's corrosive influence emerged out of the Black Legend of Spanish Cruelty; it developed in earnest during the sixteenth century in the aftermath of the Italian Wars, though its roots were set earlier.

European humanists alleged that Spain was unworthy of Renaissance culture owing to its perceived vicious excesses: violent, sexual, and emotional. Tracking this argument through seventeenth-century references to *Amadís* and *Espejo*, especially in the plays of Ben Jonson, this chapter explores how women and Spain were implicated in romance's perceived debasement of Ovidian love discourse, which effectually overtook arms as the prime determinant of the genre. Gradually, as romance also came to be regarded as a women's genre, associated with various kinds of readerly surfeits (i.e., quixoticism), an ethic of *guilty reading* emerged as a self-conscious masculine response to the genre's continued attraction.

An Intellectual Black Legend

> Who doesn't call us barbarous? Who doesn't call us mad, ignorant, and arrogant? What vice have we that we do not owe to its communication by [all other nations]?
> —Francisco Gómez de Quevedo, *España defendida* (Spain Defended) (1609–12)[2]

As such scholars as Benedetto Croce, Arturo Farinelli, Sverker Arnoldsson, and Santiago López Moreda have made plain, a major basis for the Black Legend began outside of Iberia, as the above quotation from Francisco de Quevedo also implies.[3] This narrative

---

1. See Helen Hackett, *Women and Romance Fiction in the English Renaissance* (Cambridge: Cambridge University Press, 2000), 65–68.
2. Don Francisco Gómez de *Quevedo, España Defendida, y los tiempos de ahora, de las calumnias de los noveleros y sediciosos* (Madrid: Real Academia de la Historia, 1916), 24.
3. Sverker Arnoldsson, *La Leyenda Negra: estudios sobre sus orígenes,* Acta Universitatis Gothoburgensis, Göteborgs Universitets Arsskrift, vol. 66 (Göteborg: Almqvist & Wiksell, 1960); Benedetto Croce,

particularly developed in late medieval and Renaissance Italia, where a series of Spanish conquests left a lasting impression of cruelty and vice. These accounts were further punctuated by the atrocities of the Italian Wars. As Italian power gradually consolidated under the Aragonés Crown in Sicilia, Sardegna, Napoli—and later in Milano and Genova—the region was flooded with Català merchants and soldiers. The Spanish soldiers in Italy were known for two things: their militancy and their lewdness. Such is reported, for example, by the Italian humanist scholar, diplomat, and courtier in the Aragonés court of Napoli, Giovanni Giovano Pontano:

> And indeed the sea has brought this foul way of swearing—and I wish this was the only thing our people had learned from the Catalans! From them we have acquired the dagger, nor is anything in Naples sold more cheaply than a man's life [...] We have also learned to consort shamelessly with prostitutes and put chastity on sale [...] what was once the most innocent populace, while it was delighting in amassing goods from Catalonia and the rest of Spain, while it was marveling at and assenting to the customs of that nation, became the most debased.[4]

A crucial stereotype was beginning to form. The perceived Spanish penchant for belligerency and debauchery that was attributed to the soldering class of Catalans anticipated what would later become a stereotype about Spaniards everywhere. It was ironically immortalized in the European critiques of great Spanish romance heroes as faulty paragons of chivalry, while romance's generic representation of battle-faring, and of premarital sex inspired concerns that merely reading tales of love and arms would induce readers to vice by inspiring them to imitate the books' profligate heroes.

As late medieval and early modern Napoli became, in the eyes of humanist thinkers of the time, more vicious by its integration of the Catalans, such maritime cities as Genova, Pisa, and Venezia likewise began to see their naval predominance drop via the recent arrival of the Spaniards, to whom the Italians also attributed "avarice—a typical ingredient of the merchant in all kinds of propaganda—and furthermore an infamous cunning, another classic characteristic of the same profession" (my translation).[5] For instance, when Pedro (Peter) IV of Aragón (1319–1387; ruled 1336–87) leagued with Venezia in its war with Genova, the Italian humanist scholar and poet, Francesco Petrarca (Petrarch), remarked: "The one who occupies our seacoast thirsts for and thinks about nothing but the gold in Venice and the blood of Genoa, being at the behest of avarice the satellite of one and the enemy of the other, bound by one party with gold,

---

España en la vida italiana del Renacimiento, Francisco González Ríos, trans. (Seville: Renacimiento, 2007); Arturo Farinelli, *Italia e Spagna,* 2 vols. (Torino: Fratelli Bocca, 1929); Santiago López Moreda, "'Non placet Hispania' Los orígenes de la Leyenda Negra," in *España ante sus críticos: las claves de la Leyenda Negra,* Yolanda Rodríguez Pérez, Antonio Sánchez Jiménez, and Harm den Boer, eds. (Madrid and Frankfurt: Iberoamerica and Vervuert, 2015), 67–89.

4. Giovanni Giovani Pontano, *Dialogues, Volume 1: Charon and Antonius,* Julia Haig Gaisser, ed. and trans. The I Tatti Renaissance Library, no. 53 (Cambridge: Harvard University Press, 2012), 129.

5. Arnoldsson, *La Leyenda Negra,* 17.

conquered by the other with steel."[6] This stereotype was later carried into the fictional construction of Spanish characters, including the Prince of Arragon (original spelling) from William Shakespeare's *The Merchant of Venice* (1596). Pretentious, avaricious, and entitled, the prince is inclined to discover Portia's virtue in a casket of silver. He reflects, long after the conclusion of the Italian Wars, the enduring stereotype of Spanish greed, as represented in the accounts and commentaries of the Spanish conquest of Italy.

One particularly hostile anti-Spanish and anti-romantic group was the followers of the Dutch scholar, Desiderius Erasmus. In 1516, the Cardinal and Grand Inquisitor of Castile, Fray Francisco Jiménez de Cisneros invited Erasmus to come to the University of Alcalá, but Erasmus refused the invitation, immortalizing his view, "non placet Hispania" (Spain does not please),[7] in a letter to Thomas More dated July 10, 1517.[8] In another letter to his colleague, Beatus Rhenanus, he wrote, "Cardinalis Toletanus nos invitat, sed non est animus hispanizein" (the Cardinal of Toledo invites us, but there is no inclination to become a Spaniard).[9] Erasmus's "*hispanizein*" may have been an ironic pun on *homerizein*, which means to sing Homer.[10] If so, then Erasmus's disinclination toward *hispanizein* may have more specifically encoded his fear that he would be used as a puppet of the Spanish Crown, forced to sing Spain's praises, like a rhapsode paid to recite Homeric poems. While implying Spain's antipathy to classical letters, Erasmus's "non placet Hispania" and "non est animus hispanizein" also encoded the era's radicalized fears over Spanish contact, which was heightened by the growing power of the Spanish Crown, as López Moreda reports:

> It seems more likely to think that Hispania seemed too barbaric in its customs, and in religious practices, little sincere; what's more, the false conversion of many Jews and Moors had led to an uncompromising religious policy; the Moorish and Jewish revolts in already "Christianized" territories were numerous; the Catholic Monarchs had decreed the expulsion of the latter [Jews] in 1492 and Portugal did likewise four years later, owing to the pressures exercised from Castile when marriage pacts between both Crowns were constantly being forged. (my translation)[11]

If Erasmus's comments can be taken as official statements of humanist antipathy rather than the eccentric views of a single thinker, then we may also speculate that the ethnic and intellectual arguments against Spain, which formed the basis of the Black Legend, were probably far more commonplace in the early modern period than previously suspected. Indeed, given the dating of Erasmus's comment, coupled with the probable motivations for the Dutch humanist's hesitancies as expressed to other great thinkers of the period,

---

6. Francesco Petrarca, *The Life of Solitude*, Jacob Zeitlin, trans. (Chicago: University of Illinois Press, 1924), 241.
7. Alternatively, "I do not like Spain."
8. Qtd. in López Moreda, *"Non placet Hispania,"* 67.
9. Qtd. in Carlos G. Noreña, *Juan Luis Vives I*, International Archives of the History of Ideas (The Hague: Martinus Nijhoff, 1970), 139. I have used the translation by Andrea Kouklanakis.
10. I thank Andrea Kouklanakis for drawing my attention to this possible meaning.
11. López Moreda, *"Non placet Hispania,"* 67–68.

the following inferences seem likely: (1) the English conception of what it meant to Hispanize carried negative ethnic attributes in England far earlier than the conventional turning point circa 1588, as is traditionally supposed;[12] and (2) the popular conception of "hispanizein" implied, from its early foundations, a turning away from intellectualism, a rejection of morality, and indeed, a disavowal of the very cultural, philosophical, and ideological foundation of what we would now call European humanism. Spain itself, in other words, was deemed unworthy of Renaissance culture.

Contemporary humanist thinkers, aggravated with the rude Aragonés and Català presence in Italia, thus began to complain of the apparent poverty of Hispanic letters and of the violent character of Spaniards themselves, producing the common aphorism: "España para las armas e Italia para la pluma" (Spain for arms, and Italy for the pen).[13] Versions of this aphorism circulated in the missives of European humanists: the Português scholar, Aires Barbosa, first chair of Greek at Universidad de Salamanca, once remarked that "the men of Spain who spend any time in the study of letters, they learn them not for love of Minerva, but of Mercury; they study for profit, not for wisdom" (my translation).[14] In his *Diario del viaggio in Spagna* (Diary of the Voyage in Spain) (1512), the Italian author Francesco Guicciardini likewise complained that the Spanish "are not fond of letters, and there is no knowledge among the nobles or the ladies, or very few, and there are few people who know the Latin language" (my translation).[15] In response to such humanist disavowals of Spanish intellect, López Moreda underscores that:

> We must keep in mind the reasons of personal interest of the humanists themselves, especially the Italians, to justify their role as educators and chroniclers in the court of the Catholic Monarchs; there was nothing better than talking about the cultural shortage of Spain to justify their pedagogical work and its historiographical role in a language of European dissemination, Latin. But their commitment to the diffusion of this language proved ineffective: the Castilian language was already beginning to be "partner to Empire" and the first grammar in the vernacular, that of Nebrija, proves it. (my translation)[16]

This explanation could also account for the general contempt European humanists expressed toward tales of love and arms. Usually written in vernacular languages, romances represented an obvious threat to the Italo-centric culture of early modern thinking, and of its Latin-based learning, while the growing influence of the Spanish court and of Castilian, the major language of Spanish courtliness and commerce, further instantiated the perceived connection between this newly popular vernacular literature and the potential destruction of the humanist program.

---

12. See, e.g., Eric Griffin, "Ethos to Ethnos: Hispanizing 'the Spaniard' in the Old World and the New,'" *The New Centennial Review*, 2, no. 1 (2002), 69–116, esp. 71–72.
13. Benedetto Croce, *España en la vida italiana durante el Renacimiento*, J. Sánchez Rojas, trans. (Madrid: Mundo Latino, 1915), 12.
14. Qtd. in López Moreda, *"Non placet Hispania,"* 78.
15. Qtd. in López Moreda, *"Non placet Hispania,"* 81.
16. López Moreda, *"Non placet Hispania,"* 86.

The informing context of European humanism and the pedagogical dominance of Latinity could also help to explain how the controversies of romance were grafted onto the negative character of Spain. Such was recorded in the *Discours politiques et militaires* (*The Political and Military Discourses*) (1587) by the French Huguenot captain and writer, Lord François de la Noue. The book detailed the great casualties of France's wars of religion, particularly touching on the Huguenots' suffering by the aggressions of the Catholics, and the corresponding need for military and civic education for French youth. In a section titled, "That the reading of the books of *Amadis de Gaul*, & such like is no less hurtful to youth, than the works of Machiavel to age,"[17] the author summarized four points of objection with these popular tales of love and arms: (1) their impious representation of sorcerers and enchanters, for readers "suffer themselves so far to be led as to delight to talk of them, or to see some of their proofs, they do by little and little take a custom not to abhor them;"[18] (2) their inclusion of sexually explicit content "which I term the *Poison of pleasure* [...] it consisteth in many sorts of dishonest lusts, which therein are so lively described;"[19] (3) their gratuitous violence, "which is a miserable custom brought in by this author [Montalvo], who avoweth that the highest point of knights' honor consisteth in cutting one another's throat for frivolous matters;"[20] and (4) their implausible combat tactics, "for although the wiser sort do account such knightly prowesses and giantlike strength, wherewith the reader is so importuned, to be but fables, yet the more indiscrete, under so sweet a charm of words cannot forbear, but remember some such draughts as are most conformable to their affections, to the end afterward as occasion may serve to try them, thinking thereby to be more active than others."[21]

The so-called "*Poison of pleasure*" that these books elicited was particularly concerning for moralists and theorists of the emerging field of primary education, who frequently waged war with these books over their common depiction of carnal delights. A particularly compelling mouthpiece for this argument was Spain's own humanist leader, Juan Luis Vives, who spent most of his life outside of Inquisitorial Spain, often expressing chagrin at its repressive cultural regime. He was equally appalled by the moral and intellectual failings of the country's popular romance books, as he noted in *The Education of a Christian Woman* (1524):

> I never heard of anyone who liked these books except one who had never come in contact with good books. I have read some of them myself but never found any trace of good intent or superior talent. I will lend credence to those who praise such books [...] if they say this after having had a taste of Cicero or Jerome or the sacred Scriptures, and if they

---

17. de la Noue, *The politicke and militarie discourses* (sigs. G4r–G8r). For clarity, the spelling has been modernized.
18. de la Noue, *The politicke and militarie discourses*, sig. G5v.
19. de la Noue, *The politicke and militarie discourses*, sig. G5r.
20. de la Noue, *The politicke and militarie discourses*, sig. G7v.
21. de la Noue, *The politicke and militarie discourses*, sig. G7v.

were not completely depraved themselves. For the mostpart, their only reason for awarding praise is that they see their own morals reflected in them as in a mirror and are happy to find approval.[22]

Having written his book for the instruction of Mary Tudor, Vives was particularly concerned with the negative examples that tales of love and arms gave to young women, though he was also more generally concerned that the genre represented a moral and intellectual danger to the youth.

Though undoubtedly useful in spurring men's spirits to acts of bravery and military prowess, these books also appeared to have had the undesirable effect of making society generally more violent; this danger encoded by the readerly desire toward imitation was most famously immortalized by Miguel de Cervantes's *Don Quixote of La Mancha* (1605), wherein the hero, run mad with reading books of chivalry, hacks and tilts his way across La Mancha. From the courtly pastimes of the joust to the drunken quarrels of the taverns and gentlemanly duels of the country, romance books seemed to be at the heart of Renaissance bids for honor. de la Noue claimed that the writers of books of chivalry were specifically responsible for a nostalgic revival of violent pastimes, devolving the common culture through popular emulation of a more primitive age:

> And of these tragedies [the author] maketh a sovereign pastime for *Kings, Ladies, Courts, & Cities*. Oftentimes we see in the lists the father against the son, the brother against the brother, the uncle against the nephew, where when they have hewn one upon another two long hours, they have both through faintness fallen down all tainted in blood. Sometime he feigneth they knew not one another, another time that they assailed each other to try themselves. But what gross & villainous ignorance & trials are those which procure the perpetrating of so horrible parricides [...] In old time the *Romans* toke pleasure in forcing men to fight to outrance before them, but these were transgressors that had deserved death. Where contrariwise ours are the sonnes of *Kings, Princes & Lords* that counterfeit swordplays: which can persuade unto youth that read these examples, nothing but that they still must be fighting with one or other, to the end to be esteemed of & feared. And peradventure such impressions have multiplied the quarrels in our France within these 30. years, to such quantity as we now see. Also it may be said & that justly, that such spectacles, through customable beholding the shedding of man's blood, have made our courts pitiless & cruel. Let therefore those that desire to feed their eyes with blood, imitate the manner of England, where they bring in wild beasts, as *Bears* and *Bulls* to fight with *dogs*, which pastime is without comparison far more lawful.[23]

de la Noue's observation of romance's hyperbolic violence, which readers then translated to the real world, reflected the supposition that the worst aspects of premodern culture were not only being *reflected* by romance literature, but also *reified* by it. Whereas the

---

22. Juan Luis Vives, *The Education of a Christian Woman: A Sixteenth-Century Manual*, Charles Fantazzi, trans. (Chicago: University of Chicago Press, 2000), 76. Although Vives's early life was marked by a strong adherence to Erasmianism, he distanced himself from during his residence at the English royal court, where he turned to humanism's more secular applications.
23. de la Noue, *The politicke and militarie discourses*, sig. G7v.

Romans had only promoted gladiator fights among the derelicts and condemned, the romantic duelers of the Renaissance took arms against their own kin and countrymen. Although de la Noue did not directly attribute Europe's devolving to the brutality of an earlier age as a direct result of Catholic or Spanish influence, the connection was clearly implied, particularly by his suggestion that "those that desire to feed their eyes with blood" should follow the "more lawful" manner of (Protestant) England in its bear-baiting and dogfighting entertainments.

By this observation, the French Huguenot tied Spanish romance to a rich nexus of negative Catholic associations between Spanish conquest and Roman tyranny. Although he largely blamed Spain for such inducements to violence, de la Noue also implicated France, for "to say the troth, *Spaine* bred them [the romance books], & *France* new clothed them in gay garments."[24] In other words, translation into French had effectually magnified the *"Poison of pleasure"* by elevating the quality of romantic prose and by making such works more widely available to readers. Still, the writer argued that Spaniards were the prime instigators toward warfare, which he instanced in a section complaining of Frenchmen's affection for foreign wars.[25] Having been imprisoned in Spain during the 1580s, where he wrote the *Discours politiques et militaires*, de la Noue turned his ardent anti-Spanish sentiment into a rallying cry for France to unify against the Catholic cause:

> Can the power of the *Spanish* Empire [...] force them [French Catholics] to sheath their *French* swords in the bowels of *France*? Shall the fear and complaints of the Protestants (which are not without some ground) so terrify them that they shall desist? Or may the secret practices, which tend to stirring up of great matters, fear them? Truly all this should not let them from establishing the sovereign law that bringeth health to all France which is the law of peace & concord.[26]

de la Noue's advocacy for universal "peace & concord" against the aggressions of the Spanish Empire also unearthed the Erasmian foundation for his criticism of *Amadís*, which he deemed the literary equivalent to Niccolò Machiavelli's *The Prince*.[27] Machiavelli had

---

24. François de La Noue, *The politicke and militarie discourses of the Lord de La Nouue VVhereunto are adioyned certaine obseruations of the same author, of things happened during the three late ciuill warres of France*, Edward Aggas, trans. (London, T.C., 1588), sig. G4r. Anthony Munday translated his *Declaration of the Lord de la Noue, upon his taking armes for the just defence of the townes of Sedan and Iametz, frontiers of the realme of Fraunce, and under the protection of his Majestie* (London: Iohn VVoolfe, 1589).

25. de la Noue compared his generation's inordinate bloodlust to their adoption of "a pretie Spanish saying," also quoted in Chapter 1, "Warre is my Countrie, my harnesse, my house, I am readie at all times to fight for a souse." *The politicke and militarie discourses of the Lord de La Nouue*, sig. I2v.

26. de La Noue, *The politicke and militarie discourses of the Lord de La Nouue*, sig. C5r. I have not found an earlier usage of the term Spanish Empire in print.

27. Recall that a major inspiration for *The Prince* was the ruthless Català military commander, César Borja, natural son of Pope Alexander VI (1431–1503; papal rule 1492–1503).

deemed justified warfare and cruelty as occasionally necessary for the maintenance of the state. As he wrote in *The Prince*, "the Romans, foreseeing troubles, dealt with them at once, and, even to avoid a war, would not let them come to a head, for they knew that war is not to be avoided, but is only to be put off to the advantage of others."[28] Erasmus, by contrast, had argued that the prince's prime directive was to deliver society to perpetual peace in the living example of Christ.[29] Using Rome as a key example, he described the imperial capital as "mad [...] with martial rage, and intoxicated with the vanity of military glory."[30] In this equation, war was a product of man's vanity—it was of the Earthly City, not of the Heavenly Jerusalem.[31] Although Erasmus was not strictly a universal pacifist—he called for a Christian war against the Turks—he nevertheless favored a *universal* peace for Christendom.[32] Speaking on behalf of Peace, Erasmus remarked: "when I [...] do but hear the word Man pronounced, I eagerly run to him as a being created purposely for me, and confidently promising myself, that with him I may live for ever in uninterrupted tranquility; but when I also hear the title of Christian added to the name of Man, I fly with additional speed, hoping that with Christians I may build an adamantine throne, and establish an everlasting empire."[33] By comparing *The Prince* to *Amadís*, marking it a danger to youth, de la Noue was therefore suggesting that such books had dragged society back toward the Earthly City of perpetual warfare and away from the heavenly city of perpetual Christian concord. Contrary to their common use by Spanish Catholics as guidebooks to find the Messianic kingdom, which brought conquerors to America, de la Noue found that these works instead led readers back to Rome.

Readers' impressions of Spain had been further colored by their reading of Spanish romance, which constituted a sort of firsthand testimony of the vicious Spanish character akin to the detailed accounts of Spain's enormities supplied by Iberian expats like Don António I, Prior of Crato, or Antonio Pérez, former secretary to King Philip II, two major sources of the Black Legend.[34] This, of course, seemed all-the-more reason that

---

28. Niccolò Machiavelli, *The Prince* (New York: Dover, 1992), 7.
29. In *The Complaint of Peace* (1521), Erasmus deployed prosopopoeia to have Peace directly preach the Erasmian concept of the state, which resulted from a natural human compulsion toward society and was embodied in the authority of the prince. Divinely ordained to rule over his fellow man, the prince was also honor-bound to promote and preserve the public felicity. For more information, see José A. Fernández, "Erasmus on the Just War," *Journal of the History of Ideas*, 34, no. 2 (1973), 209–226.
30. Erasmus, *The Complaint of Peace* (Chicago: The Open Court Publishing, 1917), 73.
31. This description was related to the Augustine concept of the City of God (geared toward perpetual Heavenly peace) as in conflict with the Earthly City, immersed in the cares and pleasures of the mortal realm. Augustine had treated Rome as the exemplary case of the Earthly City, the adverse of Heavenly Jerusalem.
32. Erasmus described the murder of other Christians as a prime heresy: "as there can be no victim so acceptable to the devil as a Christian sacrificed by a Christian, are not you, my good Christian, sacrificing to the devil as much as the turk?" *The Complaint of Peace*, 34.
33. Erasmus, *The Complaint of Peace*, 10.
34. For information regarding how these expats fomented the Black Legend, see Fernando Bouza, "D. António I Prior de Crato y el Horizonte Portugués de La Leyenda Negra," in Rodríguez Pérez, Sánchez Jiménez, Den Boer, *España ante sus críticos*, 117–37; Jesús M. Usunáriz, "«Envidia

Spain must be defeated. In his dedication to Sir George Clifford, 3rd Earl of Cumberland, English translator Edward Aggas wrote the following of the *Political and Military Discourses*:

> I am fully persuaded the indifferent and not curious reader shall find matter sufficient for the reestablishing of a ruinous commonwealth, if it be put in practice: wise counsel for maintenance thereof: and lastly approved documents requisite whether in civil or foreign wars, which albeit they were written particularly to relieve and restore the declining estate of the realm of France, are also in my opinion not unnecessary for ours or any other that may fall into the like, if God who is the protector and guider of all Realms should not continue among us unity and godly peace.[35]

As Aggas reasoned, war was of course to be avoided, but if the divine had willed a war against Roman Catholicism, then de la Noue's arguments could provide legal and rhetorical justifications for the Reformed League's resistance efforts against Habsburg Spain, the major military and political arm of the Holy Roman Empire.[36] Although it mainly gathered together long-standing complaints of European and especially Erasmian humanists who had contributed to a Black Legend of Spanish Cruelty, the *Discours politiques et militaires* also mobilized an ideological culture war against Spain that would partly take place in and through literary criticism. de la Noue's veiled ethnic arguments against romance books, implying that the works were vicious in part because of their common descent from Spain, therefore formed regular part of the humanist diatribes against imperial Spain, which frequently elided aesthetic issues with the political. In *Palladis Tamia* (1598), for instance, English literary critic Frances Meres concurred with "the Lord *de la Nouue* [who] in the sixe discourse of his politike and military dicourses censureth of the Bookes of *Amadis de Gaule*, which he saith are no lesse hurtfull to youth, then the workes of *Machiauell* to age."[37] The comment agreed with de la Noue over the moral constitution of ideal poetry, for which romance was perceived to

---

de la potencia del rey católico»: respuestas españolas a las críticas de sus enemigos en los siglos XVI y XVII," in Rodríguez Pérez, Sánchez Jiménez, Den Boer, *España ante sus críticos*, 45–66, esp. 50–62.

35. Edward Aggas, "To the Right Honorable his verie good Lorde, George Earle of Cumberland," in François de La Noue, *The politicke and militarie discourses of the Lord de La Nouue*, Edward Aggas, trans. (London, T.C., 1588), sigs. A2r–A3r (sig. A2v).

36. Drawing from Franz Bosbach's seminal work, *Monarchia universalis. Ein politischer Leitbegriff der frühen Neuzeit* (Vandenhoeck und Ruprecht, 1988), David Armitage observes that the "language of universal monarchy provided its opponents with a counter-theory of the Empire […] [and that] after the elevation of Charles V it became a means of understanding international politics as the competition between Habsburg and Bourbon aspirations to political hegemony through the age of Louis XIV (and indeed beyond) […] what began as an analytical theory of empire ultimately became a justification for defensive aggression within Europe." See David Armitage, "Introduction," in Armitage, ed. *Theories of Empire, 1450–1800* (Routledge, 1998), xv–xxxiii (xx).

37. Francis Meres, *Palladis tamia. Wits treasury being the second part of Wit's common wealth* (London: Cuthbert Burbie, 1598), sig. Mm4r.

fail unequivocally.[38] Intuitively Aristotelian, this argument also revealed both critics' agreement over the danger represented by romance's gratuitously violent spectacles, particularly the concern that readers would be inspired to emulate the violence described in such tales of love and arms, and so devolve by imitation of Spain's example.[39]

Guilty Reading

Romance's cultural decline in status over the course of the early modern period in England involved a number of factors: (1) the advent of the printing press and the corresponding democratization of English letters; (2) the increase in literacy throughout the sixteenth and seventeenth centuries; and (3) the contemporary politicizing of genre into intellectual hierarchies.[40] Feminist scholarship has especially taken up the question of how genre and gender intersected with theories of Renaissance reading. Lori Humphrey Newcomb observes that "two kinds of reading practices made early modern romances popular: fiction was read by increasingly diverse audiences, and their tastes were read as constituting a subordinate cultural category."[41] She traces the history of composition and reception of romance to show how the genre gradually came to be regarded as a "lesser kind of literature."[42] In particular, "a new supply of printed prose romances threatened the boundary that had previously limited pleasure reading to elite men. Writers responsive to elite interests identified these romances as more sullied by the materiality of

---

38. The books condemned by Meres were not solely of the chivalric persuasion. For instance, he censured Fernando de Rojas's sentimental romance, *Celestina* (1499; English trans. 1525), which was neither rightfully chivalric—Calisto, the bachelor protagonist, is not a knight—nor particularly immoral.
39. We usually discuss Aristotle's discourses on mimesis in terms of drama, but they of course applied to all poetry. Aristotle noted that since drama is essentially a species of poetry, it is subject to poetry's aesthetic principles; on a more universal level, he was observing and denoting praxes for ideal plots, particularly those of the tragic and epic persuasions. Correspondingly, as a species of poesy (comprising both tragic and epic elements), prose (and verse) romances could also be subjected to the Aristotelian method, particularly Aristotle's description of what constituted an ideal plot, and how the plot should be the driver of the work, not the spectacle. Romance's graphically violent episodes generally violated the Aristotelian method by fetishizing violent spectacles, which de la Noue and others attributed to their common country of origin, Spain. For instance, regarding Spaniards' notoriety for rape (a common trope in romance), Meres noted that "the Spaniardes in America rauished the women, both their owne bandes, and the Indians beholding them" *Palladis tamia*, sig. Rr6v.
40. For more information on the gendered hierarchy of romance, see, e.g., Margaret W. Ferguson, "A Room Not Their Own: Renaissance Women as Readers and Writers," in *The Comparative Perspective on Literature: Approaches to Theory and Practice*, Clayton Koelb and Susan Noakes, eds. (Ithaca: Cornell University Press, 1988), 93–116; Jacqueline Pearson, "Women Reading, Reading Women," in *Women and Literature in Britain 1500–1700*, Helen Wilcox, ed. (Cambridge: Cambridge University Press, 1996), 80–99; Mary Ellen Lamb, "Constructions of Women Readers," in *Teaching Tudor and Stuart Women Writers*, Susanne Woods and Margaret P. Hannay, eds. (New York: Modern Language Association, 2000), 23–34.
41. Newcomb, *Reading Popular Romance*, 1.
42. Newcomb, *Reading Popular Romance*, 1.

printing, distribution, sales, and consumption than the books they preferred for themselves [...] The making of popular literature, then, turns out to be an essential, but mostly suppressed, element in the making of elite literature."[43]

English romance writer Robert Greene published roughly 15 romances from 1580 to 1590, many of them drawn from English and continental sources. He acquired so much notoriety in the genre that Thomas Nashe even described him as the "Homer of women" in his 1589 *Anatomie of absurditie*.[44] Newcomb notes that in Renaissance writings, Greene's *Pandosto* (1588) was commonly used to "exemplify the category of popular literature."[45] But if Greene's *Pandosto* was called upon to represent the rabble of English romances popular with women, the Spanish *Espejo* was likewise brought forth to represent the intervening and doubly egregious body of foreign romances that threatened to overtake England's native tradition. For instance, in Thomas Overbury's satirical book, *New and choise characters, of seuerall authors* (1615), a Chambermaid "reades *Greenes* workes ouer and ouer, but is so carried away with the *Myrrour of Knighthood*, she is many times resolud to run out of her selfe, and become a Lady Errant."[46]

The comparison of a single Spanish work's profound influence over female readers to that of so large a body of English works compels us to wonder what exactly made the romance seem so dangerous. Heidi Brayman Hackel observes that the "portrayal of this servant girl seduced by a romance belongs to the early modern discourse that sexualized women's reading, particularly of this genre."[47] Helen Hackett has further traced the origins of anti-romantic stereotypes specifically to the efforts of late sixteenth- and early seventeenth-century male writers who dedicated their romances to women, thereby marketing the genre as both delectable and declassé.[48] These prefatory appeals served the rhetorical purpose of marketing romance to the predominately male readership.[49]

---

43. Newcomb, *Reading Popular Romance*, 1–2.
44. Qtd. in Hackett, *Women and Romance Fiction*, 92.
45. Newcomb, *Reading Popular Romance*, 2.
46. Thomas Overbury, *Sir Thomas Ouerburie his wife with new elegies vpon his (now knowne) vntimely death: whereunto are annexed, new newes and characters / written by himselfe and other learned gentlemen* (London: Lawrence L'isle, 1615), sig. G8r. This quotation has been amply noted in feminist scholarship of romance such as in, for example, Lori Humphrey Newcomb, *Reading Popular Romance in Early Modern England* (New York: Columbia University Press, 2002), 89; Newcomb, "Prose Fiction," in *The Cambridge Companion to Early Modern Women's Writing*, ed. Laura Knoppers (Cambridge: Cambridge University Press, 2009), 272–86 (276); Newcomb, "Gendering Prose Romance," in *A Companion to Romance: From Classical to Contemporary*, Corinne Saunders, ed. (Oxford: Blackwell, 2004), 121–39 (129); Helen Hackett, "'Yet Tell Me Some Such Fiction': Mary Wroth's *Urania* and the 'Femininity' of Romance," in *Women, Texts and Histories, 1575–1760*, Diane Purkiss and Clare Brant, eds. (London: Routledge, 1992), 39–68 (41–42); and Davis, *Chivalry and Romance in the English Renaissance*, 26.
47. Heidi Brayman Hackel, *Reading Material in Early Modern England* (Cambridge: Cambridge University Press, 2005), 153.
48. Helen Hackett, *Women and Romance Fiction in the English Renaissance* (Cambridge: Cambridge University Press, 2000), 6 and 19.
49. Hackett, *Women and Romance Fiction*, 11.

Hackett also claims that the rhetorical feminization of romance may have been influenced by England's growing interest in popular Spanish romances of chivalry, especially *Espejo*.[50] In fact, misogyny and Hispanophobia were mutually marginalizing discourses; because of the genre's strong association with inordinate lust, and because of Spaniards' established reputation for womanizing, as we have already seen, the idea that these books might be enjoyed by women was regarded merely as further evidence of Spain's attempts to conquer England (arms) by conquering its women (love). Overbury made a similar observation in his 1614 marriage tract called *A wife now the widow*. He described the attributes of a bad wife as one who "thinks shee is faire, though many times her opinion goes alone, and shee loues her glasse and the knight of the *Sunne* for lying."[51] With his imagined flatteries, the Knight of the Sun here came to stand in for not only the entire (Spanish) romance genre, but also a complete ecosystem of male erotic reading that probed diverse sources from Ovid's *Heroides* to Castiglione's *Book of the Courtier* (1528) to learn the art of seducing women. Although they read across time and space to learn the art of courtship, men found particular utility in the Spanish romances, and so the genre came to represent the vicious intentions of men's amorous reading.[52]

Mirrour of Knighthood translator Margaret Tyler had herself noted the tendency for writers to dedicate their romances to ladies, which she considered an opportunity for women like herself to read and translate these works, so to "farther wade into them in the search of truth."[53] In taking up the translation of the romance, however, Tyler was clearly conscious of her gender, which cast her in the role of a literary interloper intervening in the masculine domain of Renaissance arms:

> be it that the attempt were bold to intermeddle in arms, so as the ancient Amazons did, and in this story Claridiana doth, and in other stories not a few, yet to report of arms is not so odious, but that it may be borne withal, not only in you men which yourselves are fighters, but in us women, to whom the benefit in equal part appertaineth of your victories.[54]

Tyler's appeal to the universality of the romance's themes, of interest to both sexes, particularly struck with concerns over Spanish cultural hegemony and military prowess, or "this common fear on all parts of war and invasion. The invention, disposition, trimming, and what else in this story is wholly another man's, my part none therein but translation, as it were: only in giving entertainment to a stranger, before this time unacquainted

---

50. See Hackett, *Women and Romance Fiction*, 65–68.
51. *A wife novv the widdow of Sir Thomas Overburye Being a most exquisite and singular poem of the choice of a wife. Whereunto are added many witty characters, and conceited newes, written by himselfe and other learned gentlemen his friends* (London: Lawrence Lisle, 1614; STC 18904), sig. D1r. Overbury uses the term "a very very Woman," sig. C4v.
52. Hackett further suggests that the imagined female readers and actual male readers of romance served to personify society's general emasculation. *Women and Romance Fiction*, 86.
53. Tyler, "To the Reader," 50.
54. Tyler, "To the Reader," 49.

with our country guise."[55] Though uniquely expressed in a female voice, this defense of translation as a military strategy against imperial Spain appealed to a classical notion of translatio studii as translatio imperii.

Building on Friedrich Schleirmacher's claim that the translator has only two choices in translation, either to leave the author in peace or to move the reader toward him, Lawrence Venuti has placed a theory of translation as "domestication" in diametric opposition to what he calls "foreignization," or registering "the linguistic and cultural difference of the foreign text, sending the reader abroad."[56] Considered in light of this proposed dichotomy, Tyler's approach rather constituted foreignization with the goal of domestication, so that England might conquer Spain. It was not simply a matter of taking something Spanish and making it English, but rather of embracing certain aspects of a foreign culture so that they could be weaponized against the source nation.[57] Although related through the conventional role of the lady of the household, Tyler's polite form of *domestication* into the English language nevertheless encoded a competitive motivation, to coopt the best military insight of the "Spanish, in which nation, by common report, the inheritance of all warlike commendation hath to this day rested"[58] and reattribute it to England, as if the Spanish romance were like a great military commander, turned cloak, and regarbed in "our country guise."

The writer and translator, John Thorius, also suggested as much in his translation of the Spanish general Francisco de Valdés's martial treatise, *The sergeant maior: A dialogue of the office of a sergeant maior* (1590).[59] As Thorius noted in his dedicatory epistle to naval and military commander Sir John Norris, coming from one of the highest-ranking non-commissioned officers in the Spanish army, this firsthand testimony of Spanish military strategy might prove useful to Norris for improving England's own military campaigns against the empire:

> And forasmuch as thys booke was written to instruct those that are professed enemyes to our estate, I thought that we might reap some profit by them, if this their Sergeant Maior were

---

55. Tyler, "To the Reader," 49.
56. Lawrence Venuti, "Translation as Cultural Politics: Regimes of Domestication in English," *Textual Practice* 7.2 (1993), 208–23 (210). In coherence with Venuti's theory, this study has also maintained foreign terms or native spelling wherever possible, so "sending the reader abroad."
57. I am reminded of the preface to Peter Motteux's translation of *Don Quixote*, wherein he apologizes to Cervantes for the poor quality of Captain John Stevens's earlier translation from 1700, apparently based on the French translation, remarking that "Never did Spaniard suffer more by Drake, than our Knight of La Mancha by the Writer of that English-Spanish Quixote." Peter Motteux, "The Translator's Preface" in Miguel de Cervantes, *The History of the renown'd Don Quixote de la Mancha written in Spanish by Miguel de Cervantse Saavedra; translated from the original by several hands, and published by Peter Motteux; adorn'd with sculptures* (London: Sam Buckley, 1712), sigs. A5r–A8r (sig. A6r).
58. Tyler, transl. *The Mirrour of Knighthood*, 48.
59. Thorius also published a translation of Bartolomé Felippe's *Tratado del consejo y de los consejeros de los Príncipes* (*The Counseller, A Treatise of Counsels and Counsellors*) (1589) and an English version of Antonio del Corro's Spanish-French grammar book (1590).

as well knowne unto our men as unto themselves [...] for that theyr orders being knowen unto us, we may the better and more easily hurte them and benefit our selves by reason of this advantage. I have therefore bestowed some pains in unarming this Spanysh Sergeant and doffing his Castilian and hostile armour, and have clothed him in English apparel, to the end that our men may use him to theyr pleasure, and he finding him selfe metamorphosed, learne how to serve English men.[60]

Thorius's costume metaphor reflects a conceptual goal to domesticate Valdés, but one must also consider the sense of its usage: to identify the sources and *habits* of Spain's celebrated military strategizing, so as to coopt them for the English regiment. Using language of combat, Thorius therefore imagined his translation as disarming Valdés to the end of employing him as a servant to England, expressing a strategy of translation as reeducation that is comparable to the modern westernization of combatant nations.

In her dedication to Thomas Howard, Tyler acknowledged that *Espejo* was not a military guidebook, and indeed it differs starkly from a work like *The sergeant maior*. Therefore, her defense of the translation as a domestication of Spain (as in cultural disarmament) doesn't really fit. A fictional romance, *Espejo* was "not indeed the most profitablest, as entreating of arms."[61] In fact, as we have seen, the real interest that readers pursued with this romance was as a tale of love. This, as we also know, was a common defect attributed to such romances. According to de la Noue, works of this kind not only besmirched the rules of warfare, making society more brutal and less civilized, but they also corrupted the virtuous dimension of courtly love, producing erotic content so delectable as to yield moral corruption through indulgence in the "*Poison of pleasure*."[62] But if these famous criticisms were lodged at the books of *Amadís*, a title so popular that it often served as synecdoche, why was Overbury's Chambermaid instead reading *The Mirrour of Knighthood*?

Recall that in print *Amadís* was originally guised as a French style manual by Paynell's *Treasurie*, with Paynell further attributing its educational benefits as a rhetorical guidebook to its origins in "the french tong so pleasant, so highly commended, and so imbraced of all men."[63] de la Noue likewise observed that "to say the troth, *Spaine* bred them [the romances], & *France* new clothed them in gay garments."[64] These comments underscored the perceived *Frenchness* of Amadís, who was "of Gaul," after all. The French prestige transcended the bulk of Spanish romances printed in England, especially those by Anthony Munday, and though the works were not altogether spared from criticism (on the contrary, they were plenty criticized), they did register less directly with Spain. *Espejo*,

---

60. John Thorius, Dedication, "To the Right Honourable Knight, Sir John Norris," in Francisco de Valdes, *The sergeant maior A dialogue of the office of a sergeant maior. VVritten in Spanishe by the Maister of the Campe Francisco de Valdes. And translated into Englishe, by Iohn Thorius* (London: John Wolfe, 1590), sigs. A2r–A2v.
61. Tyler, trans., *The Mirrour of Knighthood*, 48.
62. de la Noue, *The politicke and militarie discourses*, sig. G5r.
63. Paynell, "To the Gentle Reader," in *The treasurie of Amadis of Fraunce*, iii–iiii.
64. Francois de la Noue, *The politicke and militarie discourses*, sig. G4r.

by contrast, lacked this linguistic moderation as a tale translated directly from Spanish and moreover advertised as such. Therefore, it would be easy to attribute any of the romance's perceived faults to its origins in imperial Spain, which had very obviously *bred* the work. Not only were the character names of Hispanic/Latinate origin, but they were clearly of a Spanish Catholic inspiration, with the main hero, the Knight of the Sun, particularly bearing a distinct Catholic imperial association with Philip II and his cited profligacy, which could be compared to the Knight of the Sun's simultaneous pursuit of two women. As such, Tyler's direct translation of *The Mirriour of Knighthood* from Spanish must have seemed less like *domestication*, bringing the cultural other back as the same (to make Spain more like England), and more like *foreignization*, sending the reader abroad to make the English more like the Spanish.[65]

We must also consider the wayward figure of Claridiana as contributing to the negative reputation of *The Mirrour of Knighthood*. (Overbury's Chambermaid after all sought to become a lady errant.) Ample references attest to the readerly interest inspired by Claridiana's love quest for the Knight of the Sun. For instance, in Francis Beaumont's *Knight of the Burning Pestle* (1507), a citizen's apprentice named Rafe appears onstage reading a passage from Anthony Munday's translation of *Palmerin d'Oliva*. He remarks, "I wonder why the kings do not raise an army of fourteen or fifteen hundred thousand men, as big as the army that the Prince of Portigo brought against Rosicleer, and destroy these giants; they do much hurt to wandering damsels, that go in quest of their knights" (1.229–32).[66] Although noted ironically, this confluence of danger and hurt that could befall a wandering damsel emphasized the figure's association with moral waywardness. In *The Alchemist* (1610), Ben Jonson made the association more explicit when he compared the famous *virgo bellatrix*, Claridiana, to the prostitute, Dol Common (1.1.220–1).[67] In the real world, of course, the female type most likely to be found *wandering* out of doors was the prostitute.[68] Nevertheless, there was also great appeal to a character like Claridiana, whose forwardness and hybrid sexual identity (as a woman bearing arms) presented an enticing reversal of the classic conception that virtuous women needed to be conquered either by words or deeds. So, too, must there have been some appeal to Tyler's *Mirrour of Knighthood* as the first romance published by a woman, and not only a woman, but a servant woman (like Overbury's Chambermaid) who thought of herself as something of a lady errant as well. By choosing to read the romances, women like Tyler aspired to

---

65. Nevertheless, since the work was strongly influenced by the *Orlando* and *Amadís* epics, its underscored Hispanism may have also served as convenient scapegoating.
66. Francis Beaumont, *The Knight of the Burning Pestle*, Revels Plays Edition, Sheldon P. Zitner, ed. (New York: Palgrave, 2004).
67. Unless otherwise indicated, all quotations from the works of Ben Jonson are derived from the *Cambridge Edition of the Works of Ben Jonson*, vols. 1–7, David Bevington, Martin Butler, and Ian Donaldson, eds. (Cambridge: Cambridge University Press, 2012).
68. Claridiana does take on something of the role of a bawd; in I.1, for instance, she pits Rosicleer's companions in a duel with the men of her country, and she sets her own gentlewomen as the prize (95). This scene was probably inspired by its main source, Matteo Boiardo's *Orlando innamorato*, wherein the beautiful Angelica offers herself as a prize at a duel set in the court of the Emperor Charlemagne.

the forbidden knowledge represented by the masculine genre of romance. Their invasive presence called attention to the genre's laden erotic content, thereby exposing the era's idealized perceptions of female innocence to the brute force of a masculine desire, which fetishized sexual conquest. In other words, women's interventions into romance shed light upon men's private vices.

By ironically invoking Claridiana in the form of Dol Common, Jonson thus inveighed against the masculine mentality that lauded female virtue, on one hand, eroticizing distance and inaccessibility, and sought out sexually available women (e.g., prostitutes) on the other. Furthermore, he mocked those men who claimed to read Spanish tales of love and arms to ennoble their spirits to great deeds with snippets of philosophy and classical theory, though most really read to discover, in the words of Juan Luis Vives, "some words taken from the secret archives of Venus that are spoken at the propitious moment to impress and arouse the woman you love if she shows some resistance. If they are read for that reason, it would be better to write books on the art of whoring."[69] Implicit to this criticism was the presumption that (Spanish) romance had corrupted the humanist program by mistreating the classical authorities, especially Ovid. Indeed, the "emotive Ovidian letters were staple texts in humanist male education."[70] These works provided "the path to knowledge and moral command, on the one hand, and mastery of the heroic *genus familiare*, with its base in erotic stories of women ultimately 'captured' […] by their heroes, on the other."[71] But the warlike virgin, imbued with a pronounced sexual forwardness that was attributed to Amazonia, did not well correspond to the conventional Ovidian conception of courtship as masculine conquest. In Act 4 of Jonson's *The Alchemist,* for example, Dame Pliant is brought in to play the part of a Spanish countess in order to con Surly (disguised as a Spanish nobleman) into a marriage match. She is initially resistant, remarking, "Truly, I shall never brook a Spaniard […] Never sin' eighty-eight could I abide 'em / And that was some three year afore I was born, in truth" (4.4.28–30). Pliant's Hispanophobia is a knee-jerk resistance to all things Spanish; it is an English sentiment of automatic disavowal, which then informs the play's mockery of Spanish rules of courtship, as a subsequent exchange reveals:

Kas[tril]. Must not she make curt'sy?
Sub[tle]. Ods will, she must go to him, man, and kiss him!
It is the Spanish fashion, for the women
To make first court.
Face. 'Tis true he tells you, sir:
His art knows all. (4.4.67–70)

---

69. Vives, *The Education of a Christian Woman*, 76.
70. Warren Boutcher, "'Who Taught Thee Rhetoricke to Deceive a Maid?': Christopher Marlowe's Hero and Leander, Juan Boscán's Leandro, and Renaissance Vernacular Humanism," *Comparative Literature*, 52.1 (2000), 11–52 (27).
71. Boutcher, "'Who Taught Thee Rhetoricke to Deceive a Maid?,'" 27.

In speculating upon Spanish customs, the men betray biases that are likely pulled from their (i.e., Jonson's) reading of Spanish romance, wherein warlike women like Claridiana appear as practically male in their forwardness in "first court[ing]."

In repeatedly referencing the so-called *books of the brave*, Jonson further called attention to the imperialist agenda that undergirded early modern romance reading, specifically by pricking men's desires with the promise of power and glory—and women. Sir Epicure Mammon probably best represents this stereotype. He first appears in the play with his mind firmly planted *"in Novo Orbe"* (2.1.2). He explains that he has contracted Subtle to produce for him the Philosopher's Stone, purportedly so that he can unlock the mysteries of terra incognita. He also wishes to tap all kinds of hidden knowledge, expressing universalist ideals similar to those of Christopher Marlowe's Doctor Faustus, though it's clear that what most motivates him is his desire for gold, as in "the rich Peru" (2.1.2), and his desire for women: "To have a list of wives and concubines, / Equal with Solomon, who had the stone / [...] / to encounter fifty a night" (2.1.35–9). This agenda is further underscored by his implied hedonistic pleasures with Dol Common, whom he believes to be a deranged noblewoman. He easily woos her with lofty proclamations of her virtue and beauty, though he is clearly more than happy to bed her. As a symbolic figure for the wayward romance heroine, Dol's easy corruption is representative of the *pleasure's poisons* that typically motivated men of Jonson's generation, which carried strong Spanish associations.[72] It is fitting then, that we see Dol Common taking on all of these real or symbolic roles of the masculine fancy, from the form of the Queen of Fairy that she takes for Dapper, to the likened nobility of "Austriac princes" (4.1.74), to the familiar *virgo bellatrix* (e.g., Claridiana, Bradamante, Belphoebe), to a goddess of Nature, emerging "in a free state" enjoying "in perpetuity / Of life, and lust" (4.1.156, 165–66).

In his works, Jonson repeatedly called attention to the disjuncture between the high-minded ideals that brought men to secular romance reading and the lowly pleasures that resulted from the practice, and by his repeatedly tying these contradictions to characters

---

72. These were very often paired with references to Spanish wine, which, as I discussed in Chapter 1, usually symbolized Spain's sinful excesses. To quote Meres in *Palladis tamia*, when comparing lust to wine: "the first sip of loue is pleasant, the second perillous, the third pestilent [...] I haue read that in a short space there was a towne in Spain vndermined with Conies" (sig. T1r). The coney was a common euphemism for the female pudendum, as in Robert Greene's lewd coney-catching pamphlets. In further instance, in the puppet show of *Hero and Leander* from Jonson's *Bartholomew Fair* (1614), Leatherhead explains that Cupid "because he would have their [Hero and Leander's] meeting to be merry, / He strikes Hero in love to him with a pint of sherry, / Which he tells her from amorous Leander is sent her, / Who after him into the room of Hero doth venter" (5.4.160-4). In response to this detail, Puppet Jonas exclaims *"A pint of sack! Score a pint of sack i'the Coney!"* (5.4.186). Reflecting a common confusion between Spanish sack and Spanish sherry, Cokes corrects Puppet Jonas, who earlier claimed that the wine was sherry, to which Jonas agrees. Cokes remarks, "Sherry, sherry, sherry. By my troth he makes me merry" (lines 191–92). The line refers to a common saying, also spoken by the Host in Jonson's *The New Inn*, "Be merry and drink sherry" (1.2.29). For more information on Jonson's view of Spanish romance, see Yumiko Yamada, *Ben Jonson and Cervantes: Tilting against Chivalric Romances* (Tokyo: Maruzen, 2000).

who prided themselves as great wits, he further tied the contemporary dominance of the rhetorical arts to romance's gradual debasement of humanist learning. For instance, in Jonson's great comedy about English wit, *Epicene, or the Silent Woman*, dated to the same period as *The Alchemist* circa 1610, Truewit reveals to Dauphine his secret art for getting women, remarking:

> You must leave to live i' your chamber, then a month together upon Amadís de Gaul, or Don Quixote as you are wont; and come abroad where the matter is frequent, to court, to tiltings, public shows, and feasts, to plays, and church sometimes […] In these places a man shall find whom to love, whom to play with, whom to touch once, whom to hold ever. The variety arrests his judgment. (4.1.54–62)

The period of study that Truewit recommends is not ad fuentes to Ovid's *elegaics*, but to the contemporary romances (prominently those of Spain) with their muddied representation of classical love discourse and humanist learning. With its paramount compulsion toward viciousness, this instruction underscores the perceived failure of Erasmian humanism, with its emphasis on classical learning and Christian morality, in favor of a lay humanism guised as worldliness, refinement, and eloquence. As we have seen, this Erasmian humanism was also a touchstone of anti-Spanish sentiment, a visceral expression of the common stereotype that Spaniards were intellectually and morally corrupt and, so, only useful for fighting and fornicating. Touching on the comment by Vives that these works best showed how to "arouse a woman if she shows resistance," Jonson also depicted Truewit instructing Dauphine to turn to rape if a woman seems reluctant to his sexual advances, noting that female shows of unwillingness were merely part of the rules of courtship: "their desire is to be tempted" (4.1.83). He also recommends that Dauphine be seen to excel in feats of arms: "If she love wit, give verses, though you borrow 'em […] If valor, talk of your sword, and be frequent in the mention of quarrels, though you be staunch in fighting. If activity, be seen o'your barbary often, or leaping over stools, for the credit of your back" (4.1.110–15). Of course, Truewit is not talking about actual feats of arms, but rather, as his name implies, flights of fancy and pretty words.

Romance's ample humanistic corruptions, as related by Jonson, could help to resolve the lingering problem of "how to interpret Jonson's attitude towards the figure of Ovid— as a great poet who deserves his banishment because he falls off from the moral ideal Jonson holds out for the poet, or, as a figure of sympathy, who demonstrates the vulnerability of the artist to the peremptory will of the powerful."[73] Jonson's Spanish romance comparisons specifically associate Ovid with the latter figure. For instance, in the quarto version of Jonson's play, *Poetaster* (1602), the martial figure, Tucca, refers to Ovid as "my most Magnanimous Mirrour of Knighthood" (1.2.127).[74] This was a fitting comparison

---

73. Julian Koslow, "Humanist Schooling and Ben Jonson's Poetaster," *English Literary History* 73, no. 1 (2006), 119–59 (126).
74. Ben Jonson, *Poetaster or The arraignment* (London: R. Bradock, 1602), sig. B2r. This was later changed for the 1616 folio in favor of "my flower o' the order." Gabriele Bernhard Jackson explains that "when Jonson…carried over his 'Roman' vocabulary from the quarto texts of *Sejanus* and *Catiline* into their folio printings, he 'translated' *Poetaster*'s mentions of knights

(indictment) for Ovid, who in this play assumes the role of the romantic lover and libertine. Jonson cited *The Mirrour of Knighthood* as a proof of Spain's perceived deterioration of Latin letters and of Erasmian humanism, particularly referencing English wit in such moments as when rival poet, John Marston, is depicted in the character of Crispinius to be literally vomiting up his bombastic language (5.3).[75] Such moments serve to displace anxieties about the immorality of much of Ovid's sexually explicit material by blaming Spain for its alleged corruption of the rhetorical arts.

For an elite classicist like Jonson, romance's brand of lay classicism must have seemed a prime ignorance propagated in part by Spain's seeming hegemony over Renaissance culture (frequently guised as *fashion*). In *Cynthia's Revels*, for instance, the courtier named Amorphus (possibly Anthony Munday), who is drunk of the fountain of self-love, promises to teach Asotus the art of being a courtier. Asotus says that he will call his fictional lady, "my dear Lindabrides" (3.5.24–25), adding in reference to her beloved Knight of the Sun, "she should have been married to him, but that the princess Claridiana—" (3.5.28–29). Amorphus interrupts, exclaiming, "O, you betray your reading" (3.5.30). Asotus responds, "Nay, sir, I have read history. I am a little humanitian" (3.5.31). An ironic allusion to the romance's guilty pleasures (*pleasure's poisons*), the line also has a second meaning, as the self-styled "humanitian" confuses romance with proper history and romance reading with proper humanism.

Although the books of *Amadís*, *Palmerín*, *Primaleón*, and other "Spanish inuentions"[76] were frequently condemned by romance's many detractors, *Espejo* frequently served as synecdoche for the rabble of bad romances particularly popular with readers. It was sometimes interchangeable with other titles like *Amadís* and *Palmerín*, but it was more commonly used in reference to women. This work served as the exemplar of the Spanish chivalric tradition that, for some, also represented the worst that these romances had to offer: their penchant for heroic hyperbole, their depiction of idle knights diverting themselves with damsels-in-distress, their celebration of transgressive sexual behaviors by both male and female characters, their reliance on supernatural plot devices, and perhaps most dubiously, their unique popularity with women. For instance, in his play, *The Guardian* (1655), Philip Massinger ironically mocked *The Mirrour of Knighthood* through

---

into English analogues." Gabriele Bernhard Jackson, Introduction to *Poetaster*, *The Cambridge Works of Ben Jonson, vol. 2, 1601–06*, David Bevington, Martin Butler, and Ian Donaldson, eds. (Cambridge: Cambridge University Press, 2012), 3–18 (5). Nevertheless, David Bevington also notes, in reference to the change to *Poetaster*, that Jonson was sensitive to Dekker's many *ad hominem* attacks, especially regarding Jonson's Catholic leanings. Bevington, "*Poetaster*: Textual Essay," *The Cambridge Edition of the Works of Ben Jonson Online*, https://universitypublishingonline.org/cambridge/benjonson/k/essays/Poetaster_textual_essay/.

75. Ovid's relation to the courtly love tradition, Hispanized by Spanish sources, is also invoked in Thomas Dekker's response play, *Satiromastix*. When speaking of Sir Quintillian Shorthose's affection for the widow, Mistress Miniver, Captain Tucca asks, "Dost loue her, my finest and first part of the Mirrour of Knighthood?" *Satiro-Mastix, or The vntrussing of the Humorous Poet* (London: Edward White, 1602), sig. F1v.

76. Edward Topsell, *Times lamentation: or An exposition on the prophet Ioel, in sundry sermons or meditations* (London: George Potter, 1599), sig. E8v.

the figure of Iolante's sycophantic confidante, Calypso, who relates her affection for "all the books of *Amadis de Gaul,* / The *Palmerin,* and that true Spanish story / The *Mirror of Knighthood,* which I have read often, / Read feelingly, nay more" (1.2.67–70).[77]

As is generally the case, however, the stereotype little corresponded with the reality. These idle tales of love and arms continued to be read by an eager masculine reading public; and so, the growing feminization and foreignization of the genre also produced a readerly culture of guilty romance reading as a self-conscious masculine response to the elite invectives against the practice. For example, as publisher and author Francis Kirkman wrote of the tenure of his law apprenticeship in his pseudo-biographical work, *The Unlucky Citizen* (1673):

> They that came into our Shop, might by the outside of the Books, imagine that we were well furnished with Law Books according to our practice, but if they had searched their inside, they would have found their mistake, when in stead of the *Statutes at large,* and *Cooks Reports,* they should see *Amadis de Gaul,* and *Orlando Furioso,* and in stead of *Brooks Abridgment,* and some such old Law Books, they would have found the *Mirrour of Knighthood,* they would have been much mistaken when instead of Gown-men pleading at the Bar, they found Sword-men fighting at the Barriers.[78]

Kirkman wrote *The Unlucky Citizen* in the style of the Spanish picaresque novel, *Lazarillo de Tormes* (1554), "that famous Book, of the Fryar and the Boy."[79] In this beloved Spanish bestseller, the narrator presents the story of his wicked life in the form of a confession of former transgressions; as the above passage implies therefore, the period of Kirkman's law apprenticeship corresponded with his secret indulgence in what de la Noue called the *"Poison of pleasure"* reading, though Kirkman's collective pronouns also emphasized that he was by no means alone in his readerly errantry. Indeed, Kirkman's account of the foreign romances hidden within the bindings of English law tomes bespeaks England's early modern fascination with these beloved tales of love and arms, which was concealed beneath the decorous veneer of the country's statutory culture. Furthermore, since the three works listed, *Amadís, Orlando* and *Espejo,* had been intimately involved in the portrayal of Spain as God's chosen empire, as previous chapters have detailed, these particular titles lend additional irony to the activities of those seemingly loyal Englishman. His allusion to "Sword-men fighting at the Barriers"

---

77. Philip Massinger, *The Plays and Poems of Philip Massinger,* vol. IV, Philip Edwards and Colin Gibson, eds. (Oxford: Clarendon Press, 1976).
78. Francis Kirkman, *The unlucky citizen experimentally described in the various misfortunes of an unlucky Londoner calculated for the meridian of this city but may serve by way of advice to all the cominalty of England, but more particularly to parents and children, masters and servants, husbands and wives: intermixed with severall choice novels: stored with variety of [brace] examples and advice, president and precept* (London: Francis Kirkman, 1673), sig. M7v.
79. *The Unlucky Citizen,* sig. B6r. Kirkman listed *Lazarillo* as the first such book that he purchased with some spare sixpence. This work was so impressive to Kirkman in his youth that it ultimately propelled him into a concentrated period of quixotic romance reading, covering the corpus of popular books of chivalry of diverse nations.

therefore provides evidence of an English masculine culture of covert quixoticism and veiled Hispanophilia that required a degree of secrecy and concealment in order to be reconciled to the larger cultural shifts that had cast these works as inordinately vicious—hence, guilty reading.

Quixotic Figures

As I have suggested, Overbury's wandering Chambermaid reflected a larger phenomenon within European criticisms of romance literature, whereby general concerns about tales of love and arms became intertwined with concerns about errant femininity and errant masculinity, and correspondingly, with Spanish excess. As arms referred to the rules of combat, they were coded as masculine, and were associated with a kind of physical and intellectual rigor (both feats of physical prowess and military strategy). Love, meanwhile, was coded feminine, as associated with courtly behaviors, and the carnal desires of the body. Imbued with the Ovidian conception of desire as performative suffering, tales of love and arms essentially eroticized conquest as *romantic*. As romance books came to be adopted as rhetorical guidebooks, however, laying the foundations of literary quixoticism with love's overtaking arms, the books of the *brave* gradually came to be regarded as books of the *depraved*. This transformation was undoubtedly related to a gendered hierarchy of letters. We find evidence of this gendering in chapter 32 of *Don Quixote of La Mancha*, wherein Don Quixote, Sancho, the Priest and Cardenio are staying at an inn where they meet the innkeeper's daughter named Maritornes. Although she is illiterate, Maritornes has had many romances read to her, and so, she relates her strong preference for love over arms:

> On my faith I also much delight to hear of such things, which are very pretty, and even more when they relate that the one lady is underneath some orange trees in the arms of her knight, and that a waiting lady is standing guard for them, dying of envy and much shock. I say that all that is as sweet as honey […] but I don't take delight at all in the blows that my father enjoys, but rather the lamentations that knights make when they are absent from their ladies; for they in truth sometimes make me cry, for the compassion that I have for them.[80]

From an unlearned innkeeper's daughter whose life is as removed from the sphere of chivalry as it can possibly be, this response by Maritornes affirms the gendered stratification between matters of sentimentalism (attractive to women) and matters of chivalry (attractive to men).[81] As arms referred to the rules of combat, they were coded as masculine, and they were associated with a kind of physical and intellectual rigor. Love,

---

80. Miguel de Cervantes, *Don Quixote de la Mancha, tomo 1,* John Jay Allen, ed. (Madrid: Catedra Letras Hispánicas, 2005), 442. Translation is mine.
81. Her reference to knights' "lamentations […] when they are absent from their ladies" recalls, for example, the famous complaint of Amadís upon Peña Pobre upon the rejection of Oriana, which was taught to students of rhetoric. Her preference for such lamentations further underscores love's opposition to arms because Amadís has literally discarded his arms for love.

meanwhile, was coded as feminine, as it associated with courtly behaviors and the carnal desires of the body, and of the body conquered by desire. An artificial construct, this gendered stratification of both romance types, sentimental or chivalric, depicting matters of courtliness (love) and battle-faring (arms), was part of a larger historical phenomenon of gendered philosophies of reading, as Barbara Weissberger has suggested. Even the modern division between sentimental and chivalric romance reflects an entrenched "patriarchal ideology of gender," based in part on the largely false historicizing of sentimental romance as women's reading.[82]

Maritornes's sentimental description of romances of chivalry as dealing illicitly of love and courtliness provokes a debate about the goals of reading among the Priest, the barber, the innkeeper, and others present, concerning matters of verisimilitude and narratology. The innkeeper treats these romances as factual, failing to distinguish true histories from pure fictions:

> Well your worship would have me believe that all that happens in these good books is just nonsense and lies, when they're printed with the license of the gentlemen of the Royal Council, as if they were people in the habit of printing such a bundle of lies and so many battles and enchantments that would deprive you of judgment.[83]

The innkeeper's reference to battle-faring as a marker of historicity is a direct callback to an earlier conversation Don Quixote has with the Canon of Toledo, in which the Canon attempts to persuade Quixote that romance books are not real, to which the foolish Don impassively responds:

> You would have it believed that Amadís never walked the earth, nor any of the other adventurous knights that are in the histories, you would persuade men that the Sun doesn't brighten, nor the earth sustain, nor ice cools […] and if it is a lie, then so must it be that there was no Hector, nor Achilles, nor the Trojan War, nor the twelve Peers of France, nor King Arthur of England, who wanders the world in the shape of a crow, awaited at all times in his kingdom.[84]

Cervantes pointed out the difficulty in finding the boundary between fact and fiction, particularly for his generation, which frequently played fast and loose with those categories. Like the innkeeper, Quixote expresses a vulgar misconception that anything that is printed is true, and that there are no clear-cut hierarchies of truth in the realm of fiction. Although his syllogism is effectually illogical, his confusion of fables, myths, and vaguely verifiable events and personages points to the tendency for history to be written through the lens of masculine heroism, which is measured in feats of bravery, and for which traditionally masculine arts, especial war, provide proof of historicity. Although he fails as a reader by overly esteeming these lying histories, he nevertheless succeeds as an

---

82. Barbara F. Weissberger, "The Gendered Taxonomy of Spanish Romance," *La corónica: A Journal of Medieval Hispanic Languages, Literatures, and Cultures* 29, no. 1 (2000), 205–29 (208).
83. Cervantes, *Don Quijote de la Mancha*, 445.
84. Cervantes, *Don Quixote de la Mancha*, 438.

Aristotelian critic by esteeming truth-telling as the prime determinant of poesy's value. Maritornes, by contrast, has no interest in historicity. She reads for stories of courtship, strongly associated with love rhetoric and sentimentality; she readily admits her uninterest in battles (and thus, in historicity); she is an anti-dialectical reader.

Like Overbury's Chambermaid, the innkeeper and Maritornes embody a host of readerly caricatures that were informed by the print era and its vulgar introduction of works into vernacular languages. Most interesting is how these gendered controversies correlated with the growing perception that rhetoric (associated with sentimentalism) was emasculating, as it was vulgarly connected to whoring. This stereotype furthermore reflects a gendered bifurcation of Renaissance reading habits between love (coded feminine) and arms (coded masculine), and between rhetoric (artifice) and dialectic (truth). A romance's critical reception seemed to depend on where along those two polarities it was perceived to lie.

Don Quixote himself reveals romance's largely artificial gender hierarchies, for by his own admission, he reads as much for love as he does for arms. This is further evidenced by his inventing a love interest for himself in the form of Dulcinea del Toboso and acting out feigned torments for his imagined rejection by her, styling himself as a combination of Amadís, the Knight of the Sun, and Orlando.[85] This facet of Quixote's character most informed the character's cult following in England. In *Knight of the Burning Pestle*, for instance, Rafe also performs a quixotic role that highlights romance's dual function to convey tales of love and arms, in the process revealing himself of the stock of male readers who were more enamored with courtly love themes. Like many English readers of Spanish romance, he reads to follow the hero's example to "pursue feats of arms, and through his noble achievements procure such a famous history to be written of his heroic prowesse" (1.3.41–3). But he mistakes the genre's efficacy, for in the vein of the foolish Don Quixote, Rafe quickly bumbles each chivalric adventure, losing duels, mistaking an inn for "an ancient castle" (2.6.38), confusing a barber's clients for prisoners of a giant, and trading a beloved princess for a mere cobbler's maid. The play attributes his cognitive dissonance to his reading of Spanish romances, which provokes him to confuse the genre's binary themes:

> RAFE. There are no such courteous and fair well-spoken knights in this age; they will call one "the sonne of a whore" that Palmerin of England would have called "fair sir"; and one that Rosicleer would have called "right beauteous damsel" they will call "damned bitch." (1.244–48)

Representing the English everyman, Rafe indicts his society through citation from popular Spanish romances, but in criticizing English faults, he confuses courtesy (rhetoric in kind), with bravery (dialectic in action). He expresses a shared sensibility with

---

85. He tells Sancho Panza that he will imitate Amadís, but he copies an episode from *Espejo* during the period of the Caballero del Febo's hermitage in which the hero abandons his horse. Quixote copies the knight by freeing his horse Rocinante, and he further emulates the madness of Orlando by carving verses on trees.

Don Quixote, who has no patience for vulgarity, and in the vein of a cultural critic, he commends Spanish characters for their superior courtesy, furthermore voicing the common complaint against English knights "of the Jacobean inflation of honors—drunk, gambling, foul-mouthed and impecunious."[86] In Jonson's 1605 play, *Eastward Ho!*, Gertrude, the goldsmith's daughter, likewise invokes the virtues of the "the Knight o'the Sunne, or Palmerin of England [...] or sir Lancelot? or sir Tristram?" (5.1.29–31) to complain that the "The Knighthood now a daies, are nothing like the Knighthood of old time" (lines 34–35). Gertrude notably mentions knights who are most famously depicted as great lovers. Here again, the comparison draws a connection between literary representations of chivalry, recently dominated by foreign authors, and the conduct of actual English knights, implicitly tying the devaluation of English knighthood (manhood) to an imbricated dimension of love discourse.

Spanish romances, especially *Amadís*, were marketed for English boys and gentlemen training in rhetoric and courtliness. At the same time, they were also read by women, and, in the case of *Espejo*, translated by women. In the seventeenth century, English romances would also be written by women like Mary Wroth and Margaret Cavendish—a fact that evidently caused unease among moralists who feared the growing feminization of the genre. In Overbury's quixotic Chambermaid, therefore, the complaint is not only of women's attraction to romance, but of femininity's invasion of the masculine genre through the intervening theme of love, furthermore interpreted as a kind of Spanish invasion of England; what once served as a distraction or delay from the hero's quest now appeared as his prime objective. As romance came to be further dominated by the so-called female themes, even the masculine figure of Don Quixote, whom Cervantes had intended as a stereotype for errant masculinity, now also came to be further intersected by female caricatures. One finds echoes of this idea in *She Ventures and He Wins* (1696), written by an author under the pseudonym, "Ariadne." In Act 3, scene 5, Lovewell, "a younger Brother of small Fortune,"[87] is dining at the Blew Posts in the Haymarket. He requests his bill and discovers that it has already been paid by some ladies. In language remarkably similar to Overbury's, Lovewell quips, "I believe it is e'en some Lady errant that's run mad reading of *Don Quixot*."[88] Lovewell has been suspicious of the odd behavior of his new wife, Charlot, whom he suspects to be a fortuneless whore posing as an heiress. The revelation of her payment of the bill, however, causes Lovewell to revise his theory: Charlot must be a foolish reader of romance novels, inspired to deviate from normal femininity by reading this Spanish masterpiece of love and arms, though he fails to note that it is satire. The humor of Lovewell's comment therefore lies in the metafictional irony of a female reader "run mad" with reading a book about a mad reader of romances. As we have seen, Charlot's confusion with a prostitute, much like Claridiana's, also emerged from a common English habit of denigrating Spanish literature and its perceived surfeits of vice

---

86. Davis, *Chivalry and Romance*, 127.
87. Ariadne, *She ventures, and he wins a comedy acted at the New Theatre in Little Lincoln's Inn Fields by His Majesty's servants / written by a young lady* (London: Hen. Rhodes, 1696; Wing S3054), sig. A4v.
88. Ariadne, *She ventures, and he wins*, sig. E1v.

through common references to errant femininity and especially to bawdry. This so-styled *Claridiana effect* meant that Spanish romance, embodied in a woman, could be made either virtuous or vicious based on the agenda of the writer: for Spenser, rewriting Spanish romance as English epic, she was a militant virgin. For Jonson and Overbury, mocking the vulgar English attraction to the foreign corpus, she was a lowly whore.

This phenomenon helps to explain why critiques of romance so frequently conveyed a conspicuous Spanishness in spite of romance's pan-European origins, and in light of the simultaneously situated and un-situated nature of the genre's plots, themes, and settings. Used in this way, works like *Amadís*, *Espejo* and *Don Quixote* could lend critical specificity to so large and capacious a genre, and thereby be weaponized against imperial Spain. Characters like Amadís, Primaleón, Claridiana, the Knight of the Sun, and of course Don Quixote had the additional appeal of embodying Spanishness even while they pointed to larger phenomena within the pan-European genre. As a work of satire, *Don Quixote* especially provided firsthand testimony of Habsburg Spain's commonly attributed faults as a nation symbolically run mad with its own imperial romanticism.

Although the concern over romance's vicious representation of love themes and inordinate attraction to idle readers was shared by Spanish critics, in England, misogyny and Hispanophobia worked together to implicate Spanish literature within the humanist and nationalist controversies of the era. More specifically, the guilty reading of Spanish romance prompted an impulse to suppress the genre's profound impact upon the literature that followed, as Cavendish famously remarked in her work of witty satires, *Natures Fancies* (first published in 1656):

> Time, which is the Dissolver of all Corporeal Things, yet is the Mother, Midwife, and Nurse to Knowledg; whereby we find all Modern Romancy-Writers, although they seem to laugh and make a scorn of *Amadis de Gall*, yet make him the Original-Table, or Ground, from whence they draw their Draughts, and take out covertly their Copies from thence. Indeed, *Amadis de Gall* is the *Homer* of Romancy-writers.[89]

What Robert Greene was to English women, Spain was to English romance, foundational to the canon of great English literature "which could be set against a discarded apocrypha."[90] Insofar as the denial of *Amadís* (or rather of Spain) constituted a *residual* effort at national self-definition in and through literature, English romance can be said to have "established its generic identity and credentials in large part through a rhetorical repudiation of Iberian romance."[91]

---

89. Margaret Cavendish, Duchess of Newcastle, *Natures Picture Drawn by Fancies Pencil to the Life being several Feigned Stories, Comical, Tragical, Tragi-Comical, Poetical, Romanicical, Philosophical, Historical, and Moral : Some in Verse, some in Prose, some Mixt, and some by Dialogues / Written by … the Duchess of Newcastle* (London, A. Maxwell, 1671), sigs. MMMM1v–MMMM2r.
90. Trevor Ross, *The Making of the English Literary Canon: From the Middle Ages to the Late Eighteenth Century* (Montreal: McGill-Queen's University Press, 1998), 77.
91. Helen Moore, *Amadis in English: A Study in the Reading of Romance*, 178. In these concluding paragraphs, I am referring to Raymond Williams's comments on the literary origins (residual, dominant, and emergent culture) of British imperialism, as defined in *Marxism and Literature*. As

This, moreover, is what made *Don Quixote* so attractive. It was a model for negating romance that conspicuously set itself against much of the worst of Spain, so described, and so it served as a model for a new type of literature that was being posited at the beginning of the seventeenth century, by no means a set genre, certainly a far cry from what would one day be the novel, especially the English novel, but something in formation nonetheless. It has often sufficed to say that *Don Quixote* either initiated or marked a crucial hinge period of repudiation of the dominant form of romance that preceded the novel. In England, however, that repudiation also took the form of a concerted outcry against imperial Spain, having dictated not just the English revival of romance in the late sixteenth century, but also the dominant fashions of the era, and the *empire of wit*, so to speak; in process, this rejection of Spain reconstituted what English literature *was* and *should be* for a politically ascendant nation eager for self-definition. Therefore, Spanish romance was not just an archetype for England's novelistic fictions, but an antitype. As Cavendish noted in *Natures Picture*, in a witty parody of the scrutiny of Don Quixote's library, which she called "HEAVEN's Library, which is FAME's Palace, purged from Errors and Vices," "All Romances should be cast out, but *Don Quixot*, by reason he hath wittily abused all other Romances; wherefore he shall be kept, and also have his Books writ in Golden Letters."[92] Regarding, *Amadís*, however, "Jove said, That should be the first that should be cast out, by reason it was the original of all the rest."[93]

I explained in the prologue, this book concerns the residual aspects of British imperialism as expressed in literature.

92. Cavendish, *Natures Picture*, sig. 8T1v.
93. Cavendish, *Natures Picture*, sig. 8T2r.

EPILOGUE

SPANISH LITERATURE IN ENGLAND BEFORE *DON QUIXOTE*

A rocket launches into space by expelling energy from engines that provide initial uplift. Once exit velocity is supplied by the preliminary engines, those instruments are expelled to allow for greater transit force in the second stage of a rocket's journey. If *Don Quixote* was a rocket to the English novel, and from there to the deep space of an English empire, then tales of love and arms were the rocket fuel and engines used to establish initial momentum and later jettisoned in order to make way for a second phase of literary, national and imperial propulsion. As witnessed by the trans-historiography of English literature, the early jettisoning of Spanish romance therefore corresponds with England's ideological repudiation of Spain as an initial propulsive phase in the formation of the British Empire.

An Early Modern Space Race

> Look at the British Colonial empire—the most magnificent empire that the world ever saw. The old Spanish boast that the sun never set in their dominions, has been more truly realised amongst ourselves.
> —Sir Henry Ward, speech before the House of Commons, 1839

> "Contact light."
> Buzz Aldrin, first words spoken by man on lunar surface, 20 July, 1969
>
> "—magnificent desolation…"
> Buzz Aldrin, second words spoken by man setting foot on lunar surface, 20 July, 1969.

The early modern contest for global exploration and conquest strikes so eloquently with essentialist notions of European and Western supremacy that one need to look no further than to the cross-pollinating treatises over the possibility of lunar colonization to find proof of their prolificity. Space constricts me—I cannot rehearse the twentieth-century Americo-Russian competition for Cold War space travel, easily comparable to those famous Anglo-Spanish naval skirmishes and colonial contests of the sixteenth century that led to not only major innovations in maritime navigation, but also the most fertile dreams of literal and metaphorical spaceflight. Suffice it to say that this Renaissance verve began much earlier with the classical writers and philosophers who speculated about what might lie beyond the world's end at Thule and it culminated with the European conquest of America, justified as a holy war to bring the true light of Christianity to the so-regarded dark places of the world, cast in metaphorical night. This early chapter in England's global colonization planted the seeds of a mythos of destined English supremacy—*Contact light*—that would bear fruit in much later generations in places unknown and far remote. This *magnificent desolation* would form the crux of Britain's imperial conquests, based on an entrenched narrative of the country's exceptionalism and a complex of white saviorism, which was propelled in and by the tales of love and arms.[1]

As I have already shown, sixteenth- and seventeenth-century England's efforts to translate and adapt material from Spanish authors shed light on the high degree of English anxiety over the spread of Spanish imperial culture, which was pillaged and transformed with the prerogative of a conqueror. Focusing on English translations, adaptations, and references to the famous *books of the brave* deployed by Spaniards to support their own colonial empire, this book has further revealed that the complex of English fears and envy of Spain was neither uniformly felt nor consistently enforced, but nonetheless became part and parcel of the early modern English imaginary as it reflected official positions derived from the royal court. David Read explains that:

> ...the Tudor proponents of the American venture exploited the matter of Spain to declare their independence from the essence of Spain. This unacknowledged debt to the Spaniards helps to account for the reticence of Elizabethan writers in talking about "empire." Before such a term could be applied to England, there had to be some assurance that England stood apart from its imperial prototype. This assurance was long in coming, not only because the rift with Spain took the form of a gradual deterioration rather than a sudden rupture, but also because England's literary and intellectual connections with Spain declined much more slowly than its political and religious connections.[2]

Indeed, one truly remarkable feature of the period of the first Anglo-Spanish War in England is that it coincides with the upsurge in translation and printing of Spanish literature, as I discuss in Appendix I. Correspondingly, the emergence of an idea of the *Spanish Empire* in the English imaginary coincided with a period of increased translation and publication of Spanish romances and of English readership and imitation of *books of the brave*.

In later recollection, these works would be denigrated and disregarded in spite of their demonstrable influence over Tudor- and Stuart-era writers, especially in ways that amount to a kind of patriotic counterintelligence as Peter Heylyn's selective commentary on the books of chivalry in the *Cosmographie* well shows. We cannot discount an element of the Black Legend at work here, particularly the humanist depiction of Spain

---

1. I have deliberately mislaid Aldrin's meaning in both quotations.
2. David Read, *Temperate Conquests: Spenser and the Spanish New World* (Detroit: Wayne State University Press, 2000), 33.

as a cultural void that could be alternately looted, ignored or scapegoated with impunity. Heylyn's works also point to the incomplete or biased historicizing of Spenser's *Faerie Queene*, a canonical work deeply connected to the self-fashioned ethos of Elizabethan England but perhaps not fully appreciated for its profound impact on English imperial posterity. As I have shown, for example, the poem not only celebrated England's patron, Saint George, but also it contributed to an a priori myth of George's Britishness—this alongside of its cooption of Spanish romance heroines as literary and historical forebears for Elizabeth. Spenser's epic poem was not published with the expressed title of "history," but it was clearly received as a work of British national myth-making or rather of imperial *dreams*. These were further developed by Shakespeare, Dryden, and others, who collectively constructed an alternative poetic or allegorical historicity of the British nation that was eventually received as historical fact. For instance, the Cambridge edition of *The Faerie Queene: A Reader's Guide* (1999), a work marketed to college students, says only this of the passage from Book 1, canto x.61 when Redcrosse receives his mission to be the "thine owne nations frend / And Patrone:" "St. George's connection with England is familiar. Not only was he the patron saint, but he was also closely connected with the monarchy as patron of the prestigious Order of the Garter. *This particularly English*, and particularly royal, dimension to Redcrosse […] suggests that at this point in the story, the reader is fully justified in finding historical allegory in the events described" (my emphasis).[3] The problem with this statement is not that it isn't demonstrably true, but that it doesn't acknowledge that *demonstrable truthfulness* was precisely what Spenser was seeking to concretize in the English imaginary with his patriotic Anglicizing of universal myths and legends.

Similar truisms surround William Shakespeare's *The Tempest*, whose proposed Spanish influences have received little attention by scholars, most strikingly in the case of the fourth chapter of Antonio de Eslava's *Noches de invierno (Winter Nights)*. This chapter's profound similarity with *The Tempest* should permanently dismiss the notion that *The Tempest* lacks a direct source for its plot, and yet the myth of the play's originality persists. Among scholars of Iberia, *Noches* is generally accepted as Shakespeare's source, as propelled by the famous pronouncement of Marcelino Menéndez y Pelayo in his seminal 1905 study, *Orígenes de la novela* [Origins of the novel]: "[t]he similarities between this plot with that of *The Tempest* are so obvious that it would be difficult to deny a direct imitation."[4] And yet some have persisted to deny it. In a criticism from 1965, H. R. D. Anders acknowledged that the "resemblances [of *Noches* to *The Tempest*] are obvious, [but] it is by no means certain that the tale is Shakespeare's source."[5] Writing in 1972,

---

3. Elizabeth Heale, *The Faerie Queene: A Reader's Guide*, second edition (Cambridge: Cambridge University Press, 1999), 24.
4. Menéndez y Pelayo, *Orígenes de la Novela* (Madrid, Consejo Superior de Investigaciones Científicas, 1943), vol. II, 120–38 (135). Where scholars of Iberia have rejected *Noches*, another Spanish romance is usually offered as the likely source of *The Tempest*, as in the case of de Armas, who argues persuasively for the play's debts to *Amadís*, though less convincingly to the exclusion of *Noches*.
5. H. R. D. Anders, *Shakespeare's Books: A Dissertation on Shakespeare's Reading and the Immediate Sources of His Works* (New York: AMS Press, 1965), 76.

Frank Kermode also challenged the proposed Spanish source, as already discussed, and writing in 1975, Geoffrey Bullough was similarly perfunctory, noting that "there are certain likenesses [of *Noches*] to *The Tempest*... but [Shakespeare] handled the material with unusual economy and ballasted it with oblique topical allusions and ethical ideas scarcely hinted at in [Eslava's version]."[6] Such comments point to the privilege which has been generally afforded to Shakespeare, whose superiority to his contemporaries is tacitly assumed in virtually any discussion of early modern source studies.

With regard to Shakespeare's less venerated work, *The Two Gentlemen of Verona* (1590–91), there has been far less resistance to entertain a Spanish source.[7] And yet, when the hypothesis was first being seriously tested during the nineteenth century, there was, somewhat expectedly, a desire to valorize the inventiveness of Shakespeare, who according to Karl Simrock, "may only have drawn upon his general knowledge of the poems and popular books belonging to this cycle of ideas, but still more upon his own imagination."[8] Even if this scholar was willing to accept the Spanish source, he also was compelled to point out that Montemayor's *Diana* "had the rare merit of escaping the flames that consumed the greater portion of the library of Don Quixote."[9] In other words, Shakespeare's use of a Spanish source was a rare and remarkable thing, which seemingly occurred only because of the unusual quality of the Spanish work—one good apple—and because, of course, "the celebrated Sir Philip Sidney" had used it in his books of the *Arcadia*.[10] As a further implication of the English writer's presumed improvements upon the Spanish gem, Simrock quoted Thomas Wilson's

---

6. Geoffrey Bullough, *Narrative and Dramatic Sources of Shakespeare*, vol. 8 Romances: Cymbeline, The Winter's Tale, The Tempest (London and New York: Routledge and Columbia University Press, 1975), 247. This tacit neglect of *Winter Nights* is reflected in its general absence in modern *Tempest* editions. Among other proposed and accepted influences, including the Bermuda pamphlets, Montaigne's *Essais*, and Ovid's *Metamorphoses*, the Norton edition (2004) only includes relevant sections from *Primaleon of Greece* and from Gaspar Gil Polo's *The Enamoured Diana*, but not the story from *Winter Nights*. The Oxford edition (2010) includes sections from *Purchas his Pilgrimes*, Montaigne, Ovid, and Shakespeare's earlier works, but not from *Winter Nights*. Regarding *Winter Nights*, the Folger edition (2004), the Bedford edition (2008), and the Cambridge edition (2008) are likewise silent. See *The Tempest*, Barbara A. Mowat and Paul Werstine, eds. (New York: Simon & Schuster Paperbacks); *The Tempest: A Case Study in Critical Controversy*, 2nd edition, Gerald Graff and James Phelan, eds. (New York: Bedford/St. Martins, 2008); The *Tempest*, ed. Stephen Orgel (Cambridge: Cambridge University Press, 2008).
7. Shakespeare borrowed material from Gaspar Gil Polo's *Diana in Love* (1564). Bartholomew Young's English translation of both *Diana* parts did not appear in print until 1598, but Shakespeare likely accessed the translation in manuscript. See, e.g., Thomas A. Perry, "The Two Gentlemen of Verona and the Spanish Diana, in *Modern Philology* 87, no. 1 (1989), 73–6; and T. Harrison, "Shakespeare and Montemayor's Diana," *Studies in English* 6, no. 1 (1927), 72–120.
8. Karl Simrock, Introductory comments to *The Two Gentlemen of Verona*, in James O. Halliwell, Esq. F.R.S., ed. *The Works of William Shakespeare, The Text formed From A new Collation of the early Editions...*, vol. II *The Two Gentlemen of Verona. The Merry Wives of Windsor...* (London: C. and J. Adlard, Bartholomew Close, 1854), 6.
9. Simrock, Introductory comments to *The Two Gentlemen of Verona*, 6.
10. Simrock, Introductory comments to *The Two Gentlemen of Verona*, 6.

manuscript translation of the first book of *Diana*, which originally bore the title, "Diana de Montemayor done out of Spanish by Thomas Wilson esquire in the year 1596, and dedicated to the Erle of Southampton, who was then uppon the Spanish voiage with my Lord of Essex; wherein, under the names and vailes of sheppards and their lovers, are covertly discovried manie noble actions and affections of the Spanish nation, as is of the English of that admirable and never enough praised booke of Sir Philip Sidneyes Arcadia…"[11] He added:

> Sir Philip Siddney did very much affect and imitate the excellent author thereof, who might well tearme his book *Diana* as the Suter of Apollo and the twin borne with him, as his *Arcadia*, which by your noble virtue the world so happily enjoyes, might well have had the name of *Phoebus*, for never was our age lighted with two starres of such high and eminent witt, as are the books of these two excelling authors, which doe resemble one another as the sonne and the moone doth, but with this contrariety, that as the moone takes here light from the sonne, soe here this sonne, taking some light from this moone, grewe much more resplendent than that from whence it had it.[12]

Thus was the proof made. Sidney had taken the bulk of his ideas from Montemayor, but for this, his English adaptation was celebrated for superseding the Spanish original. The message was further reinforced by appeal to the familiar binary of Diana and Apollo, here made suitors once again. Wilson suggested that Sidney's *Arcadia* shone as bright as the sun, though it was formed in the light of the Spanish moon—a reversal of the common Anglo-Spanish metaphor of the time. Although these comments were authored by Wilson during the late 1500s, they also served in the nineteenth century to cast Sidney's adaptation of a Spanish source as evidence of English literature's general supremacy over Spanish literature and so, of England's supremacy over Spain. As this cosmic metaphor argued for the *Arcadia*'s super-transcendent improvement over the *Diana*, likewise it was used by Simrock to argue for Shakespeare's improvement upon his Spanish source. This presumed supremacy was further predicated upon the assumption of *Diana*'s exceptionalism with respect to the corpus of sixteenth-century Spanish romances, as illustrated by the reference to *Don Quixote*. Again, in the early twentieth century, one scholar wrote, in reference to Shakespeare's debt to *Diana*, "You will remember that it was highly praised by Cervantes and saved by the priest from the fate of the greater part of Don Quixote's books."[13]

---

11. Thomas Wilson, esq., qtd. in Simrock, Introductory comments to *The Two Gentlemen of Verona*, 22. Wilson notably placed this comparison in the competitive context of the Anglo-Spanish War, as revealed by his reference to Southampton's accompanying Essex on the 1596 "Spanish voiage," i.e., the Islands Voyage to the Azores, though largely unsuccessful on the part of England and the United Provinces.
12. Wilson, esq., qtd. in Simrock, Introductory comments to *The Two Gentlemen of Verona*, 22.
13. The Shakespeare Society of New York, *New Shakespeareana: A Critical Contemporary and Current Review of Shakespearean & Elizabethan Studies*, vol. III (New York and Westfield: 1904), 56.

Spanish Romance before *Don Quixote*

The readiness with which Cervantes condemned the bulk of Spanish and other continental romance works to the flames makes it is unsurprising that his novel was so immediately embraced in England, where, for reasons this book has explored, there was also a very ready disposition to simultaneously coopt Spain's beloved tales of love and arms and to denigrate them as complete trash. This suggests that part of what made Cervantes attractive was his heated criticism of the Spanish Church state, from his extended critiques of the *books of the brave*, which had so thoroughly served the interests of Spanish imperialism, to his parodic harangue of the Roman Inquisition, which had kept Spain's subjects in thrall to a politico-religious regime. If this comedy book was initially found humorous in England, then it was likely because audiences were well disposed to turn Spain into an object of derision (with the knee-jerk anti-Hispanism of Jonson's Dame Pliant) and to regard Cervantes as an ideal spokesperson for the backwardness of Roman Catholicism. This reception correlated with the anti-Spanish narratives promulgated through the Black Legend, which still informs the recent if not modern tendency to qualify Spanish influence through the critical lens of Cervantes. Ironically, although Cervantes's great opus has come to be treated as another rare Spanish gem in English criticism, especially in scholarship of the early novel, in its own time it was probably received as a work of burlesque entertainments, not as a work of great scholasticism or critical erudition. In 1611, bookseller Edward Blount entered the title into the Stationers' Register as *The Delightfull History of the Witty Knighte Don Quishote*.[14] This wording implies that the Spanish book was "at the outset introduced as a work intended to entertain. Nor should one forget that *Don Quixote* was received in Spain itself as a humorous, entertaining book. When the figures of Don Quixote and Sancho Panza appeared in early street festivals, they were clearly objects of mirth."[15] In other words, at least initially, *Don Quixote* did not initiate some kind of new and sustained engagement with Spanish literature that was unprecedented at the time. It simply put a time stamp on a phenomenon of eager Spanish romance reading that had been playing out across England, Europe, and the Americas for around a century.

For *this* reason only, it is absolutely telling that Shakespeare was himself a reader of *Don Quixote*, having coauthored with John Fletcher the lost play, *Cardenio* (1613), a work purportedly inspired by Cervantes's lovelorn character by the same name. This lost Shakespearean play is, in the words of Barbara Fuchs, "the absent center, the purloined letter, the missing link, the huge gaping O. Exhibit A for the connection between the two foremost representatives of early modern English and Spanish literature."[16] Lewis Theobald's *Double Falsehood* (1727) provides soft proof of what one

---

14. Edward Arber, ed., *A Transcript of the Registers of the Company of Stationers of London 1554–1640 A.D.* (repr. Gloucester, MA: Peters Smith, 1967), 3: 451.
15. Dale B. Randall and Jackson C. Boswell, *Cervantes in Seventeenth-Century England: The Tapestry Turned* (Oxford: Oxford University Press, 2009), xvi.
16. Fuchs, *Poetics of Piracy*, 1.

might also suppose: Shakespeare and Fletcher borrowed the mostly self-contained story about a stilted lover whose intended bride was forced to the altar. Performed before King James I during the 1612–13 holiday season, when England and Spain were at peace and when there was, moreover, early talk of an Anglo-Spanish royal marriage, there would have been little appetite to turn Spain into an object of ridicule, even by criticizing its romances, or to engage in any heavy-handed criticism against the country.[17] For this reason, I do not believe that the original *Cardenio* would have reflected the authors' belief in *Don Quixote*'s exceptionalism. As something widely read, and as a famous part of Cervantes's beloved opus, the Cardenio episode was readily available, easily recognizable and certainly timely, but, most important, it was easily adaptable to the stage, and this is probably why it was chosen. The same could not be said of the larger plot of *Don Quixote*, as the flop of Francis Beaumont's 1607 *Knight of the Burning Pestle* had already proven. Moreover, given the current climate of warming Anglo-Spanish relations and blossoming Anglo-Spanish courtship, it was an opportune tale to perform during the chilly winter season of 1612–13.

What *Cardenio does* mean is that we need to take more seriously the idea that the Spanish romances that preceded *Don Quixote* had a rich literary tradition and English cult following beyond their conventional treatment as pre-*Quixote* primordia. Accepting this premise should make Shakespeare's use of Spanish sources less remarkable and less surprising, and therefore less commensurate with a criterion of exceptionalism. Certainly, when it comes to *The Tempest*, Shakespeare's co-authorship of *Cardenio* is reason enough to entertain his debt to Eslava.[18] But we don't actually *need Cardenio*. There is already evidence enough to contemplate a possible connection in the atmosphere of avid English readership of Spanish romance. And, moreover, there is a direct connection between

---

17. Just as Elizabeth was wed to Frederick on February 14, 1613, James considered another match for Prince Charles with the Spanish Infanta, Maria Anna (1606–46), the talks for which began seriously that same year when James entertained competing French, Spanish, and Savoyard bids for the Prince of Wales. Originally, James had sought a Spanish Match for his eldest son, Henry (1594–1612), but when Henry died, James shifted his plans to Charles. Over the next decades, he attempted to negotiate a match for Charles to Maria Anna. From the Court to the country estates, from the parliament to the pulpit, the issue lie at the forefront of English political discourse for nearly two decades.

18. Shakespeare's association with Fletcher, a known Hispanist, may also explain how Shakespeare discovered *Noches*. For information on his Spanish literacy, see Edward M. Wilson, "Did Fletcher Read Spanish?" *Philological Quarterly* 27 (1948), 187–90. For information on Fletcher and Spain, see David Carnegie and Gary Taylor, eds., *The Quest for Cardenio: Shakespeare, Fletcher, and the Lost Play* (Oxford: Oxford University Press, 2012). See also Terri Bourus and Gary Taylor, eds. *The Creation and Re-Creation of Cardenio: Performing Shakespeare, Transforming Cervantes* (New York: Palgrave Macmillan, 2013). For more about Fletcher's adaptation of Spanish exemplary novels, see Joyce Boro, "Blessed with a Baby or "bum-fidled with a bastard"? Maternity in Fletcher's *The Chances* and Cervantes' *Novela de la señora Cornelia*," in Bourus and Taylor, eds. *The Creation and Re-Creation of Cardenio*, 61–72; and Boro "John Fletcher's *Women Pleased* and the Pedagogy of Reading Romance," in *Staging Early Modern Romance: Prose Fiction, Dramatic Romance, and Shakespeare*. Mary Ellen Lamb and Valerie Wayne, eds. (London: Routledge, 2009), 188–202.

Eslava's title and Shakespeare's *The Winter's Tale*, also composed sometime between 1609 and 1611. The play's title bears no direct relation to its plot but rather categorizes the play as an idle tale with which to divert oneself through the long nights of winter. As Mamillius remarks in the play, "a sad tale's best for winter" (2.1.25). This also corresponds with Eslava's purpose "to entertain you [the reader], and relieve you of the great sorrow of the nights of winter."[19] Correspondingly, each chapter is related by one of four gentleman who are engaged in a narrative competition, similar to the premise of Boccaccio's *Decameron* or Chaucer's *Canterbury Tales*.[20]

Even in scholarship that has accepted the *Noches* hypothesis, comparison never fully destabilizes the notion of the play's supreme originality, or at least of Shakespeare's supremacy. Even the Spanish scholar Menéndez y Pelayo also tended toward this view, remarking of the *Noches* chapter, "this is undoubtedly the outline of the Shakespearean work, but how far it is from the work itself! All that is deep and symbolic, all that is musical and ethereal, is the personal creation of the genius of Shakespeare" (my translation).[21] The charge that Eslava's version lacks depth is patently exaggerated. This Spanish work offers numerous metaphysical discussions, touching on diverse matters from the vagaries of fortune to the nature of magic and the occult. In fact, these prolonged discussions brought the work to the attention of the Spanish Inquisition, which ordered that all references to necromancy, the art of communing with the dead, be expurgated.[22] Curiously, the blots and purges from the censored Spanish chapter are echoed in Shakespeare's elusive

---

19. Antonio de Eslava, *Parte primera del libro intitulado Noches de inuierno. Compuesto por Antonio de Eslaua, natural de la Villa de Sanguessa* (Barcelona: 1609), t4r–t4v (t4r).
20. To date, no contemporary English translation or adaptation of *Winter Nights* has been found, but translations regularly circulated in manuscript, often many years or decades before they were published, if they were ever published at all. Thomas Shelton's manuscript translation of *Don Quixote* entered circulation in 1607, roughly five years prior to its publication. The manuscript translation by James Mabbe of Rojas's *Celestina* (1499), which was based on the Antwerp edition, predated its 1633 publication by at least 30 years. Bartholomew Young's translation of *La Diana* circulated in manuscript for almost two decades prior to its publication in 1598, while Thomas Wilson's partial translation never found its way to print. Eslava's collection was moreover very popular, appearing in three editions in just two years: two published in Barcelona in 1609 (with various reprints) and a third in Brussels in 1610. The Brussels edition was most likely to be translated because the Spanish Netherlands were a common point of origination for Spanish print works that were destined for export. For example, Thomas Shelton's 1612 translation of *Don Quixote* was based on the 1607 edition printed in Brussels. For more information, see Stijn Van Rossem, "The Verdussens and the International Trade in Catholic Books (Antwerp, Seventeenth Century)," in *Books in the Catholic World During the Early Modern Period*, Natalia Maillard Álvarez, ed. (Brill, Leiden: 2014), 1–50.
21. Menéndez y Pelayo, *Orígenes de la Novela*, 136.
22. See, e.g., *Novissimus librorum prohibitorum et expurgatorum: index pro Regis catholici Hispaniarum* (Madrid: Diego Díaz de la Carrera, 1640), sig. F4r. *Winter Nights* also appeared as a censored book in *Final Index of Prohibited Works* of 1780; see *Índice ultimo de los libros prohibidos y mandados expurgar: para todos los reinos y señorios del católico rey de las Españas, el señor Don Carlos IV* (Madrid: Antonio de Sancha, 1780), sig. M5v.

references to Prospero's "secret study," and in his final revelation, "graves at my command / Have waked their sleepers, oped, and let 'em forth" (5.1.48–9).[23]

I also reject the claim that the Spanish work lacks Shakespeare's famed ethereal elements. For instance, as narrator Fabricio describes Serafina's magical wedding festivities, the gentleman Leonardo interrupts to question whether "in that Magical Palace the royal wedding of the Prince Valentiniano was attended by many nymphs, dryads, naiads, and mermaids, who with their soft music captivated the listeners."[24] This description is directly correspondent with Shakespeare's dramatization of the betrothal masque in Act 4, scene 1, particularly the "Soft music" conjured at the stage direction at line 58 and Prospero's own captivation, so strong that he "forgot that foul conspiracy / Of the beast Caliban and his confederates" (4.1.139–40). It has been suggested that Shakespeare added the marriage masque for the occasion of the play's performance during the royal nuptials of Princess Elizabeth Stuart (1596–1662) and Frederick of Palatine (1596–1632), but this supposition is challenged by Stephen Orgel, who finds no textual evidence to support a revision.[25] If we accept the *Noches* chapter as a pre-*Tempest*, then we can agree with Orgel that the masque was probably not a later addition.

---

23. Although Shakespeare was shielded from the privations of Catholic Inquisition, he was probably concerned about provoking the displeasure of King James, a known critic of the occult arts who had specifically condemned necromancy in his *Daemonologie* (1597) and made necromancy a capital offense with the 1604 Witchcraft Act. Whereas Shakespeare could be reasonably certain that his depiction of the colluding Weird Sisters in *Macbeth* (1607) would be understood as a condemnation of witches and necromancers, he had to take a different approach with *The Tempest*, wherein Prospero functions as the moral center of the play. This anxiety could help to explain Prospero's constant repetitions that he will give up his magic once the business of the play is concluded. One major difference between Prospero and Dárdano is that Dárdano never renounces his magic. Nor does he use his magic irresponsibly. As Fabricio explains, "Well could the wise King Dárdano vanquish Nicíforo if he wanted to use magical arts, for in that era there was no better necromancer than he, except that he had promised to the Lord Almighty that he would not utilize his magic to the offense of God" (105). Prospero, by contrast, is guilty of having excessively reveled in his magic; by too fully occupying himself with his "secret studies" he fed his brother's treachery—"in my false brother / Awaked an evil nature" (1.2.92–3)—and provoked his own deposal. By emphasizing Prospero's error in dabbling in the occult, Shakespeare transformed the original tale from a supernatural exposition on divine vengeance to a Faustian drama about the dangers of hubris. In Christopher Marlowe's 1592 tragedy, the infamous necromancer vows to burn his books as devils drag him off to hell. This tragically belated decision by Doctor Faustus illustrates the folly of pursuing forbidden knowledge, which Faustus must purchase with his immortal soul. Thus, the noble hero falls from grace. This idea is echoed in *The Tempest*, first by Caliban's insistence on burning Prospero's books as a way of depriving his master of his power, and again by Prospero's final determination, "I'll drown my book" (5.1.57). Voluntarily relinquishing the keys to his power, Prospero appears to have learned a valuable lesson about reaching too high, and thereby avoids the catastrophe that ought to have been provoked by his venture into the occult arts.
24. Eslava, *Noches de invierno*, 109.
25. Stephen Orgel, "Introduction," in William Shakespeare, *The Tempest* (Oxford: Oxford University Press, 1987), 1–88 (44, note 1).

The point here is not to enforce Eslava's chapter as *the* source, but rather to reincorporate it into the critical conversation surrounding *The Tempest*, not merely as one among Spain's other so-styled primitive originals but as a work of value in itself. This was precisely the problem when Richard Garnett and Edmund Gosse admitted the *Noches* chapter's parity with *The Tempest*, clarifying, however, that it was a "most dull and pedantic production" greatly improved by Shakespeare's genius.[26] This needless valorizing of Shakespeare in relation to his sources is emblematic of a phenomenon observed by Dennis Britton and Melissa Walter, whereby "[u]nwittingly perhaps, our anxieties about Shakespeare source study are linked to our inability (or unwillingness) to divorce our current understandings of Shakespeare from the long history of what Shakespeare has 'stood' for: the quintessential genius, the greatest writer in English, and England and Englishness."[27] Perhaps no play better emblematizes this phenomenon than *The Tempest*, which has given life to more than one false aphorism.[28]

I don't imagine that these scholarly truisms are ill-spirited, motivated by modern hatred of Spain, or deliberately intended to denigrate Spanish literature. I do profess, however, that since historical myths have a tendency to be self-replicating, modern scholarship has more than once fallen victim to the circular nature of British imperial mythmaking, which tacitly assumes a priori creation.[29] Thankfully, as the citations in this book well indicate, the *turn to Spain* in English studies is already well underway, largely led by scholars of Spanish romance, and this work has collectively contributed to a greater scholarly willingness to *gaze beyond the Pyrenees*, especially in the last 20 years. Yet, there is much left to discover.

By unpacking the political and cultural anxieties that Spain's beloved tales of love and arms activated in England, coupled with their equally transcendent propulsion of England's masculine conquest desires, this book has further uncovered an important but understudied aspect of the romantic pre-history of *Don Quixote* in England. It has also shown how Spain's imperial fictions propelled England's own symbolic probing of the cosmos and of the classical past for theories of empire. But a future study might consider more deeply how these early experiments with romanticizing the empire would eventually transform into fully fledged colonial projects. We might further consider how England's rewriting of Spain's imperial past anticipated and responded to the ample

---

26. Richard Garnett and Edmund Gosse, *English Literature: From the Age of Henry VIII to the Age of Milton,* part II of IV (London: Macmillan, 1904), 251.
27. Dennis Britton and Melissa Walter, "Rethinking Shakespeare Source Study," in *Rethinking Shakespeare Source Study: Audiences, Authors, and Digital Technologies* (New York: Routledge, 2018), 1–16 (4).
28. For instance, as Shakespeare's last solo play, *The Tempest*, is still affectionately referred to as Shakespeare's so-called *farewell to the stage,* even if this has also repeatedly served as a point of contention. It is the perception of Shakespeare's exceptionalism that motivates the continued attention that is given to this virtually groundless biographical reading.
29. Fuchs laments that early modern England's attempts to culturally distance itself from Spain have made a long-standing impact on the critical apparatus, whereby scholars, too, have historically negated or ignored the Spanish connections in some of the most canonical English works. *The Poetics of Piracy* (Philadelphia: University of Pennsylvania Press, 2013), 1–12.

criticisms expressed against the British Crown at the height of its power, such as in the opening quotation by Sir Henry Ward, in which he proclaimed that the British Empire had at last coopted the Spanish "boast" of *empire upon which the sun never set*, only to criticize the Crown for lacking a working colonial policy or ethic of care for its subjects.[30]

I am personally curious to know how the Tudor and Stuart Black Legends of Spain informed the works of British Romantic and Victorian writers. I am thinking, for example, of Robert Southey's *Madoc* (1805), in which the Welsh knight is imagined to voyage to America three centuries before the Spaniards, remobilizing a myth that had risen to prominence in the sixteenth and seventeenth centuries with Columbus's famous misreading of *Medea*. The poem specifically features the knight conquering the bloody, human-sacrificing tribes of Aztlān, ancestral home of the Mexica people, and himself converting them to Christianity. Reading *Madoc* in light of the *books of the brave* certainly breaks open these residual aspects of British Empire that were born in the sixteenth century. But what of Britain's other imperial fictions? How might they be traced to Spain's beloved tales of love and arms?[31] Indeed, what else might we discover if we were to probe the *books of the brave* English beyond their conventional treatment as pre-*Quixote* primordia?

---

30. Henry Ward, "Waste Lands of the Colonies," in *Hansard's Parliamentary Debates, Third Series, Commencing with the Accession of William IV* (London: House of Commons, 1839) 841–919 (847).
31. For instance, how might we connect Mary Shelley's contributions to *Lives of the Most Eminent Literary and Scientific Men of Italy, Spain and Portugal* (ca. 1835–39) to her references to Italian and Iberian romances in *Frankenstein* (1818)? More specifically, when Shelley described Henry Clerval, best friend to Victor Frankenstein, as a composer of plays based on his favorite books, what prompted her to note that "the principal characters of [these books] were Orlando, Robin Hood, Amadis, and St. George," and what episteme of European civilization did these characters encode? *Frankenstein: The 1818 Text* (New York: Penguin Random House, 2018), 26. This line does not appear in the 1831 version by Percy Byshe Shelley (London: Colburn and Bentley).

APPENDIX I

ENGLISH READERSHIP OF SPANISH ROMANCE, BY THE NUMBERS

The line graph in Figure 5, "Publication trends for romances and other literature translated from Spanish into English," tracks the trends in publication of Spanish literature in England from 1473 to 1640, based on STC numbers.[1] The graph shows that all Spanish–English translations, all literature translations, *and* all romance translations dramatically spiked after 1580, in the backdrop of England's first major military clashes with Spanish forces, first major ventures in global exploration, and first colonial endeavors in North America. At the turn of the seventeenth century, the total number of all categories, including romance translations, dipped. The trend in romance translation never recovered from its post-war dip.[2] I infer, therefore, that the increase in English printing of Spanish romances was a unique phenomenon, likely connected to the comingled English fascination and perturbation with Spanish conquest, and spurred on by the first Anglo-Spanish War.

If war had brought Iberian culture to the fore of the English political consciousness, it had also lent an uncanny timeliness to reading tales of love and arms. Figure 6, "Genre breakdown of printed translations from Spanish into English, 1473–1640," presents a genre breakdown of Spanish–English translations from 1473 to 1640. From 1473 to 1640, 345 Spanish titles were printed in England (including reprints); of these titles, 14.78 percent (45 titles) were romances.[3]

---

1. All statistical data pertaining to translations of Spanish works were derived from the *Renaissance Cultural Crossroads Database*: Brenda Hosington, et al., *Renaissance Cultural Crossroads*, accessed October 27, 2016, <http://www.dhi.ac.uk>. Reprints have been included (separate STC/USTC numbers) in witness to the high market demand for Spanish works. The classification of titles from the database as romances is based on the determination of the database's creators. All works were either translated directly from Spanish or from an intermediary language, most commonly French, Italian, Spanish, or Latin.
2. The number of literature translations increased with the onset of the first (formally declared) Anglo-Spanish War of 1624–31, but romances translations continued to decline.
3. In fact, during this period, the total number of romance translations was larger than the number of travel, grammar, political, historical, rhetorical, conduct, military, law, and medicinal books

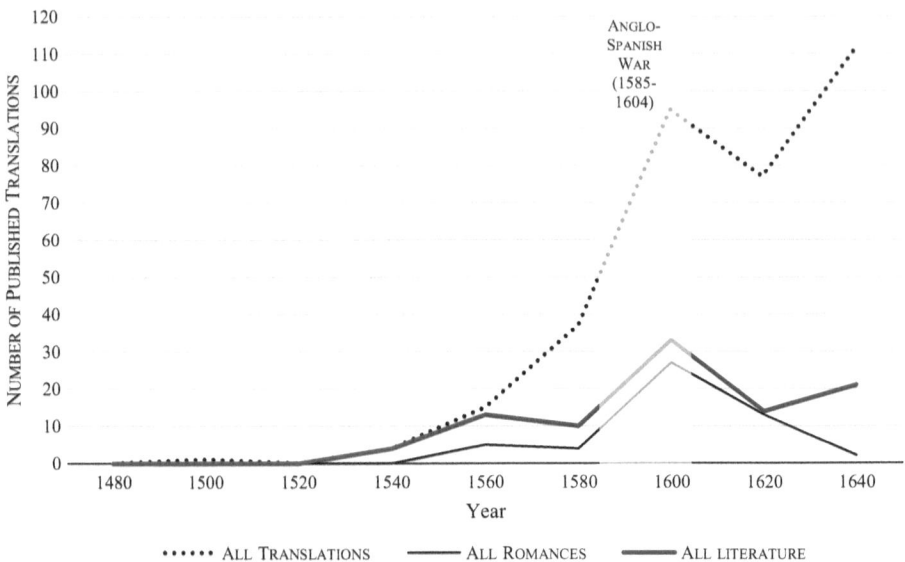

Figure 5 Publication trends for romances and other literature translated from Spanish to English.

Figure 7, "Language and genre breakdown of literature translations printed in English, 1473–1640" tracks the number of literature translations from Spanish, French, Italian, Portuguese, and Latin, separated by genre. Unsurprisingly, French titles predominated the market for foreign romances with a total of 62 titles, including reprints.[4] At 45 titles, Spanish romances comprised the second largest category, though French was also the intermediary language for 17 of these works. In fact, during the second half of the sixteenth century, the period when romances started to gain renewed popularity, more Spanish-authored romances were published in English than French-authored romances, once again highlighting a ready connection between romance and Spain, particularly during the period of the Spanish Monarchy's most concentrated global expansion.[5]

---

combined (99 titles, or 29.12 percent of all Spanish translations); Spanish romances were even more commonly printed than news tracts (or relations of events), of which there were 41 titles (12.05 percent); they were also more common than travel narratives, of which there were 26 titles (8 percent). The only single larger category was religious works, of which there were 110 titles (32.35 percent).

4. This number corresponds with the popular conception of romance as a largely Francophone genre as well as the well-documented roots of romance in French troubadour poetry and other Norman traditions.
5. From 1473 to 1549, there were 28 French romances and only two Spanish romances. Around 1550, however, the ratio started to shift, with 34 more French titles and 43 more Spanish titles published by 1640. During the first Anglo-Spanish War, 38 total romance translations

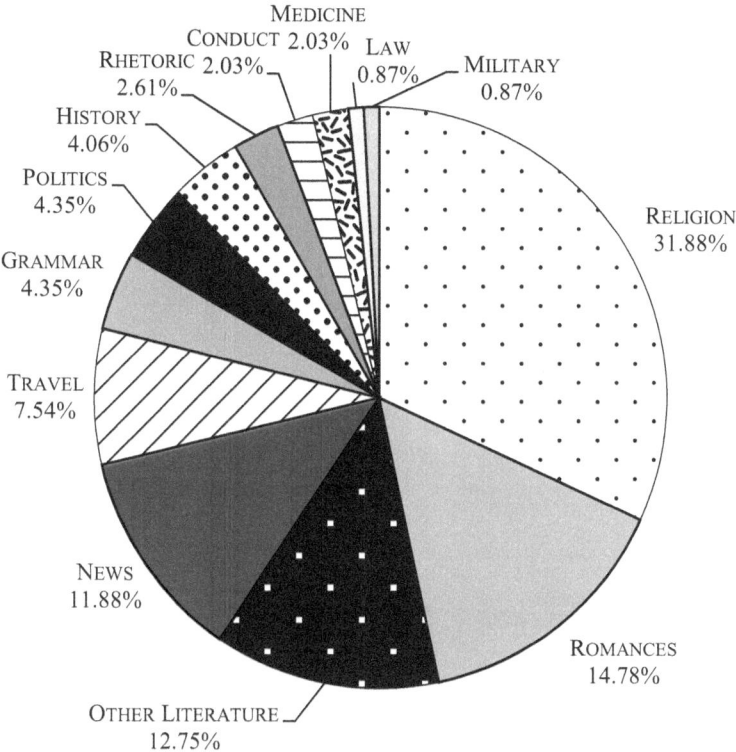

Figure 6 Genre breakdown of printed translations from Spanish into English, 1473–1640.

Somewhat surprising, however, is the relative scarcity of Italian romances on the English print market. From 1473 to 1640, there were only four Italian romance titles printed in English, all of them editions of *Orlando furioso* (1516). Although the number of reprints is a testament to the enormous popularity of Ariosto's great opus, one wonders why so few other Italian romances followed. It was certainly not for a lack of Italian translators. In fact, during the Anglo-Spanish War, there were more total translations from Italian (105 titles) than total translations from Spanish (93 titles). Nor was there a scarcity of Italian romances to translate. In addition to *Orlando Furioso*, there was, for example, Luigi Pulci's *Morgante Maggiore* (1483) and Francesco Cieco da Ferrara's *Il Mambriano* (1509). The data suggests that the market for Italian romance in translation may have been more restricted than is commonly believed, perhaps constrained to just a few titles, and appealing more specifically to certain elite bilingual readers.[6]

---

were printed in England. Among these, only 8 romances were originally composed in French (21.05 percent), while 24 (63.16 percent) were written in Castilian, 2 (5.26 percent) in Portuguese, and the rest in Latin and Italian.

6. Nevertheless, Italian literature greatly influenced English writers even where documentary evidence is scant, as in the case of Boccaccio's *Decameron*, which was an important source for Shakespeare, but was seemingly not translated into English during his lifetime.

APPENDIX I

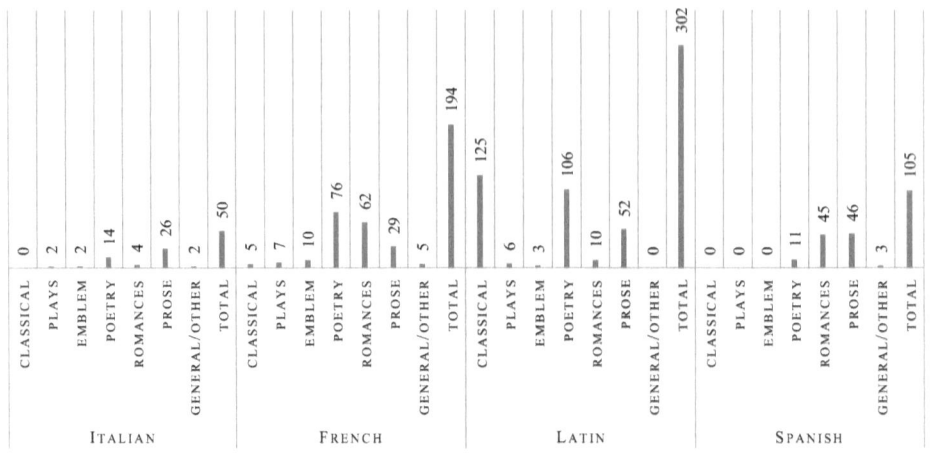

Figure 7 Language and genre breakdown of literature translations printed in English, 1473–1640.

Orlando Furioso and *Orlando innamorato* certainly were defining works of the era, also serving as fodder for major works of criticism theorizing the newly popularized genre of romance, namely the *Discorso intorno al comporre dei romanzi* (1554) by Giraldi Cinzio and *I romanzi* (1554) by Giovan Battista Pigna. But these famous defenses of Ariosto against the outcry of Italian humanists may also point to another reason why Spain and France gained an edge.[7] Jane Everson has observed, for example, that Italian humanists were "at best silent about vernacular literature [...] and at worst scathing in their hostility towards all such fables and fictions, especially in verse and in Italian."[8]

Then again, the validity of such data also depends on what one considers a *romance*. The *Renaissance Cultural Crossroads Database*, from which I have derived my figures, seemingly defines the genre as pertaining to fictional works only of the sentimental, pastoral, or chivalric persuasion, based on a posteriori definition.[9] This means that, for example, Robert Tofte's partial translation of *Orlando innamorato* (1598) is categorized under poetry rather than romance, skewing the figures against Italy. And what of the dominant verse epic, *La Gerusalemme liberata* (1581) of Torquato Tasso (1493–1569)? RCC gives

---

7. In fact, owing to the belatedness of Italian romance translations on the print market, works like *Huon of Bourdeaux, The Mirrour of Knighthood,* and *Amadis de Gaul* may have been more representative primers for English readers, at least during the 1580s, when the Anglo-Spanish War was gaining speed.
8. Jane E. Everson, *The Italian Romance Epic in the Age of Humanism* (Oxford: Oxford University Press, 2001), 112.
9. For a summary of the evolution of romance's definition, see Christine S. Lee, "The Meanings of Romance: Rethinking Early Modern Fiction," *Modern Philology* 112, no. 2 (2014): 287–311, esp. 306–7.

no classification,[10] though translator Richard Carew's pronouncement of the work as a "heroicall poeme" somewhat obviates its classification. (For instance, "heroic poem" was also how Ariosto's proponents classified his work.) Whether this choice is correct depends on how one constitutes romance, whether as a concrete set of themes and historical contexts, as a specific literary form, as a vernacular tradition in fiction, as a series of strategies, or as a combination of all of these. A related question concerns what constituted a romance during the sixteenth century, a time when the genre was heavily in flux and lacked a standardized name. It was only later and especially in modern usage, largely through scholarly convention, that romance has come to specifically mean a vernacular tradition of fiction writing in prose.[11]

In other words, the significance of this data is not that it provides us with wholly concrete and indisputable figures for English translation and readership of foreign romance. In fact, as creators Brenda Hosington, et al. remark, even "the definition of what constitutes a translation has a long and contentious history."[12] What it does allow us to infer with reasonable confidence, however, is that the most popular romances of Iberia arrived in England during a time when political relations with the Spanish Crown were deeply strained; that the English demand for Spanish literature was higher during the war years; and that, correspondingly, Spanish and Portuguese romances competed with French, Italian, and English romances, perhaps briefly dominating the market for a short time during the Anglo-Spanish War.

---

10. As of the final revision of this study, the records for Godfrey of Bulloigne (ESTC S117565; STC 23698) bore a status of "still being revised," though the most recent record updates were from 2008 and 2009. Brenda Hosington, et al. *Renaissance Cultural Crossroads* http://www.dhi.ac.uk, accessed September 4, 2020.
11. Lee, "The Meanings of Romance," 306–7.
12. Brenda Hosington, et al. *Renaissance Cultural Crossroads* http://www.dhi.ac.uk, accessed May 23, 2020.

SELECTED BIBLIOGRAPHY

A wife novv the widdow of Sir Thomas Overburye Being a most exquisite and singular poem of the choice of a wife. Whereunto are added many witty characters, and conceited newes, written by himselfe and other learned gentlemen his friends (London: Lawrence Lisle, 1614).
Adams, H. M. *Catalogue of Books Printed on the Continent of Europe 1501–1600 in Cambridge Libraries* (Cambridge: Cambridge University Press, 1967).
Adorno, Rolena. *Colonial Latin American Literature: A Very Short Introduction* (Oxford: Oxford University Press 2011).
Alcoy I Pedrós, Rosa. *San Jorge y la princesa: diálogos de la pintura del siglo XV en Cataluña y Aragón* (Barcelona: Biblioteca de la Universitat de Barcelona, 2004).
Alexander, Sir William. *An Encouragement to Colonies* (London: William Stansby, 1624).
Álvarez Recio, Leticia. "Spanish Chivalric Romances in English Translation: Anthony Munday's Palmendos (1589)," *Cahiers Élisabéthains: A Biannual Journal of English Renaissance Studies* 91, no. 1 (2016), 5–20.
Álvarez Recio, Leticia, "Anthony Munday's *Palmendos* (1589) in the Early Modern English Book Trade: Print and Reception," *Atlantis: Journal of the Spanish Association of Anglo-American Studies* 38, no. 1 (2016), 53–69.
Anders, H. R. D. *Shakespeare's Books: A Dissertation on Shakespeare's Reading and the Immediate Sources of His Works* (New York: AMS Press, 1965).
Aptekar, Jane. *Icons of Justice: Iconography and Thematic Imagery in Book V of* The Faerie Queene (New York: Columbia University Press, 1969).
Ariadne, *She ventures, and he wins a comedy acted at the New Theatre in Little Lincoln's Inn Fields by His Majesty's servants / written by a young lady* (London: Hen. Rhodes, 1696).
Ariosto, Ludovico. *Orlando furioso,* Oxford World's Classics edition, Guido Waldman, trans. (Oxford: Oxford University Press, 2008).
Aristotle, *On the Art of Fiction,* L. J. Potts, trans. (Cambridge: Cambridge University Press, 1953).
de Armas, Frederick. "Galeoto Fu 'l Libro: Don Quixote, Amadis, and The Tempest," *Cervantes: Bulletin of the Cervantes Society of America* 37, no. 2 (2017), 9–34.
Armitage, David, ed. *Theories of Empire, 1450–1800* (London: Routledge, 2016).
Arnoldsson, Sverker. *La Leyenda Negra: estudios sobre sus orígenes,* Acta Universitatis Gothoburgensis, Göteborgs Universitets Arsskrift, vol. 66 (Göteborg: Almqvist & Wiksell, 1960).
Aske, James. *Elizabetha triumphans* (London: Thomas Gubbin, 1588).
Bacon, Francis. *Lord Bacon's Essays with an introductory dissertation and notes*, Joseph Devey, ed. (London: George Bell and Sons, 1888).
Barella Vigal, Julia. "Antonio de Eslava y William Shakespeare: historia de una coincidencia," in *El Crotalón: Anuario de Filología Española*, vol. 2 (Madrid: Crotalón, 1985), 489–501.
Beaumont, Francis. *The Knight of the Burning Pestle* (London: Nicholas Okes, 1613).
Bergvall, Åke. "The Theology of the Sign: St. Augustine and Spenser's Legend of Holiness," *Studies in English Literature* 33 (1993), 21–42.
Bevington, David. "*Poetaster*: Textual Essay," *The Cambridge Edition of the Works of Ben Jonson Online*, September 3, 2014, https://universitypublishingonline.org/cambridge/benjonson/k/essays/Poetaster_textual_essay/.

Bland, Mark. "The London Book-Trade in 1600," in *A Companion to Shakespeare*, David Scott Kastan, ed. (Oxford: Blackwell, 1999), 450–63.

Boadas, Sònia. "Lucian of Samosata and Celestial Journeys in Spanish Golden Age Literature," *Dix-septième siècle*, 286, no. 1 (2020), 135–51.

Bohun, Edmund. *A Geographical Dictionary* (London: Charles Brome, 1693).

Boro, Joyce. "John Fletcher's *Women Pleased* and the Pedagogy of Reading Romance," in *Staging Early Modern Romance: Prose Fiction, Dramatic Romance, and Shakespeare*. Mary Ellen Lamb and Valerie Wayne, eds. (London: Routledge, 2009), 188–202.

Boruchoff, David A. "New Spain, New England, and the New Jerusalem: The 'Translation' of Empire, Faith, and Learning (Translatio Imperii, Fidei Ac Scientiae) in the Colonial Missionary Project," *Early American Literature* 43, no. 1 (2008), 5–34.

Bourus, Terri and Gary Taylor, eds. *The Creation and Re-Creation of Cardenio: Performing Shakespeare, Transforming Cervantes* (New York: Palgrave Macmillan, 2013).

Boutcher, Warren. "'Who Taught Thee Rhetoricke to Deceive a Maid?': Christopher Marlowe's Hero and Leander, Juan Boscán's Leandro, and Renaissance Vernacular Humanism," *Comparative Literature* 52.1 (2000), 11–52.

Boyle, A. J. ed., *Seneca's Medea* (Oxford: Oxford University Press, 2014).

Brayman Hackel, Heidi. *Reading Material in Early Modern England* (Cambridge: Cambridge University Press, 2005).

Brennan, Michael. *The Sidneys of Penshurst and the Monarchy, 1500–1700* (Aldershot: Ashgate, 2006).

Britton, Dennis and Melissa Walter, eds. *Rethinking Shakespeare Source Study: Audiences, Authors, and Digital Technologies* (New York: Routledge, 2018).

Buchanan, Henry. "'India' and the Golden Age *in A Midsummer Night's Dream*," *Shakespeare Survey* 65, no. 1 (2012), 58–68.

Bullough, Geoffrey. *Narrative and Dramatic Sources, vol. 8* (New York: Columbia University Press, 1975).

Burton, Richard. *Ultima Thule: or, A Summer in Iceland*, vol. 1 (London: William P. Nimmo, 1875).

B[urton], R[obert] (Nathaniel Crouch). *The English Empire in America by R.B.* (London: Nathaniel Crouch, 1685).

Camden, William. *Britain, or A Chorographicall Description of the Most flourishing Kingdomes, England, Scotland, and Ireland, and the Ilands adioyning, out of the depth of Antiquitie: Beautified with Mappes of the several Shires of England: Written first in Latine by William Camden,* Philémon Holland, trans. (London: George Bishop, 1610).

Camden, William. *The historie of the life and reigne of that famous princesse Elizabeth containing a briefe memoriall of the chiefest affaires of state that haue passed in these kingdomes of England, Scotland, France or Ireland since the yeare of the fatall Spanish invasion to that of her sad and ever to be deplored dissolution* (London: William Webbe, 1634).

Camden, William. *The History of the Most Renowned and Victorious Princess Elizabeth Late Queen of England; Containing All the Most Important and Remarkable Passages of State, Both at Home and Abroad (so Far as They Were Linked with English Affairs) During Her Long and Prosperous Reign. The Fourth Edition, Revised and Compared with the Original, Whereby Many Gross Faults are Amended, Several Periods Before Omitted are Added in Their Due Places,... with a New Alphabetical Index of All the Principal Things Contained in the History* (London: R. Bentley, 1688).

Campanella, Tommaso. *A discourse touching the Spanish monarchy. Wherein vve have a political glasse, representing each particular country, province, kingdome, and empire of the world, with wayes of government by which they may be kept in obedience. As also, the causes of the rise and fall of each kingdom and empire. VVritten by Tho. Campanella. Newly translated into English, according to the third edition of this book in Latine* (London: Philemon Stephens, 1654).

Carnegie, David and Gary Taylor, eds. *The Quest for Cardenio: Shakespeare, Fletcher, and the Lost Play* (Oxford: Oxford University Press, 2012).

Carrión, Maria Mercedes. *Subject Stages: Marriage, Theatre, and the Law in Early Modern Spain* (Toronto: University of Toronto Press, 2010).

Casale, Giancarlo. "Did Alexander the Great Discover America? Debating Space and Time in Renaissance Istanbul," *Renaissance Quarterly* 72, no 3 (2019), 863–909.

Cavendish, Margaret. *Natures Picture Drawn by Fancies Pencil to the Life being several Feigned Stories, Comical, Tragical, Tragi-Comical, Poetical, Romanicical, Philosophical, Historical, and Moral: Some in Verse, some in Prose, some Mixt, and some by Dialogues / Written by ... the Duchess of Newcastle* (London, A. Maxwell, 1671).

Certaine miscellany works of the Right Honourable Francis Lo. Verulam, Viscount S. Alban. (London: William Rawley, 1629).

de Certeau, Michel. *Writing of History*, Tom Conley, trans. (New York: Columbia University Press, 1988).

de Cervantes Saavedra, Miguel. *Don Quijote de la Mancha, tomo 1*, John Jay Allen, ed. (Madrid: Catedra Letras Hispánicas, 2005).

de Cervantes Saavedra, Miguel. *The History of the renown'd Don Quixote de la Mancha written in Spanish by Miguel de Cervantse Saavedra; translated from the original by several hands, and published by Peter Motteux; adorn'd with sculptures* (London: Sam Buckley, 1712).

Chapman, George. "De Guiana carmen Epicum," in Richard Hakluyt, *The Principal Navigations Voyages Traffiques and Discoveries of the English Nation In Twelve Volumes*, vol. X, reprinted from the 1600 edition (Glasgow: James MacLehose and Sons, 1904), 446–50.

Chartier, Roger. *Cardenio between Cervantes and Shakespeare: The Story of a Lost Play*, English edition, Janet Lloyd, trans. (Cambridge: Polity Press, 2013).

Checa Cremades, Fernando and Laura Fernández-González, eds. *Festival Culture in the World of the Spanish Habsburgs* (Farnham, Ashgate Publishing, 2015), 87–113.

Cheney, Donald, A. C. Hamilton, David Richardson, and A. C. Barker, *The Spenser Encyclopedia* (Toronto: University of Toronto Press, 1990).

Clay, Diskin. "Columbus' Senecan Prophecy," *The American Journal of Philology*, 113, no. 4 (1992), 617–20.

Codex Mendoza, Bodleian Library, Oxford University, MS Arch. Selden A. 1. (fol. 71v), Codex Mendoza Online. (INAH: National Institute of Anthropology and History).

Columbus, Christopher, and Roberto Rusconi, *The Book of Prophecies edited by Christopher Columbus*, vol. III, Roberto Rusconi, ed., Blair Sullivan, trans. (Berkeley: University of California Press, 1997).

Cortés, Hernán. *Cartas y relaciónes de Hernan Cortés al emperador Carlos V*, Pascual de Gayangos, ed. (Paris: A. Chaix y Ca., 1866), 101-102.

Cortés, Hernán. *Letters of Cortes: The Five Letters of Relation from Fernando Cortes to the Emperor Charles V*, vol. I, Francis Augustus MacNutt, ed. (New York: G. P. Putnam's Sons, 1908).

Craft, Peter. "Peter Heylyn's Seventeenth-Century World View," *Studies in Medieval and Renaissance History*, 3rd ser., 2 (2014), 325–44.

Croce, Benedetto. *España en la vida italiana durante el Renacimiento*, J. Sánchez Rojas, trans. (Madrid: Mundo Latino, 1915).

Cromwell, Oliver. "Speech V. Meeting of the Second Protectorate Parliament, 17 Sept. 1656," in Thomas Carlyle, *Oliver Cromwell's Letters and Speeches with Elucidations, in Four Volumes, vol. III* (London: Chapman and Hall, Ltd., 1897), 267–310.

Crowley, Tim. "Contingencies of Literary Censorship: Anglo-Spanish Diplomacy and *Amadís de Gaula* in January 1569," *Sixteenth Century Journal* (2015), 891–926.

Crowley, Tim. "Sidney's Legal Patronage and the International Protestant Cause," *Renaissance Quarterly* 71, no. 4 (2018), 1298–350.

Cruz, Anne, ed., *Material and Symbolic Circulation Between Spain and England, 1554–1604, Transculturalisms, 1400–1700* (Fanham: Ashgate, 2008).

Cummings, Stephan. "Encountering Spain in Early Modern Naples: Language, Customs and Sociability" in *The Spanish Presence in Sixteenth Century Italy: Images of Iberia*, Piers Barker-Bates and Miles Pattenden, eds. (Fanham: Ashgate, 2015), 43–62.

Curbet, Joan. "Repressing the Amazon: Cross-Dressing and Militarism in Edmund Spenser's *The Faerie Queene*," in *Dressing Up for War: Transformations of Gender and Genre in the Discourse and Literature of War*, A. Usandizaga and A. Monnickendam, eds. (Amsterdam: Rodopi Press, 2001).
Curione, Celio Secondo. *Pasquine in a Traunce* (London: W.P. Seene, 1566).
Davenant, William. *The Cruelty of the Spaniards in Peru* (London: Henry Herringman, 1658).
Davis, Alex. *Chivalry and Romance in the English Renaissance* (Cambridge: D. S. Brewer, 2003).
Dekker, Thomas. *Satiro-Mastix, or The vntrussing of the Humorous Poet* (London: Edward White, 1602).
Desai, R. W. "England, The Indian Boy, and the Spice Trade in *A Midsummer Night's Dream*," in *India's Shakespeare: Translation, Interpretation, and Performance*, Poonam Trivedi and Dennis Bartholomeusz, eds. (Delhi: Pearson Education India, 2005), 127–41.
de Montaigne, Michel. *Essais*, John Florio, trans. (London: Edward Blount, 1603).
Díaz del Castillo, Bernal. *The History of the Conquest of New Spain*, David Carrasco, ed. (Alburquerque: University of New Mexico Press, 2008), 466–73.
Doran, Susan. *Monarchy and Matrimony: The Courtships of Elizabeth I* (London: Routledge, 1996).
Dorer, Edmund. *Das Magazin für die Litteratur des In- und Auslandes*, January 31, 1885.
van Dorsten, J. A., Dominic Baker-Smith, and Arthur F. Kinney, eds., *Sir Philip Sidney: 1586 and the Creation of a Legend*, Publications of the Sir Thomas Browne Institute, New Ser., no. 9 (Leiden: J. Brill/Leiden University Press, 1986).
Drake, Francis. *Sir Francis Drake's West Indian Voyage, 1585–86* (Kiribati: Hakluyt Society, 1981).
Dryden, John. *Troilus and Cressida* (London: Able Swall and Jacob Tonson, 1679).
Dryden, John. "*The Indian Emperour, or The Conquest of Mexico by the Spaniards* (1665): Connexion of the Indian Emperour, to the Indian Queen," in *The Works of John Dryden*, Vol. 9: Plays; *The Indian Emperour; Secret Love; Sir Martin Mar-all*, John Loftis and Vinton A. Dearing, eds. (Berkeley: University of California Press, 1996), Oxford Scholarly Editions Online (2015).
Durán, Diego. *The History of the Indies of New Spain*, Doris Heyden, trans. (Norman: University of Oklahoma Press, 1994).
The eighth booke of the Myrror of knighthood. Being the third of the third part. Englished out of the Spanish tongue… (London: Cuthbert Burby, 1599).
Eisenberg, Daniel, ed. *An Edition of a Sixteenth-Century Romance of Chivalry: Diego Ortúñez de Calahorra's 'Espejo de príncipes y cavalleros ['El Caballero del Febo']* (Baltimore: Johns Hopkins, 1971).
Ellison, James. *George Sandys: Travel, Colonialism, and Tolerance in the Seventeenth Century*, Studies in Renaissance Literature, 8 (Rochester: D. S. Brewer, 2002).
Erasmus, Desiderius. *The Complaint of Peace* (Chicago: The Open Court Publishing, 1917).
de Eslava, Antonio. *Noches de invierno*, Julia Barrella, ed. (Zaragoza: Iberoamericana, 2013).
de Eslava, Antonio. *Parte primera del libro intitulado Noches de inuierno. Compuesto por Antonio de Eslaua, natural de la Villa de Sanguessa* (Barcelona: Miguel Menescal, 1609).
Español Bouché, Luis. *Leyendas Negras. Vida y obra de Julián Juderías (1877–1918); la leyenda negra antiamericana* (Salamanca: Junta de Castilla y León, 2007).
Everson, Jane. *The Italian Romance Epic in the Age of Humanism* (Oxford: Oxford University Press, 2001).
Fallows, Noel. *Jousting in Medieval and Renaissance Iberia* (Woodbridge: The Boydell Press, 2010).
The Famous and Renowned History of Amadis De Gaule Conteining the Heroick Deeds of Armes and Strange Adventures, Aswell [Sic] of Amadis Himself, as of Perion His Son, and Lisvart of Greece, Son to Esplandian, Emperor of Constantinople […] Translated Out of French into English by Francis Kirkman (London: Jane Bell, 1652).
Farinelli, Arturo. *Italia e Spagna*, 2 vols. (Torino: Fratelli Bocca, 1929).
Farmer, Alan and Zachary Lesser, "The Popularity of Playbooks Revisited," *Shakespeare Quarterly* 56 (2005), 1–32.
Farmer, Alan and Zachary Lesser, eds. *DEEP: Database of Early English Playbooks*. Created 2007. http://deep.sas.upenn.edu.

Ferguson, Margaret W. "A Room Not Their Own: Renaissance Women as Readers and Writers," in *The Comparative Perspective on Literature: Approaches to Theory and Practice*, Clayton Koelb and Susan Noakes, eds. (Ithaca: Cornell University Press, 1988), 93–116.

Finke, Laurie. "Spenser For Hire," in *Culture and the King: the Social Implications of the Arthurian Legend*, Martin B. Shichtman and James P. Carley, eds. (New York: University of New York Press, 1994).

Foulkes, Richard. *Performing Shakespeare in the Age of Empire* (Cambridge: Cambridge University Press, 2002).

Foxe, John. *Actes and monuments of these latter and perillous dayes touching matters of the Church,…* (London: John Day, 1563).

Friedrich, Hugo. "On the Art of Translation," in *Theories of Translation*, Rainer Schulte and John Biguenet, eds. (Chicago: University of Chicago Press, 1992), 11–16.

Frye, Northrop. *Anatomy of Criticism* (Princeton: Princeton University Press, 1957).

Frye, Susan. "The Myth of Elizabeth at Tilbury," *The Sixteenth Century Journal* 23, no. 1 (1992), 95–114.

Fuchs, Barbara. *Exotic Nation: Maurophilia and the Construction of Early Modern Spain* (Philadelphia: University of Pennsylvania Press, 2009).

Fuchs, Barbara. *The Poetics of Piracy* (Philadelphia: University of Pennsylvania Press, 2013).

Fuchs, Barbara. *Romance* (New York: Routledge, 2004).

Fuchs, Barbara. "Spanish Lessons: Spenser and the Irish Moriscos," *SEL: Studies in English Literature, 1500–1900* 42.1 (2002), 43–62.

Garnett, Richard and Edmund Gosse, *English Literature: From the Age of Henry VIII to the Age of Milton*, part II of IV (London: Macmillan, 1904).

García Càrcel, Ricard and Lourdes Mateo i Bretos, *La leyenda negra* (Madrid: Compañía Europea de Comunicación e Información, 1991).

Gawdy, Philip. *Letters of Philip Gawdy of West Harling, Norfolk, and of London to Various Members of his Family 1579–1616*, Isaac Herbert Jeayes, ed. (London, J. B. Nichols and Sons, 1906).

Gillies, John. *Shakespeare and the Geography of Difference* (New York: Cambridge University Press, 1994).

Gilman, Stephen. "Bernal Díaz del Castillo and Amadís de Gaula," in *Studia Philologica: Homenaje ofrecido a Dámaso Alonso*, vol. II (Madrid: Gredos, 1960), 99–114.

Goldberg, Jonathan. *Endlesse Worke: Spenser and the Structures of Discourse* (Baltimore: Johns Hopkins University Press, 1981).

Gómez de Quevedo, Francisco. *España Defendida, y los tiempos de ahora, de las calumnias de los noveleros y sediciosos* (Madrid: Real Academia de la Historia, 1916).

Goodman, Jennifer R. *Chivalry and Exploration: 1298–1630* (Woodbridge: The Boydell Press, 1998).

Graziani, René. "Philip II's *Impresa* and Spenser's Souldan," *Journal of the Warburg and Courtald Institutes* 27 (1964), 322–4.

Greenblatt, Stephen. *Sir Walter Ralegh: The Renaissance Man and His Roles* (New Haven: Yale University Press, 1973).

Greene, Roland. "The 'Scrienne' and the Channel: England and Spain in Book 5 of *The Faerie Queene*," *Journal of Medieval and Early Modern Studies* 39, no. 1 (2009), 43–64.

Greene, Roland. *Unrequited Conquests: Love and Empire in the Colonial Americas* (Chicago: University of Chicago Press, 1999).

Greenstadt, Amy. *Rape and the Rise of the Author: Gendering Intention in Early Modern England*, reprint (Abingdon, Routledge, 2016).

Greer, Margaret, Walter D. Mignolo, and Maureen Quilligan, eds. *Rereading the Black Legend: The Discourses of Religious and Racial Difference in the Renaissance Empires* (Chicago: University of Chicago Press, 2007).

Griffin, Eric J. *English Renaissance Drama and the Specter of Spain: Ethnopoetics and Empire* (Philadelphia: University of Pennsylvania Press, 2009).

Griffin, Eric J. "Ethos to Ethnos: Hispanizing 'the Spaniard' in the Old World and the New,'" in *The New Centennial Review*, 2, no. 1 (2002), 69–116.

Haase, Wolfgang and Meyer Reinhold, eds,. *The Classical Tradition and the Americas, vol. 1: European Images of the Americas and the Classical Tradition, vol. I: European Images of the Americas and the Classical Tradition* (Berlin: Walter de Gruyter, 1994).

Habib, Imtiaz. "Bengal as Shakespeare's India and the Stolen Indian Boy: The Historical Dark Matter of *A Midsummer Night's Dream*," *Early Modern Literary Studies* 20, no. 1 (2018), 1–27.

Hackett, Helen. *Women and Romance Fiction in the English Renaissance* (New York: Cambridge University Press, 2000).

Hadfield, Andrew. *Edmund Spenser: A Life* (Oxford: Oxford University Press, 2012).

Hakluyt, Richard. *The Principal Navigations Voyages Traffiques and Discoveries of the English Nation In Twelve Volumes,* vol. X, reprinted from the 1600 edition (Glasgow: James MacLehose and Sons, 1904).

Hale, Edward Everett. "The Queen of California," *Atlantic Monthly*, March 1864, 265–78, rpt. in *The Queen of California: The Origin of the Name of California* (San Francisco: Colt, 1945), 1–47.

Hall, Kim F. *Things of Darkness: Economies of Race and Gender in Early Modern England* (Ithaca: Cornell University Press, 1995).

Halliwell, James O. *The Works of William Shakespeare, The Text formed From A new Collation of the early Editions…, vol. II The Two Gentlemen of Verona. The Merry Wives of Windsor…* (London: C. and J. Adlard, Bartholomew Close, 1854).

Hamilton, Donna. *Anthony Munday and the Catholics, 1560–1633,* second edition (New York: Routledge, 2016).

Hansard's Parliamentary Debates, Third Series, Commencing with the Accession of William IV (London: House of Commons, 1839).

Harington, John. trans. *Ludovico Ariosto's Orlando Furioso: Translated into English heroical verse by Sir John Harington,* R. McNulty, ed. (Oxford: Oxford University Press, 1972), Oxford Scholarly Editions Online (2012).

Hariot, Thomas. *A briefe and true report of the new found land of Virginia …* (London: R. Robinson, 1588).

Hawkins, Richard. *The Observations of Sir Richard Hawkins, Knt. in his Voyage into The South Sea in the Year 1593, reprinted from the edition of 1622,* C. R. Drinkwater Bethune, ed. (London: Hakluyt Society, 1847).

Hay, Peter. *An Aduertiseme[nt] to the Subjects of Scotland of the Fearfull Dangers Threatned to Christian States…* (Aberdeen: Edward Raban, 1627).

Heale, Elizabeth. *The Faerie Queene: A Reader's Guide,* second edition (Cambridge: Cambridge University Press, 1999).

Hendricks, Margo. "'Obscured by Dreams': Race, Empire, and Shakespeare's *A Midsummer Night's Dream*," in *Shakespeare Quarterly* 47, no. 1 (1996), 37–60.

Heng, Geraldine. *Empire of Magic: Medieval Romance and the Politics of Cultural Fantasy* (New York: Columbia University Press, 2003).

Heylyn, Peter. *Cosmographie in Four Bookes: Containing the Chorographie and Historie of the Whole Vvorld, and all the Principall Kingdomes, Provinces, Seas and Isles Thereof* (London: Henry Seile, 1652).

Heylyn, Peter. *The historie of that most famous saint and souldier of Christ Iesus; St. George of Cappadocia…* (London: Henry Seyle, 1631).

Higden, Henry. *A modern essay on the tenth satyr of Juvenal* (London: T. Milbourn, 1687).

Higginbotham, Jennifer. *The Girlhood of Shakespeare's Sisters: Gender, Transgression, Adolescence* (Edinburgh: Edinburgh University Press, 2013).

Highley, Chris. *Shakespeare, Spenser, and the Crisis in Ireland* (Cambridge: Cambridge University Press, 1997).

Hill Boone, Elizabeth. "This New World Now Revealed: Hernán Cortés and the Presentation of Mexico to Europe," *Word & Image* 27, no. 1 (2011), 31–46.

Hosington, Brenda, et al. *Renaissance Cultural Crossroads,* http://www.dhi.ac.uk.

Índice ultimo de los libros prohibidos y mandados expurgar: para todos los reinos y señorios del católico rey de las Españas, el señor Don Carlos IV (Madrid: Antonio de Sancha, 1780).

James I, *Daemonologie in forme of a dialogue, divided into three bookes* (Edinburgh: Robert Walde-grave, 1597).

Jameson, Fredric. "Magical Narratives: Romance as Genre," *New Literary History*, 7, no. 1 (1975), 135–63.
Jonson, Ben. *The Cambridge Edition of the Works of Ben Jonson, vols. 1–7* (Cambridge: Cambridge University Press, 2012).
Jonson, Ben. *Poetaster or The arraignment* (London: R. Bradock, 1602).
Juderías, Julián, *La leyenda negra y la verdad histórica* (Madrid: Rev. de Arch., Bibl. y Museos, 1914).
Kelsey, Sean. "Staging the Trial of Charles I" in *The Regicides and the Execution of Charles I*, Jason Peacey, ed. (Hampshire: Palgrave, 2001), 71–93.
Kermode, Frank, ed. *William Shakespeare's The Tempest*, reprint (London: Routledge, 1994).
King, John. "Queen Elizabeth I: Representations of the Virgin Queen," *Renaissance Quarterly* 43 (1990), 30–74.
King, John. *Tudor Royal Iconography: Literature and Art in an Age of Religious Crisis* (Princeton: Princeton University Press, 1989).
Kirkman, Francis. *The unlucky citizen…* (London: Francis Kirkman, 1673).
Knapp, Jeffrey. *An Empire Nowhere: England, America, and Literature from Utopia to The Tempest* (Berkeley: University of California Press, 1992)
Koslow, Julian. "Humanist Schooling and Ben Jonson's Poetaster," *English Literary History* 73, no. 1 (2006), 119–59.
Lamb, Mary Ellen. "Constructions of Women Readers," in *Teaching Tudor and Stuart Women Writers*, Susanne Woods and Margaret P. Hannay, eds. (New York: Modern Language Association, 2000), 23–34.
Lamb, Mary Ellen. "The Red Crosse Knight, St. George, and the Appropriation of Popular Culture," *Spenser Studies* 18, no. 1 (2003), 185–208.
de Las Casas, Bartolomé, *Historia de las Indias,* tomo I, segunda edición (México: Fondo de Cultura Económica, 1965).
Lee, Christine. "The Meanings of Romance: Rethinking Early Modern Fiction," *Modern Philology* 112, no. 2 (2014), 287–311.
Leland, John. *A Learned and True Assertion of the original, Life, Actes, and death of the most Noble, Valiant, and Renoumed Prince Arthure, King of great Brittaine*, Richard Robinson, trans. (London: John Wolfe, 1582).
Leonard, Irving A., *Books of the Brave: Being an Account of Books and of Men in the Spanish Conquest and Settlement of the Sixteenth-Century New World*, second edition (Berkeley: University of California Press, 1992).
Leycesters Common-Wealth Conceived, Spoken and Published with most Earnest Protestation of all Dutifull Good Will and Affection Towards this Realme, for Whose Good Onely, it is made Common to Many (London: s. n., 1641).
Lightfoot, William. *The Complaint of England, Wherein it is clearely prooued that the practices of Traitrous Papists against the state of this Realme, and the person of her Maiestie, are in Diuinitie vnlawfull, odious in Nature, and ridiculous in pollicie…later by the Spaniards outrages, in his exactions raised vpon Naples, and his tyrannies executed in the* Indies (London: John Wolfe, 1587).
Llull, Ramón. *The Book of the Order of Chivalry*, Noel Fallows, trans. (Woodbridge: The Boydell Press, 2013).
Lockey, Brian. *Early Modern Catholics, Royalists, and Cosmopolitans: English Transnationalism and the Christian Commonwealth* (London: Routledge, 2016).
López de Gómara, Francisco. *The Pleasant Historie of the Conquest of VVeast India, now called new Spain, Atchieued by the vvorthy Prince Hernando Cortes Marques of the valley of Huaxacac, most delectable to Reade*, Thomas Nicholas, trans. (London: Henry Bynneman, 1578).
Loomba, Ania. "The Great Indian Vanishing Trick: Colonialism, Property, and the Family in *A Midsummer Night's Dream*," in *A Feminist Companion to Shakespeare*, Dympna Callaghan, ed. (London: Wiley, 2016), 181–205.
Machiavelli, Niccolò. *The Prince* (New York: Dover, 1992).

MacPhail, Eric. "Ariosto and the Prophetic Moment," *Modern Language Notes* 116, no. 1 (2001), 30–53.
Madrigales the triumphes of Oriana, to 5 and 6 voices: composed by divers severall aucthors (London, Thomas Morley, 1601).
Malory, Thomas. *Le morte darthur, Emprynted and fynysshed in thabbey Westmestre* (London: Caxton, 1485).
Maltby, William S., *The Black Legend in England* (Durham: Duke University Press, 1971).
Marino, John A. "City Solidarities and Nodes of Power," in *Becoming Neapolitan: Citizen Culture in Baroque Naples* (Johns Hopkins University Press, 2011).
Martyr of Angleria, Peter. *The Decades of the newe worlde or west India ...*, Rycharde Eden, trans. (London: Guilhelmi Powell, 1555).
Massinger, Philip. *The Plays and Poems of Philip Massinger, vol. IV*, Philip Edwards and Colin Gibson, eds. (Oxford: Clarendon Press, 1976).
McCarthy-King, Erin. "The Voyage of Columbus as a 'Non Pensato Male,'" in *New Worlds and the Italian Renaissance: Contributions to the History of European Intellectual Culture*, Andrea Moudarres and Christiana Purdy Moudarres, eds. (Leiden: Brill, 2012), 25–44.
Menéndez y Pelayo, Marcelino. *Orígenes de la Novela*, vol. II (Madrid: Consejo Superior de Investigaciones Científicas, 1943).
Meres, Francis. *Palladis tamia. Wits treasury being the second part of Wit's common wealth* (London: Cuthbert Burbie, 1598).
Miles Gloriosus, the Spanish Braggadocio, Or, the Humour of the Spaniard Lately Written in French, and Newly Translated into English, with the French Annexed, I.W. trans. (London: I.E., 1630).
Milton, Anthony. *Laudian and Royalist Polemic in Seventeenth-Century England: The Career and Writings of Peter Heylyn* (Manchester: Manchester University Press, 2007).
Mínguez, Victor. *Los reyes solares: iconografía astral de la monarquía hispánica* (Publicacions de la Universitat Jaume I, 2001).
Montrose, Louis. "The Work of Gender in the Discourse of Discovery," *Representations*, 33 (1991), 1–41.
Moore, Helen, ed., *Amadis de Gaule, translated by Anthony Munday* (Aldershot: Ashgate, 2004).
Moore, Helen. *Amadís in English: A Study in the Reading of Romance* (Oxford: Oxford University Press, 2020).
Moore, Helen. "The Eastern Mediterranean in the English *Amadis* Cycle, Book V," *The Yearbook of English Studies* 41, no. 1 (2011), 113–25.
Munday, Anthony, trans. *The Fift Booke of the most Pleasant and Delectable Historie of Amadis De Gaule*. (London: Hugh Jackson, 1598).
Mundy, Barbara. "Mapping the Aztec Capital: The 1524 Nuremberg Map of Tenochtitlan, Its Sources and Meanings," *Imago Mundi*, 50 (1998), 11–33.
Muñoz, Victoria. "'De-Naturalizing' Rape in Translation: Margaret Tyler's *Mirrour of Princely Deedes and Knighthood* (1578)," *Modern Language Studies* 44 no. 2 (2015), 10–27.
de Nebrija, Antonio. *Gramática castellana* (Salamanca: Juan de Porras, 1492).
Newcomb, Lori Humphrey. *Reading Popular Romance in Early Modern England* (New York: Columbia University Press, 2002).
Nicholas Canny, ed. *The Oxford History of the British Empire, Vol. I: The Origins of Empire* (Oxford: Oxford University Press, 2001), 1–33.
Nohrnberg, James. "Raleigh in ruins, Raleigh on the rocks," in *Literary and Visual Ralegh*, Christopher Armitage, ed. (Manchester, England: Manchester University Press, 2016), 31–88.
Noreña, Carlos G. *Juan Luis Vives I*, International Archives of the History of Ideas (The Hague: Martinus Nijhoff, 1970).
Novissimus librorum prohibitorum et expurgatorum: index pro Regis catholici Hispaniarum (Madrid: Diego Díaz de la Carrera, 1640).
de La Noue, François. *The politicke and militarie discourses of the Lord de La Nouue VVhereunto are adioyned certaine obseruations of the same author, of things happened during the three late ciuill warres of France*, Edward Aggas, trans. (London: T.C. and E.A., 1587).

O'Connor, John. *Amadis de Gaule and Its Influence on English Literature* (New Brunswick: Rutgers University Press, 1970).
Ordóñez [Rodríguez] de Montalvo, Garci. *Las Sergas del virtuoso caballero Esplandián, hijo de Amadís de Gaula* (Sevilla, 1510) (Madrid: Biblioteca de Autores Españoles, 1857).
Ortelius, Abraham. *Theatrum orbis terrarium* (London: John Norton, 1606).
Ortúñez de Calahorra, Diego. *Espejo de príncipes y cavalleros, Parte I*, Daniel Eisenberg, ed. (Madrid, Espasa-Calpe, 1975).
Overbury, Thomas. *A Wife Now the Widdow of Sir Thomas Overburye being a most Exquisite and Singular Poem of the Choice of a Wife. Whereunto are Added Many Witty Characters, and Conceited Newes, Written by Himselfe and Other Learned Gentlemen His Friends London* (London: Lawrence Lisle, 1614).
Overbury, Thomas. *New and choise characters, of seuerall authors together with that exquisite and unmatcht poeme, The wife (With many other things added this sixt impression.)* (London: Lawrence Lisle, 1615).
Parker, Geoffrey. *Emperor: A New Life of Charles V* (New Haven: Yale University Press, 2019).
Parker, Geoffrey. *Imprudent King: A New Life of Philip II* (New Haven: Yale University Press, 2014).
Parker, Geoffrey. *The World Is Not Enough: The Imperial Vision of Philip II of Spain*, The Twenty-Second Charles Edmondson Historical Lectures (Waco: Baylor University, 2000).
Parker, Patricia. *Inescapable Romance: Studies in the Poetics of a Mode* (Princeton: Princeton University Press, 1979).
Parry, Robert, trans. *The second part of the first booke of the Myrrour of knighthood in which is prosecuted the illustrious deedes of the knight of the Sunne, and his brother Rosicleer, sonnes vnto the Emperour Trebatio of Greece: With the valiant deedes of armes of sundry worthie knights, very delightfull to bee read, and nothing hurtfull to bee regarded. Now newly translated out of Spanish into our vulgar tongue by R[obert] P[arry]* (London: Thomas Este, 1599).
Paynell, Thomas, trans. *The moste excellent and pleasaunt booke, entituled: The treasurie of Amadis of Fraunce...* (London: Henry Bynneman, 1572).
Pearson, Jacqueline. "Women Reading, Reading Women," in *Women and Literature in Britain 1500–1700*, Helen Wilcox, ed. (Cambridge: Cambridge University Press, 1996), 80–99.
Peat, Derek. "Falstaff Gets the Sack," *Shakespeare Quarterly* 53, no. 3 (2002), 379–85.
de Perott, Joseph. *The Probable Source of the Plot of Shakespeare's* The Tempest (Worcester: Clark University Press, 1905).
Petrarca, Francesco. *The Life of Solitude,* Jacob Zeitlin, trans. (Chicago: University of Illinois Press, 1924).
Pigna, Giovanni Batista. *I Romanzi di Giovanni Battista Pigna: divisi in 3 libri, ne'quali della poesia e della vita dell'Ariosto si tratta* (Vinegia: Vincenzo Valgrisi, 1554).
Pinet, Simone. *Archipelagoes: Insular Fictions from Chivalric Romance to the Novel* (Minneapolis: University of Minnesota Press, 2011).
Polk, Dora. *The Island of California: A History of the Myth* (Lincoln: University of Nebraska Press, 1995).
Pontano, Giovanni. *Dialogues, Volume 1: Charon and Antonius,* Julia Haig Gaisser, ed. and trans. The I Tatti Renaissance Library, no. 53 (Cambridge: Harvard University Press, 2012).
Praeclara Ferdinadi Cortesii de Noua maris Oceani Hyspania narratio... Carolo Romanoru imperatori... M.D. XX transmissa... per Petru Saguorgnanu [sic] ex Hyspano idiomate in Latinu versa anno Dni, M.D. XXIIII Kl. Martii. [Explicit secunda Ferdinandi Cortesii Narratio... (Nuremberg: Friedrich Peypus, 1524).
Pujante, Ángel-Luis. *La Tempestad* (Barcelona: Austral, 2012).
Purchas, Samuel. *Purchas his Pilgrimes* (London: H. Featherstone, 1625).
Raleigh, Sir Walter. *Sir Walter Raleigh's Discovery of Guiana,* Joyce Lorimer, ed. (London: The Hakluyt Society, 2006).
Raman, Shankar. *Framing "India": The Colonial Imaginary in Early Modern Culture* (Stanford: Stanford University Press, 2001).
Randall, Dale and Jackson Boswell. *Cervantes in Seventeenth-Century England: The Tapestry Turned* (Oxford: Oxford University Press, 2009).
Raymond, Joad. *Pamphlets and Pamphleteering in Early Modern Britain* (Cambridge: Cambridge University Press, 2003).

Read, David. *Temperate Conquests: Spenser and the Spanish New World* (Detroit: Wayne State University Press, 2000).
Restall, Matthew. *Seven Myths of the Spanish Conquest* (Oxford: Oxford University Press, 2003).
Riley, E. C. *Cervantes's Theory of the Novel* (Oxford: Clarendon Press, 1962).
Río Torres-Murciano, Antonio. "«Aquestos y Otros Triunfos». Historia de Indias e Historia de Europa En La Épica Cortesiana," *Revista de Indias* 80, no. 278 (2020), 29–61.
Roach, Joseph. *Cities of the Dead: Circum-Atlantic Performance* (New York: Columbia University Press, 1996).
Rodríguez Lobo, Francisco. *Corte en Aldea y Noches de Invierno* (Valencia: Salvador Faulí, 1798).
Rodríguez Pérez, Yolanda and Antonio Sánchez Jiménez, and Harm den Boer, eds. *España ante sus críticos: las claves de la Leyenda Negra* (Madrid and Frankfurt: Iberoamerica and Vervuert, 2015).
Romo Feito, Fernando. "Ideology and Image of Peninsular languages in Spanish Literature," in *A Comparative History of Literatures in the Iberian Peninsula* (Amsterdam: John Benjamins, 2010), 456–74.
Ross, Trevor. *The Making of the English Literary Canon: From the Middle Ages to the Late Eighteenth Century* (Montreal: McGill-Queen's University Press, 1998).
van Rossem, Stijn. "The Verdussens and the International Trade in Catholic Books (Antwerp, Seventeenth Century)," in *Books in the Catholic World during the Early Modern Period*, Natalia Maillard Álvarez, ed. (Brill, Leiden: 2014), 1–50.
Rowe, Nicholas. *Some Account of the Life of Mr. William Shakespeare* (Ann Arbor: Augustan Reprint Society, 1948).
Ruscelli, Girolamo. *Le Imprese Illustri con espositioni, et discorsi* (Venice: Franciscus Rampazetto, 1566).
de Sahagún, Bernardino. *Conquest of New Spain: 1585 revision*, S. L. Cline, ed. (Salt Lake City: University of Utah Press, 1989).
Said, Edward. *Orientalism* (New York: Random House, 1978).
Samson, Alexander. "A Fine Romance: Anglo-Spanish Relations in the Sixteenth Century," *Journal of Medieval and Early Modern Studies* 39, no. 1 (2009), 65–94.
Samson, Alexander. *The Spanish Match: Prince Charles's Journey to Madrid, 1623* (Aldershot: Ashgate, 2006).
Saulnier Duverdier, Gilbert. *The love and armes of the Greeke princes. Or, The romant of the romants. Written in French by Monsieur Verdere, and translated for the Right Honourable, Philip, Earle of Pembroke and Montgomery, Lord Chamberlaine to his Majesty*, n. n., trans. (London: Thomas Walkley, 1640).
Schleiner, Louise. "Margaret Tyler, Translator, and Waiting Woman," *English Language Notes* 29 (1992), 1–9.
Schleiner, Winfried. "'Divina Virago': Queen Elizabeth as an Amazon" *Studies in Philology* 75, no. 2 (1978), 163–80.
Scott Kastan, David. *Shakespeare after Theory* (New York: Routledge, 1999).
Sebek, Barbara. "'More natural to the nation': Situating Shakespeare in the "Querelle de Canary" in *Shakespeare Studies, vol. 42*, James R. Siemon and Diana E. Henderson, eds. (Madison: Farleigh Dickinson University Press, 2014), 106–21.
The Second Booke of Amadis De Gaule Contaning the Description, Wonders, and Conquest of the Firme-Island. the Triumphs and Troubles of Amadis. His Manifold Victories… L[azarus] P[iot] (Anthony Munday), trans. (London: C. Burbie, 1595).
Seneca, Lucius Annaeus. *Seneca His Tenne Traigedies, Translaited into Englysh*, John Studley, trans. (London: Thomas Marsh, 1581).
Shakespeare, William. *Henry IV, Part I*, David Bevington, ed. Oxford World Classics Edition, Stanley Wells, ed. (Oxford: Oxford University Press, 2008).
Shakespeare, William. *Henry IV, Part 2*, René Weis, ed. Oxford World's Classics Edition, Stanley Wells, ed. (Oxford: Oxford University Press, 1997).
Shakespeare, William. *The Tempest*, Stephen Orgel, ed. (Oxford: Oxford University Press, 1987).
The Shakespeare Society of New York, *New Shakespeareana: A Critical Contemporary and Cvrrent Review of Shakespearean & Elizabethan Stvdies,* vol. III (New York and Westfield: 1904).

Shapiro, James. "Revisiting Tamburlaine: *Henry V* as Shakespeare's Belated Armada Play," *Criticism* 31, no. 4 (1989), 351–66.
Shahani, Gitanjali. "The Spiced Indian Air in Early Modern England," *Shakespeare Studies* 42 (2014), 122–40.
Shepherd, Simon. *Amazons and Warrior Women: Varieties of Feminism in Seventeenth-Century Drama* (Sussex: Harvester Press, 1981).
Sherburne, Edward. *Medea: A Tragedie. Written in Latine by Lucius Annaeus Seneca. Englished by E. S. Esq with annotations*, Edward Sherburne, trans. (London: Humphrey Moseley, 1648).
Sidney, Philip. *An Apology for Poetry (or The Defence of Poesy)*, R. W. Maslen, ed. (Manchester: Manchester University Press, 2002).
Sidney, Philip. *The Countess of Pembroke's Arcadia* (London: William Ponsonbie, 1590).
de la Sierra, Pedro. *The second part of the Myrror of knighthood Containing two seuerall bookes, wherein is intreated the valiant deedes of armes of sundrie worthie knights, verie delightfull to be read, and nothing hurtfull to bee regarded. Now newly translated out of Spanish into our vulgar tongue by R.P.* (London: Thomas East, 1583).
de Silva, Oliveira. "Recurrent Onomastic Textures in the *Diana* of Jorge de Montemayor and the *Arcadia* of Sir Philip Sidney," *Studies in Philology* 79, no. 1 (1982), 30–40.
de Silva, Oliveira. "Sir Philip Sidney and the Castilian Tongue," in *Comparative Literature* 34, no. 2 (1982), 130–45.
Singh, Jyotsna. *Colonial Narratives/Cultural Dialogues: "Discoveries" of India in the Language of Colonialism* (London: Routledge, 1996).
Skura, Leslie. "Discourse and the Individual: The Case of Colonialism in *The Tempest*," *Shakespeare Quarterly* 4, no. 1 (1989), 42–69.
Smith, Jeremy L. "Music and Late Elizabethan Politics: The Identities of Oriana and Diana," *Journal of the American Musicological Society* 58, no. 3 (2005), 507–58.
Spenser, Edmund. *The Faerie Queene*, second edition, A. C. Hamilton, ed. (London: Routledge, 2007).
St. Clair, William. *The Reading Nation in the Romantic Period* (Cambridge: Cambridge University Press, 2004).
Stationers' Company, *A Transcript of the Registers of the Company of Stationers of London, 1554–1640 AD*, vol. 5, Edward Arber, ed. (Birmingham: Priv. print, 1896).
Strickland, Agnes. *Lives of the Queens of England, from the Norman Conquest*, Volume 4 (Philadelphia: Lippincott, 1893).
Strong, Roy. *Artists of the Tudor Court: The Portrait Miniature Rediscovered*, 1520–1620 (London: Victoria & Albert Museum, 1983).
Strong, Roy. *The Cult of Elizabeth: Elizabethan Portraiture and Pageantry* (London: Thames & Hudson, 1977).
Strong, Roy. *Gloriana: The Portraits of Queen Elizabeth I* (New York: Thames and Hudson, 1987).
Strong, Roy. "Queen Elizabeth I as Oriana," *Studies in the Renaissance* 6 (1959), 251–60.
Thomas, Henry. *Spanish and Portuguese Romances of Chivalry: The Revival of the Romance of Chivalry in the Spanish Peninsula, and Its Extension and Influence Abroad* (Cambridge: Cambridge University Press, 1920).
Thompson, Ayanna. *Performing Race and Torture on the Early Modern Stage* (New York: Routledge, 2008).
Topsell, Edward. *Times lamentation: or An exposition on the prophet Ioel, in sundry sermons or meditations* (London: Edm. Bollifant, 1599).
Tottel's Miscellany: Songs and Sonnets of Henry Howard, Earl of Surrey, Sir Thomas Wyatt and Others, Amanda Holton, ed. (New York: Penguin Books, 2012).
Tyler, Margaret, trans. *The Mirror of Princely Deedes and Knighthood*, Margaret Tyler, trans., Joyce Boro, ed. (London: The Modern Humanities Research Association, 2014).
Uman, Deborah and Belén Bistué, "Translation as Collaborative Authorship: Margaret Tyler's *The Mirrour of Princely Deedes and Knighthood*," *Comparative Literature Studies* 44, no. 3 (2007), 298–323.
Ungerer, Gustav. *Anglo-Spanish Relations in Tudor Literature* (Bern: Francke Verlag, 1956).
de Valdes, Fancisco. *The sergeant maior…* (London: John Wolfe, 1590).

Valencia-Suárez, María Fernanda. "Tenochtitlán and the Aztecs in the English Atlantic world, 1500–1563," *Atlantic Studies*, 6, no. 3 (2009), 277–301.

Vanhoutte, Jacqueline. *Age in Love: Shakespeare and the Elizabethan Court* (Lincoln: University of Nebraska Press, 2019).

Venuti, Lawrence. "Translation as Cultural Politics: Regimes of Domestication in English," *Textual Practice* 7.2 (1993), 208–23.

Vickers, Brian. "Shakespeare and Authorship Studies in the Twenty-First Century," *Shakespeare Quarterly* 62, no. 1 (2001), 106–42.

Virgil, *The Eclogues and Georgics*, R. D. Williams, ed. (New York: St. Martin's Press, 1979).

Vitkus, Daniel. "The Unfulfilled Form of The Faerie Queene: Spenser's Frustrated Fore-Conceit," *Renaissance and Reformation* 35, no. 2 (2012), 83–112.

Vives, Juan Luis. *The Education of a Christian Woman: A Sixteenth-Century Manual*, Charles Fantazzi, trans. (Chicago: University of Chicago Press, 2000).

de Voragine, Jacobus. *The Golden Legend: Readings on the Saints*, William Granger Ryan, ed. (Princeton: Princeton University Press, 2012).

Weatherby, Harold L. "The True Saint George," *English Literary Renaissance* 17, no. 2 (1987), 119–41.

Weissberger, Barbara F. "The Gendered Taxonomy of Spanish Romance." *La corónica: A Journal of Medieval Hispanic Languages, Literatures, and Cultures* 29, no. 1 (2000), 205–29.

Whitbourne, Richard. *A Discourse Containing a Louing Inuitation both Honourable, and Profitable to all such as Shall be Aduenturers, either in Person, Or Purse, for the Aduancement of His Maiesties most Hopeful Plantation in the Nevv-found-Land, Lately Vndertaken. Written by Captaine Richard Whitbourne of Exmouth, in the County of Deuon* (London: Felix Kyngston, 1622).

Williams, Raymond. *Marxism and Literature*, reprint (Oxford: Oxford University Press, 2009).

Wilson, Louise. "I maruell who the diuell is his Printer": Fictions of Book Production in Anthony Munday's and Henry Chettle's Paratexts, in *The Book Trade in Early Modern England: Practices, Perceptions, Connections*, J. Hinks and V. Gardner, eds. (Newcastle: British Library and Oak Knoll Press, 2014), 1–18.

Wilson, Louise. "Playful Paratexts: The Front Matter of Anthony Munday's Iberian Romance Translations," in *Renaissance Paratexts*, Helen Smith and Louise Wilson, eds. (Cambridge: University of Cambridge Press, 2014).

Wilson, Louise. "The Publication of Iberian Romance in Early Modern Europe," in *Translation and the Book Trade in Early Modern Europe*, José María Pérez Fernández and Edward Wilson-Lee, eds. (Cambridge: Cambridge University Press, 2014).

Wilson-Okamura, David Scott. "Errors about Ovid and Romance," *Spenser Studies* 23 (2008), 215–34.

Wilson-Okamura, David Scott. "When did Spenser Read Tasso?" *Spenser Studies* 23 (2008). 277–82.

Yamada, Yumiko. *Ben Jonson and Cervantes: Tilting against Chivalric Romances* (Tokyo: Maruzen, 2000).

Yates, Frances A. *Astrea: The Imperial Theme in the Sixteenth Century*, second edition (London: Routledge, 1999).

Yong, Bartholomew. *Diana of George of Montemayor: translated out of Spanish into English* (London: G[eorge] B[ishop], 1598).

INDEX

1 Henry IV play 34

Aggas, Edward 173
The Alchemist 179–80, 182
Alexander, Sir William 120–1
Aleyn, Charles 121–2
altísimas torres (extremely tall towers) 52
Amadís 15–16, 18–22, 44, 46, 68, 83–5, 99
Amadís de Gaula 8, 11, 14–16, 17–23, 33, 45,
  47–8, 51–2, 54, 67–8, 132, 135, 137, 165,
  170, 178, 183–4, 189
  caused diplomatic scandal 17
  comparison to 172
  criticisms lodged at the books of 178
  as French style manual 178
  myths of 160
  pinnacle of Díaz's romanticism 47
  sequel of 135
  Spanish romances 188
  synonymous with American colonization 14
  used as reference to Spanish king 18
Amazon woman 29, 76, 85, 135, 138, 151, 160
America 1–2, 4–6, 24, 27–8, 32–4, 40–1,
  43–9, 52, 54, 58, 60–5, 81, 87–8,
  95–9, 101–5, 108, 121, 126, 129, 131–2,
  158–61, 201
  allegorical presence in romance 134, 145
  Christian Church's Restoration in 108
  Christianization of the 107
  colonial exploits in 49
  colonial project in 27, 40
  colonization of 120
  Columbus's writings on 120
  contacts with Saint George 117
  contemporary mystification of 146
  discovery of 81, 96, 122–3
  England's desired conquest of 141
  England's destiny in 124
  holy cross was prime symbol of 111
  inordinate cruelty in 60
  madmen willing to dream of 132

Messianic kingdom in 108
new mythology in 48
origins of English settlements in 125
post-Columbian conception of 104
Spain's conduct in 121–2
Spanish conquest of 5, 105
Spanish vernacular romance 1
"strange" was a common description of 132
under the Stuarts 120
Amoret 77–9, 83
Anatomie of absurditie 175
Anders, H. R. D. 193
Andronica 101, 103–5
Anglo-Dutch War 152
Anglo-Spanish War 11, 21, 120, 126, 132,
  140, 143, 148, 152, 192, 203, 205, 207
Anti-Spanish sentiment 165–190
  an intellectual black legend 165–174
  guilty reading 174–185
  Quixotic figures 185–190
António I, Don, Prior of Crato 172
Anzaldúa, Gloria, tradition of 148
Apolidon, Prince 46, 52
Apollo's challenger 24–37, 52, 71–4, 148, 150
April Eclogue 71
Arabic caliph 136
Aragón 2, 11–12, 100, 113–14, 117, 166
The Arcadia 92, 194–5
Arcaláus 15, 17–18, 68
Archimago 68, 74, 112–13, 116
argonauts 128–9
Ariosto, Ludovico 104–5, 206
Aristotle 134, 154, 174
Armada 9, 37, 73, 119, 140
de Armas, Frederick 51, 54, 199
Armato, Persian king 135
Arnoldsson, Sverker 165
Artegall 31, 73, 85, 88–93
Arthur, King 7, 13, 48–9, 68–70, 73, 95, 108,
  113, 134
Astolfo 101–3, 105

INDEX

Astrophel 17
Atawallpa (Atahualpa), Inca Emperor 24, 139, 142
Athens 132, 148–9
Atlantis 47–9, 119
Australia 131, 151–4, 158, 163
Aztec Empire 39–40, 49, 57. *See also* Tenochtitlán

Bacon, Sir Francis 120, 131, 151, 153
Baja California Sur 137, 156–8, 160–3. *See also* California
Barbosa, Aires 168
Barker, Christopher 33
Baronius, Cardinal Caesar 116
Battle of Alcoraz 114
Battle of the Puig 114
Battle of Zutphen 16
Beaumont, Francis 179, 197
Belphoebe 15, 67, 71, 72, 74, 78, 81, 83, 86
  characterization in conversation with Spanish romance 75
  conspicuous evolution of character 76
  faerie analogs 67
  famed for her rare chastitee 75
  first entrance in *Faerie Queene* 76
  formidable defense against rape 76
  improvement of Claridiana 76
  kinship with Claridiana 75
  love and honor for 78
  militant chastity 82
  militant resistance of 77
  personified virginity as permanent state 71
  rejection of Timias 15, 83
  self-fashioned English ethos 77
  Timias's betrayal of 83
Bergvall, Åke 111
The Black Legend in England 5
Black Legend of Spanish Cruelty 4, 6, 165, 173
Black Legend 5, 80, 121, 165
  anti-Spanish narratives promulgated through 196
  arguments against Spain's conduct 121
  emerged of Spanish Cruelty 165
  intellectual responses of 5, 165–74
  major basis for 165–6
  realm of California 137
  sources of 172
  tracing roots of 5
Blount, Edward 196

The Book of Prophecies 97–8, 108
Book of the Courtier 176
Books of the brave 8, 14–17, 31, 181, 185, 192, 196, 201
The Book of the Order of Chivalry 11, 80
Boone, Elizabeth Hill 43
Boro, Joyce 30
Bottom, Nick 47
Braggadocchio 73–4
Brasil 110
Braun, Georg 42
Britannia 124
British Isles 124–5, 129
Britomart 31, 67, 72, 74, 77–8, 88–93, 141
Britton, Dennis 200
Bruno, Giordano 72
Bullough, Geoffrey 194
Burton, Richard 128–9

El Caballero del Febo 22, 34. *See also* Knight of the Sun
Cádiz 9, 31, 35
Calafia, Queen 135–7, 140, 160–3
Caliban 52, 54, 56–9, 62, 199
California 135, 137, 157–63
  distinction between California and Nova Albion 160
  as an English port for trade 158
  enmity between England and Spain, proof of 164
  going to 156–63
  gynocratic race of warrior women 137
  romantic origins 162
  Spanish explorers on the name of 163
Cambridge University Library 49
Camden, William 18, 25, 124
Campanella, Tomasso 120
Canny, Nicholas 126
Canterbury Tales 198
Cappadocia 113, 118
Cardenio 196–7
Carew, Richard 207
Carlos, Don 19
Carrasco, Davíd 42
Carrión, Maria Mercedes 19
Castilla (Castile) 1, 12
Catholic monarchs (Reyes Católicos), Isabella and Ferdinand 2, 12, 96, 167–68
Catholicism 112, 119, 155, 173
Cavendish, Margaret 188
Cavendish, Sir Thomas 108

Caxton, William 13
Cecil, Thomas 119
Cecil, William 17
de Certeau, Michel 28
de Cervantes, Miguel 170–71
Chambermaid 175, 178, 185, 187–8
Chapman, George 87, 108, 141, 143, 148
Charles I, King of England 109, 120, 121, 152, 156, 197
Charles V, Holy Roman Emperor 42, 57, 81, 103–4, 109, 112, 120–1, 132, 137, 142
Chaucer, Geoffrey 69, 134, 198
Christendom 74, 114, 172
Christianity 4, 29, 49, 65, 101, 110, 113, 128, 192
   cross, dearest symbol of 110
   establishment in England 128
   European conquest of America 192
   fight against the forces of evil 113
Cinzio, Giraldi 206
Cisneros, Fray Francisco Jiménez de 167
Civitates Orbis Terrarum 42
Claridiana, Princess 23, 28–31, 33–4, 67, 72, 75–7, 83, 85, 89, 92, 179–181, 183, 188–9
Clifford, Sir George 173
Códice Mendoza 41, 46, 48
Coldock, Francis 33
Columbus, Christopher 88, 96–9, 104, 107–8, 119, 123, 126, 129, 135, 201
   interpretation of his discovery of America 123
   misreading of *Medea* 119, 122
   writings vital to Spain's American dominium 120
Columbus, Ferdinand 98–99
Conquest of Mexico 59–60
Constantinople 22, 135–6, 140
Corinthians 47, 134
Cortés, Hernán 5, 39–40, 81, 103, 137, 139, 142, 156
   brokered agreement with Moctezuma 39
   city plan of 42
   correspondence with Charles V 40
   defeated Cuauhtémoc 39
   description of Tenochtitlán's religious sector 40
   emphasized wealth of Aztec Empire 40
   at the entry of Tenochtitlán 45
   expedition led by his men 137
   identifying site of principal "mosque" 41
   imprisonment of Moctezuma by 49
   letters of 42, 49
   small retinue led by 39
Cortés, Martín 24, 29
Cortez, Hernando (character) 60
Cosmographie in four bookes 131, 152, 160–2, 192
Critias 48
Croce, Benedetto 165
Cromwell, Oliver 7
Crouch, Nathaniel (Robert Burton) 125–6
Crowley, Tim 18
The Cruelty of the Spaniards in Peru 59–60
Crusaders, Christian 39
Crusades 12–13, 41, 73, 102, 110, 113–14, 116
Cuauhtémoc, Aztec Emperor 39
Culhua-Mexica map 42
cultural imperialism 1, 9
Cupid 79, 81–2, 151
Curbet, Joan 92
Cynthia 74, 146
Cynthia's Revels 183

Dárdano, King 52–3
Davenant, William 59–60, 65
de Armas, Frederick 51, 54, 199
De consolatione philosophae 80
De Guiana, carmen Epicum 87
Decades of the Newe Worlde or West India 49, 139
Decameron 198
Defence of Poesy 16
Devereux, Sir Robert 21, 81
Diana, Amazonian empress (character) 23, 29, 91
Diana, classical moon goddess 30, 32, 71, 146–47, 195
Diana, Elizabethan avatar 34, 71–72, 74–75
Diana, pastoral romance 67, 71, 92, 194–95
Diario del viaggio in Spagna 168
Díaz del Castillo, Bernal 5, 44–7, 50
Diogenes, Antonius 103
Discourse on Western Planting 122
Discourse touching the Spanish monarchy 120
The Discovery of Guiana 139, 142, 152
Dol Common 180–1
domestication 177–9
Don Quixote of La Mancha 14, 55, 163, 170, 185, 190, 195, 197
Double Falsehood 196
Dourado, Fernao Vaz 157

Drake, Sir Francis 27, 35, 82, 104–5, 108, 135, 145, 152, 157–9, 163
Dryden, John 49, 59–60, 126, 132, 193
Duffet, Thomas 59
Duke of Athens. *See* Theseus
Duke of Milan. *See* Prospero
dynastic legitimacy 109

East, Thomas 31
Eclogues 121, 124
Eden, Richard 49
The Education of a Christian Woman 169
Edward III, King of England 109, 116
El Dorado 61, 101, 108, 139–40, 143, 151, 163–4
Elizabeth I, Queen of England 17–18, 20–1, 25, 27, 30, 34–5, 70–1, 73–4, 75–8, 81–2, 86, 88–9, 90–1, 108, 112, 119, 140, 143, 148–9, 151
  Amazonian identification 76, 140
  Anglo-Spanish relations in reign 17
  Armada portrait 25–7
  as a "Matamoros" 119
  as a great conqueror 140
  as a pacifist Amazon 141
  as an empress of "peace & plenty" 142
  association to Diana cult 30, 75, 92
  avatars 71
  characterization as eternally virginal 71
  conquest of New Albion 145
  court politics 18
  defend reputation of 21
  Elizabethan premises, Building on 120
  England, the seat of 108
  English empire ruled by 89
  exceptionalism 88
  expelled ambassador in Ridolfi plot 18
  favorite Shakespearean characters 35
  female sovereignty 91
  foreign policy towards Spain 34
  honorary title of 70
  in Armada portrait 27, 73
  in the tradition of the martial George 119
  antagonism with Philip II 18, 143
  militant chastity 77–8, 81–2
  oft-quoted speech to the troops 140
  Raleigh's strained relationship with 151
  representation as an Amazon 76, 141
  resist the tyranny of Spanish imperialism 90
  right to rule 142
  royal entertainments 20
  royal iconography 25
  Sea Dogs 35
  separatist gynocratic politics 88
  Shakespeare characterized as 148
  Spes associating Oriana and 17
  supreme wisdom of 20
  true leader of Christendom 74
  virtuous imperialism 86, 91
Eliza Trimphans 90
An Encouragement to Colonies 120
England 3–5, 7, 9, 11–15, 18, 21–2, 25–7, 30–7, 40, 42, 49–50, 58, 60, 62, 65–6, 67–8, 87–8, 91, 95, 105, 108, 111, 116, 127, 132, 135, 140–1, 160, 164, 168, 171, 176–8, 186, 190, 193, 196, 200, 203, 207. *See also* George, Saint
  Amadís's mystique in 15
  American conquest 109
  appropriation of Spanish literature 4
  Black Legends in 5
  books of brave 11
  colonial aspirations 62
  colonial interventions in America 40
  colonial project in America 27
  cosmic empire of virtue 67–8
  country's flag 119
  crypto-Catholic communities in 30
  defeat of 1588 Armada 31
  destined arrival as a salvation from Spanish tyranny 60
  destiny in West 87
  disappearance of illustrious civilization 50
  divided by courtly and political ruptures 12
  dynasty of the Stuarts 109
  European tradition 110
  first plantation colony 49
  glory at Agincourt 37
  historical identification with Saint George 110
  holds the chase 143–51
  imperial rise of 65–6
  imperialism 11
  oppression of Catholics 18
  Philip's venture to conquer 26
  project of global conquest 132
  real-world encounters with the Spanish 21
  Red Cross for 95, 109–119
  religious and legal traditions of 91
  revive masculine spirit 13
  role in Messianic kingdom 68
  romance adaptations produced in 42

romance's meteoric rise to prominence in 22
scandals and disappointments of 88
self-fashioning as a world savior 9
significance of Raleigh voyage to 88
Signs of England 104–5
Spanish invasion of 188
Spanish literature in 191–201, 203–5
Spanish romance in 3, 14, 33
traditions of 25
triumph over Spanish imperialism 68
Union Jack 119
ventures in global exploration, navigation, and sea piracy 34
victories of 7, 104
virtue ethic of supreme civility 58
The English Empire in America 125
Epicene, or the Silent Woman 182
Erasmus, Desiderius 167, 172
de Eslava, Antonio 52–5, 193–4, 197–8, 200
España defendida 165
Espejo de príncipes y cavalleros 8, 11, 14, 22–3, 67, 132, 165, 178, 183–4, 189. *See also The Mirrour of Knighthood*
Esplandián 63, 135–6, 138, 161–3
Europe 1, 5, 19, 22, 25, 40–1, 43, 66, 95, 101–2, 112–13, 142–3, 152, 196
Everson, Jane 206

Fabricio, Don 52–3, 199
The Faerie Queene 15, 67, 71, 73, 76, 78, 81–2, 84, 88–9, 91, 95, 107–109, 116, 118, 132–3, 146, 153–4, 193
  anticipated the arrival of the English in America 107
  Artegall's voyage 88
  Book V of 73
  Britomart's relationship with Artegall 88
  characterization of Red Cross Knight 95
  Christianization of the Americas 107
  comparison with the Passion 107
  contemporary mystification of America 146
  discover a vision for English futurity 89
  Elizabeth in 71
  extolls female virtue 81
  first edition of 67
  interpretations of Britomart 88–9
  militant virgins 78
  most successful fiction 109
  second edition of 88
  self-fashioned ethos of Elizabethan England 193

Timias's supreme melancholy 84
transformed Oriana into Gloriana 67–72
used the imaginative space of Faerieland 95, 108
Faerieland 106–109
Farinelli, Arturo 165
Ferdinand II, King of Aragón 2, 55, 96, 99, 100, 110
Ferdinand, Prince (character) 55–6
Fletcher, John 59, 196–7
Florisel de Niquea 14
foreignization 177, 179, 184
François, duc Alençon 71
Frobisher, Sir Martin 35
Frye, Northrop 14
Frye, Susan 140
Fuchs, Barbara 4–5, 7, 196

Galilei, Galileo 131
Garnett, Richard 200
Gaspar de Carvajal, Fray 138
Gawdy, Philip 20
gentlemen of the shade 34–5
George, Saint 95, 105, 109–111, 117–8. *See also* England
  cross of 109
  Crusades vision of 116
  devilish imposture 112
  doughtie Conqueror 109
  figure of English popular culture 109
  as a martial figure 116
  as a prophetic sign of English conquest 120
  in reformed England 109
  reincarnation of 108
  Spanish American plantation colony, patron saint of 110
  tapestry of Saint George and the dragon 113–14
  Viceroyalty of Brasil 110
  city of Coventry 118
Georgic red cross 105, 111, 119
Gibson, Edmund 124
Gilman, Stephen 41, 45
gleaming teocalli. *See* medieval towers
Gloriana 67–70, 72, 74–6, 112
Goldberg, Jonathan 111
Golden Fleece 100–1, 111
Golden Lion 31
de Gómara, Francisco López 44, 47, 49, 120, 138
Gómez de Quevedo, Francisco 165

INDEX

Gosse, Edmund 200
Gower, George 26
Gramática de la lengua castellana 1
Graziani, René 74
Greene, Robert 175, 189
Greene, Roland 56, 80
Grey, Lord Deputy Arthur 82
Griffin, Eric 7
The Guardian 183
Guerau de Espés del Valle. *See* de Spes Ambassador
Guiana 10, 87, 90, 108, 137, 139–41, 143, 151
Guicciardini, Francesco 168
guilty reading 8, 165, 174–185
Guyon, Sir 73

Habsburg dynasty 49, 117
Hackel, Heidi Brayman 175
Hackett, Helen 136, 175
Hadfield, Andrew 88
Hakluyt, Richard 122
Hall, Joseph 153
Hall, Kim 146
Hamilton, Donna 32
Harington, John 104–5
Hawkins, Sir John 35
Hawkins, Sir Richard 35
Hendricks, Margo 148
Heng, Geraldine 7
Henry V 37
Henry VIII, King of England 81
Herberay, Nicolas de 162
Hercules Octaeus 149
Heroides 176
Heylyn, Peter 116–8, 122–3, 131–2, 152, 154–5, 157–64, 192–3
    accepted the *Medea* passage 122
    commended the creations of Spenser and Shakespeare 154
    credited Spenser for English Saint George 118
    depiction of Baja California 160
    English hopes in exploration 152
    English patriotic literature 120
    for Renaissance readers 121
    inclined to doubt *Amadís*'s historicity 162
    omitting the California of romance 163
    romance maxim, using of 132
Hispano-Roman regime 72
Historia general de las Indias 49, 138
The Historie of Cambria, now called Wales 122
The History of the Indies 120
The History of the World 153
Hogenberg, Franz 42
Hosington, Brenda 207
House of Busirane 78–9
House of Commons, 1839 191
House of Habsburg 81
House of Tudor 81
Howard, Robert 59
Howard, Thomas 30–1, 178
Humour of the Spaniard 72

I romanzi 206
Iberia 8, 11, 13, 22, 110, 114, 165, 193, 207
Iceland 128–9
Il Mambriano 205
imperial conflict, on moon 75
India 101, 135, 146, 148, 162
The Indian Emperour, or the Conquest of Mexico by the Spaniards 59–60, 126
The Indian Queene 59
inhuica atl (celestial water) 52
Instauratio Magna (Great Renewal) 131
Ínsula Firme (Firm Island) 46–8, 51–2, 132, 162. See also *Amadís de Gaula*
Isabel I, Queen of Castle (Isabella I) 1–2, 96, 99, 110
Island of Glass Towers 48
Israel 98, 107
Italian Wars 165–6

James I, King of Aragón 11
James I, King of England 3, 57, 109, 114, 120, 127, 131, 151, 192, 197
James, Saint 110–1, 114
Jameson, Fredric 3
Johnson, Richard 118
Jonson, Ben 153, 165, 179–83, 188–9

Kermode, Frank 54, 194
King of the Moon 103
King of the Sun 103
Kino, Eusebio 159
Kirkman, Francis 184
Knapp, Jeffrey 87
Knight of Chastity. *See* Britomart
Knight of Justice. *See* Artegall
Knight of the Burning Pestle 179, 187, 197
Knight of the Chariot (Knight of the Sun) 31

INDEX

Knight of the Sun 22–3, 27–9, 31–3, 77, 83, 85, 89, 92, 176, 179, 183, 187, 189

La Chanson de Roland (Song of Roland) 137
de Laet, Johannes 157
La Gerusalemme liberata 206
languages 1–37, 41, 47, 57, 58–9, 168, 177–8, 183, 187–8
de Las Casas, Fray Bartolomé 4–5, 44, 120
Lazarillo de Tormes 184
Le Morte D'Arthur 13
Leonardo da Vinci 131, 199
Leonard, Irving 8, 131, 136, 199
Lindabrides 31, 33, 83, 85
Lisuarte de Grecia 14, 162
Llull, Ramón 11–12, 80, 82
Lockey, Brian 91
López de Gómara, Francisco 44, 47, 49, 120, 138
López Moreda, Santiago 165, 167–68
Louis IX, King of France 12
Lucian of Samosata 75, 103, 153

Machiavelli, Niccolò 171–2
Madoc 201
Magellan, Ferdinand 104, 143
La Malinche (Doña Marina) 24, 57, 63, 81
Malory, Thomas 13
Maltby, William S. 5
Mammon, Sir Epicure 181
maps 52, 111, 153, 155–7, 160, 162
Maria Anna, Spanish Infanta 120
Marlowe, Christopher 181
Marston, John 183
Martyr, Peter 49, 139
Mary I, Queen of England 18, 24–5, 112, 170
Mary I, Queen of Scotland 17–18, 30
Massinger, Philip 183
matrimonial imperialism 67, 75, 77, 91. *See also* Philip II, King of Spain
Matter of Britain cycle 68
Medea 8, 96–7, 99, 104, 119–21, 122–3, 126, 128, 201
Menéndez y Pelayo, Marcelino 193, 198
Mercator, Gerard 124, 157
The Merchant of Venice 167
Meridian, Prince 31
Meres, Frances 173
Mesoamerica 49–50, 60, 108
Messianic kingdom 106, 172
México 15, 40–1, 67, 71–2, 74–8, 81–3, 86

civilization 40
cultural richness and pagan Otherness of 40
European imperial program 41
historical chronicles by Spanish 42
major manuscript history of precolonial culture 41
places of worship 40
Microcosmos: a Little Description of the Great World 152
A Midsummer Night's Dream 47, 132, 134, 143, 153
Miles Gloriosus 72, 79
Miranda 51, 53, 55–8
The Mirrour of Knighthood 14, 22–3, 27–31, 33, 35, 54, 71–2, 75–7, 85, 89, 155, 162, 176, 178–9, 183
Amazonian princess Claridiana of 75–6
amorous princess Claridiana in 72
Christian Knight of the Sun in 77
crucible of meaning and of conflict 30
enormous growth on English market 33
Falstaff's references to 35
first and second edition of 22
forebear in form of Claridiana 89
heliotypic symbols with Spain and Spanish Catholicism 27
rise in print market 71–2
shaped the Elizabethan tradition of Diana 71
strong resemblance to *Orlando* epics 33
translations of 33
The Mock Tempest, or the Enchanted Castle 59
Moctezuma II, Aztec Emperor 39, 48–50, 57, 59–60, 65–6, 98, 107, 126, 139, 142–3
Montaigne, Michel de 57
Montalvo, Garci Rodríguez de 14–15, 18, 54, 71, 135, 137, 156
Montemayor, Jorge de 71, 92, 194–5
Montrose, Louis 91
Moore, Helen 6, 33
More, Thomas 153, 167
Morgante Maggiore 205
Morley, Thomas 70, 141
mosques (mezquitas) 40–1
Munday, Anthony 3, 33, 46, 83, 178–9
Mundy, Barbara 42
Mutability Cantos 148

Napoli 58, 166
Nashe, Thomas 175
Natures Fancies 189

de Nebrija, Antonio 1, 168
New and choise characters, of seueral authors 175
New England 6, 106, 108
New Jerusalem 95, 97–99, 104, 106, 108, 123
Newberry Library in Chicago, U.S.A 42
Newcomb, Lori Humphrey 174–5
Nicoll, Charles 87
Noches de invierno (*Winter Nights*) 52, 54, 193, 198–9
Norris, Sir John 177
de la Noue, Lord François 169, 172–3, 178, 184
Nova Galicia 160

Oberon 143–9
Old and New Worlds 30
de Olid, Cristóbal 137
de Ordaz, Don Diego 39, 55, 61, 106, 138
Order of the Garter 116, 119
de Orellana, Francisco 138
Orgel, Stephen 199
Oriana, Princess (character) 15, 17, 19–20, 67–8, 70–1, 76, 83–4
Orientalism 40–1
Orlando epics 9, 33, 67, 89, 194
Orlando furioso 75, 101, 103–4, 205–6
Orlando Innamorato 206
Ortelius, Abraham 119, 122, 124, 157
Ortúñez de Calahorra, Diego 22–4, 27–8
Otherness 44
Overbury, Thomas 175–6, 185, 187–9
Ovid 176, 180, 182–3

Palladis Tamia 173
Palmerín de Oliva 33, 179, 183
Pandosto 175
Parry, Robert 32
Pardo Bazán, Emilia 4
Patrick, Saint 110
Paynell, Thomas 15–16, 155, 161, 178
Paynim king 73
Peat, Derek 36–7
Pedro (Peter) I, King of Aragón 114
Pedro IV, King of Aragón 166
Pérez, Antonio 172
Perú 2, 10, 24, 49, 50–6, 61, 99, 111, 134, 139, 142–3, 153, 181
Petrarca (Petrarch), Francesco 142, 166, 205
Peypus, Friedrich 42
Philip II, King of Spain 18–20, 23, 25, 71, 80, 111–2, 131, 143, 146–7, 156, 172, 179
Phoebus 25, 34, 74, 147, 150

Pigna, Giovan Battista 206
Pillars of Hercules 26–7, 48, 72, 100, 103, 131
Pinet, Simone 48
Pizarro, Francisco 24, 62, 64, 81, 139
Pliant, Dame 180
Poetaster 182
The Poetics of Piracy: Emulating Spain in English Literature 4
Poison of pleasure 169, 171, 178, 184
Political and Military Discourses 173
Pontano, Giovanni 166
Popocatépetl 39, 45, 55, 107
Powel, David 122
Praeclara Ferdinandi 48
Primaleón de Grecia 33, 183
The Prince 171–2
Promised Land 47, 88, 109, 132
Prospero/ King James 50–9, 62, 199
Protestant Reformation 110
Pulci, Luigi 205
Purchas, Samuel 41
Pyramus and Thisbe 149

Queen of Scots. *See* Mary I, Queen
Quixote, Don 14, 170, 186–9

Raleigh, Sir Walter 35, 74, 81–2, 86–8, 91, 108, 135, 137–40, 142–3, 145, 149, 151, 153
Ramusio, Giovanni 42
Read, David 192
Real Maestranza de Zaragoza (Royal Order of Chivalry of Zaragoza) 113
Red Crosse 108
red saltire cross 110
Redcrosse 106–7, 109, 111–2, 117, 128, 193
  allegorized New World adventurer 106
  costume of 113
  discovered identity as an English Saint 117
  divine plan for 106
  doubt upon the Catholic Church 116
  identified as Saint George 112
  Spenser described as 110
Redcrosse knight 111, 113
Remón, Alonso 44
Rhenanus, Beatus 167
Richard I, King of England 116
Rodríguez de Montalvo, Garci 14–15, 18, 54, 71, 135, 137, 156
Rogers, William 90
Roman Catholicism 119, 196

Romance of Romances 162–3
romance strategies 7–8
Romm, James 99

sack (wine) 35–7
Said, Edward 40–1
Santiago Matamoros 114
Santo Domingo 27
Saracens 74, 102, 116
de Sas, Andrés Marzal 115
Schleiner, Louise 30
Schleirmacher, Friedrich 177
Scott, Ann, Duchess of Monmouth and Buccleuch 60
Sea Dogs 35
The Sea Voyage 59
Second Protectorate Parliament 7
Seneca, Lucius Annaeus 8, 96–7, 99, 100, 119, 122, 124, 134, 149
Serafina 52–3, 199
Las sergas de Esplandián (*Exploits of Esplandian*) 14, 48, 135
Shakespeare Association of America 6
Shakespeare, William 34, 37, 47, 49–55, 59–63, 65, 69, 132, 148–9, 153–4, 167, 193–4, 196–9
Shapiro, James 37
She Ventures and He Wins 188
Shepherd, Simon 93
Sherburne, Edward 123
Sibbald, Sir Robert 124
Sidney, Sir Philip 16–17, 77, 92, 194–5
de la Sierra, Pedro 31–32
Siglo de Oro 13
de Silva Feliciano 136
Simrock, Karl 194
Solitarie Iland 33
Souldan (*Faerie Queene*) 73–4
Southey, Robert 201
Spain 1–2, 5–7, 9–10, 12–13, 17, 27, 36, 59–60, 67–8, 70, 73, 81, 95, 97–100, 103, 105, 110–11, 119–21, 126, 128, 148, 151, 165, 168, 171–4, 177–8, 183–4, 189–90, 192, 196–201, 206
  Anglo- Hispanist approach 6
  Armada 111
  attempts to conquer England 176
  Braggadocio 72, 79
  Catholicism 27, 155
  conflicts with 86
  contemporary romances 13
  conventional enmity with England 164
  coat of arms 100
  Crusades in 12–13
  downfall goes to England 128
  Elizabethan chastity 67
  Elizabethan stand against Spain 143
  England's supremacy over 195
  English strategy of pirating 36
  first war 5
  galleons dashed and scattered in naval battle 73
  global westward expansion with 129
  God's chosen empire 95
  Golden Age reinterpretations 103
  growing cultural influence in Europe 5
  historiographical studies of early modern literature 6
  imperial matrimony 67–8, 70
  imperialist designs of 10
  in New Jerusalem 97–99
  inordinate cruelty in America 60
  intellectual arguments against 167
  love stories 67
  matrimonial imperialism 67
  moral fall from grace in New World 81
  negative character of 169
  negotiations for a Spanish royal marriage 120
  notorious excesses 81
  own humanist leader 169
  perceived dominance 165
  perception of 165
  progressive decline in 131
  rapid unification 12
  Renaissance translation 1
  romance 166
  royal arms 27
  seizure of English shipping in the Low Countries 17
  self-fashioning as global empire 9
  Spaniards 59
  Spanish 99
  Spanish Armada invasion 7
  Spanish Empire 117, 192
  symbolic nodes of power 70
  to English romance 189
  transatlantic colonization 143
  translating empire and culture following Roman model 2
  unvirtuous conquests 148
  unworthy of Renaissance culture 165, 168

Spanish literature 4–5, 188–9, 191–202, 207
Spanish romance 3, 11, 14, 21, 33–5, 64, 68–70, 75–6, 166, 171–2, 176–8, 180–2, 187–90, 192–3, 195
Spenser, Edmund 15, 60–2, 65, 69–70, 105, 107–8, 110, 116–7, 119, 133–4, 146, 154, 189, 193
  adaptation of Oriana into Gloriana 70
  allegorizes the reformation of the Amazonian realm 90
  characterization of Red Cross Knight 95
  claims the Red Cross for England 109
  condemn men 85
  constructed fictional mythology of England 95
  created analogue for Astolfo/Columbus/Tiphys 108
  created Archimago 68
  defend cruelty against Catholic aggressors 82
  description of Belphoebe 76
  Elizabethan characters 67
  failed to discover Diana 75
  fictional space of 95
  forceful challenge to Philip 74
  forecast England's triumph in virtue 68
  introduced a verve for weaponizing the red cross 119
  lack of royal patronage 67
  literary divinations from 108
  managing colonial projects 82
  masculine rule 91
  poetics of piracy 67
  popularizing English myth of Saint George 95, 105, 109, 112, 118
  quirk of compound naming 75
  reclaiming heraldic symbol of the red cross for England 95
  romances of 65
  so-styled prophetic romance 117
  speech from *Treasurie of Amadis* 83
  subtle rebuke of Elizabeth 88
  symbol for English victory 105
  symbol of Saint George 109
  technique of recovering English myths 112
  vision of Spanish romance 70
  warlike women 72
Spes, Ambassador de 17–18, 20, 67–9
Stuart, James 3, 109, 120, 127, 131, 151, 192
Studley, John 123

Summer Isle 52, 54, 59
Sun King. *See* Charles V

tales of love and arms 7–8, 10–14, 99, 101, 152, 166, 168–70, 174, 180, 184–5, 187, 191–2, 196, 200–1. *See also The Book of the Order of Chivalry*
  contemporary romances 13
  global conquest of sixteenth century 14
  lust and fortitude 11–12
  marriage of Castilla and Aragón 12
  masculine wanderlust 14
  naïve romance 14
  origins of knighthood 11
Tasso, Torquato 206
The Tempest 50–4, 57, 59, 62–3, 87, 193–4, 197, 200
temples (templos) 40
Tenochtitlán 39–42, 44–47, 49–50, 52, 60–1, 106, 108, 132
  built entirely of crystal and precious metal 61
  city on lake 44
  construction 52
  cosmic modeling 42
  English map of 49
  fabled grandeur compared to England 108
  fall of 44
  features as cosmic center 42
  fertile subject matter for romantic mythology 47
  first sights of 45
  great towers, cues and buildings 50
  Huey Teocalli 46, 107
  incomparable wonders of 46
  religious sector 40
  Spaniards' first encounter of 44
  Spaniards' first sights of 45
  Spanish descriptions of 60
  spherical shape 50
  water paradise of 47
  wonders of 55
  woodcut map and city plan of 42
  world savior 49
Teocalli, Huey (Templo Mayor) 46, 107
terra cotta roofs 42
Terra Incognita 108, 148, 153–5, 181
Terzo Volvme delle Navigationi et Viaggi 42
Theatrum Orbis Terrarum 119
Theobald, Lewis 196

Theseus, Duke of Athens (character) 132–4, 147
Thirty Years War 9, 120
Thorius, John 177–8
Thule 101, 119–29, 146, 148, 192
Timias 15, 82–6
  enacts symbolic castration 85
  flees to Solitary Island 85
  masculine violence (unruly desire) 83
  passions 82
  swayed by carnal impulses 82
  torment at rejection of Belphoebe 15, 83–4
  wounding by group of men 82
Tiphys 96–7, 99, 102, 104, 108, 121–2, 129
Titania 134, 143–51
Topas, Sir 69, 134
Torres-Murciano, Antonio Río 103
Tottel's Miscellany 80
translations. *See* cultural imperialism
Treasurie of Amadis 15–16, 22, 83, 155, 161–2, 178
Trionfi 142
Triumphes of Oriana 70, 141
The True History 44, 75, 103, 153, 155, 163
Tudor, Mary (Queen of England) 18, 24–5, 112, 170
The Two Gentlemen of Verona (1590–91) 194
Tyler, Margaret 28, 30–1, 76, 176–9

Ulloa, Francisco de 157
Ultima Thule; or, A Summer in Iceland 128
The Unlucky Citizen (1673) 184

Urganda la Desconocida (Urganda the Unknown) 15, 48

de Valdés, Fancisco 177–8
Valentiniano, Prince 53, 199
de Valois, Isabel (Elizabeth) 19
Venuti, Lawrence 177
Virgil 84, 97, 101, 117, 121, 124, 126, 128, 134
virgo bellatrix 72, 88–9, 92, 140, 179, 181
virtuous imperialism 67–8, 75, 86, 91. *See also* Elizabeth
Vives, Juan Luis 169–70, 180
de Voragine, Jacobus 118

Waller, Edmund 126
Walter, Melissa 200
War of the Roses 12
Ward, Sir Henry 191, 201
Weatherby, Harold 110
Weissberger, Barbara 186
A wife now the widow 176
Wilbye, John 141
Williams, Raymond 9, 189
Wilson, Thomas 194–5
The Winter's Tale 198
The Wonders beyond Thule 103
wrath 72
Wroth, Mary 188
Wyatt, Sir Thomas 80

Yates, Frances 104

www.ingramcontent.com/pod-product-compliance
Lightning Source LLC
Chambersburg PA
CBHW021825300426
44114CB00009BA/324